The Man in Seat Sixty-One – Worldwide

The Man in Seat Sixty-One – Worldwide

A guide to train travel beyond Europe

Mark Smith

BANTAM PRESS

LONDON • TORONTO • SYDNEY • AUCKLAND • JOHANNESBURG

TRANSWORLD PUBLISHERS
61–63 Uxbridge Road, London W5 5SA
A Random House Group Company
www.rbooks.co.uk

First published in Great Britain
in 2011 by Bantam Press
an imprint of Transworld Publishers

A CIP catalogue record for this book
is available from the British Library.

ISBN 9780593059432

Addresses for Random House Group Ltd companies outside the UK
can be found at: www.randomhouse.co.uk
The Random House Group Ltd Reg. No. 954009

The Random House Group Limited supports the Forest Stewardship
Council (FSC), the leading international forest-certification organization. All our
titles that are printed on Greenpeace-approved FSC-certified paper carry the FSC logo.
Our paper procurement policy can be found at
www.rbooks.co.uk/environment

Typeset in 11/16 pt Caslon
by Falcon Oast Graphic Art Ltd.
Printed and bound in Great Britain by
CPI Mackays, Chatham, ME5 8TD

2 4 6 8 10 9 7 5 3 1

The train times and fares shown in this book are examples, to help you understand the options and plan your train journeys around the World. Timetables and fares change regularly, so always check them for your own dates of travel using the websites or travel agency phone numbers provided.

All currency conversions are approximate and you should check individual exchange rates at the time of planning your journey.

To Nicolette, Nathaniel and Katelijn

Contents

Introduction

TRAVEL BROADENS THE MIND. At least it does when you travel overland by train, when the journey reflects the culture and history of the country through which you're travelling, with local people around you and all the sights and sounds passing by the window. Train travel is often the most practical option, cheap, safe, civilised and comfortable, far less environmentally damaging than an easily avoidable short-haul flight. But these days, budget airlines are well established in Europe, the USA, Australia and New Zealand, and are now springing up even in India and Thailand. They're backed by persuasive adverts, cheap prices and flashy internet sites. Meanwhile, trains and ferries in places such as China or Thailand are often run by government-subsidised organisations without the budget or commercial drive for overseas marketing or even (in many cases) online booking. They seldom feature in package holidays, as tour companies find it easier to containerise tourists in planes and tour buses. It almost requires a conscious effort to avoid flying and rediscover the pleasure of, well, actually seeing and experiencing the country you're supposed to be visiting, instead of hanging around westernised airports and seeing little more than the inside of a Boeing or Airbus. It can be very tempting to jet everywhere and miss all that the journey has to offer.

This book sets out to make a difference. It aims to explain the principal overland travel options to, from and within the most popular countries in Africa, Asia, the Americas and Australasia, with information on trains and where necessary connecting buses and ferries. This will help you stay firmly on the ground, travelling comfortably and affordably by regular scheduled train, meeting local people and getting far more out of your travel experience than if you flew or stayed within the package-tour 'bubble'.

Train travel between the UK and other European countries is covered in my first book, *The Man in Seat 61: A guide to taking the train from the UK through Europe*. This book covers train travel beyond Europe, in the Middle East, Africa, Asia, the Americas and Australasia. However, I've included a summary of the London–Moscow and London–Istanbul train journeys for the benefit of overland travellers bound for the Far East via the Trans-Siberian Railway or the Middle East, and you'll also find details of the train and ferry journey from London to Morocco, Tunisia and Egypt in North Africa.

Both this book and the seat61 website are intended to be a resource for travellers rather than a personal travelogue, so I have aimed to include all the most popular destination countries, whether my own travels have taken me there or not. I have included some less often visited countries too. However, personal experience inevitably sways the content. Although I have tried to cover popular destinations in more detail than obscure ones, under-rated destinations such as Syria sometimes get more coverage than their popularity (or lack of it) at first seems to warrant. But if this inspires you to travel off the beaten track to some fascinating places, I need make no apology! I must also confess that countries which I have yet to visit, and those which have only a very limited rail service, are unavoidably covered in less depth than those I have been to, and which have extensive rail systems. Much of South America falls into the former category, although the scenic journeys to Machu Picchu in Peru and to the Copper Canyon in Mexico are described in the South America section and are well worth seeking out. If this book inspires you to do your own research, to leave the tourist 'bubble' behind and explore the world at ground level, I will reckon it a job well done.

How to use this book

For many if not most people, a long-haul flight is the only practical option for reaching Southeast Asia, Australia or the USA, for example, within the holiday time available. But once you are there, the information in this book will help you stay on the ground, using local transport to see the sights, thereby getting much more out of the experience than if you used domestic flights. You should turn to the chapter dealing with your destination country, which gives information on train travel within that country, and, in many cases, train or ferry travel onward to neighbouring countries too.

For those travellers who wish to avoid flying completely, whether for environmental reasons, medical reasons, or simply for the experience, the options for surface travel from the UK to each country are covered in the relevant chapter of the country-by-country section of the book. In addition, there is a separate section on the principal overland routes from the UK to Asia: the Trans-Siberian Railway (a key link between Europe and the Far East), the less well-travelled 'Silk Route' from Europe to China via Central Asia, and the classic UK–Istanbul–Tehran–Pakistan route to India.

This book is intended equally for both types of traveller.

Who is the Man in Seat Sixty-One?

I'm a time-served rail traveller, ex-railwayman and editor of the website **www.seat61.com**. I set up my website in 2001, to try to plug the gap between how simple, swift and affordable train travel from the UK to Europe can be, and how difficult (and on occasion downright impossible) it is to find anyone who can tell you how to do it or where to buy tickets. The site soon expanded to cover train travel outside Europe, where I found a similar problem: it's so easy, inexpensive and rewarding to explore countries such as India, Thailand, China or the United States by train, but the commercial world of travel agents and tour companies only seems to sell flights and coach tours and the occasional expensive tourist 'cruise train'. The train operators themselves are often government-subsidised organisations that do not have the budget for overseas advertising, flashy websites or even in many cases online booking. Finding even basic information about local scheduled train travel can be very difficult.

It all started at the tender age of thirteen. From time to time my family would drive across London from our home in Buckinghamshire to my grandmother's in Sidcup. Keen to foster a spirit of independence in their young son, my parents would drop me off at Waterloo East and let me take the short ride to Sidcup on my own by local train and double-decker bus. I can't recall what it was that first attracted me to the Isle of Wight, perhaps I thought it would count as my first trip overseas, but I secretly saved my pocket money for ages and ages (several weeks, at least), and on our next trip I invested my life savings (about £2.73) in a half-fare day return from London to Ryde. The train journey remains a blur. What I *can* remember is sitting on the deck of the ferry at Portsmouth, heading out to sea, knowing I shouldn't be there, and not realising then that the Isle of Wight was just over there across the water. How I got away with this adventure I do not know – it seems my mother was too relieved to scold me when I finally appeared in Sidcup, safe and sound.

Several school trips followed in subsequent years, planned by schoolmasters who chose traditional rail and sea over air travel, in the years before budget airlines. An exchange visit with a French school in Nîmes meant an overnight trip from Calais to the south of France in couchette compartments shared with pupils from the local girls' school. Wild tales of bravado with the opposite sex, all (unfortunately for us) grossly exaggerated, were whispered up and down the train next morning. A school trip to Russia later that year was my first grand tour of the Continent. We crossed the North Sea from Tilbury to what was then still Leningrad on a beautiful but ageing Russian steamship of 1940 vintage, thence by sleeper train to Moscow, onwards to Berlin and back to London Victoria by train and ferry.

On that trip I saw what I still regard as the most moving train departure I have ever witnessed, when Train Number 1, the *Krasnaya Strela* (Red Arrow) left Leningrad for Moscow. For a full minute before departure, martial music blared from every station loudspeaker and everyone turned to watch the gleaming red train standing in glorious isolation in the middle of the station. As the dramatic chords rose to a fortissimo, the brakes of the Soviet Union's most prestigious train hissed off and its immaculate maroon coaches eased their way out of the station towards the capital, spot on time at exactly five minutes to midnight. Needless to say, our school party followed this vision of luxury on the somewhat less prestigious Relief Train 52, complete with chipped Formica panelling and the odd cracked window.

The trip back from Russia to London was made memorable by another event, as a younger fellow pupil took it upon himself to shout 'Solidarity! Solidarity!' light-heartedly out of our carriage window. Maybe this wouldn't ordinarily provoke a diplomatic incident, but when it's 1982, the station is Warsaw Central and the train is the *Moscow Express*, the time and place could have been better chosen. I have never seen a woman go as berserk as our Russian train conductress – the East Germans who pulled her off the unfortunate schoolboy may well have saved his life.

If these early trips taught me anything, it was that overland travel allows you to experience each country in a way you can't by air, and the journey is often an interesting experience in itself. Perhaps that's why so many films are set on ships and trains, but the only ones set on planes seem to be disaster movies.

After school came university at Oxford, and like many students I spent my summer holidays exploring the four corners of the Continent thanks to the European railways' InterRail scheme. There was nothing to rival an InterRail pass for the freedom it gave you to discover Europe, and the same holds good today. In other vacations, I found work in London with Transalpino, a company that sold European train tickets both directly to the public and through other travel agencies. Now I was on the other side of the counter, discovering how European rail ticketing systems worked. No fares manual or timetable was left unturned! Word got around, and travel agencies soon started asking for me by name to sort out their trickier train-travel problems.

When the time came for a permanent career, I knew exactly what I wanted to do. I ran away from Oxford to join the circus. Or British Rail, as it was then called. I applied for their General Management Training Scheme, widely regarded as the best people-management experience you could get, and having been through it I wouldn't disagree. My first appointment was as Station Manager for local stations around Ashford in Kent, a delightful job that involved travelling round the local countryside, checking each station's ticket office accounts, passenger information, maintenance and cleanliness, and signing the signal-box train register. Every job on the railways produces its fair share of strange stories. During the first Gulf War in 1990, I started rummaging through the rolled-up posters on top of the cupboard in my office on the platform at Ashford, looking for a replacement for a faded car-park poster. Minutes later, I was in the supervisor's office next door asking, 'Tony, what are these top-secret military maps of Kuwait doing on top of my cupboard?' Truth is often stranger than fiction, though I still have absolutely no idea how those maps got into my office.

In 1991 I was promoted to Station Manager for Charing Cross, and a few years later for London Bridge as well. This was perhaps the most rewarding but stressful job I've ever had. It certainly had its moments, not least when the Duke of Edinburgh arrived early at Charing Cross for a special train to Sevenoaks. Instead of finding me on the forecourt to meet him, he made his own way to the train and found me still in his compartment, carefully arranging the timetable card I'd been given for him and the copy of the *Evening Standard* I'd purloined from the manager in WH Smith. 'In here?' he said. If he noticed my lower jaw hitting the linoleum, he was too polite to mention it. 'Yes, sir . . .' I stepped off the train to allow him to enter, cringing inwardly. Moments later my station supervisor came rushing up, desperate to tell me that our member of staff at the platform entrance had stopped the Duke and asked him for his ticket. I was lucky not to end up in the Tower for that one . . .

I eventually switched from poacher to gamekeeper, and spent several years with the Office of the Rail Regulator and the Department for Transport, managing the regulation of UK rail fares and ticketing. This had its moments too, briefing ministers and getting front-row seats in the officials' box in both Houses of Parliament when rail-fare questions were being asked (and trying to resist the temptation to join in!). However, it was in my spare time that I decided to set up the website seat61.com, purely as a hobby.

Seat61.com was the result of two things. First, on a grey and drizzly day in 2001 I found myself in WH Smith at Marylebone with nothing to read on the commuter train home. I spotted a 'Teach Yourself HTML' book for £2.99, bought it, and surprised myself as much as anyone when my following the instructions for publishing a webpage actually worked. Second, I thought I'd put this new-found skill to work to do something about the huge gap between how simple it was to travel to Europe by train, and how difficult it was to find out about. I can remember drafting the first pages, typing lines such as 'You can reach Africa in 48 hours from London, without flying' almost tongue-in-cheek, a cry in the wilderness, thinking that no one would ever read it. Then I answered a question on a travel website, about train travel to Hamburg. The questioner said she was the internet travel editor of the *Guardian* newspaper; she loved seat61 and announced that it would be 'Website of the Week' in the next Saturday's travel section. I have to admit that at first I didn't believe it. How would a simple personal site like seat61 get to be featured in a national newspaper? Or, put another way, which of my so-called friends was winding me up? I bought a copy of that Saturday's *Guardian* in my local supermarket, turned to the travel section, and there it was, seat61.com Website of the Week. I think I may have burst out laughing in the middle of the fruit and veg aisle.

Since then seat61 has grown beyond anything I could have imagined, and I have left work to run the site full-time. It now receives almost a million visitors each month, and has featured in many national newspapers both in the UK and in the USA, Canada, South Africa, Israel, Italy, Norway and Australia amongst other countries. More recently, it has received several awards, 'Best Low-Carbon Transport and Technology Initiative' in the Virgin Holidays Responsible Travel Awards 2010, 'Top Travel Website' in the Wanderlust Travel Awards in 2007 and again in 2008, plus the Bronze Award in 2009 and Silver in 2010, and 'Best Travel Website' in the Guardian & Observer Travel Awards 2008. I've been asked to write articles for the *Observer, Sunday Times, Guardian, The Times, Daily Telegraph* and *Wanderlust Magazine*, amongst others.

Concern over aviation's impact on the environment has become a major issue in the last couple of years, and flying is no longer perceived as either glamorous or fun. The need to find alternatives to flying has never been greater. I sincerely hope that this book will continue the work of the website, namely to encourage people to lessen their impact on the environment and in so doing to rediscover what I have known for years: that the journey itself can be as much fun as the destination.

PART

1

GETTING STARTED

1
Key resources

Thomas Cook Timetables

A RESOURCE THAT I WOULD recommend to anyone for journeys across Europe as far as Istanbul, Moscow or even (by ferry) to North Africa and the Middle East is the Thomas Cook European Rail Timetable. This has train timetables and route maps for every country in Europe, and ferry information for European ferries and ferries across the Mediterranean to Africa and the Middle East. Train, bus and ferry information for countries outside Europe used to be contained in its sister publication, the Thomas Cook Overseas Timetable, which was both an aid and an inspiration for my own travels beyond Europe. Sadly, the Overseas Timetable ceased publication after the winter 2010/2011 edition, after a run of twenty years. If you can get hold of a winter 2010/2011 copy then do so, as it will stand you in good stead in understanding rail and bus services worldwide for some years to come, even if the exact times it quotes gradually become outdated. However, some of the most popular train routes beyond Europe may be incorporated into the Thomas Cook European Timetable. Thomas Cook rail timetables can be obtained for around £14 ($21) from the bureau de change section of any high-street branch of Thomas Cook in the UK, or online at **www.thomascookpublishing.com** with shipping to any country worldwide.

Guidebooks

If there is one thing worth not skimping on, it's a good guidebook. Buy a good one, and you will see far more and understand more about what you see. It's best to buy a guidebook as soon as you've decided to visit a country, but before you have settled exactly what you want to do or where you want to go within the country. The guide will help you with that! Avoid guidebooks with glossy pictures but little in-depth information. For serious independent travel, I'd recommend either the Lonely Planet series or the Rough Guides.

Freighter travel

Airlines have pretty much devastated the world of long-distance passenger shipping. Cunard's *Queen Mary 2* operates a monthly passenger service across the Atlantic from Southampton to New York, at least from April or May to November, but other than that, long-distance travel by sea now means a trip on a passenger-carrying freighter. Many container lines have space for up to twelve passengers, usually in 1- or 2-bed cabins with private facilities. There may be a guest lounge and you might share the dining room with the ship's officers. Don't expect the cost to be cheaper than flying – ten days' food, transport and accommodation in a private cabin doesn't cost less than 8 hours in a cramped seat. Freighter travel typically costs in the region of £75–£100 per day including meals, which is not unreasonable from that point of view.

- A good place to start looking for freighter routes, costs and booking is Strand Travel, **www.strandtravelltd.co.uk**, or call +44 (0)20 7921 4340.

Other sites to try include:

- www.geocities.com/freighterman.geo

- www.cruisepeople.co.uk

2
Planning a trip

WITH PACKAGE HOLIDAYS, you can walk into a travel agency and they'll sort it all out for you. With flights, a single internet site can probably book your itinerary all in one place. Travel by train and ferry, however, normally means travelling independently, putting the trip together yourself. Personally, I find researching and arranging a trip part of the fun, but if you're a first-time traveller it can be a bit daunting. So here's how I plan out a trip, from the initial idea that I'd like to visit a particular country or area.

STEP 1: Research the destination
Use your guidebook to work out where to go and what you want to see. It'll give you an idea of when to travel direct and when to stop off somewhere en route. It will also give you an idea of what there is to see in any given place, and hence how long you might want to stay there.

STEP 2: Research the transport options, routes, timetables and prices
You'll find plenty of information in this book, on the website **www.seat61.com**, and in the relevant Lonely Planet or Rough Guides guidebook.

STEP 3: Sketch out an itinerary and work out a budget
Personally, I use a simple spreadsheet on my PC. The idea of the spreadsheet is to:

- *make sure your itinerary works logistically*. For example, if it takes 48 hours to reach Moscow, and if the Moscow–Beijing train runs only on Tuesdays and takes six days, while the Beijing–Hanoi train runs only on Sundays and Thursdays, how long will the whole journey take and will this fit into your three weeks' annual leave from work? The only way to be sure is to plan it out for yourself.

- *see if you're happy with how long you get in each place*. Many people want to stop everywhere and see everything, but haven't thought through how long they'll actually get in each place after allowing for travelling time. Again, plan it out, and if necessary adjust your itinerary, trading off longer stays in key places to give a more relaxed journey against trying to stop everywhere to see everything.

- *plan a budget*. I'm often asked, 'How much does a trip like this cost?' This is independent travel, not an inclusive package, and the answer is usually 'It's as long as a piece of string.' Do you want a long, leisurely trip with 5-star hotels and lots of stopovers, sightseeing tours and three-course restaurant meals? Or a budget trip with fewer stopovers, travelling second class, staying in backpacker hostels and living on snacks? The only way to work out costs is to work out an itinerary and a budget yourself and adjust what you would ideally like to what you can realistically afford.

- *make sure you book the right trains, ships or buses for the right date*. Obvious, really. But with independent travel you'll often have to put the trip together yourself, booking each leg of the journey separately via a different agency or website, and it pays to make sure you get it right.

Here's a sample itinerary and budget:

A	B	C	D	E	F	G
Date	Day	Activity or journey	Fares (£)	Hotels (£)	Food etc. (£)	Other (£)
28 August	Monday	London depart 12:39 Brussels arrive 16:10, Eurostar Brussels depart 17:25 Cologne arrive 19:45, Thalys Cologne depart 22:28 by sleeper to Moscow...	69 25 180	0	20	
29 August	Tuesday	On board sleeper via Warsaw...	0	0	10	
30 August	Wednesday	Arrive Moscow 10:59 Day in Moscow	0	40	20	
31 August	Thursday	Day in Moscow	0	40	20	10 entrance fees
1 September	Friday	Day in Moscow. Depart Moscow 23:00 by train to Irkutsk	70	0	20	
2 September	Saturday	On train in Siberia...	0	0	10	
3 September	Sunday	On train in Siberia...	0	0	10	
4 September	Monday	On train in Siberia...	0	0	10	
5 September	Tuesday	Arrive Irkutsk 04:30 (08:30 local time). Day in Irkutsk	0	30	20	
6 September	Wednesday	Day in Irkutsk. Day tour to Lake Baikal	0	30	20	20 Baikal day tour
7 September	Thursday	Depart Irkutsk 15:00 by sleeper for Ulan Bator	80	0	20	
8 September	Friday	On train in Siberia...	0	0	10	
9 September	Saturday	Arrive Ulan Bator 06:00. Day in UB	0	30	20	15 day tour
10 September	Sunday	Depart UB 09:30 for Beijing by sleeper train	80	0	10	
11 September	Monday	Arrive Beijing 15:00	0	40	20	
12 September	Tuesday	Day in Beijing. Visit Forbidden City	0	40	20	10 entrance fees
13 September	Wednesday	Day in Beijing. Day tour to Great Wall	0	40	20	25 Great Wall tour
14 September	Thursday	Flight Beijing–London: Beijing depart 21:30	450	0	20	20 taxi to airport

Then add one-off items to the bottom of your table:

One-off items	Cost (£):
Guidebooks	30
Belarus transit visa	50
Russian visa	70
Mongolian visa	40
Chinese visa	40
Travel insurance	45

Column A shows the date. If you need to pre-book any part of your itinerary, you can now book it for the right date.

Column B shows the days of the week. If you need to take a train or ferry that runs only on certain days of the week, you can check whether you've got the day right!

Column C shows journey details plus a rough idea of what you might do that day. You can see how long you get in major stops, and can adjust the itinerary if you think it's not long enough. You are sketching out activities for planning purposes only – you don't have to stick to this programme rigidly once you're travelling!

Column D shows likely train, bus or ferry costs. Use rough estimates if you're not a hundred per cent sure.

Column E shows likely hotel costs. The hotel cost is zero when you're on a sleeper train. If you know where you want to stay, use the actual cost, otherwise use a rough estimate, higher for staying in an expensive western city, less in a cheaper Asian or African city.

Column F is for daily spending on food, local transport, normal museum entrance fees and so on. Some people try to plan a whole trip using a flat 'budget per day' which never changes, but I adjust my budgeted amount according to whether I'm on a train or in a city, in a western city or a developing-world city, likely to want a restaurant meal or happy with snacks, and so on.

Column G is for large and predictable one-off costs, like expensive entrance fees to major attractions. For example, the entrance fee to Petra in Jordan is about 30 dinar (£30 or $45). If you've budgeted only £30 a day to cover everything including food, then that's a problem, but if you've made provision for predictable large one-off costs like this, your budget won't be blown, you won't be stressed, and you won't feel compelled to go without food that day. Your guidebook will help you identify these expenses.

PART

2

OVERLAND ROUTES FROM EUROPE TO ASIA

To China, Japan and the Far East by Trans-Siberian Railway

The Trans-Siberian Railway is no mere curiosity or expensive summer-only tourist route. It's a real, working railway with regular year-round passenger trains linking Moscow with Mongolia, China and Vladivostok, from where ferries sail to Japan and Korea. You can use it to travel from London to Beijing overland in around nine days or Tokyo in around fourteen days. You can reach Vietnam or even Bangkok and Singapore this way. If you travel independently it's not prohibitively expensive, either, as a Moscow–Beijing ticket will set you back only £555 or so, for 5,000 miles (9,000 km) of travel and six nights' accommodation. This chapter will help you plan and book a journey from the UK to the Far East via the fabled Trans-Siberian Railway.

OVERVIEW

There is no such train as the 'Trans-Siberian Express'. Instead, there's a whole range of trains across Siberia, including many Russian domestic trains plus several direct international trains to Mongolia and China (and even a through sleeping-car to North Korea). The route map overleaf shows where the Trans-Siberian Railway runs, along with its principal connecting routes. Here's a summary of the train service:

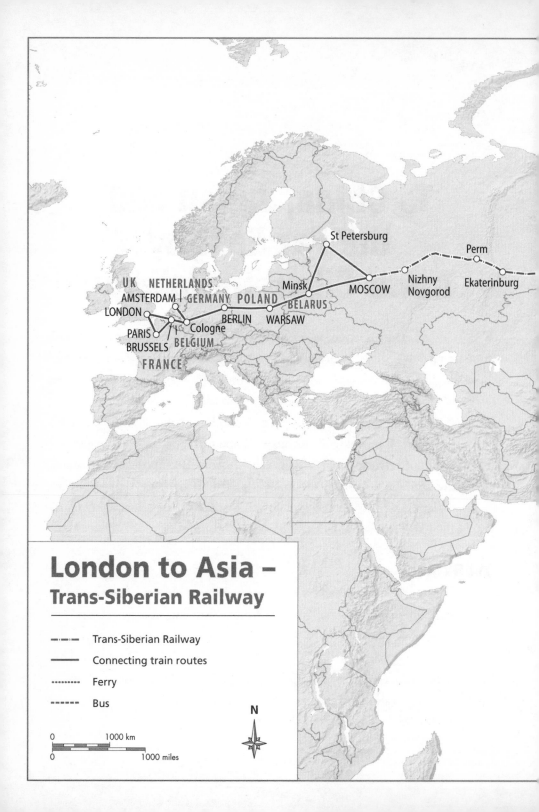

London to Asia –
Trans-Siberian Railway

St Petersburg

Perm

Nizhny
Novgorod

MOSCOW

Ekaterinburg

Minsk

BELARUS

UK   NETHERLANDS

AMSTERDAM

GERMANY   POLAND

LONDON

BERLIN   WARSAW

PARIS   Cologne

BRUSSELS   BELGIUM

FRANCE

N

-··-··- Trans-Siberian Railway

——— Connecting train routes

·········· Ferry

------ Bus

0   1000 km

0   1000 miles

RUSSIAN FEDERATION

Omsk
Krasnoyarsk
Novosibirsk
Irkutsk
Chita
Ulan-Ude
Khabarovsk
ULAN BATOR
MONGOLIA
Harbin
Vladivostok
JAPAN
BEIJING
Donghae
Golmud
Incheon
TOKYO
CHINA
Xian
Shanghai
Sakaiminato
Lhasa
To Kobe
or Osaka
Guilin
Nanning
Guangzhou
HANOI
HONG KONG
THAILAND
BANGKOK
VIETNAM
CAMBODIA
PHNOM
PENH
Saigon
Penang
MALAYSIA
KUALA LUMPUR
SINGAPORE

PACIFIC

OCEAN

INDIAN

OCEAN

London to Moscow

Take a lunchtime Eurostar to Brussels, a connecting high-speed train to Cologne, then a modern air-conditioned sleeping-car of the Russian Railways with 1-, 2- and 3-bed compartments that links Cologne and Moscow daily, taking two nights, one day. For details of this 1,924-mile (3,097-km) journey, see page 66. A one-way ticket costs around £296 with a bed in a 3-berth sleeper.

Moscow to Vladivostok

The *Rossiya* (train 1 westbound, train 2 eastbound) links Moscow, Irkutsk and Vladivostok every second day, taking seven nights for the 6,152-mile (9,258-km) journey. A ticket in the summer months costs around 18,629 rubles (£423 or $630) in a 4-berth *kupé* sleeper or 31,175 rubles (£708 or $1,062) in a *spalny vagon* 2-berth sleeper. Another train, the *Baikal* (trains 9 and 10), links St Petersburg with Irkutsk every second day, and there are many other Russian domestic trains every day between the various cities along the Moscow–Vladivostok line. In fact, there's even a daily slow train from Moscow to Vladivostok, train 904, that takes nine days – not one you want to get on by mistake!

Moscow to Beijing via Mongolia

This is the most popular route, and arguably the most interesting of all. A weekly Chinese train (train 4 eastbound, train 3 westbound) links Moscow with Beijing via Ulan Bator in Mongolia, taking six nights for the 4,735-mile (7,621-km) journey. Bought through a local Russian agency, the fare costs around £555 ($800) one-way in a second class 4-berth sleeper or £780 ($1,130) in a first class 2-berth sleeper. In addition to the direct train there's a Russian/Mongolian train between Moscow and Ulan Bator once a week (trains 5 and 6), a daily Russian train from Irkutsk to Ulan Bator (trains 362 and 263), and a twice-weekly Chinese/Mongolian train between Ulan Bator and Beijing (trains 23 and 24).

Moscow to Beijing via Manchuria

A weekly train, this time Russian, runs between Moscow and Beijing via the Trans-Manchurian route. This is the *Vostok* (train 20 eastbound, train 19 westbound) with 2-berth *spalny vagon* sleepers and 4-berth *kupé* sleepers. The *Vostok* covers 5,623 miles (8,986 km) in seven nights, and prices are broadly similar to those for the Trans-Mongolian route.

Onward connections by train within China

From Beijing there are daily overnight trains to Shanghai or Xian, a daily train to Lhasa in Tibet taking 48 hours, and a train every second day to Hong Kong taking 24 hours. For details of these onward trains, see the chapter on China pages 293–303.

Onward connections by ferry to Japan and Korea

Two ferry companies sail weekly from Shanghai to Osaka or Kobe in Japan taking two nights, fares starting at around RMB1,300 (£130 or $195) one-way. From Vladivostok, the ferry *Eastern Dream* sails once a week via Donghae in South Korea to Sakaiminato in Japan, taking two nights, with fares from £155 ($235) one-way including sleeping berth. For details see pages 63 and 65.

Onward connections by train to Vietnam

There's a direct twice-weekly train from Beijing to Hanoi in Vietnam, taking two nights and costing around £200 ($300) in soft sleeper. Details are shown in the Vietnam chapter, page 438.

PLANNING YOUR TRIP

1. Decide on your final destination. Vladivostok? Beijing? Tokyo? Hong Kong? Even Saigon, Bangkok or Singapore can be reached overland this way, if you have the time: the route map on pages 34–5 shows you the places you can reach by Trans-Siberian Railway. Vladivostok is an interesting place for a day or two, but not in itself worth a seven-day journey from Moscow. Beijing is a wonderful destination, with Shanghai or Xian just an overnight train ride away.

How about Tokyo? There are passenger ships from both Vladivostok and Shanghai to Japan. If Southeast Asia is your choice, you can get to Hanoi in Vietnam by twice-weekly train from Beijing (see the Vietnam chapter, page 426), then travel onwards by train and the occasional bus to Phnom Penh, Bangkok or Singapore (see the chapters on Cambodia, Malaysia and Singapore, and Thailand, pages 281, 343, 401).

2. Do you want to make the whole trip in one go, or to stop off on the way?
Travelling to Vladivostok in seven days without stopovers can be tedious, and it is better to break up the journey and see something of Siberia. On the other hand, the more varied scenery and the camaraderie on board the direct Moscow–Beijing trains makes non-stop travel on this route a thoroughly enjoyable option, and maximises your time in China. If you'd like to break your journey, the most usual stopovers are Irkutsk in Siberia and Ulan Bator in Mongolia. Ekaterinburg and Ulan Ude are also worth a stop.

To help decide whether to stop off and where, buy a copy of Bryn Thomas's excellent *Trans-Siberian Handbook*, which contains journey planning information, town guides, the history of the line, and best of all, a mile-by-mile guide to the sights you can see from the train, to help you get the most from your trip. The Lonely Planet guide to the Trans-Siberian Railway is also excellent.

3. What time of year to go? What class of sleeper to use? What's Trans-Siberian travel like? The section 'Trans-Siberian travel tips' will help with this: see page 70.

4. Plan your Trans-Siberian trains. Plan your trains using the Trans-Siberian timetable below (see page 58). Within Russia, there are fast, quality trains (known as Firmeny) and slower, cheaper trains.

5. Plan your overall itinerary and budget. How much will a trip like this cost? Do you need a six-month sabbatical or is two weeks off work enough? It depends on what you want to do. The only way to find out is to write down your proposed itinerary and a realistic budget for each stage: see 'Planning a trip', page 25.

6. Book your Trans-Siberian train. When you have planned your journey, decide how you are going to buy your Trans-Siberian tickets. There are several ways to buy tickets, some cheaper but more effort, others easier but more expensive. The section 'How to buy tickets' on page 44 explains the options.

7. Book connecting trains, ships and flights. Now book any onward trains in China or ferry to Japan. You may also need a one-way flight if you're not returning overland.

8. Arrange visas. Once you have booked the Trans-Siberian train, you need to arrange your visas: see page 53. You can usually only get visas within three months of travel.

9. Book your train from London to Moscow. Finally, arrange train travel from London to Moscow to connect with the Trans-Siberian. Bookings for European trains open 60 days before departure; you can't book until reservations open, so do this bit last. The London–Moscow train journey takes less than 48 hours: see page 66.

HOW MUCH DOES IT COST?

The good news is that a Trans-Siberian journey needn't be expensive if you travel independently and not with an inclusive tour. It's a regular railway with regular fares, not expensive tourist fares. For over 5,000 miles (9,000 km) of travel, a bed for five to seven nights and a world-class experience, it's a bargain! However, what you pay will vary enormously, depending on:

- which class you travel in. Most western travellers use second class 4-berth sleepers, known in Russia as *kupé*. The third class, known as *platskartny*, with berths arranged in open-plan coaches, is a bit basic for most western travellers, though more adventurous types may enjoy it. First class 2-berth sleepers, known as *spalny vagon*, give twice as much space per passenger as *kupé* berths do, but the fare is twice the price so only worth it if money is no object.

- whether you travel independently (cheaper) or book an all-inclusive tour (more expensive).

- if travelling independently, whether you buy your ticket through a Russian travel agency (cheaper), a western travel agency (more expensive), or at the ticket office (cheapest, but not always practical, see below).

- if booking through an agency, which agency you use. Demand for the direct Moscow–Beijing trains exceeds supply, and Russian Railways sells off blocks of tickets to travel agencies before bookings open to the public. The agencies then sell those tickets at whatever price they can get for them. So shop around!

- for journeys wholly within Russia, whether you travel on a fast, quality Firmeny train such as trains 2 (the *Rossiya*) and 10 (the *Baikal*) or a slow, ordinary, unnamed, lower-quality train such as trains 340 and 350, which have cheaper fares. As a general rule, low train numbers are quality trains, whereas slower, low-quality trains have three-digit train numbers. When you contact an agency, make sure you know what train number you're being quoted a fare for!

If you buy tickets at the ticket office in Moscow

One-way fare, per person, in rubles	*Platskartny* 3rd class bunks	*Kupé* 2nd class 4-berth	*Spalny vagon* 1st class 2-berth
Moscow to Vladivostok (Firmeny train 2 *Rossiya*)	7,574 (£172)	18,629 (£423)	31,175 (£708)
Moscow to Irkutsk (Firmeny train 2 *Rossiya*)	5,917 (£134)	14,533 (£330)	24,336 (£553)
Moscow to Irkutsk (slow train 340 or 350)	3,594 (£81)	8,859 (£201)	17,660 (£401)
St Petersburg to Irkutsk (Firmeny train 10 *Baikal*)	5,303 (£121)	13,012 (£295)	23,329 (£530)
Moscow to Ekaterinburg (Firmeny train 2 or 16)	2,299 (£52)	5,583 (£127)	11,189 (£254)
Ekaterinburg to Irkutsk (Firmeny train 10 *Baikal*)	3,801 (£86)	9,294 (£211)	16,665 (£379)
Irkutsk to Vladivostok (Firmeny train 2 *Rossiya*)	5,254 (£119)	12,901 (£293)	16,900 (£384)
Irkutsk to Ulan Bator (train 362)	About £27/$40	About £40/$60	–

Buying tickets at the ticket office is a practical option for most Russian domestic journeys, such as Moscow–Irkutsk or Irkutsk–Vladivostok or even Moscow–Vladivostok, provided that you are prepared to take a different train or travel a day later than planned if your first choice of train is fully booked. However, if you have limited time and a settled itinerary, pre-booking your trains via an agency is a better option.

Demand for the direct Moscow–Beijing and Moscow–Ulan Bator trains exceeds supply and these particular trains get fully booked even before bookings open to the public, as travel agencies buy up all the tickets to re-sell them. This means you'll almost certainly have to use an agency if you want to travel on these direct trains. The official fare for these trains is therefore irrelevant, as agencies charge whatever they think their market will bear.

With or without 'services'? On the best Russian trains you can buy tickets 'without services', meaning without any meals, or 'with services', meaning with all your meals included, either served in the restaurant or in your compartment. All the fares shown above are 'without services'. Expect to pay an extra 1,336 rubles (£31) in *kupé* or 2,211 rubles (£50) in *spalny vagon* for a 'with services' ticket on train 2 from Moscow to Irkutsk for example – not bad value for a four-day trip!

If you buy tickets from a Russian travel agency

Unless you have lots of time and can afford to take pot luck when you get to Moscow, you'll probably want to book your trains in advance. Russian Railways sells tickets online, but only in Russian, so most westerners buy tickets through a travel agency, either a local Russian agency (cheapest) or a specialist western agency (more expensive). Different agencies charge completely different prices for the same journey, but to give you a very rough idea, here are the sorts of fares you can expect to pay if you shop around and book through the cheapest Russian agency. Depending on the agency, you may need to add a courier fee or a credit card charge (up to 12 per cent) to these fares. Be aware that agencies' websites aren't always kept up to date, so you may be quoted a higher price when you actually contact them.

One-way fare, per person	*Platskartny* 3rd class bunks	*Kupé* 2nd class 4-berth	*Spalny vagon* 1st class 2-berth
Moscow to Beijing (Trans-Mongolian, train 4)	–	£555 ($804)	£780 ($1,131)
Moscow to Beijing (Trans-Manchurian, train 20)	–	£564 ($817)	£857 ($1,242)
Moscow to Vladivostok (Firmeny train 2, *Rossiya*)	£228 ($330)	£556 ($806)	£1,037 ($1,503)
Moscow to Irkutsk (Firmeny train 2, *Rossiya*)	£179 ($259)	£434 ($629)	£724 ($1,049)
Moscow to Ulan Bator (train 4 or 6)	–	£330 ($478)	£498 ($722)
Irkutsk to Ulan Bator (train 362)	–	£161 ($233)	–
Irkutsk to Beijing (train 4 via Mongolia)	–	£303 ($439)	£467 ($677)
Irkutsk to Beijing (train 20 via Manchuria)	–	£386 ($559)	£568 ($823)
Ulan Bator to Beijing (train 4)	–	£204 ($295)	£345 ($500)
Ulan Bator to Beijing (train 24)	–	£165 ($239)	£268 ($388)

If you buy tickets from a western travel agency

There are various western agencies who specialise in Trans-Siberian travel. They can arrange a tailor-made tour for you, but will sell you just a train ticket if you like. Their prices vary enormously, so shop around.

If you buy tickets in Ulan Bator

A ticket for Ulan Bator to Irkutsk costs about 33,000 togrog (£20/$30) if bought at the station.

If you buy tickets at the station or through China Travel Service (CITS) in Beijing

You can buy tickets in person at Beijing main station or via CITS (the Chinese state tourist agency). You can check fares at **www.cits.net** (click 'Train' at the top).

One-way fare, per person	2nd class 4-berth (hard class)	1st class 4-berth (soft class)	1st class 2-berth (deluxe soft class)
Beijing to Moscow (train 3)	£417 ($608)	£605 ($881)	£661 ($963)
Beijing to Moscow (train 19)	£488 ($711)	–	£745 ($1,085)
Beijing to Irkutsk (train 3)	£268 ($391)	£387 ($564)	£420 ($611)
Beijing to Irkutsk (train 19)	£280 ($407)	–	£423 ($616)
Beijing to Ulan Bator (train 3 or 23)	£141 ($206)	£187 ($272)	£208 ($301)

Child fares

In Russia, children under 5 sharing a berth with an adult go free, children aged 5 to 10 travel at half the adult fare.

On the Trans-Manchurian and Trans-Mongolian international trains (trains 3, 4, 19, 20), children under 4 go free if they share a berth with an adult, children aged 4 to 11 inclusive travel at three quarters of the adult fare.

For journeys wholly within China, children under 120 cm tall travel free, children 120–150 cm tall travel for half fare, children over 150 cm tall pay full fare.

HOW TO BUY TICKETS – EASTBOUND

There are three ways to book a trip on the Trans-Siberian Railway, each with advantages and disadvantages:

- Option 1: Buy a ticket yourself at the station ticket office – the cheapest method, but the most uncertain and not always practical.

- Option 2: Buy tickets in advance through a Russian agency – quite easy, fairly cheap, arguably the best option.

- Option 3: Let a specialist western travel agency arrange it all for you – least hassle, but the most expensive.

OPTION *1: Buy tickets at the ticket office*

You can walk up to the ticket office at any Russian station and buy a ticket or tickets for any journey within Russia, including the Trans-Siberian Railway. This is the cheapest way to book because you pay the real Russian Railways price. It is not usually too difficult to get a ticket for internal Russian journeys a day or two before departure, for example Moscow–Ekaterinburg, Moscow–Irkutsk or even Moscow–Vladivostok, especially if you can be a bit flexible about your exact departure date or class of travel. The daily Irkutsk–Ulan Bator train is not too difficult to book at the ticket office, either. To avoid language problems, it's a good idea to learn the Russian alphabet so you can write down your requirements to show to the ticket office staff – see page 555. When writing dates, use roman numerals for the month, e.g., for '3 June 2011' write '3 VI 2011'. Many big Russian stations now have a *servis tsentr* (service centre) where you pay a small fee (about 100 rubles) to book your ticket in a relaxed air-conditioned environment. It might well be worth it! Russian railway reservations are computerised, so you can arrange any journey from any station, as long as the journey starts in Russia or one of the ex-Soviet states.

For the weekly direct Moscow–Beijing Trans-Mongolian and Trans-Manchurian trains (trains 4 and 20) and the weekly Moscow–Ulan Bator train (train 6) demand exceeds supply, especially in the busy May–September peak season. Travel agencies buy up all the tickets on these trains, so you'd often find them fully booked even if you went to the ticket office the moment bookings opened to the public 45 days before departure. So these particular trains should be booked through an agency; see the next section.

For information on buying train tickets at the station in Ulan Bator (Mongolia), see page 49.

OPTION *2: Buy tickets from a local Russian agency*

Unless you're on a six-month sabbatical with time no object, you'll probably want to arrange your Trans-Siberian tickets in advance before you leave home. A good option is to buy tickets over the internet through a local Russian travel agency. Naturally, these agencies charge more than you'd pay at the ticket office, but not always that much more. Prices vary enormously, so shop around. Make sure that any quote you get is inclusive of any credit card fees, and that you know whether it's for a slow, low-quality train (three-digit train numbers) or one of the fast, quality trains such as the *Baikal* or *Rossiya* (one- or two-digit train numbers and usually a name).

As far as the popular Moscow–Beijing and Moscow–Ulan Bator direct trains are concerned, here's how the system works: Russian Railways open up bookings to travel agencies for these and other trains 60 days before departure, whereas bookings don't open to the public until 45 days before departure. The travel agencies know that demand for these particular trains exceeds supply, so they buy up blocks of tickets, which means hardly any are left for sale at the ticket office when public bookings open. The agencies then re-sell these tickets for whatever price they can get, which often bears no relation to the face value of the ticket. Trans-Mongolian Moscow–Beijing train 4 is particularly popular, and first class deluxe 2-berth sleepers on this train can sell out very quickly indeed, such is the demand from rich, privacy-loving westerners. Travel agencies keep their own waiting lists and will take Trans-Siberian bookings months in advance, well before the 60-day point when they can purchase the actual ticket, so contact a booking agency as far ahead as you can. If you're booking closer to the departure date, you may find that one travel agency says the train is full, but another agency has bought a block of tickets speculatively and has some left, or knows a rival agency that it can buy tickets from – another reason to shop around.

Here are some reputable Russian agencies to try:

Real Russia, **www.realrussia.co.uk/trains**, a good Russian/British agency
Svezhy Veter, **www.sv-agency.udm.ru/sv/trains.htm**
G&R International, **www.hostels.ru**
Way to Russia, **www.waytorussia.net/Services/TrainTickets.html**, also known as **www.trainline.ru**
All-Russia Travel Service, **www.rusrailtravel.ru**
Ost-West, **www.ostwest.com**

Real Russia, Svezhy Veter, G&R International and Ost-West have all been highly recommended by seat61 correspondents, and are all reputable companies. Tickets can be picked up at their offices in Moscow or sent to you for a courier fee of about £27 ($40). You may be asked to fax them a photocopy of your credit card and/or passport, which sounds dodgy, but for some reason this is quite normal when dealing with Russian companies. Be prepared for a credit card fee of between 7 and 12 per cent, but this is still a safer way to buy tickets than using a money transfer.

However far ahead you place your order with an agency, bear in mind that they cannot make the actual booking with Russian Railways (and therefore cannot absolutely guarantee your reservation) until 60 days before departure. Usually there's no problem at all, but very occasionally there are more tourists wanting berths than there are berths on the train; as noted above, this is true especially of the deluxe 2-berth first class on Trans-Mongolian trains 3 and 4. If deluxe first class is your preferred option but you would accept a first or second class 4-berth ticket (or you would be willing to pay for a whole 4-berth compartment) should the deluxe 2-berth be sold out, then it's worth telling the agency so at the outset.

These Russian agencies can also book hotels in Moscow and other Russian cities, and they can arrange a visa support letter for Russia (if you're not using the recommended visa service at **www.realrussia.co.uk**). Most of them can arrange hotels or train bookings in Mongolia or China too, through their contacts there. If you prefer to arrange these separately, see the advice on page 49.

OPTION 3: *Let a specialist western agency arrange your trip*

The most hassle-free way of booking a Trans-Siberian trip, but the most expensive, is to arrange a tailor-made itinerary through one of the western travel agencies who specialise in independent travel to Russia, a few of which are detailed below. They can arrange your Russian visa, your hotel in Moscow, your Trans-Siberian train reservation, stopovers and tours if you want them in places like Irkutsk or Mongolia, connecting trains in China and even the ship to Japan.

- Real Russia, **www.realrussia.co.uk**. This is a joint UK/Russian company, whose business was originally just arranging visas, then selling Russian train tickets, and now they've started doing inclusive Trans-Siberian tours as well. They know what they're doing, and have tours with better-class hotels and more feature-laden itineraries at cheaper prices than many other western operators. For example, a Moscow–Beijing 'Three capitals' trip with visits, city tours and hotels in Moscow, Ulan Bator and Beijing starts at £1,335 per person for two people travelling together or £1,450 for a solo traveller, with two tour departures a month, departure dates guaranteed, with no minimum group size, but there's a maximum group size so (as their site puts it) you're a small group not a 'herd'.

- The Russia Experience, **www.trans-siberian.co.uk**, telephone 020 8566 8846. Another reliable and experienced agency, The Russia Experience charges about £509 for a ticket from Moscow to Beijing in second class 4-berth accommodation on train 20, including two nights in a hotel in Moscow. Travelling first class in a 2-berth room on this train costs about £750. The cost of getting to Moscow, hotels in China, visas and return trains/flights are all extra – you can arrange these yourself or the agency can do this for you. Unfortunately, The Russia Experience no longer books places on the Chinese Trans-Mongolian train (train 4), but they can book you on the Moscow–Ulan Bator and Ulan Bator–Beijing trains with a stopover in Mongolia.

- Intourist, **www.intouristuk.com**, telephone 0870 112 1232. A well-established and experienced UK agency, Intourist can arrange tailor-made Trans-Siberian itineraries. It charges about £720 per person for a Moscow–Beijing ticket on the Trans-Mongolian train in second class 4-berth, including one night in a hotel in Moscow. First class deluxe 2-berth costs about £1,013. Intourist can also book westbound Beijing–Moscow trains (which for some reason cost a few pounds more than eastbound), stopover tours along the Trans-Siberian Railway, the Vladivostok–Japan ferry and key trains in China. Getting to Moscow, hotels in China, visas and return trains/flights are extra – you can arrange these yourself or the agency can do this for you. For Moscow to Vladivostok, Intourist charges about £792 one-way in second class 4-berth or £1,445 in first class 2-berth.

- Vodka Train, **www.vodkatrain.com**. An Australian agency offering budget Trans-Siberian tours.

- Sundowners, **www.sundownerstravel.com**. Sundowners offers all sorts of tours, including trips covering just train travel plus a night or two in a hotel at each end.

- Trans-Sputnik, **www.trans-sputnik.nl**. This is a Dutch agency, but very good value so they are worth contacting even if you're not Dutch! They offer one-way Moscow–Beijing fares from €510 (£465) second class 4-berth or €750 (£680) first class 2-berth on train 4, a bit more for train 20. They can also arrange an Amsterdam–Moscow ticket from €265 (£240) one-way with sleeper.

How to buy train tickets in Ulan Bator, Mongolia

You can buy tickets at the International Railway Ticketing Office on Zamchyd Gudamj, a couple of roads over from the railway station. The foreigners' booking office is in room 212, open 08:00–20:00 Monday to Friday (at weekends use the normal booking window). International trains to Irkutsk, Moscow and Beijing can be booked up to 30 days in advance, except for berths on the Moscow–Beijing and Beijing–Moscow trains 3 and 4, which only become available the day before departure.

A good starting point for arranging hotels and travel in Mongolia is the official Mongolia tourist board website, **www.mongoliatourism.gov.mn**, or you can also try **www.discover.mn**. To reserve trains starting in Ulan Bator from outside Mongolia, try contacting a hotel or guesthouse who may book the train for you, or try one of the Russian agencies (see pages 46–7) as they may have contacts in Mongolia who can arrange tickets starting in Ulan Bator.

How to buy train tickets onwards to Shanghai, Xian, Hong Kong, Vietnam

If you book your Trans-Siberian trip through a travel agency (either a western or a Russian one) they may be able to book connecting trains within China for you, to Xian, Shanghai, Hong Kong or even Hanoi in Vietnam. Or you can book trains in China yourself at the ticket office when you get there. Alternatively, you can pre-book using **www.chinatripadvisor.com**. For train times, fares and how to book trains in China, see the China chapter, page 286. Train times and fares for the twice-weekly train from Beijing to Hanoi are given in the Vietnam chapter, pages 438–9.

How to buy tickets for the ship to Korea or Japan

If you arrange your journey through a UK travel agency, they may be able to book the ferries from Vladivostok to Korea/Japan or from Shanghai to Japan for you. However, it's cheaper to book these ships yourself by emailing or telephoning the ferry company. See pages 63–5.

HOW TO BUY TICKETS – WESTBOUND

OPTION 1: Buy tickets in person at Beijing

The absolute cheapest way to buy westbound Trans-Siberian tickets is in person at one of the reservation offices in Beijing. However, the two weekly Beijing–Moscow trains get booked up very early, so buy tickets as far in advance as you can. It is easier to get berths on westbound trains than on eastbound, and easier in winter than in the peak summer season from May to September. Train 3 to Moscow via Mongolia is often fully booked a couple of weeks in advance, especially in summer; train 19 via Manchuria occasionally has berths available even a few days before departure (but not always!). The basic message is this: if you positively have to be on a specific train on a specific date, forget booking at the ticket office; you should pre-book via CITS or some other agency and pay their extra fee. But if you're living in Beijing, or plan to be there for some time, and can be a bit flexible about exactly what date you leave, booking in person can be a good option. You can buy Trans-Siberian train tickets in person in Beijing at:

- The international train booking office on the ground floor of the Beijing International Hotel. This is about five minutes' walk north of Beijing main station on Jianguo Men Nei Dajie, open 08:30–12:00 and 13:30–17:00 Monday to Friday, 09:00–11:00 and 14:00–16:00 at weekends and holidays. The staff speak basic English and leaflets are available with international train times in English.

- BTG Travel and Tours, on Fwai Dajie between the New Otani and Gloria Plaza hotels, open 08:00–20:00. They have a desk for Trans-Siberian tickets, with information in English.

OPTION 2: *Buy tickets by phone or email with China Travel Service (CITS)*

CITS is the official Chinese state tourist agency, and this is probably the cheapest way to buy westbound Trans-Siberian tickets starting in Beijing, other than buying in person at the ticket office. You can book trains from Beijing to Moscow, Irkutsk or Ulan Bator by emailing support-en@cits.com.cn (you can check details on the CITS website, **www.cits.net**) or by calling CITS on +86 10 6512 0507 or +86 10 6512 0503. Expect to pay by bank transfer rather than credit card. Reports also suggest that CITS can't book Beijing–Irkutsk tickets on train 3, only Beijing–Krasnoyarsk and beyond, so by all means ask for Beijing–Irkutsk, but be prepared to accept an offer of a Beijing–Krasnoyarsk ticket and simply get off in Irkutsk; this will still be the cheapest option.

OPTION 3: *Buy tickets through an agency in China or Hong Kong*

If you're in China or Japan and want an agency to arrange your westbound Trans-Siberian trip, try one of these two agencies:

- Chinatripadvisor, **www.chinatripadvisor.com**. If you just want the Trans-Siberian train ticket, a cheap option is to buy it through this website. Typical costs for Beijing to Moscow are £420 ($610) one-way on Trans-Mongolian train 3 or £495 ($719) on Trans-Manchurian train 19 in second class 4-berth; £675 ($979) on train 3 or £764 ($1,109) on train 19 in first class 2-berth.

- Monkey Shrine, **www.monkeyshrine.com**. Monkey Shrine is an experienced China-based tour agency that can arrange a tailor-made itinerary with stopovers and hotels along the way, plus help with visas. Monkey Shrine offers a good service, but is naturally more expensive than booking it all yourself via CITS. A key advantage is being able to arrange onward tickets, not just tickets starting in Beijing, and to arrange hotels or tours along the way.

OPTION 4: *Buy Russian train tickets from a Russian agency*

If you want a ticket from Vladivostok to Moscow, or intend stopping off within Russia and need some tickets for Trans-Siberian travel wholly within Russia, you can book through several Russian agencies: see pages 46–7 for details. They can often arrange westbound Beijing to Moscow tickets through their contacts in China, too.

For travel from Japan to Europe via Vladivostok, you can book the ship from Japan to Vladivostok directly with the shipping company via **www.dbsferry.com**, then book the Vladivostok–Moscow train through one of these Russian agencies.

OPTION 5: *Let a specialist western agency arrange your trip*

The most hassle-free way to book Trans-Siberian travel, but the most expensive, is to arrange a tailor-made itinerary with a western agency specialising in Trans-Siberian trips. They can arrange your whole journey, either eastbound or westbound, with stopovers and hotels along the way if you want them, plus visa support. See pages 48–9 for agency details, links and sample prices.

How to buy train tickets in Ulan Bator, Mongolia

See page 49 for details.

How to buy train tickets for onwards travel from Moscow to western Europe

Don't cheat! Finish your Trans-Siberian journey by train all the way to London St Pancras. You can book onwards travel by train from Moscow to Berlin, Brussels, Prague, Vienna and many other European cities through a Russian agency (see pages 46–7 for suggestions), though the final Eurostar leg to London will need to be booked separately online. See pages 66–8 for train information from Moscow to London.

VISAS

After sorting out your Trans-Siberian tickets, you need to get your visas.

Arranging a Russian visa

You will need a Russian visa. Always check the latest visa information, as it changes from time to time. But here's a quick run-down of the arrangements as at 2010:

- **Tourist, transit or business visa?** A tourist visa allows stays of up to 30 days, and is usually what you need. A business visa allows a longer stay, but is more expensive. A transit visa allows up to 10 days in transit, but you aren't allowed to spend time in Moscow, as most Trans-Siberian travellers do, so a tourist visa is usually better.

- **When to apply?** Visas are only issued three months or less before your intended date of entry to Russia, so there's no need to apply before then. Ideally, allow a month for the visa processing, but if you have less time than this, don't panic, various agencies offer 'express' services that will help you get a visa much faster.

- **Letters of invitation and visa support:** A hangover from Soviet times is that to get a visa you need supporting documentation, usually just called 'visa support'. In theory, this is a letter of invitation from your travel agency setting out confirmed travel and accommodation arrangements for your entire stay in Russia or (for independent travellers) an accommodation voucher issued by your hotel(s) showing confirmed accommodation for each and every night you plan to spend in Russia. Having to pre-book all this would be ridiculously restrictive, so here's how it *really* works. You go to an agency such as **www.realrussia.co.uk** or one of the Russian agencies listed on page 46 and they sell you the necessary visa support for a small fee, which allows you to get a visa without any genuine hotel bookings, so you can travel around freely just as you would in any other country, buying tickets and finding hotels as you go. Behind the scenes, the agency usually has an arrangement with a local hotel; they make a dummy 'reservation' for the period you want to be in Russia so they can legally issue the visa support, though of course you don't pay for the hotel and everyone knows (apart from the Russian government) that you have no intention of ever using that hotel room. Crazy, eh?

- **The easy way to get a Russian visa,** and the fastest, is to ask **www.realrussia.co.uk** to get it for you. Real Russia is a reliable UK agency based in Russia which arranges Russian visas simply and cheaply, with all the necessary visa support included in the price. They have been recommended by several seat61 correspondents. (Incidentally, seat61 gets a small commission if you buy through the link from the seat61 website.) Real Russia can also arrange visas for Belarus, Mongolia and China, and arrange train tickets too.

- **Dates of entry and exit:** Make sure you get these right. It should be obvious, but I've known people date their visa for the date they arrive in Moscow, then get thrown off their sleeper train when it arrives at the Russian frontier the night before, as their visa wasn't valid for entering Russia until the next day. Your date of entry into Russia is *the date you physically enter Russian territory*, in other words the date your train rolls across the frontier, not the date you reach Moscow, which is irrelevant. Similarly, your date of exit is the date you physically leave Russian territory, which on a westbound sleeper train could be the day *after* you leave Moscow. Double-check train times to see when you will reach the frontier, and double-check that the embassy have given you the right dates when you get your passport back with the visa.

- **More information:** The website of the Russian embassy in London is **www.rusemblon.org**. There is also good information on Russian visas at **www.waytorussia.net**.

Arranging a Belarus transit visa

You'll need a Belarus transit visa if you are travelling between London and Moscow on the direct London–Cologne–Berlin–Warsaw–Moscow route, as all the direct trains from Cologne, Berlin or Warsaw to Moscow or St Petersburg pass through Belarus. However, getting a Belarus transit visa is relatively straightforward. Note that if you plan to stop off in Belarus you'll need a tourist visa.

You will need to get your Russian visa before applying for the Belarus one, although you can apply for both together if you go through **www.realrussia.co.uk**.

- **Cost:** The Belarusians significantly increased visa fees in 2007 and again in 2008. A Belarus transit visa now costs £63 one-way or £114 return if you arrange it yourself direct with the embassy, or £83 one-way or £133 return arranged through Real Russia. It takes six working days, or there's an extra-fee express option which takes two days. Before you accuse Belarus of profiteering, be aware that the high costs are in retaliation for stringent visa requirements imposed on Belarusians by the UK Foreign Office.

● For official visa information see the Belarus embassy website, **http://belembassy.org/uk/**, or call 020 7938 3677. The embassy address in London is 6 Kensington Court, London W8 5DL, visa section open 09:00–12:30 Monday to Friday.

● If you live in the UK, the easiest and fastest way to get a Belarus visa is to use Real Russia, **www.realrussia.co.uk** (see page 48).

● **Should you avoid Belarus?** If the high visa fees are an issue you might want to try (and some people go to great lengths to do so). Just remember that if you pay the visa fee, you can travel quickly and simply from western Europe to Moscow on a direct train through Belarus, saving time and expense. To avoid Belarus by travelling via the Baltic states entails an awkward and time-consuming relay race of trains and buses, taking at least 48 hours longer, with two extra hotel nights. The route via Ukraine (Ukraine no longer requires EU citizens to buy a visa) is faster, but will still take at least an extra 24 hours, with a change of trains in Kiev and with no easy way to pre-book the Kiev–Moscow train before you get to Kiev. In other words, the detour might be interesting if you have the time and particularly want to see Ukraine or Lithuania/Latvia on the way, but it will take longer and in the end cost more than simply buying the visa and travelling direct.

● **Getting a Belarus transit visa in Moscow:** If you're travelling westbound and want to arrange a Belarus visa in Moscow, here's how. The Belarus embassy is at Maroseika 17/6, 101990, Moscow. It's a couple of blocks from Kitai Gorod and Lubyanka metro stations. You will need photocopies of your passport, your Russian visa and your train ticket through Belarus, one passport photo, US$45 for same-day visa issue or US$36 for next-day visa issue (for EU citizens), payable in clean post-1995 US dollar bills, no change given. The visa office is open 10:00–12:00 Monday, Tuesday, Thursday and Friday (allow plenty of time) and you pick up your passport and transit visa between 16:00 and 16:30 on those days. The visa office entrance is down the side, the door on the right, then walk up the stairs to the second floor. If you don't already have the necessary US dollars, there is an exchange office nearby. US passport holders are currently charged $177 for a same-day visa, because of charges imposed by the USA on Belarusians. Visa regulations and costs change from time to time; the above is current at the time of writing.

There is also a Belarus consulate in St Petersburg, at 8/46 Naberezhnaya Robespiera, Apt. 66.

Arranging a Mongolian visa

If you are taking the Trans-Mongolian route and you're an EU citizen, you'll need a Mongolian transit visa (if crossing Mongolia non-stop) or tourist visa (if you intend stopping off).

- See **www.embassyofmongolia.co.uk** for information on how to obtain a Mongolian visa in the UK. US, Singaporean and Malaysian citizens and some other nationalities do not now need a visa for Mongolia; check on the website for details.

- As of October 2008 the Mongolian embassy in London no longer accepts visa applications by post, so either take your passport round to the embassy in person and collect it again some days later, or use a visa service agency such as Real Russia, **www.realrussia.co.uk**. The Mongolian embassy in London is at 7–8 Kensington Court, London W8 5DL, open Monday to Friday 10:00–12:30.

Arranging a Chinese visa

You'll need a Chinese visa if you're visiting China.

- You should apply for a visa at least a month before you leave, but less than three months before entering China.

- In the UK, the Chinese embassy (**www.chinese-embassy.org.uk**) has outsourced visa issuing, and UK citizens should apply for a visa via **www.visaforchina.org.uk**. It costs about £30 for a single-entry tourist visa. Alternatively, you can use a visa service agency such as Real Russia, **www.realrussia.co.uk**.

- Chinese visa requirements were tightened in 2008 for the Olympics, but were relaxed again afterwards. You no longer need confirmed tickets into and out of China, or confirmed hotel bookings for every night in China.

- The Chinese embassy in Moscow will now only issue Chinese visas to Russian nationals, so don't plan to get your Chinese visa there.

- Note that the validity window (the period for which a visa is valid when issued) has been reduced to just a couple of months, so don't plan on months and months of travelling around before you reach China, as your visa will have expired by then!

TRANS-SIBERIAN TIMETABLE

This is a summary of the most important Trans-Siberian trains between Moscow, Irkutsk, Vladivostok, Ulan Bator and Beijing. You can check all Russian and Trans-Siberian train times at **www.realrussia.co.uk** or **www.poezda.net**. A complete timetable can also be found in the Thomas Cook Overseas Timetable, if you can get hold of one. All trains run to Moscow time, and the times below are Moscow time except where shown – remember that local time can be up to 8 hours ahead of Moscow time! Trains normally stop at each station for 5 to 15 minutes, a bit longer at the more important stations.

Moscow → *Ulan Bator, Beijing and Vladivostok*

Distance from Moscow (km)	Hours ahead of Moscow			Train 2 *Rossiya* Every 2nd day	Train 4 Tuesday	Train 6 Wednes-day	Train 20 *Vostok* Friday	Train 10 *Baikal* Every 2nd day	Trains 340/350 Daily	Train 362 Daily	Train 24 1 or 2 per week
				Note A	Notes B, I	Notes C, I	Notes D, I	Note E	Note F	Note G	Note H
0	0	Moscow (Yaroslavski station)	dep	21:25 day 1	21:35 day 1	21:35 day 1	23:55 day 1	–	13:35 day 1	–	–
	0	St Petersburg (Ladozhski station)	dep	|	|	|	|	16:22 day 1	|	–	–
1,397	+2	Perm	dep	17:45 day 2	17:55 day 2	17:55 day 2	20:37 day 2	22:34 day 2	15:24 day 2	–	–
1,778	+2	Ekaterinburg (Sverdlovsk)	dep	23:29 day 2	23:39 day 2	23:39 day 2	02:24 day 3	04:30 day 3	21:14 day 2	–	–
2,676	+3	Omsk	dep	11:28 day 3	11:51 day 3	11:51 day 3	15:26 day 3	17:30 day 3	12:16 day 3	–	–
3,303	+4	Novosibirsk	dep	19:27 day 3	19:13 day 3	19:13 day 3	23:12 day 3	01:59 day 4	21:20 day 3	–	–
4,065	+4	Krasnoyarsk	dep	07:40 day 4	07:06 day 4	07:06 day 4	11:02 day 4	13:48 day 4	10:35 day 4	–	–
5,152	+5	Irkutsk	arr	01:14 day 5	23:55 day 4	23:55 day 4	04:02 day 5	07:39 day 5	04:38 day 5	–	–
			dep	01:39 day 5	00:25 day 5	00:25 day 5	04:32 day 5	–	05:19 day 5	16:50 day 1	–
5,608	+5	Ulan Ude	dep	08:54 day 5	08:30 day 5	08:30 day 5	11:35 day 5	–	12:29 day 5	01:55 day 2	–
6,265	+5/+4*	Ulan Bator (local time)	arr	|	06:30 day 6	07:30 day 6	|	–	–	06:10 day 3	–
			dep	|	07:15 day 6	–	|	–	–	–	08:05 day 1
6,780	+5/+4*	Erlian (Chinese frontier) (local time)	arr	|	21:00 day 6	–	|	–	–	–	22:00 day 1
7,574	+5/+4*	Harbin (local time)	dep	|	|	–	12:50 day 7	–	–	–	–
7,622**	+5/+4*	Beijing (local time)	arr	|	14:04 day 7	–	05:31 day 8	–	–	–	14:33 day 2
8,492	+7	Khabarovsk	dep	11:10 day 7	–	–	–	–	–	–	–
9,258	+7	Vladivostok	arr	23:23 day 7	–	–	–	–	–	–	–

* China and Mongolia have no daylight saving time, so are 4 hours ahead of Moscow in summer, 5 hours ahead in winter.

** Moscow–Beijing is 7,622 km (4,735 miles) via Ulan Bator or 8,986 km (5,623 miles) via Harbin.

Note A: *Rossiya*. Firmeny quality train. Runs every second day, leaving Moscow on odd-number dates (1st, 3rd, 5th etc.), except 31st of the month. 2-berth *spalny vagon* and 4-berth *kupé* sleepers, *platskartny* berths and restaurant car.

Note B: Moscow–Beijing express via the Trans-Mongolian route. Leaves Moscow every Tuesday. Chinese coaches. First class 2-berth, first class 4-berth, second class 4-berth sleepers. Restaurant car (Russian in Russia, then Mongolian, then Chinese).

Note C: Runs from Moscow on Wednesday, also Thursday in summer. 2-berth and 4-berth sleepers and restaurant car. Russian and Mongolian coaches.

Note D: *Vostok*. Trans-Manchurian Moscow–Beijing express. Leaves Moscow every Friday. Russian coaches. 2-berth *spalny vagon*, 4-berth *kupé* sleepers. Russian restaurant car in Russia, Chinese restaurant car in China.

Note E: *Baikal*. Firmeny quality train. Runs from St Petersburg on odd-number dates (1st, 3rd, 5th etc.), except the 31st. 2-berth *spalny vagon*, 4-berth *kupé* sleepers, *platskartny* berths and restaurant car. The Baikal used to run from Moscow, but was diverted to start from St Petersburg as of June 2010.

Note F: This is a slower, cheaper, lower-quality alternative to the top-quality *Rossiya* and *Baikal* for journeys within Russia. 2-berth *spalny vagon*, 4-berth *kupé* sleepers and *platskartny* berths. Train number is 340 on some dates, 350 on others.

Note G: Runs daily. 4-berth *kupé* sleepers and *platskartny* berths from Irkutsk to Ulan Bator.

Note H: Runs from Ulan Bator to Beijing on Thursday all year round. Please double-check days of running when you book as Chinese Railways have changed the days several times over the last few years. Soft class 2-berth and 4-berth sleepers and hard class 4-berth sleepers.

Note I: Trains 4, 6 and 20 from Moscow to Ulan Bator and Beijing can generally only be used by passengers making an *international* journey (for example, Moscow to Beijing, Irkutsk to Beijing or Moscow to Ulan Bator), not for internal journeys within Russia (for example, Moscow to Irkutsk), where there are plenty of domestic trains available. So if you want to stop off at Irkutsk (for example), you will need to take a Russian internal train (the *Rossiya* or the *Baikal*) between Moscow and Irkutsk.

There are many other slower trains not shown here, including a daily slow train (Train 904) from Moscow to Vladivostok taking nine days in all. You can find these using the online train timetable at **www.realrussia.co.uk/trains** or **www.poezda.net**.

Vladivostok, Beijing and Ulan Bator → *Moscow*

Hours ahead of Moscow			Train 1 Rossiya	Train 3	Train 5	Train 19 Vostok	Train 9 Baikal	Train 23	Train 263	Trains 339/349
			Every 2nd day	Wednes-day	Tuesday	Saturday	Every 2nd day	1 or 2 per week	Daily	Daily
			Note J	Notes K, S	Notes L, S	Notes M, S	Note N	Note P	Note Q	Note R
+7	Vladivostok	dep	14:52 day 1	–	–	–	–	–	–	–
+7	Khabarovsk	dep	03:44 day 2	–	–	–	–	–	–	–
+5/+4*	Beijing (local time)	dep	I	07:45 day 1	–	22:56 day 1	–	07:40 day 1	–	–
+5/+4*	Harbin (local time)	dep	I	I	–	15:10 day 2	–	I	–	–
+5/+4*	Erlian (frontier) (local time)	arr	I	20:37 day 1	–	I	–	20:39 day 1	–	–
+5/+4*	Ulan Bator (local time)	arr	I	13:20 day 2	–	I	–	13:15 day 2	–	–
		dep	I	13:50 day 2	13:50 day 1	I	–	–	21:10 day 1	–
+5	Naushki (Russian frontier)	arr	I	19:14 day 2	19:14 day 1	I	–	–	xx:xx day 2	–
+5	Ulan Ude	dep	05:32 day 4	03:40 day 3	03:40 day 2	06:33 day 4	–	–	17:10 day 2	05:43 day 1
+5	Irkutsk	arr	12:20 day 4	10:40 day 3	10:40 day 2	13:10 day 4	–	–	02:31 day 3	13:25 day 1
		dep	12:50 day 4	11:05 day 3	11:05 day 2	13:40 day 4	14:20 day 1	–	–	14:05 day 1
+4	Krasnoyarsk	dep	06:42 day 5	04:07 day 4	04:07 day 3	07:24 day 5	08:48 day 2	–	–	08:27 day 2
+4	Novosibirsk	dep	19:54 day 5	16:17 day 4	16:17 day 3	19:37 day 5	21:09 day 2	–	–	21:40 day 2
+3	Omsk	dep	03:33 day 6	23:56 day 4	23:56 day 4	03:14 day 6	06:36 day 3	–	–	06:02 day 3
+2	Ekaterinburg (Sverdlovsk)	dep	15:58 day 6	12:08 day 5	12:08 day 4	15:38 day 6	21:05 day 3	–	–	20:57 day 3
+2	Perm	dep	21:35 day 6	17:45 day 5	17:45 day 4	21:26 day 6	03:11 day 4	–	–	03:01 day 4
0	St Petersburg (Ladozhski station)	arr	I	I	I	I	10:00 day 5	–	–	I
0	Moscow (Yaroslavski station)	arr	17:58 day 7	14:28 day 6	14:28 day 5	18:13 day 7	–	–	–	04:11 day 5

You can check the times and days of running of these and other, slower trains not shown here using the online train timetable at **www.realrussia.co.uk/trains** or **www.poezda.net**.

* China and Mongolia have no daylight saving time, so are 4 hours ahead of Moscow in summer, 5 hours ahead in winter.

xx:xx = exact time not available

Note J: *Rossiya*. Firmeny quality train. Runs from Vladivostok on even-numbered dates from the 8th of each month onwards, plus the 2nd, 4th, 6th of March, May, July, October, December, and the 1st, 3rd, 5th of other months. 2-berth *spalny vagon* and 4-berth *kupé* sleepers, *platskartny* berths and restaurant car.

Note K: Beijing–Moscow express via the trans-Mongolian route. Chinese coaches. First class 2-berth (deluxe soft class), first class 4-berth (soft class), second class 4-berth (hard class). Chinese restaurant car in China, Russian restaurant car in Russia.

Note L: Runs from Ulan Bator on Tuesday, also Thursday in summer. 2-berth *spalny vagon* and 4-berth *kupé* sleepers and restaurant car. Russian and Mongolian coaches.

Note M: *Vostok*. Trans-Manchurian route. Russian coaches. 2-berth *spalny vagon*, 4-berth *kupé* sleepers. Restaurant car (Chinese, then Russian).

Note N: *Baikal*. Firmeny quality train. Runs from Irkutsk on odd dates (1st, 3rd, 5th etc.), except the 31st. 2-berth *spalny vagon* and 4-berth *kupé* sleepers and restaurant car.

Note P: Runs from Beijing to Ulan Bator on Tuesday, or maybe Saturday. Please double-check days of running as it has changed several times over the last few years. The train has deluxe 2-berth, soft class 4-berth and hard class 4-berth sleepers.

Note Q: 4-berth *kupé* sleepers and *platskartny* berths from Ulan Bator to Irkutsk.

Note R: This is a slightly slower, cheaper, lower-quality alternative to top-quality *Rossiya* and *Baikal* for journeys within Russia. Train number is 339 on some dates, 349 on others.

Note S: Trains 3, 5 and 19 from Beijing and Ulan Bator to Moscow can only be used for *international* journeys. They *cannot* be used for internal journeys wholly within Russia. If you want to stop off at Irkutsk (for example), book a Russian internal train (for example the *Rossiya* or the *Baikal*) for the journey between Irkutsk and Moscow. Train 3 may also not take passengers from Beijing to Ulan Bator, at least in the peak summer season, as it is largely reserved for passengers going through to Russia. Beijing–Ulan Bator passengers should take train 23 instead.

Alternatives between Ulan Bator and Beijing

If you're trying to travel the Trans-Mongolian route flexibly, buying tickets as you go, you will find there are daily trains between Moscow, Irkutsk and even Ulan Bator, making this section relatively easy without pre-booking, but between Ulan Bator and Beijing there are just two direct trains a week, one a through train from Moscow (so there are limited berths available for passengers joining at Ulan Bator), the other a weekly train whose day of running Chinese Railways keeps changing from one year to the next so no one's quite sure. However, there are alternatives, so you're unlikely to be completely stuck. A hard class sleeper train runs from Ulan Bator to Hohot four times a week, leaving Ulan Bator around 20:05 and arriving at Jining Nan (Jining South) around 19:00 next day; from Jining Nan to Beijing there are several daily trains, journey time 9 hours, fare about £6 ($8) with soft class seat. There may also be a daily overnight train from Ulan Bator to Saynshand, 40 km from the Chinese frontier at Erlian; you can get from Saynshand to Erlian by local bus or taxi, then take one of the daily trains from Erlian to Jining Nan (Jining South) and from Jining Nan to Beijing. You can confirm train times for any journey within China at **www.chinahighlights.com/china-trains/** (click 'trains between 2 of all stations'; note that this system recognises 'Jining South', not 'Jining Nan', and be aware that trains 3, 4, 23, 24 aren't daily). There is no way to check Mongolian train times online.

FERRY CONNECTIONS FROM CHINA TO JAPAN

Two shipping companies sail weekly year-round from Shanghai to either Kobe or Osaka in Japan, from where there are 'bullet trains' to Tokyo. A third shipping line links Tianjin (only half an hour or so from Beijing by train) with Kobe.

OPTION 1: *The Shanghai Ferry Company*

The Shanghai Ferry Company sails between Shanghai and Osaka, one a week in either direction, taking two nights. From Shanghai the boat departs at 11:00 every Tuesday, arriving in Osaka at 09:00 on Thursday; from Osaka it departs every Friday at 12:00, arriving at Shanghai at 12:00 on Sunday. For details see **www.shanghai-ferry.co.jp**, and look for the 'English' button.

Their ship gets good reports. You can book a ticket on the Shanghai Ferry Company by emailing them, at pax@shanghai-ferry.co.jp for departures from Japan, or at zhangyz@suzhaohao.com for departures from Shanghai. You will be given a reference number and can pick up and pay for your ticket at the port. Fares start at around 20,000 Japanese yen (about £150) for a one-way ticket in an open-plan economy room, ¥22,000 (£170) in a standard cabin (4-berth) or ¥40,000 (£300) in a deluxe 2-berth cabin. Return tickets are available costing 50 per cent more than one-way fares. Check both sailing dates and fares at **www.shanghai-ferry.co.jp**.

OPTION 2: *The China-Japan International Ferry Company*

The other shipping company linking Shanghai and Japan is the China-Japan International Ferry Company, **www.chinajapanferry.com**, which also sails weekly, going alternately to Kobe and Osaka, taking two nights. The ship leaves Shanghai every Saturday at 13:00, arriving in Osaka or Kobe at 09:30 on Monday. From Osaka or Kobe it sails at 12:00 on Tuesday, arriving at Shanghai on Thursday (exact time varies). See **www.chinajapanferry.com** for schedules and to confirm fares.

Fares start at ¥20,000 or RMB1,300 (£130 or $195) one-way for a berth in a shared Japanese-style room accommodating 8–15 passengers or ¥25,000/RMB1,600 (£165 or $245) for a berth in a western-style 4-berth cabin. There's a 10 per cent discount for students, and children 6–11 travel at half fare. A range of cabins is available on board, with restaurants, café, and so on.

You can book via their online application form at **www.chinajapanferry.com** from 2 months (but no less than 7 days) before departure.

Alternatively, for sailings from China, you can telephone the Shanghai branch on +86 2165 957 988. There is someone who can speak English and the only information you need to give is your name, date of birth, class of travel and passport number. They will then make a reservation and you can buy the ticket at the port. If you are travelling from Japan to China the number to call is +81 3 5489 4800. This is the company's Tokyo branch, as unfortunately nobody can speak English at their Osaka office.

If you are booking a Trans-Siberian train through an agency such as The Russia Experience (**www.trans-siberian.co.uk**), the agency can also book a ferry crossing with either of these shipping lines. Prices start at around £230 in a second class cabin (8-berth, open-plan), £250 in a first class 4-berth, or £375 in a deluxe 2-berth cabin.

OPTION 3: *China Express Line*
This ferry links Tianjin (near Beijing) in China with Kobe in Japan every week, taking two nights. It leaves Tianjin at 11:30 on Monday, arriving in Kobe at 14:00 on Wednesday; from Kobe it sails at 10:30 on Friday, arriving in Tianjin at 14:00 on Sunday. See **www.celkobe.co.jp** for more information and to confirm sailing dates, times and fares. Tianjin is only 30 minutes (120 km) from Beijing South Station by frequent 350km/h Hexie train.

Fares for the ferry start at ¥22,000 (£170) one-way or ¥33,000 (£250) return for a basic passage, and you can book by email to pax@celkobe.co.jp. The Beijing–Tianjin train fare is only about RMB69 (£8 or $12) in a soft seat.

FERRY CONNECTIONS FROM VLADIVOSTOK TO JAPAN
The time-honoured weekly ferry run by Russia's Far East Shipping Company (FESCO) fell victim to the recession in late 2009. FESCO no longer operates, but a new year-round weekly ferry from Vladivostok to South Korea and Japan started in 2009. The *Eastern Dream* is a good modern ship, built in 1993. The official website is **www.dbsferry.com/02_ticket/ticket03.asp**.

Vladivostok → Donghae (Korea) → Sakaiminato (Japan)
The *Eastern Dream* sails from Vladivostok every Wednesday at 15:00, arriving Donghae at 12:00 on Thursday and Sakaiminato at 09:00 on Friday. You can confirm sailing times and days at **www.dbsferry.com/02_ticket/ticket03.asp**.

Sakaiminato (Japan) → Donghae (Korea) → Vladivostok

The *Eastern Dream* sails from Sakaiminato at 19:00 on Sunday, calls at Donghae from where it leaves at 15:00 on Monday, arriving Vladivostok at 12:00 on Tuesday. You can confirm sailing times and days at **www.dbsferry.com/02_ticket/ticket03.asp**.

Fares and how to buy tickets

The cheapest fare from Vladivostok to Japan is £157 or $235 one-way, £290 or $435 return, for economy class with a berth in a shared open-plan sleeping area. For a berth in a 2-berth cabin the fare rises to £323 or $485 one-way, £550 or $825 return. Deluxe suites are also available. You can book the ferry through **www.dbsferry.com/02_ticket/ticket03.asp** or via an agency such as The Russia Experience (**www.trans-siberian.co.uk**). Alternatively, perhaps the easiest way to book is to telephone the shipping line on +82 2 548 5502. Ask for an English speaker, reserve your place by phone, and collect and pay for the tickets at the ferry terminal.

Train connections in Japan

You can check train times from Sakaiminato to any station in Japan at **www.hyperdia.com** (English button upper left). You are unlikely to have any problems buying a train ticket to Tokyo when you arrive in Japan, though unfortunately Sakaiminato is not a Japan Rail Pass exchange office, which means that you can't start using a Japan Rail Pass there even if you've pre-purchased one. For more information about train travel in Japan, see the Japan chapter, page 332.

THE LONDON CONNECTION, LONDON–MOSCOW

The Trans-Siberian Railway starts at your local station, so don't cheat by flying the first few hundred miles! It's easy to travel from London to Moscow using Eurostar to Brussels, a connecting train to Cologne and the daily Russian sleeping-car direct from Cologne to Moscow, total journey about 48 hours. The sleeping-car is comfortable, modern and air-conditioned, with 1-, 2- and 3-bed compartments with washbasin. European travel is covered in depth in my first book, *The Man in Seat 61: A guide to taking the train from the UK through Europe*, but here are details of the quickest and most direct route from the UK to Moscow. The train passes through Minsk, so you'll need a transit visa for Belarus. Sleeper trains also run direct to Moscow from Amsterdam, Paris, Vienna, Prague, Warsaw, Berlin, Budapest, Helsinki and many other cities; you can check train times using the journey planner at **http://bahn.hafas.de**.

London → Moscow

Travel from **London** to **Brussels** by Eurostar, leaving London St Pancras daily except Saturdays at 14:34, arriving Brussels Midi at 17:33. On Saturday, leave London at 12:58, arriving Brussels at 16:05.

Travel from **Brussels** to **Cologne** by high-speed ICE train, leaving Brussels at 18:25 and arriving in Cologne at 20:15. On Saturday, you can also take the earlier 17:28 Thalys high-speed train from Brussels, arriving in Cologne at 19:15. You'll have time for a meal in Cologne.

Travel from **Cologne** to **Moscow** by direct Russian Railways sleeping-car, which leaves Cologne daily at 22:28, travelling across Germany, Poland and Belarus, and arriving into Byeloruski station in Moscow on the second morning at 10:33. In other words, you leave London on day 1 and arrive in Moscow on day 3.

Moscow → London

The daily sleeper train leaves **Moscow** at 21:09 and arrives in **Cologne** at 06:14 two nights later.

Take the ICE train from **Cologne** to **Brussels**, leaving Cologne at 07:43 and arriving in Brussels at 09:35.

Travel from **Brussels** to **London** by Eurostar. On Monday to Friday, a Eurostar leaves Brussels Midi at 12:29 and arrives London St Pancras at 13:33. On Saturday, a Eurostar leaves Brussels Midi at 11:29 and arrives London St Pancras at 12:26 and on Sunday, a Eurostar leaves Brussels Midi at 12:20 and arrives London St Pancras at 13:33.

Fares

Eurostar+ICE fares from London to Cologne start from £53 one-way, £97 return. You must book in advance to get the cheapest fares, as the price rises as the cheaper seats sell out. Approximate fares for the sleeper train to Moscow are shown in the table below.

Cologne to Moscow approximate fare per person	Sharing 3-berth sleeper	Sharing 2-berth sleeper	Single berth sleeper
Normal one-way fare	£243	£291	£417
Saver return	£367	£463	£723
Saver for 2 people together, per person	£293	£389	–

How to buy tickets

Call Deutsche Bahn's UK office on 08718 80 80 66 (no booking fee) or Europeanrail.com on 020 7619 1083 to buy tickets. Europeanrail.com charge a £35 booking fee, but they are more expert in making this type of booking. You can only book these trains 2 months in advance or less, so buy your train tickets to Moscow after you have arranged everything else. Travelling westbound, you can also use an agency such as Real Russia, **www.realrussia.co.uk**, to arrange tickets from Moscow to Cologne, then book onward tickets using **www.raileurope.co.uk**. For advice on how to obtain visas see page 53.

THE JOURNEY: Moscow–Beijing on train 4

I found train 4 to Beijing surprisingly modern, clean and comfortable. On the journey I made there were at least fifty westerners aboard, with a pleasant party atmosphere all the way. There were plenty of Chinese, Russians and Poles to meet, too.

For the first three days, the train travels across the vastness of Siberia, passing from Europe to Asia 1,777 km east of Moscow. On day 4, the train rounds Lake Baikal, the deepest freshwater lake in the world, with excellent views of the lake. In summer, the countryside appears green and pleasant, though in some parts the permafrost lies only inches below the surface. It can be quite humid (train 4 is not air-conditioned). On day 5, after passing through Mongolian customs late at night, you wake up to a complete change of scenery: grassy steppe, covered in dew, giving way south of Ulan Bator (Mongolia's capital) to the open wastes of the Gobi Desert. Look out for camels and yurts – the circular tents used by Mongolian nomads. Reaching the Chinese frontier at midnight to the sound of triumphant martial music played at full volume over the station loudspeakers, the train is taken away and jacked up to have its bogies changed from Russian 5' gauge to standard (4' 8½") gauge. You can remain on board or wander round the station while this is being done. The next and last day, the train crosses the mountains north of Beijing, and at the time I travelled it passed through the Great Wall of China at Qinglongqiao (the train now takes a slightly different route). Arrival at Beijing's main station, due at 15:33 on day 6, was 4 hours late. A Russian restaurant car is attached to the train for the first four days; a Mongolian restaurant car is available for day 5; and an excellent Chinese restaurant car is available on day 6.

THE JOURNEY: Moscow–Vladivostok on the *Rossiya*

My journey on the *Rossiya*, travelling to Japan via Vladivostok, was a completely different experience. My first class 2-berth car was comfortable, spotlessly clean and even air-conditioned. Meals in the restaurant cost around £3.50 ($5). I was the only westerner on the train until Irkutsk, where I was joined by two professors from Alabama. And unlike on the Moscow–Beijing train, where almost everyone is making the complete journey, the *Rossiya* is used for all sorts of intermediate journeys, with Russians getting on and off at every station. The carriages were replaced in the early 2000s. The train makes several stops a day, usually only for 10–20 minutes, but you can stretch your legs and take photographs. Approaching Ekaterinburg (known as Sverdlovsk during the Soviet era) at the kilometre post exactly 1,777 km from Moscow, the *Rossiya* passes the obelisk marking the boundary between Europe and Asia.

Arrival in Vladivostok was two minutes ahead of schedule, seven days after leaving Moscow. The ocean terminal is adjacent to the station, but you may need to spend a night in Vladivostok to be sure of a safe connection. Vladivostok is an interesting city, and a day or two spent there will not be wasted.

Overall, the Moscow–Vladivostok route is seven days of Siberia on a train with few fellow westerners and indeed few Russians making the whole trip. This makes for a much less interesting journey than the Moscow–Beijing train, and one that it would be good to break up with stopovers rather than make in one go.

TRANS-SIBERIAN TRAVEL TIPS

When should you go?

The Trans-Siberian Railway runs all year round, so you can go at any time of year. May to September are the peak months for foreign tourists, with the warmest weather and the longest hours of daylight. This means booking a specific date is more difficult in the summer (you need to book well ahead) but you might like the party atmosphere amongst like-minded travellers on Moscow–Beijing trains 4 and 20. On the other hand, Siberia in winter is a sight to see – the trains are well heated, warm and cosy; you'll just need to wrap up well when you get off for a stroll at station stops.

Should you travel first or second class?

On the Russian internal trains there are normally three classes: *spalny vagon* 2-berth compartments, often described as first class (and sometimes called *myagky* or *lyux*), *kupé* 4-berth compartments, usually described as second class, and *platskartny* open-plan dormitory cars, sometimes described as third class. The Russian Trans-Manchurian train (trains 19 and 20) has *spalny vagon* 2-berth and *kupé* 4-berth compartments, but no *platskartny*. *Kupé* is the way most travellers go, and can be considered the normal class of travel. *Spalny vagon* gives you much more privacy, with 2 people instead of 4 in the same size compartment, but it costs twice as much. The choice is yours. *Platskartny* is a bit rough for most western travellers, but some budget-minded backpackers enjoy it. The Chinese Trans-Mongolian train (trains 3 and 4) has first class deluxe

2-berth compartments (known in China as 'deluxe soft sleeper'), first class 4-berth compartments ('soft sleeper') and second class 4-berth compartments ('hard sleeper'). First class deluxe 2-berth is expensive but worth the extra if you can afford it as it has two beds, an armchair, and a private washroom with showerhead shared with the next-door compartment. This accommodation gets booked out very quickly! First class 4-berth on trains 3 and 4, on the other hand, is virtually identical to second class 4-berth and is probably not worth the extra.

What do you do on a train for six or seven days?

This is the question most people ask. Well, you put your feet up and relax. You read, watch the scenery, look out for the sights listed in your *Trans-Siberian Handbook*, go to meals in the restaurant car, sleep in your own comfortable bed at night, meet people, talk, play chess, drink tea, drink vodka, get off at station stops and take photographs. The Moscow–Mongolia–Beijing route is arguably the most interesting, both in the sights and scenery it offers on the way, and in the on-board company. You are unlikely to be bored – the time just goes!

- *The Trans-Siberian Handbook* by Bryn Thomas has a kilometre-by-kilometre account of the sights to look out for from the train. Highly recommended, as this helps you get the most from your journey. You can tell where you are from the black and white kilometre posts all along the line, usually on the south side of the tracks.

- Take plenty of reading books – Tolstoy's *War and Peace* is the most predictable title, but it's a great read. The funny thing is, you probably won't finish it – there's so much else to do!

Is not speaking Russian a problem?

No, it isn't. Very few western travellers on the Trans-Siberian Railway can speak Russian or, for that matter, Chinese or Mongolian. However, even if you don't speak Russian, it is worth learning the Cyrillic (Russian) alphabet. You will then be able to read place names and understand many Russian words. For example, 'РЕСТОРАН' is pronounced 'restoran' and means (surprise surprise) 'restaurant'. 'АВТОБУС' is pronounced 'avtobus' and means 'bus'. You'll also realise that 'СССР', the old acronym for the Soviet Union, is not 'see see see pee' but 'SSSR'.

What about food?

All the main Trans-Siberian trains have a restaurant car, a Russian one when in Russia, a Mongolian one in Mongolia and a Chinese one in China. Few people go to Russia for the cuisine, but contrary to what you might have heard, Russian restaurant-car food is quite edible and not expensive. Allow about £4–£6 ($6–$9) for a two-course meal with beer, to be paid in local currency. Some Moscow–Beijing tickets include meals for the Russian part of the journey, so ask your booking agency if meals are included. Don't expect an extensive menu: typical meals include ham and fried eggs for breakfast, schnitzel and potatoes for lunch or dinner, with soups and salads for starters. The restaurant car also sells beer, Russian champagne and (of course) vodka, chocolate and snacks. The Mongolian diner will probably offer you rice and mutton. The Chinese dining car has a selection of excellent Chinese dishes. You can also buy food from the many vendors on station platforms when the train stops.

- Unlimited boiling water is available free of charge from the samovar at the end of each coach, so remember to bring a mug, spoon, coffee, tea and a selection of cuppa soups or even dried pasta.

- My personal favourite: water-based drinking chocolate for a relaxing night-time drink each evening.

What about security? Is it safe for families or women travelling alone?

The Trans-Siberian is a very safe way to travel, even for families and women travelling alone. After all, the train is full of Russian families and women travelling alone, it's how the Russians themselves get around! Just use common sense as you would anywhere else: lock the compartment door at night and don't leave your wallet or camera lying unattended in your compartment while you go to the toilet or the restaurant car. In addition to the normal lock on the compartment door, Russian *spalny vagon* and *kupé* compartments have a security latch which stops the door opening more than an inch or two, and which cannot be released from outside even with a staff key. There's also a safe place for your bags at night – if you have a bottom bunk, there is a metal box underneath the bunk which you can only get to by lifting up the bunk. In other words, for anyone to get to your bags, they will have to shift you off your bunk first! Your carriage attendants may also lock the access doors at each end of the corridor at night to prevent intruders. So don't worry, you'll be safe and snug. Men and women share the same compartments, but on some routes you can now ask for a ladies-only compartment. If you're a woman travelling alone and do happen to find yourself sharing with men who make you uncomfortable, ask the carriage attendants if they can move you to another compartment and they normally will, without too much problem.

Do the trains have electrical outlets?

To answer what has become a FAQ, all the trains have 2-pin shaver sockets in the washrooms which can be used to recharge mobile phones or cameras, and the best trains have a 2-pin socket or two in the corridor that can be used for recharging if you keep an eye on your equipment. Remember to take a multi-purpose travel adaptor. However, you're unlikely to find any specific powerpoints for charging laptops, mobile phones or digital cameras in your compartment. Your carriage attendant may be willing to charge items using the socket in their own compartment, for a small tip.

Toilets and showers

Each sleeping-car has at least two western-style toilets and a washroom with sinks. The carriage attendants (*provodniks*) will keep the toilet clean during the journey. How clean depends on both the *provodniks* and the passengers in your car(!), but there's normally no problem, especially on high-quality Firmeny trains like the *Rossiya* and *Baikal*. There are no showers on Trans-Siberian trains, with two exceptions: on the Trans-Mongolian Moscow–Beijing train (trains 3 and 4), there's a shower hose in the small washroom shared between each adjacent pair of deluxe first class 2-berth compartments; and on the *Baikal* from St Petersburg to Irkutsk (trains 9 and 10) there's a shower that you have to pay for in car 7. There may now be a similar shower on the Moscow–Vladivostok *Rossiya* (trains 1 and 2). Remember that the need to take a shower every single day is a relatively recent western social trend, not a human necessity; that not so many generations ago, Sunday night was bath night, whether you needed it or not! Just lock yourself into the washroom halfway across and make good use of the sink and a cup of water.

Smoking
If you're a rabid anti-smoker, don't worry. There isn't a problem in the compartments, corridor or restaurants. But if you're a smoker, don't worry either. You can grab a smoke in the vestibules between the cars.

Do Trans-Siberian trains run on time?
Within Russia, the trains are remarkably punctual. My train from Moscow arrived in Vladivostok two minutes ahead of schedule. However, on international trains you should expect an hour or two's delay when crossing frontiers. For example, on the Trans-Mongolian route it is not unusual to arrive in Ulan Bator perhaps 1 or 2 hours late and in Beijing 2 to 5 hours late. Allow for this when planning any connections.

Can you stop off on the way?
All Trans-Siberian trains stop at stations every few hours for between 5 and 20 minutes, enough time to get off the train, stretch your legs, take photos and buy something from the vendors on the platform. But not enough time for a tour of the town!

Many people travel the whole way from Moscow to Beijing or Vladivostok in one go on one of the direct trains. Other people prefer to stop off along the way, breaking up the long journey and seeing something of Siberia or Mongolia. Ekaterinburg, Irkutsk (for Lake Baikal) and Ulan Bator (Mongolia) are the most usual stopovers.

On the direct Moscow–Beijing trains, the varied scenery and friendly atmosphere on board make travelling straight through without stopovers perfectly bearable and indeed fun. There are usually lots of westerners on board as well as Russians, Chinese and Mongolians, almost all of them making the whole trip, like yourself. However, on a Moscow–Vladivostok train, you might be the only westerner on board for much of the journey, the whole trip is made within Russia, and relatively few of your fellow-travellers will be making the whole journey to Vladivostok. It may be better to break up this trip with one or two stopovers, perhaps at Ekaterinburg or Irkutsk.

Remember that Trans-Siberian trains are 'reservation obligatory'. Every time you step on board a train you must have a confirmed sleeping-berth reservation for that specific journey on that specific train on that specific date – you *cannot* hop on and off trains spontaneously without a reservation. So if you want to travel from, say, Moscow to Beijing stopping off at Irkutsk you need a ticket/reservation from Moscow to Irkutsk and a second separate ticket/reservation for the train you want to take from Irkutsk to Beijing. Think of these as two separate journeys, not one. You can arrange all the tickets and reservations before you go.

If you are stopping off, remember that the weekly direct international trains between Moscow and Beijing (trains 4 and 20 eastbound, trains 3 and 19 westbound) can only be used by passengers making the complete international journey; you cannot use them for domestic trips within Russia – although train 4 does carry passengers between Ulan Bator and Beijing, and allows passengers for Beijing to join at Russian stations en route, such as Irkutsk. In practice, a typical trip from Moscow to Beijing with stopovers at Irkutsk and Ulan Bator can be made using the *Rossiya* or other Russian domestic train from Moscow to Irkutsk, the daily train 362 from Irkutsk to Ulan Bator and the weekly Ulan Bator–Beijing train.

In theory, Russian Railways have a system whereby if you hold a ticket/reservation from A to C, and get off the train at B, you can get the ticket endorsed by the station manager, then make a second reservation and pay a small reservation charge when you want to resume your journey. However, this does not work with international tickets. The Russians themselves don't often use this facility, so Russian railway staff may not be familiar with it. I recommend buying separate tickets/reservations for each leg of your journey before you go, but if you really want to try this system out, you had better practise your Russian language skills!

Can you take your bike, car or motorcycle?

Believe it or not, this gets asked from time to time. Trans-Siberian passenger trains do not carry cars or motorbikes, full stop. However, you can take bicycles with you, zipped up in a bike bag with pedals removed and the handlebars turned, free of charge as hand luggage. Bear in mind that it will take up space in your sleeping compartment, so it may be less antisocial to book a berth in a more spacious 2-berth compartment than to inflict your bike on three fellow travellers in a 4-berth compartment.

Is this the longest train ride in the world? No. Well. Sort of . . .

You'll sometimes hear Moscow–Vladivostok in seven days on the *Rossiya* referred to as the longest train ride of them all. It isn't. Nor is Moscow–Vladivostok in nine days on the daily lower-quality slow train 904 (not a train normally used by foreigners, or one you want to get on by mistake). Once a week the *Rossiya* conveys a through sleeper from Moscow to Pyongyang in North Korea; it is detached at Ussuryisk just an hour or so before Vladivostok, then it heads south all the way into Korea, a considerably longer continuous train ride than Moscow–Vladivostok. But this isn't the longest train ride either. There is a through train from Donetsk and Kharkov in Ukraine to Vladivostok, and this appears to be the longest scheduled continuous train ride of them all. Unless you know differently, of course!

A BRIEF HISTORY OF THE TRANS-SIBERIAN RAILWAY

In the late nineteenth century, Japan, Britain and America all managed to gain footholds on the Chinese coast as bases for their trade with China and the Orient. Russia too needed to establish its foothold on the east as well as securing the vast expanses of Siberia, so in 1891 Tsar Alexander III approved a plan for a trans-continental line linking Moscow and St Petersburg with Vladivostok on the Pacific coast, as this was the only year-round ice-free port on Russian territory.

A railway had been built as far as Ekaterinburg as early as 1878, and this was steadily extended eastwards. Omsk was reached in 1894, Irkutsk and Lake Baikal in 1898. The Trans-Siberian Railway finally reached Vladivostok in 1901, but for several years passengers had to cross Lake Baikal by ice-breaking ferry to connect with a second train on the other side – only in 1904 was the line around Lake Baikal completed and the whole journey from Moscow to Vladivostok possible on a single train. Until 1916, the eastern end of the journey involved cutting across China, over part of what is now the Trans-Manchurian route – you can see from the route map on pages 34–5 how the Trans-Manchurian line initially heads towards Vladivostok. The Russians secured the right to build and maintain this route across China thanks to a treaty signed after they had made a generous loan to the Chinese to help them pay off their debts to Japan. From 1916, the journey from Moscow to Vladivostok could be made entirely within Russia, taking the route followed by today's *Rossiya* and skirting the Chinese border to the north via Khabarovsk. The Trans-Mongolian line is a relatively recent addition to the Trans-Siberian network: construction started in 1940, it reached Ulan Bator in 1949, and it was completed into China by 1956.

The Trans-Siberian Railway today

Today, the Trans-Siberian Railway is a key part of the massive Russian railway system. It is not a tourist line – it is a real, working railway, carrying a huge amount of freight and passenger traffic. It is double-track and electrified all the way from Moscow to Vladivostok, and on some parts of the line freight trains rumble past every few minutes. It is not the only line in Russia – on the contrary, if you saw a map of Russian railways you would be hard pressed to decide which of the many routes Trans-Siberian trains actually take for the first few thousand miles east of Moscow. There is in fact now a second route across Siberia that runs north of the Trans-Siberian, to Sovetskaya Gavan on the Pacific coast, known as the BAM (Baikal–Amur–Maestral railway). Started in the 1930s, it was only completed in 1991. However, this route is of little interest to most Western travellers.

The best resource for further information about the Trans-Siberian Railway is **www.transsib.ru/Eng/**.

TRANS-SIBERIAN WEB RESOURCES

www.transsib.ru/Eng/ – the Trans-Siberian web encyclopaedia.

www.trans-siberia.com – an independent site, based on a traveller's experiences.

www.myazcomputerguy.com/everbrite/Page9.html – excellent advice from Ruth Imershein, an experienced and regular traveller to Russia.

To China via Central Asia and the 'Silk Route'

The most usual route from Europe to China is via the classic Trans-Siberian Railway, shown in the map on pages 34–5. But there is another route now open to foreigners, the so-called 'Silk Route' via Kazakhstan, shown on the map overleaf. Unlike on the Trans-Siberian, there is no direct train covering the whole route from Moscow to Beijing, so this chapter deals with the individual sections one by one. Most travellers will opt to book this journey through a specialist agency, given the complexities of the visas needed, which usually require travel to be pre-planned and for you to hold onward tickets.

LONDON TO MOSCOW

It's easy to travel from London to Moscow by train, in 48 hours with comfortable sleepers for the overnight sections. For times, fares and how to buy tickets, see pages 66–8. You will need a Belarus transit visa and Russian tourist visa, see pages 53–7.

MOSCOW TO ALMATY OR ASTANA (KAZAKHSTAN)

Two direct trains link Moscow with Kazakhstan every second day, the *Kazakhstan* to Almaty (also written Alma-ata) and the *Tselina* to Astana. Of the two, the Moscow–Almaty route offers the better train, as it is a quality Firmeny service; however, both trains are safe and comfortable. A couple of other trains which link Moscow with Astana on the way to somewhere else are not shown here.

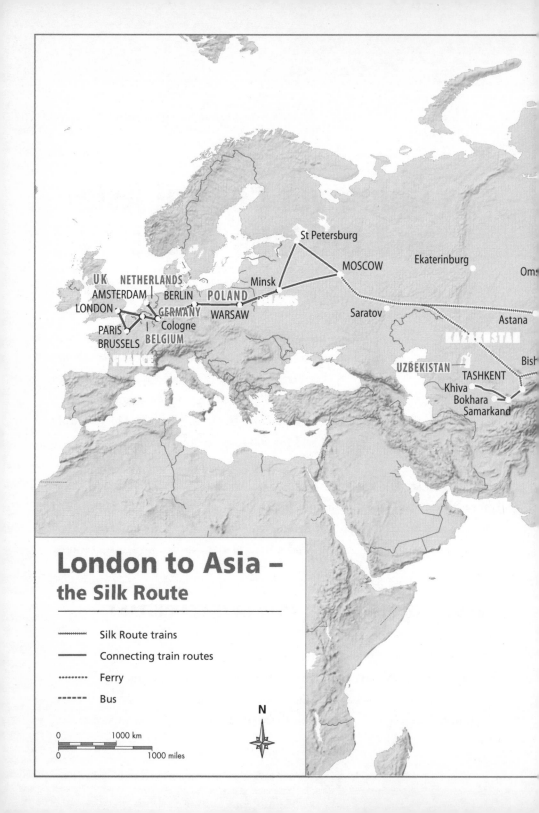

London to Asia –
the Silk Route

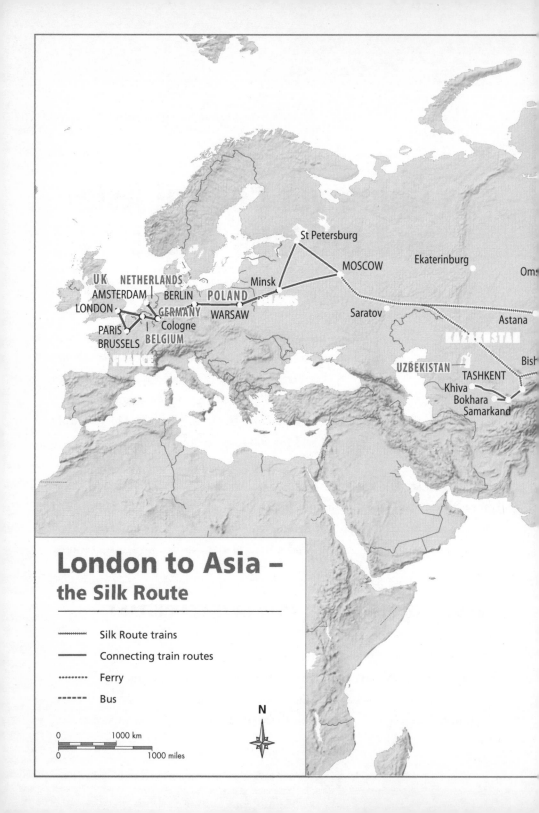
Silk Route trains
Connecting train routes
Ferry
Bus

0   1000 km
0   1000 miles

N

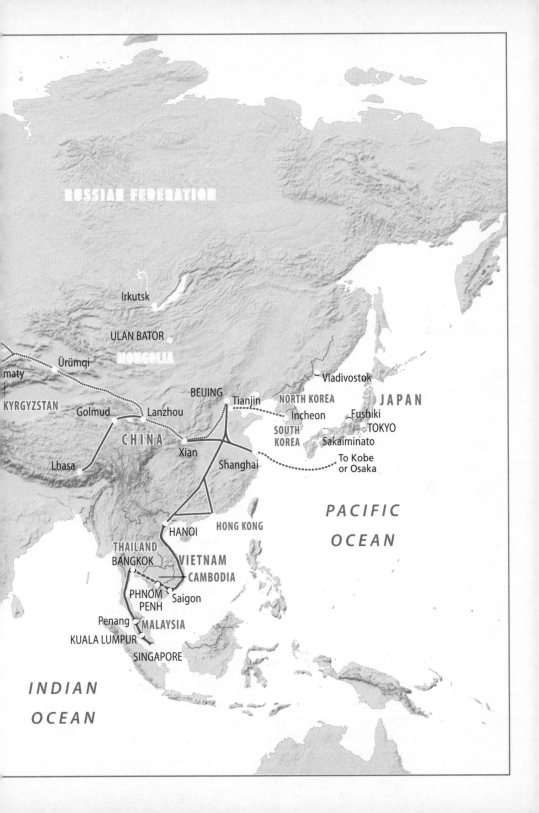

Moscow → Almaty and Astana

Each train runs every 2 days		Train 8 *Kazakhstan* Note A	Train 72 *Tselina* Note B	Train 84 Note C
Moscow	depart	22:50 day 1	22:45 day 1	22:45 day 1
Yaisan (Kazakh frontier)	arrive	13:04 day 3	I	I
Kustanay (Kazakh frontier)	arrive	I	22:55 day 3	22:55 day 3
Almaty (Almaty I)	arrive	06:51 day 5	I	I
Astana	arrive	–	11:57 day 4	08:42 day 4

Almaty and Astana → Moscow

Each train runs every 2 days		Train 7 *Kazakhstan* Note A	Train 71 *Tselina* Note B	Train 83 Note C
Astana	depart	–	07:35 day 1	11:05 day 1
Almaty (Almaty I)	depart	06:19 day 1	I	I
Kustanay (Russian frontier)	arrive	I	20:10 day 1	20:10 day 1
Yaisan (Russian frontier)	arrive	01:07 day 3	I	I
Moscow	arrive	10:30 day 4	15:30 day 3	15:30 day 3

Note A: *Kazakhstan.* Train 8 departs Moscow (Paveletskaya station) on odd-numbered dates (1st, 3rd, 5th etc. of each month, but not the 1st following a 31st). Train 7 departs Almaty on even-numbered dates (2nd, 4th, 6th etc.). The train is a quality Firmeny service with 2-berth *spalny vagon* and 4-berth *kupé* sleepers, and *platskartny* open-plan dormitory cars, plus restaurant car. The train passes from Russia into Kazakhstan, then briefly transits another part of Russia before re-entering Kazakhstan. However, it is reported that you need only a single-entry visa for Russia and a single-entry visa for Kazakhstan to travel on this train, i.e. multiple-entry visas for Russia and Kazakhstan are not required just because of this (but please double-check this). Moscow to Almaty is 4,017 km.

Note B: *Tselina.* Train 72 departs Moscow (Kazanski station) on odd-numbered dates (1st, 3rd, 5th etc. of each month, but not the 1st following a 31st). Train 71 departs Astana on odd-numbered dates (1st, 3rd, 5th etc. of each month, but not the 31st). The train is a 'fast' service (but not a Firmeny top-quality service) with 2-berth *spalny vagon* and 4-berth *kupé* sleepers, and *platskartny* open-plan dormitory cars, plus restaurant car. Moscow to Astana is 3,105 km.

Note C: Train 84 leaves Moscow on even-numbered dates (2nd, 4th, 6th etc. of each month). Train 83 leaves Astana on even-numbered dates. 2-berth *spalny vagon* and 4-berth *kupé* sleepers, and *platskartny* open-plan dormitory cars, plus restaurant car.

You can double-check train times and days of running using the online timetable at **www.realrussia.co.uk/ trains** or **www.poezda.net**. Train 8 is sometimes shown as train 7!

How much does it cost?

Moscow to Almaty or Astana costs £200 in 4-berth *kupé*, booked with Real Russia, **www.realrussia.co.uk**.

How to buy tickets

You can book these trains through several reputable Russian agencies, including:

Real Russia, **www.realrussia.co.uk**, who can also help with visas

Svezhy Veter, **www.sv-agency.udm.ru/sv/trains.htm**

G&R International, **www.hostels.ru**

Way to Russia, **www.waytorussia.net/Services/TrainTickets.html**

For more information on these agencies, see pages 46–7.

You can make arrangements for trains, hotels and tours in Kazakhstan and Uzbekistan through local agencies such as **www.tourasia.kz**. You will need Russian and Kazakh tourist visas for this journey.

ALMATY OR ASTANA (KAZAKHSTAN) TO ÜRÜMQI (CHINA)

Two trains a week link Kazakhstan with China, one from Almaty and one from Astana, running to Ürümqi. The Almaty–Ürümqi train is named the *Zhibek Zholy* and has modern air-conditioned soft class (4-berth sleeper compartments) and hard class (open-plan bunks). A Kazakh restaurant car runs from Almaty to the frontier at Druzhba, and a Chinese restaurant car runs from Druzhba to Ürümqi. Trains 53 and 54, Astana–Ürümqi, use Kazakh coaches, with 2-berth and 4-berth compartments.

Almaty → Ürümqi

		Train N896	Train 54
Almaty (Almaty II)	depart	22:58 Sat	–
Astana	depart	I	15:55 Tue
Chinese frontier	arrive	22:10 Sun	22:10 Wed
Ürümqi	arrive	08:58 Mon	08:58 Thur

Ürümqi → Almaty

		Train N895	Train 53
Ürümqi	depart	23:58 Mon	23:58 Thur
Kazakh frontier	arrive	09:20 Tue	09:20 Fri
Astana	arrive	I	13:55 Sat
Almaty (Almaty II)	arrive	06:40 Wed	–

How much does it cost?

Almaty to Ürümqi costs £123 in hard class or £138 in soft class, booked with Real Russia.

How to buy tickets

You can book these trains in either direction through Real Russia, **www.realrussia.co.uk/trains** or (for eastbound journeys) through a local agency such as **www.tourasia.kz**.

ÜRÜMQI TO XIAN AND BEIJING

Trains T69 and T70 have soft class (4-berth sleeper compartments) and hard class sleepers (open-plan bunks). There are other trains available between Xian and Beijing; see the China chapter, pages 295–6.

Ürümqi → Beijing

		Train T70 Daily	Train 1044 Daily
Ürümqi	depart	20:03 day 1	23:58 day 1
Xian	arrive	01:08 day 2	11:26 day 3
Beijing	arrive	13:38 day 3	–

Beijing → Ürümqi

		Train T69 Daily	Train 1043 Daily
Beijing	depart	18:44 day 1	–
Xian	depart	07:09 day 2	21:25 day 2
Ürümqi	arrive	10:50 day 3	07:18 day 3

How much does it cost?

Ürümqi to Beijing costs around RMB970 (£105) in soft sleeper or RMB630 (£70) in hard sleeper if bought at the station.

MOSCOW TO TASHKENT (UZBEKISTAN)

There is a train running three times a week from Moscow to Tashkent in Uzbekistan. This is the *Uzbekistan*, with 2-berth *spalny vagon* and 4-berth *kupé* sleepers, and *platskartny* open-plan dormitory cars, plus restaurant car. The train passes from Russia into Kazakhstan, briefly transits another part of Russia before re-entering Kazakhstan, then it enters Uzbekistan. You will need a Russian visa, Kazakh transit visa and Uzbek visa. It is reported that it is not necessary to have multiple-entry visas for Russia and Kazakhstan just because this train transits part of Russia after entering Kazakhstan, but please double-check this. You can check train times and days of running using the online timetable at **www.realrussia.co.uk/trains** or at **www.poezda.net**.

Moscow → Tashkent

Uzbekistan		Train 6
Moscow (Kazanski station)	depart	23:25 Mon, Wed, Fri
Yaisan (Russian/Kazakh frontier)	arrive	10:36 Wed, Fri, Sun
Tashkent (Uzbekistan entry point)	arrive	19:05 Thur, Sat, Mon

Tashkent → Moscow

Uzbekistan		Train 5
Tashkent	depart	19:35 Tue, Fri, Sun
Yaisan (Kazakh/Russian frontier)	arrive	07:51 Thur, Sun, Tue
Moscow (Kazanski station)	arrive	14:10 Fri, Mon, Wed

How much does it cost?

Moscow to Tashkent costs £295 in 4-berth *kupé* or £385 in 2-berth *spalny vagon*, booked with Real Russia.

How to buy tickets

You can book these trains through several reputable Russian agencies, including:

Real Russia, **www.realrussia.co.uk,** who can also help with visas

Svezhy Veter, **www.sv-agency.udm.ru/sv/trains.htm**

G&R International, **www.hostels.ru**

Way to Russia, **www.waytorussia.net/Services/TrainTickets.html**

For more information on these agencies, see pages 46–7.

You can make arrangements for trains, hotels and tours in Kazakhstan and Uzbekistan through local agencies such as **www.tourasia.kz**. You will need a Russian tourist visa, Kazakhstan transit visa and Uzbekistan tourist visa for this journey.

TASHKENT TO SAMARKAND, BOKHARA, URGENCH FOR KHIVA (UZBEKISTAN)

Urgench (also known as Urganch) is the railhead for Khiva, 35 km or 30 minutes away. A taxi will cost around £6 ($9). There are no direct trains from Bokhara to Urgench, as they are on different lines.

Tashkent ➜ Samarkand, Bokhara, Urgench

		Train 2 Note A	Train 10 Note B	Train 50 Note C	Train 56 Note D	Train 662 Note C
Tashkent	depart	07:05	08:20	19:05	19:25	20:10
Samarkand	arrive	10:30	12:00	23:50	00:33	01:43
Bokhara	arrive	–	14:45	–	I	06:50
Urgench	arrive	–	–	–	13:22	–

Samarkand, Bokhara, Urgench ➜ Tashkent

		Train 55 Note D	Train 49 Note C	Train 9 Note B	Train 1 Note A	Train 661 Note C
Urgench	depart	15:15	–	–	–	–
Bokhara	depart	I	–	08:05	–	19:10
Samarkand	depart	04:33	07:05	11:10	17:00	00:49
Tashkent	arrive	09:13	12:25	14:39	20:30	05:55

Note A: *Registan*. Runs on Monday, Thursday, Friday, Saturday and Sunday; consists of luxury air-conditioned cars.

Note B: *Sharq*. Air-conditioned, runs daily.

Note C: Runs daily, with 2-berth *spalny vagon* and 4-berth *kupé* sleepers.

Note D: Runs three times a week (train 56 on Monday, Tuesday, Friday; train 55 on Tuesday, Wednesday, Saturday) with 2-berth *spalny vagon* and 4-berth *kupé* sleepers.

There are several other irregular trains between Tashkent and Samarkand. You can check times and days of running for all these trains using the online timetable at **www.realrussia.co.uk/trains** or **www.poezda.net** (Bokhara may appear as 'Bukhara' or 'Buhara 1').

How much does it cost?

Tashkent to Samarkand costs around £20 in *kupé* or £30 in *spalny vagon*, if bought through Real Russia.

How to buy tickets

You can buy tickets at the station, or from outside Uzbekistan through Real Russia, **www.realrussia.co.uk/trains**.

TASHKENT TO ALMATY

There is no direct train service between these cities, though it's possible to go by train, changing at Arys, or by train+bus via Chimkent. Use **www.poezda.net** to check train times. Traveller Helmut Uttenthaler reports: 'It's possible to go by train with changing at Arys. We did this, we had 53 minutes for our connection from daily train 23 (to Aktjubinsk) to the twice-weekly train 381 (Ufa–Tashkent). Although train 23 left Almaty with 40 minutes' delay, we arrived at Arys on time. The connecting train was also on time, so no problem. However, getting tickets in advance from Arys to Tashkent on train 381 can be difficult. Free places for getting on at Arys are very rare and appear in the "express" booking system only a few days before departure (as the train comes from Ufa in Russia). We were three people, and when we booked our trip to Arys 8 days ahead it was not yet possible to buy tickets from Arys to Tashkent. Some days later (4 days ahead) we tried it again and now just 3 free places appeared for Arys–Tashkent. Two in *platskartny*, one in *kupé*. We bought all of them . . . However, if we had failed to buy tickets or had missed our connection we would have made the way from Arys to Tashkent by taxi, as it's only about 150 km. From locals we heard that they usually take the train to Chimkent and from there a bus to Tashkent. But we wanted to go by train all the way.'

MOSCOW TO BISHKEK (KYRGYZSTAN)

A twice-weekly train, with 2-berth and 4-berth sleepers and restaurant car, links Moscow with Bishkek in Kyrgyzstan.

Moscow → Bishkek

Kirgizia		Train 18
Moscow (Kazanski station)	depart	23:25 Thur, Sun
Yaisan (Kazakh frontier)	arrive	10:44 Sat, Tue
Kaindy (Kirgiz frontier)	arrive	22:50 Sun, Wed
Bishkek (Bishkek II)	arrive	02:41 Mon, Thur

Bishkek → Moscow

Kirgizia		Train 17
Bishkek (Bishkek II)	depart	10:07 Mon, Thur
Kaindy (Kazakh frontier)	arrive	13:09 Mon, Thur
Yaisan (Russian frontier)	arrive	07:41 Wed, Sat
Moscow (Kazanski station)	arrive	14:10 Thur, Sun

How much does it cost?

Moscow to Bishkek costs £251 in 4-berth *kupé*, booked with Real Russia.

How to buy tickets

You can book this train in either direction with Real Russia at **www.realrussia.co.uk/trains**.

SILK ROUTE AND CENTRAL ASIA RESOURCES

To check train times (and days of running) in any of the ex-Soviet states, use the online timetable at **www.realrussia.co.uk** or **www.poezda.net**.

There's an excellent personal account of a journey via the Silk Route at **www.johndarm.clara.net/silkroute**.

The Silk Route by Rail by Dominic Streatfield-James is a guidebook specifically designed to help you plan and book a trip to China via the Silk Route.

To Pakistan and India overland

There were newspaper articles a few years ago about the possibility of train travel from London to India or even Dhaka in Bangladesh, prompted by Calcutta–Dhaka trains resuming after forty years and the planned completion of the final missing link in the rails between Bam and Zahedan in southeast Iran. The Bam–Zahedan section was finally completed in early 2009 (having been 'under construction' for decades), so the rails do indeed now stretch all the way from St Pancras to Karachi, Lahore, Delhi and Dhaka, with just a short hop by ferry necessary across the Bosphorus in Istanbul (a gap due to be filled by the Bosphorus tunnel now under construction) and a ferry ride across Lake Van in eastern Turkey.

However, you can't just buy a London–Delhi train ticket and hop on a train to India. Far from it. Such a two- or three-week trip should not be undertaken lightly, as it will take a lot of DIY organisation, including the bureaucracy involved in getting an Iranian visa, and there are security concerns with bandit attacks in southeast Iran near the Pakistan border. But for more adventurous travellers willing to brave this, it promises to be an epic trip.

You currently also need to check the Pakistan visa situation, as in late 2009 and early 2010 westerners were not being granted visas for Pakistan if they wanted to use trains or any other form of surface travel. This may or may not be a temporary measure.

OVERVIEW

The itinerary outlined below assumes you're travelling eastbound, but it would work exactly the same way westbound.

Days 1–4: Travel from **London** to **Istanbul** (3–4 nights) by train. There are daily departures via a choice of routes, the best being London–Paris–Munich–Vienna–Budapest–Bucharest–Istanbul. The whole journey (which involves at least six separate trains) can be booked via one of several European rail ticketing agencies in the UK, and we're talking a minimum of £350 one-way, £550 return. See the Turkey chapter, pages 127–38, for times, fares, and how to buy tickets.

Days 5–8: Istanbul–Tehran. Take an evening ferry across the Bosphorus to Haydarpaşa station on the Asian side and travel from Istanbul to Tehran in Iran on the comfortable weekly *Trans-Asia Express* (3 days); see the Iran chapter, page 102. This train departs every Wednesday, so your timetable will need to be built around this. The fare is around £40 one-way including sleeper, plus maybe £15 booking fee.

Day 9: Travel from **Tehran** to **Kerman** in southeast Iran by daily overnight train leaving Tehran at 16:50 and arriving at Kerman at 07:00 next morning. The train has comfortable air-conditioned sleepers (4-berth compartments). There's also an earlier train if this train is full. Times and fares can be confirmed at **www.raja.ir** (click the 'house' logo then 'English' top right). Fares are very cheap, less than £10, though an agency may charge more.

Day 10: Kerman–Bam. The railway was extended a further 225 km to Bam in 2004, so change trains at Kerman on to the 08:00 connecting train to Bam, arriving 11:00. The journey takes you through spectacular desert. The fare is only a few pounds.

Day 10–11: Bam–Zahedan. This section of line has been under construction for some time, but was reported as physically complete in May 2009. A train service was supposed to have started running over it in June 2009, but details have yet to be released, and in fact

UK

GERMANY

FRANCE

TURKEY

Passengers cross
Lake Van by ferry

London to India

Only relevant rail routes are shown here

0   500 km

0   500 miles

N

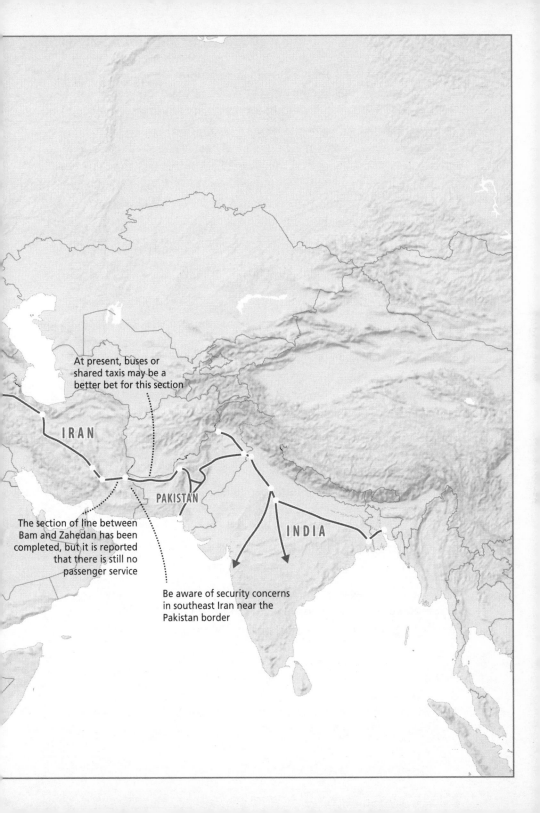

At present, buses or shared taxis may be a better bet for this section

IRAN

PAKISTAN

INDIA

The section of line between Bam and Zahedan has been completed, but it is reported that there is still no passenger service

Be aware of security concerns in southeast Iran near the Pakistan border according to the most recent report in 2010 no passenger train service has yet begun. What form this train service will take when it does arrive is not yet clear – possibly a direct train from Tehran to Zahedan, maybe weekly, maybe daily, maybe several times per week, who knows. In the meantime, there are buses from Kerman or Bam to Zahedan. A bus reportedly leaves Kerman daily at 20:00, calls at Bam a few hours later and arrives in Zahedan at 04:00 next morning. The fare is just a few pounds.

Day 11+: Zahedan–Quetta. From Zahedan, a mixed passenger and goods train leaves on the 3rd and 17th of every month at 10:00, arriving in Quetta (in Pakistan) at 20:30 the next day. This train consists of several very basic passenger cars (seats only) attached to a freight train, with no sleeping berths or restaurant. The fare is about 30,000 Iranian rials (£2 or $3). The more frequent *Taftan Express* on this route, which had sleepers, was withdrawn due to security problems a few years ago. Take plenty of food and, above all, lots of drinking water, as it gets very hot in the desert and there's nothing available on board. There are overnight buses on this route, but the train will show you great desert scenery in daylight – treat it as an adventure. Expect an arrival in Quetta 3–6 hours late. However, please check locally that the twice-monthly train is running, as there have been reports that even that has been temporarily suspended because of bombing. If it isn't running, buses may be available as an alternative. A third possibility would be to take one of the share taxis available from Zahedan to the Pakistani frontier, then more taxis from there to Quetta, and this option can be a good bet.

Day 13+: From **Quetta**, the *Quetta Express* runs daily trains with comfortable air-conditioned sleepers to **Lahore**, taking 24 hours; see the Pakistan chapter, page 379, for times. Expect this to cost less than £20.

Day 15+: From **Lahore** there is a twice-weekly train to **Amritsar** in India, the *Samjhota Express*, which takes 7 hours to make the 46 km journey (for details see the Pakistan chapter, page 380). The time taken is down to the border formalities, not the distance! Alternatively you could travel by the daily buses or taxi. Spend the night in Amritsar, and perhaps visit the Golden Temple.

Day 16+: Travel by one of the regular daily trains from **Amritsar** to **Delhi**; journey time 6 to 8 hours, a dozen trains daily.

Onwards to Dhaka in Bangladesh: Take the prestigious overnight *Rajdhani Express* train from **Delhi** to **Calcutta**, and the new *Maitree Express* train (currently running Saturday and Sunday only, an all-day journey) or one of the daily buses from **Calcutta** to **Dhaka**.

Onwards to Kathmandu in Nepal: Take a train from **Delhi** to **Gorakhpur**, then a bus; see the Nepal chapter, pages 369–70, for more information.

Onwards to Burma, Thailand, China: Unfortunately, there are no easy overland routes from India or Bangladesh into either Burma (Myanmar) or Thailand. It is possible, visas and permits permitting, to travel to Kathmandu in Nepal then take a £200 ($300) tour (you can't go independently, it's not allowed) across the Himalayas to Tibet, then a train into China; see the Nepal chapter, page 371. For overland travel from Europe to China the easy way, see the chapter on the Trans-Siberian Railway, page 33.

PLANNING YOUR TRIP

- Read through the arrangements for getting an Iranian visa detailed in the Iran chapter, page 105. The process is quite bureaucratic, but doable.

- You'll also need to understand visa requirements for Pakistan and India, particularly any 'onward ticket' requirements which annoyingly assume everyone travels by air so can pre-book everything. Read the visa pages on the Pakistan and Indian embassy websites carefully (see **http://in.vfsglobal.co.uk** for India and **www.phclondon.org** for Pakistan). If necessary call the embassies to ask advice. Buying refundable air tickets then cancelling them is one dodge to get round such requirements. To be honest, the visa requirements are likely to be the most difficult part of making this trip; sorting out the transport arrangements is the easy bit!

- In summer 2009 and early 2010 I received reports that Pakistan is not allowing westerners to use trains or other surface travel within Pakistan, to avoid the potential embarrassment of a westerner being involved in a terrorist incident. My correspondents were refused visas for Pakistan by the Pakistani High Commission in London when officials realised they planned to enter Pakistan overland using surface transport. This situation clearly curtails the possibility of travelling overland to India through Pakistan – I do not know whether it is a temporary measure. It was later reported by one of the same correspondents that the Pakistani consulate in Birmingham had also refused a visa on those grounds, but that the Bradford Pakistani consulate had no problem issuing a visa for overland travel, and he can now travel!

- I'd suggest planning the trip out carefully before you start to book anything, using a simple spreadsheet, so you can see which days you'll be in which place – see the chapter 'Planning a trip', page 25.

- The Istanbul–Tehran train runs only once a week, on Wednesday nights, and this will probably determine the rest of your timetable.

- Each leg of the journey is ticketed separately, even on the London–Istanbul section, so you can stop off wherever you like for as long as you like, be it Paris or Vienna or Budapest or Istanbul or Tehran. Where, how often, and for how long you stop off on the way is entirely your decision.

- If you want to research this trip further, buy a copy of the Lonely Planet Istanbul to Kathmandu guide, which covers Turkey, Iran, Pakistan, India and Nepal.

- A key issue when considering whether to make this trip is the security situation in southeast Iran and Pakistan. Check the Foreign Office advice on Iran and Pakistan at **www.fco.gov.uk**, although this errs on the paranoid side. Noelle Virtue, who travelled from India to Europe in March 2009, reported: 'Although we didn't have any problems in Quetta itself, we were told by a member of the police and several others that it wasn't a safe place for foreigners to be. We left Quetta on an overnight bus to Taftan with no problems and no escort. However, once we crossed the border into Iran we were told that we needed an escort to Zahedan and that we would have to pay for a taxi to take us and the escort there as buses wouldn't take foreigners. Once we got to Zahedan we were taken to the police station where we awaited a squad car to take us to the bus station for onward travel to Kerman. This involved changing into three different squad cars and showing our passports again to each police officer. The whole process from the border to Zahedan should take 1.5 hours but took us about six. We heard from fellow travellers that the train is still in operation between Zahedan and Quetta but that it's not a great experience and they had difficulty finding a hotel in Zahedan that would take foreigners. They also had to be escorted everywhere in Zahedan during their stay there.'

BOOKING YOUR TRIP

It's not so much a question of 'buying a ticket to India' as an exercise in project management, arranging all the various tickets from a variety of sources and being prepared to buy some on the way as you go.

- The critical administrative issue is getting an Iranian visa. See the Iran chapter, page 105, for advice on agencies in Iran to contact for this.

- You'll also need to arrange visas for Pakistan and India. For Pakistan visa arrangements, see **www.phclondon.org**. Turkish tourist visas can be bought when the train reaches the Turkish frontier, so they present no problem.

- Train tickets for the London–Istanbul portion of the journey can all be arranged through a European rail ticketing agency in the UK such as Deutsche Bahn's UK office or europeanrail.com. See the Turkey chapter, pages 127–38, for more advice and information.

- Istanbul–Tehran train tickets can be arranged through an Istanbul travel agency such as Tur-Ista, see the Iran chapter, pages 102–4.

- The agency you use to obtain support for your Iranian visa may be able to organise the Tehran–Kerman–Bam trains, and perhaps the Kerman/Bam to Zahedan bus and train or bus ticket from Zahedan to Quetta. If they can't do the train out of Iran, you can book this at the station in Zahedan, but check that you can still get a visa without onward tickets.

- Trains within Pakistan and India are best left to be booked at the ticket office once you arrive in those countries.

- Good luck!

PART

3

THE MIDDLE EAST

IRAN

Watching the television news or reading the newspapers, you could be forgiven for thinking that Iran is a dangerous place. In fact, apart from some bandit problems in the southeast, it's one of the safer countries to visit, with some of the most hospitable people you'll find anywhere. And with a comfortable weekly train from Istanbul to Tehran, the *Trans-Asia Express*, you can even get there by train. Don't miss the fabulous city of Esfahan, easily reached from Tehran by a daily overnight train. Getting a visa to visit Iran still requires a certain amount of legwork, but it's now much easier than it was.

Train operator:	Iranian Islamic Republic Railways (IR: 'Raja Trains'), **www.raja.ir** Unofficial site, with times and fares for trains in Iran: **www.msedv.at/rai/** Map of Iranian rail network: **http://commons.wikimedia.org/wiki/ Image:Iran_railway_en.png**
Time:	GMT+3½
Currency:	£1 = approx. 15,000 Iranian rials, $1 = approx. 8,780 Iranian rials
Visas:	Required by everyone. See the Iranian embassy website, **www.iran-embassy.org.uk**, and the advice on page 105. Consulate address: 50 Kensington Court, Kensington High Street, London W8 5DB, telephone 020 7937 5225 or 020 7361 0823 Recorded visa information (60p a minute): 0906 802 0222
Travel advice:	Check Foreign Office advice for southeastern Iran at **www.fco.gov.uk**.

EUROPE TO IRAN, overland

If you can get an Iranian visa, it's now fairly straightforward to travel from

London to Iran overland, using the *Trans-Asia Express* from Istanbul to Tehran. First, you need to reach Istanbul. The journey from London to Turkey takes three or four nights, and departures from London are daily. For details of the London to Istanbul journey, see pages 127–38. Once in Istanbul, you take the weekly *Trans-Asia Express* from Istanbul to Tabriz and Tehran.

ISTANBUL TO TEHRAN, by train

There is a safe, modern and comfortable weekly train from Istanbul to Tehran, the *Trans-Asia Express*, introduced in March 2001. The train is actually two connecting trains: you take a Turkish train from Istanbul to Tatvan pier, then a ferry across Lake Van, then an Iranian train from Van pier to Tehran. Only one baggage van actually goes all the way, being conveyed across Lake Van on the ferry. Both the Turkish train and the Iranian have modern air-conditioned first class 4-berth couchettes and an elegant modern restaurant car. The total distance from Istanbul to Tehran is 2,968 km excluding the 90 km length of Lake Van.

Istanbul → Tehran

Trans-Asia Express, eastbound		
Istanbul (Haydarpaşa)	depart	23:55 Wednesday
Ankara	arrive	08:45 Thursday
Ankara	depart	10:25 Thursday
Tatvan Pier (train)	arrive	14:50 Friday
Tatvan Pier (ferry)	depart	15:00 Friday
Van Pier (ferry)	arrive	21:00 Friday
Van Pier (train)	depart	21:30 Friday
Tabriz	arrive	06:35 Saturday
Tabriz	depart	08:23 Saturday
Tehran	arrive	20:20 Saturday

Tehran → Istanbul

Trans-Asia Express, westbound		
Tehran	depart	21:25 Thursday
Tabriz	arrive	09:26 Friday
Tabriz	depart	10:56 Friday
Van Pier (train)	arrive	19:56 Friday
Van Pier (ferry)	depart	20:00 Friday
Tatvan Pier (ferry)	arrive	02:00 Saturday
Tatvan Pier (train)	depart	04:52 Saturday
Ankara	arrive	08:30 Sunday
Ankara	depart	09:30 Sunday
Istanbul (Haydarpaşa)	arrive	18:34 Sunday

You can confirm these train times at **www.raja.ir** (click the 'house' logo then 'English' top right). Allow for an arrival an hour or two (or three) late, so don't plan any tight connections. Travelling westbound, always allow for a night in Istanbul; don't plan onward travel to Belgrade/Bucharest/Thessaloniki the same day. If you want to stop off, there are other trains between Istanbul and Ankara (see the Turkey chapter, pages 142–4), and between Tabriz and Tehran (see **www.raja.ir** for train times and fares).

Fares

One-way, per person, including couchette	
Istanbul to Tehran	€49.40 (£45 or $67)
Istanbul to Tabriz	€40.90 (£37 or $55)
Ankara to Tehran	€43.20 (£39 or $58)
Ankara to Tabriz	€34.70 (£32 or $48)

The Turkish Railways website (**www.tcdd.gov.tr**) quotes fares in euros, as shown above. The Iranian Railways website (**www.raja.ir**) quotes the one-way fare from Tehran to Istanbul as 404,000 Iranian rials (about £25 or $40), including sleeping berth.

How to buy tickets: eastbound from Istanbul

You can book the eastbound train from Istanbul to Tehran at the international booking office at Istanbul Haydarpaşa station. The ticket office in Istanbul accepts Turkish lira, euros, US dollars and Visa/MasterCard, but not pounds sterling. It's often possible to find berths available even booking a day or two before departure, but as this train runs only once a week it's probably best to book in advance before you get to Istanbul. You can do this by asking a travel agency in Istanbul to buy the tickets for you. Try either of these two reliable agencies:

- **Tur-ISTA Tourism Travel Agency**, Divan Yolu Caddesi No. 16/B, 34410 Sultanahmet, Istanbul, Turkey. Telephone +90 (212) 527 7085 or 513 7119. Fax +90 (212) 519 3792. Email erdemir@tur-ista.com. I can recommend their service – please mention seat61.com when booking. They charge about €65 for an Istanbul–Tehran ticket.

- **Viking Turizm**, Mete Caddesi No. 24, Taksim, Istanbul, Turkey. Telephone +90 (212) 334 2600. Fax +90 (212) 334 2660. Email info@vikingturizm.com.tr. Please mention seat61.com when booking.

How to buy tickets: westbound from Tehran

You can book the westbound Tehran to Istanbul train at Tehran station – you will need to show your passport. Alternatively, you can book this train through a number of Iranian travel agencies, such as **www.irantravelingcenter.com**.

Currency

The Turkish restaurant car accepts Turkish lira, US dollars and euros, but not

Iranian rials. The Lake Van ferry accepts both lira and rials, and it is reported that lira can be exchanged for rials on board the ferry. The restaurant car on the Iranian train will accept Iranian rials or euros, but not Turkish lira. There is no exchange possible on board the train or at the frontier, but the train stops for 1–2 hours at Tabriz and euros or US dollars (but not Turkish lira) can be exchanged for rials there. Rials are freely available at banks and exchange bureaux in Ankara and may be available in Istanbul.

Visas for Iran

Before booking your travel, check that you can get an Iranian tourist visa. Iran used to grant tourist visas only if you made tour arrangements within Iran through a recognised tour agency, but it is now getting a lot easier for independent travellers to get visas. The Iranian embassy website, **www.iran-embassy.org.uk/?l=e**, has a list of travel agencies who can help you obtain a visa, such as **www.magic-carpet-travel.com**, **www.iranianvisa.com** or **www.persianvoyages.com**. One seat61 correspondent has recommended www.iranianvisa.com, saying their service fee is only €30. You may be able to find an agency who will tailor-make arrangements for you, allowing you to arrive in Iran on the *Trans-Asia Express*. There is absolutely no problem reported in crossing the border into Iran by train; border officials are said to be very friendly!

TRAIN TRAVEL WITHIN IRAN

Iran has a good and growing network of intercity trains, many with air-conditioning, and travelling by train is a great way to explore the country in comfort. For example, there is a daily overnight service linking Tehran with Esfahan, one of the most historic and beautiful cities of Iran. This train leaves Tehran at 22:40, arriving in Esfahan at 06:10 the next morning; in the other direction it departs from Esfahan at 22:50 and arrives in Tehran at 06:15. It has air-conditioned first class 4-berth sleepers and second class seats.

You can buy tickets at the station; just remember to take your passport with you.

The Iranian Railways website, **www.raja.ir**, will give times and fares for all services.

MOVING ON FROM IRAN

For onward travel to Pakistan and India, see the 'To Pakistan and India overland' chapter, page 90.

ISRAEL

Getting to the Holy Land by sea or overland may currently be problematic (the options are explained below), but once there you'll find a rapidly developing standard-gauge rail network with modern trains linking all the main cities, including Haifa, Tel Aviv and Jerusalem. Indeed, the line to Jerusalem has recently been totally rebuilt and a new faster line is under construction.

Train operator:	Israel Railways (IR), **www.israrail.org.il**
Ferries to Israel:	None currently operating
Time:	GMT+2 (GMT+3 from last Sunday in March to last Saturday in October)
Currency:	£1 = approx. 5.7 shekels
Tourist information:	**www.goisrael.com** For the latest security situation, check travel advice on the Foreign Office website, **www.fco.gov.uk**.
Visas:	UK, EU, US, Canadian, Australian and NZ citizens do not need a visa to visit Israel.

EUROPE TO ISRAEL, without flying

There are two options for surface travel from London or anywhere else in Europe to Israel, although unfortunately there are problems with both options.

You can travel by train and bus via Syria and Jordan. This works in the outward direction from London to Israel, but can only be done in the return Israel to London direction if you are careful to avoid any indication in your passport (or anywhere else) of your visit to Israel. This is because you are not allowed to enter Syria with any evidence of a visit to Israel in your passport. The route is London–Paris–Vienna–Budapest–Istanbul–Aleppo–Damascus–Amman–Allenby Bridge–Jerusalem.

The second option is to travel by train+ferry to Athens, then by sea from Piraeus to Israel. The catch here is that the direct ships from Piraeus to Israel stopped running in 2001, and still show no signs of resuming in 2010. You can check the latest situation with UK ferry booking agents **www.viamare.com**. However, there's now a glimmer of hope for ferry travel to Israel, as a new Rhodes–Cyprus and Cyprus–Israel service started in summer 2008.

London ➤ Jerusalem, via Istanbul, Syria and Jordan

Travel by train from **London** to **Istanbul**. Departures are daily, and the journey takes three or four nights; see the Turkey chapter, pages 127–38. You arrive in Istanbul at 07:50; by all means then head onwards the same evening, but I'd recommend an overnight stop in Istanbul both for comfort and to allow you two days for sightseeing.

The next stage (day 5 from London if you overnight in Istanbul) is to go by train from **Istanbul** to **Adana** in southern Turkey (with a night in a sleeper), then by bus from **Adana** via **Antakya** to **Aleppo** in Syria. From **Aleppo** travel on to **Damascus** by train – there are several a day taking 4–5 hours. For times, fares and information, see the Syria chapter, pages 117–22. At the Syrian border, be sure not to give any indication that you plan to visit Israel. In all the Istanbul–Damascus journey takes two nights, two days, so you can expect to reach Damascus on the evening of day 7 from London.

The next stage is to travel by bus from **Damascus** to **Amman** in Jordan. There are several buses daily and the journey takes 5 hours. See the Jordan chapter, pages 113–14.

Take a local bus or taxi from **Amman** to the **Allenby Bridge** border crossing with Israel. Pass through customs and passport control. Take another bus or taxi into central Jerusalem.

How to buy tickets

You can book the London to Istanbul train journey through any UK European rail ticketing agency, for example European Rail (**www.europeanrail.com**) on 020 7619 1083. You can book the train from Istanbul to Adana either at the station when you get to Istanbul, or through a travel agency in Istanbul, as shown in the Syria chapter, page 120. Onward buses from Adana to Aleppo can be booked when you get to Adana. You will need to book the Aleppo–Damascus train at the station in Aleppo, and the Damascus–Amman bus or train when you get to Damascus.

London ➜ *Israel, via Athens and Cyprus*

It used to be possible to travel from London to Israel via Greece in about seven nights: taking train+ferry to Athens then picking up one of the several weekly sailings from Piraeus direct to Haifa in Israel. However, all these ferries were suspended in 2001, and remain suspended in 2010, because of the political situation in Israel. You can check the latest situation with Viamare Travel (**www.viamare.com**, 020 8206 3420).

As of summer 2008, an alternative route has become available, sailing via Rhodes and Cyprus.

Travel from **London** to **Athens** by train+ferry, via Bari, Brindisi or Ancona (or you could take the train all the way, following the same route as for London–Istanbul as far as Bucharest, then on to Thessaloniki and Athens).

You then take a ferry from **Piraeus** (the port of Athens) to **Rhodes**. You can find information on the journey London–Rhodes at **www.seat61.com/Greece.htm**.

A passenger cruise ferry (which started operating in summer 2008) sails at least once a week between June and October from **Rhodes** (and on some dates Crete) to **Limassol** in Cyprus, taking one night, then weekly between April and October from **Limassol** to **Haifa** in Israel, taking one night.

Fast air-conditioned trains link **Haifa** with **Tel Aviv**, and Tel Aviv with **Jerusalem**.

Fares and how to book

For the ferry from Rhodes to Limassol and Haifa you can find sailing dates and prices at **www.varianostravel.com/Cruises/ferry_service.htm**.

For train and ferry travel from the UK to Rhodes, see **www.seat61.com/Greece.htm**.

For trains from Haifa and Tel Aviv, see **www.rail.co.il**.

TRAIN TRAVEL WITHIN ISRAEL

Israel has a modern and rapidly expanding train network. The line from Tel Aviv to Jerusalem, closed for some years, reopened in early 2005, and fast air-conditioned trains also link Tel Aviv with Haifa. However, there are no international train services to or from Israel. For train routes, times and fares in Israel, see **www.rail.co.il**.

Tel Aviv → Jerusalem

Trains leave Tel Aviv's Merkaz station (also known as Tel Aviv Central–Savidor) for Jerusalem every hour from 05:54 to 19:54, Monday–Thursday and Sunday, journey time 1 hour 40 minutes for the 82-km (51-mile) journey. They call at Tel Aviv Hashalom station 2 minutes after leaving Merkaz. Trains return from Jerusalem to Tel Aviv every hour from 05:43 to 21:43 on Monday–Thursday and Sunday. On Friday, trains run hourly in each direction until around 13:00; there is no service on Friday afternoon and just one late-night service on Saturday after dark. The fare is 21.5 shekels (£3.70 or $5.50) one-way, 39 shekels (£6.70 or $10) return. Children under 10 travel for 17 shekels (£3 or $4.50) one-way, 34 shekels return.

Haifa → Tel Aviv → Ben Gurion airport, Be'er Sheva

On Monday–Thursday and Sunday, two trains an hour link Haifa (Hof HaKarmel station) with Tel Aviv (Merkaz station) and Ben Gurion airport. Journey time is 50–60 minutes for the 85 km (53 miles) from Haifa to Tel Aviv; Tel Aviv to Ben Gurion airport takes 19 minutes. One train an hour links Tel Aviv Merkaz with Be'er Sheva, some trains starting back in Haifa. On Friday, trains run hourly in each direction on both routes until around 13:00; there is no service on Friday afternoon, or on Saturday until after dark. Haifa to Tel Aviv costs 28.5 shekels (£5 or $7.50) one-way, 51.5 shekels (£9 or $13) return. Children under 10 travel for 23 shekels (£4 or $6) one-way, 46 shekels return.

JORDAN

Jordan is a gem. Its modern capital, Amman, is worth a brief visit, but Jordan's premier attraction is 240 km (150 miles) to the south at Petra, the ancient capital of the Nabataeans. Approached through a narrow defile in the rock, the ruined city will take your breath away. Equally breathtaking is the wild beauty of the desert and sandstone outcrops at Wadi Rumm, another 115 km (72 miles) south of Petra and once the haunt of Lawrence of Arabia. Indeed, Lawrence fans will also wish to visit the fort at Aqaba on the Red Sea, and perhaps the fort at Azraq, an hour's taxi ride east of Amman, where Lawrence set up his headquarters for a while, sleeping in the room above the gatehouse. Believe it or not, Jordan can be reached by train from the UK via Istanbul and Syria: this chapter explains how. You may need to use a bus for part of the journey, including from Damascus to Amman if you cannot find a suitable train on the Damascus–Amman Hedjaz Railway, the weekly train having been suspended in 2006 and only partly reinstated. Once in Jordan you'll need to use buses or taxis to get around as it has virtually no rail network.

Train operator:	Hedjaz Jordan Railway (HJR), **www.jhr.gov.jo**
Time:	GMT+2 (GMT+3 from last Sunday in March to last Saturday in October)
Currency:	£1 = approx. 1.09 Jordanian dinars (JD), $1 = approx. 0.7 dinars
Tourist information:	**www.see-jordan.com** Information on Petra: **http://nabataea.net/petra.html**
Visas:	UK, EU, US, Canadian, Australian and NZ citizens need a Jordanian visa. You can get this in London from their embassy at 6 Upper Phillimore Gardens, Kensington, London W8 7HA, telephone 020 7937 3685.

EUROPE TO JORDAN, overland

It's possible to travel overland from the UK to Jordan, by train and bus. The journey takes around six or seven nights, via Istanbul, Aleppo and Damascus, though you may well want to stop off and see something of Turkey and Syria on the way.

London → Amman

Step 1: London to Istanbul. The train journey from London or Paris to Istanbul takes three or four nights, with daily departures all year round. For details, see pages 127–38.

Step 2: Istanbul to Aleppo and Damascus. At the time of writing, the weekly direct sleeping-car from Istanbul to Aleppo in northern Syria is still suspended, but a daily air-conditioned sleeper train links Istanbul with Adana in southeastern Turkey. Spend the night in Adana then take a bus onwards to Aleppo next day. Total journey time from Istanbul to Aleppo is two nights, two days; see the Syria chapter, pages 117–20, for details. Several air-conditioned 160km/h trains link Aleppo with Damascus every day, and there's a sleeper train too: details are shown in the Syria chapter.

Step 3: Damascus to Amman. There used to be a wonderful twice-weekly narrow-gauge train service from Damascus to Amman over the historic Hedjaz Railway. However, the service was suspended in 2006 due to track damage (allegedly by Syrian tanks on manoeuvres!). However, there are a few positive signs: a weekly train resumed running in May 2010 from Deraa to Amman, leaving Deraa at 18:00 on Monday, arriving in Amman at 21:45; and one (unconfirmed) report suggests that a weekly Damascus–Amman train may now have been reintroduced, leaving Damascus Kadem station at 08:00 on Monday, arriving in Amman at 17:00. It's therefore worth asking at the Syrian Railways booking office at the Hedjaz station in Damascus city centre, or at the Kadem station when you arrive from Aleppo. Alternatively, several daily buses link Damascus with Amman, taking around 4 or 5 hours, details below.

Damascus ➜ *Amman by bus*

		Karnak	JETT	JETT
Damascus	depart	07:00	15:00	16:00
Amman	arrive	11:30	19:30	20:30

Amman ➜ *Damascus by bus*

		JETT	JETT	Karnak
Amman	depart	07:00	08:00	15:00
Damascus	arrive	11:30	12:30	19:30

Karnak = daily air-conditioned bus operated by Karnak bus company, Syria (no website).

JETT = daily air-conditioned bus operated by Jordan Express Tourist Transportation, www.jett.com.jo.

Damascus to Amman is 180 km by road. The fare is JD8 (£7 or $11). The JETT website is **www.jett.com.jo**, or call +962 6 5664146.

AMMAN TO PETRA AND AQABA, by bus

The Hedjaz Railway no longer operates south of Amman, except for freight trains. But there are regular buses and minibuses from Amman to Petra (Wadi Musa is the name of the modern town next door) and Aqaba.

JETT (Jordan Express Tourist Transportation) runs air-conditioned buses between Amman and Aqaba, leaving Amman (Abdali bus station) at 07:00, 09:00, 11:00, 14:00, 16:00 and 18:00, arriving in Aqaba 4 hours later. The fare is JD7.50 (£7 or $10). Additional buses run 3–5 times daily from Amman's Wehdat, Tabarbour and 7th circle bus stations. Northbound, buses leave Aqaba for Amman's Abdali bus station at 07:00, 09:00, 11:00, 14:00, 16:00 and 18:00, with additional buses to Amman's 7th circle and Wehdat bus stations.

The JETT bus to Petra leaves Amman (Abdali bus station) at 06:30, arriving at Petra (Wadi Musa) at 10:00, and returns from Petra at 17:00, arriving in Amman at 20:30. The fare to Petra is JD8 (£7 or $11). See **www.jett.com.jo** or call JETT on +962 6 5664146.

You can also travel between Amman, Petra and Aqaba by service taxi. These are usually 25-seater minibuses. The taxis leave when full and usually operate throughout the day. The fare from Amman to Petra is around JD3 (£2.75), journey time about 2 hours 40 minutes. These minibus taxis leave from Amman's Wehdat bus station.

Hiring a private taxi to take you to Petra will cost about JD40–JD50 (£36–£46) after negotiation.

MOVING ON FROM JORDAN

Amman → Cairo by bus

A daily long-distance bus leaves Amman (JETT terminal) at 03:00, taking some 19 hours to reach Cairo. It is run by Jordan Express Tourist Transportation (JETT), **www.jett.com.jo**, telephone +962 6 5664146. This bus crosses Israel – remember that you won't be able to enter Syria with any sign of a visit to Israel in your passport.

Amman → Cairo by bus+ferry

It's also possible to travel from Jordan to Egypt avoiding Israel, using a ferry. Here are details for the southbound journey – details for the northbound journey are shown in the Egypt section.

Travel from **Amman** or **Petra** to **Aqaba** by bus or service taxi as shown above.

There is a daily fast catamaran (departing 12:00, crossing 1 hour) and a daily conventional ferry (departing 15:00, crossing 3–4 hours) from **Aqaba** to **Nuweiba** in Sinai, Egypt. The fare is about JD16 (£15) for the ferry or JD21 (£19) for the fast catamaran. You must check in at least 2 hours before the ferry sails.

There are buses from **Nuweiba** to both **Cairo** and **Sharm el Sheik**, taking several hours.

SYRIA

Syria has to be one of the world's most under-rated destinations. Yet the first thing anyone asks when you tell them you're going there is, 'Is it safe?' Ironically, it's one of the safest countries to visit, safer in fact than most western countries, and it's home to some of the most hospitable people you could hope to meet. Damascus is well worth visiting with its Great Mosque, tomb of Saladin and ruined Temple of Apollo, although I personally prefer Syria's second city, Aleppo, with its wonderful labyrinthine souqs (covered Arabian markets) and the classic faded grandeur of the Baron's Hotel. However, Syria's two great attractions are outside the cities, at Palmyra, a ruined city in the desert in the northeast, and Krak des Chevaliers, a superbly preserved crusader castle overlooking a mountain pass between Syria and Palestine.

Train operator:	Chemins de Fer Syriens (CFS), **www.cfssyria.sy** (Hint: for English, click 'Call Offers' then for train times, select 'trips')
Time:	GMT+2 (GMT+3 from last Sunday in March to last Saturday in October)
Currency:	£1 = approx. 67 Syrian pounds, $1 = approx. 45 Syrian pounds
Tourist information:	**www.syriatourism.org**
Visas:	UK, EU, US, Canadian, Australian and NZ citizens need a Syrian visa. You can get one in London from the Syrian embassy at 8 Belgrave Square, London SW1X 8PH, telephone 020 7245 9012, **www.syrianembassy.co.uk**.

EUROPE TO SYRIA, by train

It's easy to reach Aleppo and Damascus overland from London or any other city in Europe.

First, you need to take the train to Istanbul. The train journey from London or Paris to Istanbul takes three or four nights with daily departures year-round. You'll find details for this journey on pages 127–38.

From Istanbul there used to be a weekly direct sleeping-car to Aleppo, but at the time of writing this service remains suspended. However, there is an alternative route with daily departures: travelling by train to Adana in southern Turkey then by bus or taxi on to Aleppo. Details of this journey are given in the next section, pages 154–5.

ISTANBUL TO SYRIA, by train and bus

Istanbul ➜ Aleppo

Step 1: Travel from **Istanbul** to **Adana** by daily air-conditioned sleeper train. The *Içanadolou Mavi Tren* leaves Istanbul's Haydarpaşa station on the Asian side of the Bosphorus at 23:50 and arrives in Adana at 18:35 next day after a remarkably scenic and comfortable journey across Turkey. It has a civilised air-conditioned sleeping-car with 1- and 2-bed compartments with washbasin, reclining Pullman seats and a restaurant car. You'll probably need to stay overnight in Adana before travelling on to Syria next day.

You can also travel to Adana via Ankara if you prefer; indeed Ankara is well worth a 24-hour stopover if you have the time. Take a modern air-conditioned daytime train from **Istanbul** (departs 11:00 daily) to **Ankara** (changing on to a high-speed 250km/h train at Eskişehir, arriving Ankara 16:40, restaurant car available for lunch), then the *Cukurova Mavi* train from **Ankara** (departing 20:05 daily) to **Adana** (arriving 07:25, sleeping-car and couchettes available, with restaurant car).

See the Turkey chapter, pages 142 and 151, for details of all these trains.

Step 2: travel from **Adana** to **Antakya** then on to **Aleppo** by air-conditioned bus. Buses run every hour from Adana to Antakya, where you change on to another bus from Antakya to Aleppo. There are at least two bus companies running at least two daily buses each from Antakya to Aleppo: Özhan Turizm (**www.ozhanturizm.com**) and Hatay Luks Nur Seyahat (**www.hatayluksnurseyahat.com**) – though their websites are only in Turkish. It's easy to buy tickets at the bus station when you get to Antakya. Özhan Turizm have departures from Antakya to Aleppo at 08:00, 11:00 and 13:00, journey time 3 hours. On their website, click '*seferlerimiz*' (timetables) then '*tarifeli*' (scheduled times). *Hergün* means daily, *hareket saati* is departure time, *variş saati* is arrival time, *dönüş saati* is return time (from Aleppo).

Instead of taking the bus from Antakya to Aleppo, you can travel by service taxi, which will take three passengers for around £5 each. The service taxis leave when they are full, mainly in the early morning or afternoon, taking 3–4 hours to reach Aleppo, including the border crossing. A seat61 correspondent took a taxi all the way from Adana to Aleppo and reports that it took 5–6 hours, including 2 hours at the border crossing, and cost $90 for all three passengers.

Alternative step 2: You can also take a weekly train between Adana and Aleppo, if it's still running by the time you read this – the Turkish Railways website **www.tcdd.gov.tr** is the place to look, in the international Middle East section. It's a Syrian train with comfortable first class seats and a sleeping-car with 1- and 2-bed compartments which leaves Adana every Friday night at 00:05, arriving at Aleppo at 08:20 on Saturday morning. It calls at Meydan Ekbez for frontier formalities from 04:44 to 05:55. If its weekly schedule fits your plans, this is the option to go for. The train in fact starts in Mersin in southern Turkey; it was initially introduced in 2009 as a twice-weekly service, then discontinued, then reintroduced in June 2010 on a weekly schedule.

Aleppo → *Istanbul*

Step 1: Travel from **Aleppo** to **Antakya** and then **Adana** by daily buses. There's a daily direct Syrian bus from Aleppo's Karnak bus station to Antakya and Adana, leaving at 05:00. Turkish company

Özhan Turizm (**www.ozhanturizm.com**) has departures from Aleppo at 12:00, 15:00 and 17:00 for Antakya, journey time 3 hours (see the Istanbul–Aleppo section for advice on how to use the website); hourly buses then connect Antakya and Adana. Or there are minibuses to Antakya with bus connection to Adana, which leave from the small bus station down a side street next to the Ramsis Hotel (opposite the Baron's Hotel) at 05:00 and 14:00, journey about 6 hours 30 minutes to Adana. If you catch a very early bus, you may manage to connect in Adana the same day, otherwise you'll need to overnight in Adana.

Alternative step 1: If it's still running by the time you read this, a weekly train leaves Aleppo at 03:00 on Friday morning, calling at Meydan Ekbez for frontier formalities from 05:51 to 07:00 and arriving at Adana at 12:20 the same day. The train has two Syrian first class seats cars and a Syrian sleeping-car with 1- and 2-bed compartments. If its weekly schedule fits your plans, this is the option to go for. Tickets can be booked on the day at Aleppo station; there will almost certainly be places available.

Step 2: Travel from **Adana** to **Istanbul** by the daily air-conditioned sleeper train, the *Içanadolou Mavi Tren*, leaving Adana at 14:00 and arriving at Istanbul at 08:58 next day.

How much does it cost?

Istanbul to Adana by train costs just 73 Turkish lira (about £33 or $50) sharing a 2-bed sleeper, TL90 (£41 or $61) in a single-bed sleeper, or TL28 (£12 or $19) in a reclining seat. See the Turkey chapter, pages 144 and 151, for fares for Istanbul–Ankara–Adana, or check fares using **www.tcdd.gov.tr**.

Adana to Aleppo by train costs €14 (£12.50) one-way in a seat, and around €25 (£22.50) for a sleeper.

Adana to Antakya by bus costs around TL15 (£7 or $10).

Antakya to Aleppo by bus costs around TL18 (£8 or $12).

Northbound, the Turkish bus from Aleppo to Antakya costs around 350 Syrian pounds (£5 or $7); travelling by minibus Aleppo–Antakya and connecting bus on to Adana costs around 800 Syrian pounds (£12).

How to buy tickets, southbound

You can buy your Istanbul–Adana ticket at the station in Istanbul – preferably a few days in advance, especially if you want a sleeper, as these can sell out – although you'll usually find Pullman seats available even on the day of departure.

If you want to make your booking earlier, to be sure of a sleeper, you can book from outside Turkey by contacting Tur-ISTA Tourism Travel Agency, Divan Yolu Caddesi No. 16/B, 34410 Sultanahmet, Istanbul, Turkey; telephone +90 (212) 527 7085 or 513 7119; fax +90 (212) 519 3792; email erdemir@tur-ista.com. I can personally recommend their service. Their office is near the Sultanahmet tram stop, a short way from the Blue Mosque. You can collect the tickets as you pass through Istanbul heading south to Syria, or they may be willing to send the tickets to you for a fee.

Buy onward bus tickets when you get to Adana.

It is not possible to pre-book the Adana–Aleppo train from anywhere except the ticket office at Adana, but there will be plenty of places available in both seats and sleeper, so just turn up and buy a ticket on the day.

How to buy tickets, northbound

Buy bus tickets or tickets for the Aleppo–Adana train in Aleppo.

Buy your Adana–Istanbul train ticket at the station when you get to Adana. There are normally Pullman seats available on the day, and often sleepers.

If you're making a round trip and are sure of your return date, you could pre-book your Adana–Istanbul tickets through Tur-ISTA Tourism Travel Agency (see above for details).

THE BARON'S HOTEL, ALEPPO

When you arrive in Aleppo, whatever your normal budget, the most wonderful and historic place to stay is the Hotel Baron, on Baron Street. Opened in 1909, it was one of the most famous hotels in the Middle East, used by Agatha Christie, Teddy Roosevelt, Mustafa Kemal Atatürk, Charles Lindbergh and T. E. Lawrence. It will cost you all of £30/$45 for a single room or £38/$55 for a double to stay there, an experience in itself! Email the hotel on hotelbaron@mail.sy or telephone +963 21 211 0880.

ALEPPO TO DAMASCUS

If you need to travel between Aleppo and Damascus, take the train. It's fast, very comfortable, and unbelievably cheap. New 160km/h diesel trains came into service in late 2006 and the number of Syrians using trains is increasing: passenger numbers in 2010 are expected to be double those carried in 2006, at over 4 million passenger journeys. There are several daytime air-conditioned trains between Aleppo and Damascus, also an overnight train with sleeping-car. All trains shown here run daily.

Aleppo → *Damascus*

Train number		170	10	12	16	230
Classes		1,2	1,2	1,2	1,2	1,2,S
Aleppo	depart	03:50	05:40	10:10	16:45	00:10
Hama	arr/dep	05:40	07:05	11:39	18:10	02:12
Homs	arr/dep	06:26	07:46	12:30	18:59	03:28
Damascus (Kadem)	arrive	08:54	09:40	14:33	21:02	06:24

Damascus → *Aleppo*

Train number		7	11	173	13	231
Classes		1,2	1,2	1,2	1,2	1,2,S
Damascus (Kadem)	depart	06:50	15:10	16:50	20:40	00:01
Homs	arrive	09:14	17:40	18:51	22:55	03:13
Hama	arrive	10:04	18:33	19:29	23:43	04:10
Aleppo	arrive	11:29	20:23	20:50	01:08	05:58

1,2 = first and second class with buffet car.

1,2,S = first and second class seats plus sleeper with 1- and 2-bed compartments.

Trains 7–16 use new 160km/h air-conditioned diesel trains delivered from South Korea in late 2006.

You should double-check all train times locally. You can check Syrian train times and fares at **www.cfssyria.sy** (in Arabic only, but you can easily translate using Google language tools). Another good resource for checking Syrian train times is **www.syrische-eisenbahn.de/SyrianRailways/CFS/Fahrplan/CFS-Fahrplan.htm**.

Damascus Kadem station is 3–4 km southwest of Damascus city centre. A taxi to or from the centre costs about 100 Syrian pounds (£1.50 or $2) and takes 25 minutes when traffic is busy. A free shuttle bus leaves the Hedjaz station one hour before the departure of each Aleppo-bound train from Damascus Kadem (confirm this at the Hedjaz station ticket office).

Be sure to arrive at your departure station with plenty of time to spare as you may need to get your tickets 'validated' and your passport details recorded.

Homs now has two stations, Homs 1 (nearer the centre) and Homs 2 (on the outskirts). Most Aleppo–Damascus trains serve Homs 2, but some may still call at Homs 1; please check locally.

Fares and how to buy tickets

Aleppo to Damascus by one of the modern daytime express trains (trains 7–16) costs just 200 Syrian pounds (£3 or $4) one-way in second class, 240 Syrian pounds (£4 or $5) in first class. If you go on the older trains (170 and 173) the one-way fare is 140 Syrian pounds (£2 or $3) in second class, 180 Syrian pounds (£3 or $4) in first class.

On the overnight train (trains 230 and 231) the one-way fare for a berth in a shared 2-bed compartment is 505 Syrian pounds (£6 or $9).

Buy your tickets at the station: in Damascus, you can buy tickets for this journey at the city centre Hedjaz station, as well as at Kadem station. Remember that you must take your passport when buying tickets.

ALEPPO TO LATAKIA

There is some spectacular mountain scenery on the route from Aleppo to Latakia, on the coast, with the best views from the north side of the train. Two modern air-conditioned trains a day make the journey in just 2½ hours, or you can choose one of the older, slower but still comfortable trains and travel first class for just £1.

Trains also run between Damascus and Latakia, Latakia and Tartous, and Hama and Tartous: see **www.cfssyria.sy** for times and fares (in Arabic only, but you can easily translate using Google language tools).

Damascus, Aleppo → Latakia

Train number		42	242	246	44	125
Classes		1,2	1,2	1,2	1,2	1,2
Damascus	depart	–	–	–	–	15:50
Aleppo	depart	06:00	06:48	15:50	17:30	I
Latakia	arrive	08:30	10:08	19:22	20:07	20:55

Latakia → Aleppo, Damascus

Train number		120	41	243	245	45
Classes		1,2	1,2	1,2	1,2	1,2
Latakia	depart	01:30	06:25	07:10	15:40	17:25
Aleppo	arrive	I	09:04	10:50	19:40	20:00
Damascus	arrive	06:46	–	–	–	–

All trains are daily, but please double-check all train times locally.

Trains 41–45 and train 120 use the same modern air-conditioned trainsets as used on the Aleppo–Damascus line.

Trains 242–246 and train 125 use older but still comfortable cars.

Fares and how to buy tickets

On fast modern trains 41–45, Aleppo to Latakia costs 135 Syrian pounds (£2) first class, 105 Syrian pounds (£1.60) second class. On older trains 242–246, Aleppo to Latakia costs 70 Syrian pounds (£1) first class, 50 Syrian pounds (£0.75) second class.

The fare for Damascus to Latakia is 120 Syrian pounds (£2) first class, 80 Syrian pounds (£1.20) second class.

Buy your tickets at the station. Remember to take your passport when buying tickets. It's reported that, as a foreigner, you may have to get your ticket stamped at another ticket window after buying it.

PALMYRA AND KRAK DES CHEVALIERS

The ruined city at Palmyra can be reached by bus or taxi from Damascus, journey time 3–4 hours. You will need to ask locally about bus times. The buses pass through Homs, but there are no direct buses between Aleppo and Palmyra.

The crusader castle at Krak des Chevaliers can be reached by minibus taxi from Homs (the nearest city) to the village of Hosn, next to the castle. You can travel to Homs by train from either Damascus or Aleppo. Hiring a car and driver for a day trip from Aleppo to Krak will cost around £70 or $100.

MOVING ON FROM SYRIA

Damascus ➜ Beirut (Lebanon) by bus

There is no railway to Beirut, but a whole range of buses daily link Damascus with Beirut (Charles Helou bus station), taking around 5 hours for the 115-km journey. Buy tickets and check exact times locally, as the bus companies do not have any website.

Damascus ➜ Amman (Jordan) by bus

There used to be a twice-weekly Damascus–Amman train over the famous Hedjaz Railway (Monday and Thursday at 08:00, arriving 17:00, were it running) but it has been suspended since 2006 following track damage. Instead, there are several daily buses from Damascus to Amman, taking about 5 hours. For details, see the Jordan chapter, pages 113–14.

Damascus and Aleppo → Tabriz and Tehran (Iran) by train

There is a weekly train with sleeping-cars and restaurant car from Damascus and Aleppo via Lake Van in Turkey (where passengers leave the Syrian train, take a ferry and join an Iranian train at the other side) to Tabriz and Tehran in Iran. Fares are not expensive. Times and fares are available at the Turkish Railways website **www.tcdd.gov.tr** (click 'English' then 'passenger' then 'trains to the Middle East'). Also try the Iranian Railways website **www.raja.ir** and **www.cfssyria.sy**. Between Syria and Lake Van the train has 1- and 2-bed Syrian sleeping cars. Between Lake Van and Tehran the train has Iranian 4-berth couchette cars, all air-conditioned.

TURKEY

Istanbul is arguably Europe's most exotic city, where east really does meet west. Minarets tower over mosques as ferries ply the Bosphorus between Europe and the edge of Asia. You won't regret making the effort to reach Istanbul by train, an epic three-night journey starting from London's St Pancras station by Eurostar, then across Europe into the Balkans by sleeping-car, culminating in a dramatic entry through the ancient city walls and around the Topkapi Palace to stop with a squeal of brakes in Istanbul's Sirkeci station on the European side of the Bosphorus, just a stone's throw from the water. A ferry ride away, modern air-conditioned trains depart from Istanbul's Haydarpaşa station on the Asian side for Ankara, Konya and eastern Turkey, often passing through superb scenery on their way. Although the rails don't reach every part of Turkey (the coastal resorts on the south being without any rail link), taking the train is a great way to travel around much of the country.

Train operator:	Türkiye Cumhuryeti Devlet Demiryollan (TCDD), **www.tcdd.gov.tr** To check European train times use **http://bahn.hafas.de**
Time:	GMT+2 (GMT+3 from last Sunday in March to last Saturday in October)
Currency:	£1 = approx. 2.25 new Turkish lira (TL), $1 = approx. 1.4 lira
Tourist information:	**www.turizm.gov.tr**, **www.turkeytravelplanner.com**
Visas:	UK, EU, US, Canadian, Australian and NZ citizens need a Turkish tourist visa, which you can buy at any frontier; see the visa advice on page 138.

UK TO TURKEY, by train

Can you still travel from London or Paris to Istanbul by train? Of course! The train journey is not only perfectly feasible, it's both safe and comfortable if you book a sleeper, and best of all it's an adventure. The journey takes three or four nights and departures from London are daily. The various options from London to Istanbul are explained in more detail in my first book, *The Man in Seat 61: A guide to taking the train from the UK through Europe*, but here is a summary for the recommended journey to Istanbul via Bucharest.

London ➜ *Istanbul*

Day 1: Travel from **London** to **Paris** by Eurostar, leaving London St Pancras at 16:02 (15:32 at weekends), arriving Paris Gare du Nord at 19:17 (18:47 at weekends). By all means take an earlier Eurostar from London if you'd like to spend some time in Paris, or if it has cheaper seats available. In Paris, it's a 10-minute walk from the Gare du Nord to the Gare de l'Est.

Day 1, evening: Travel from **Paris** to **Munich** overnight by the excellent City Night Line sleeper train *Cassiopeia*, leaving Paris Gare de l'Est daily at 20:20 and arriving in Munich at 07:16 next morning. It has sleeping-cars (1-, 2- and 3-bed compartments, either standard with washbasin or deluxe with private toilet and shower), 4- and 6-berth couchettes (basic bunks) and ordinary seats.

Day 2: Travel from **Munich** to **Budapest** by air-conditioned 225km/h Austrian RailJet train, leaving Munich at 09:27 and arriving in Budapest Keleti station at 16:49. A bar-bistro car is available, so treat yourself to lunch. If you want to stop off in Salzburg or Vienna for a day or two, no problem: this train calls at both Salzburg (arrive 10:58, depart 11:00) and Vienna Westbahnhof (arrive 13:44, depart 13:54). There are of course plenty of other trains between Munich, Salzburg, Vienna and Budapest which may suit your plans better if you're stopping off in those cities. You can check train times using **http://bahn.hafas.de**. Look out for great views of Salzburg citadel and castle on the right as

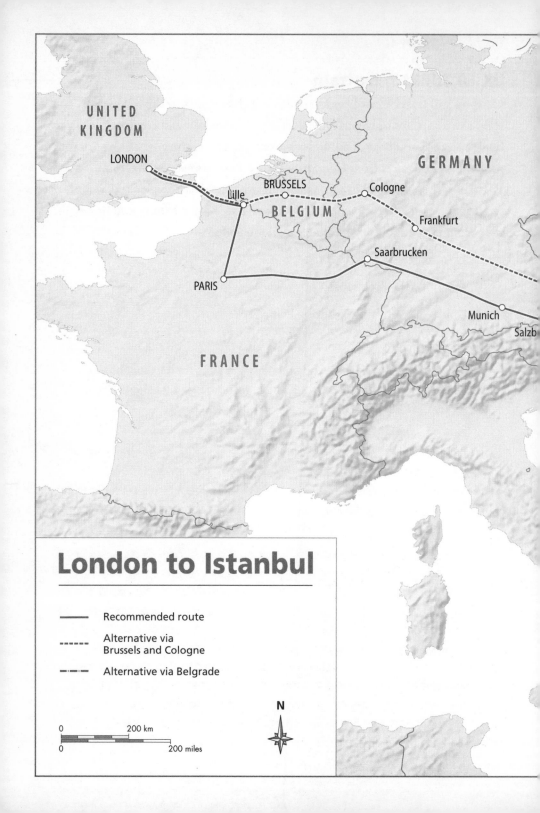

UNITED KINGDOM

LONDON

GERMANY

Lille

BRUSSELS

Cologne

BELGIUM

Frankfurt

Saarbrucken

PARIS

Munich

Salzb

FRANCE

London to Istanbul

—— Recommended route

----- Alternative via
Brussels and Cologne

—·—·— Alternative via Belgrade

N

0   200 km

0   200 miles

you cross the River Salzach approaching Salzburg. The train crosses the Danube just before arrival in Budapest.

Day 2, evening: Travel from **Budapest** to **Bucharest** overnight on the EuroNight sleeper train *Ister*, leaving Budapest Keleti station at 19:10 and arriving at Bucharest Nord station at 11:47 next morning. The Ister (*Ister* is the ancient name for the River Danube) has modernised air-conditioned sleeping-cars with safe, comfortable and carpeted 1-, 2- and 3-bed rooms with washbasin, 6-berth couchettes (basic bunks), a restaurant car for dinner and ordinary seats. Travel in ordinary seats is not recommended, a couchette is OK, but a bed in the sleeper is the recommended option. Sleepers can be converted to private sitting rooms for evening/morning use, and there's even a shower at the end of the corridor (which may or may not work). Take your own provisions in case the restaurant car doesn't show up – there usually is one but quite often isn't. The train crosses Transylvania by night, and soon after Braşov (reached at 07:02 next morning) it descends the pass through the Carpathian mountains, a wonderful, almost Alpine section of route.

Spend the night and following day in Bucharest.

Day 3: Spend the day and night in Bucharest. In theory, you could travel straight on to Istanbul on today's *Bosfor* but 37 minutes is too short a connection to be reliable, so I recommend an overnight stop.

Day 4: Travel from **Bucharest** to **Istanbul** on the *Bosfor*, which leaves Bucharest Nord daily at 12:24 and arrives at Istanbul's Sirkeci station at 07:50 next day (day 5 from London). The *Bosfor* has a modernised air-conditioned sleeping-car with safe, comfortable and carpeted 1-, 2- and 3-bed compartments with washbasin, and 6-berth couchettes (basic bunks). A bed in a sleeper is the recommended option. Bedrooms can be converted to private sitting rooms for daytime use, and there's a shower at the end of the corridor which might even work. There's no buffet or restaurant car at all on this train, so take plenty of food and bottled water, and your own supply of beer or wine.

Istanbul ➜ *London*

Day 1: Travel from **Istanbul** to **Bucharest** on the sleeper train *Bosfor*, which leaves Istanbul's Sirkeci station daily at 22:00 and arrives in Bucharest Nord at 18:30 next day. Expect an arrival an hour or two late. Remember to take your own food, water and wine or beer, as there's no restaurant or buffet car at all (there's a handy wine shop directly across the road from the entrance to Sirkeci station). Travelling in the comfort and security of the sleeping-car, this is a very pleasant journey, although be prepared to get off the train at the frontier (Kapikule) at 02:55 to have your passport stamped. In the morning the train wanders through lush green Bulgarian valleys before crossing the wide brown Danube into Romania. Relax and enjoy the ride . . .

Day 3: Travel from **Bucharest** to **Budapest** on the EuroNight sleeper train *Ister*, leaving Bucharest at 17:35 and arriving in Budapest Keleti station at 08:50 the next morning (day 4). The *Ister* has a comfortable sleeping-car with 1-, 2- and 3-bed compartments with washbasin, 6-berth couchettes and ordinary seats. Spend a few hours exploring Budapest; there is a left-luggage facility at the station.

Day 4: Travel from **Budapest** to **Munich** by air-conditioned 225km/h RailJet train, leaving Budapest at 13:10 and arriving in Munich Hauptbahnhof at 20:34. A bar-bistro car is available, so treat yourself to lunch! The train travels via Vienna (arrive 16:00, depart 16:14) and Salzburg (arrive 18:58, depart 19:02; watch for great views of the Danube and citadel soon after departure), giving opportunities for further stopovers.

Day 4, evening: Travel from **Munich** to **Paris** by the excellent City Night Line sleeper train *Cassiopeia*, leaving Munich Hauptbahnhof daily at 22:43 and arriving at Paris Gare de l'Est 09:23 next morning. Walk from the Gare de l'Est to the Gare du Nord.

Day 5: Travel from **Paris** to **London** by Eurostar, leaving Paris Gare du Nord at 11:13 and arriving London St Pancras at 12:29.

What's the journey like?

Travelling in the comfort and security of the sleeping-car, the journey from Bucharest to Istanbul is pleasant, leisurely and enjoyable. A couple of hours after leaving Bucharest the train crosses the Danube from Romania into Bulgaria on a long steel bridge (2.5 km long, in fact, making it the longest steel bridge in Europe; built in 1954), then for most of the rest of the day it meanders slowly through pleasant river valleys past small Bulgarian villages. The Turkish frontier at Kapikule is reached very late at night (01:25), and here you will need to leave the train briefly to buy a Turkish visa and then get your passport stamped: see the visa information on page 138. You'll be back in bed soon enough, but make sure you're awake for the dramatic entry into Istanbul, through the impressive Byzantine Walls of Theodosius and along the Bosphorus right underneath the walls of the Topkapi Palace, into Istanbul's historic Sirkeci station, built in 1888 in the heart of the city, within walking distance from all the sights. There's no more traditional way to arrive in Istanbul than by sleeping-car into Sirkeci station – why not hop into a taxi to the famous and equally traditional Pera Palas Hotel? Expect an arrival an hour or two late, occasionally 3 hours late or more; just relax and enjoy the ride.

How much does it cost?

Each leg of the journey is ticketed separately, so choose your class or type of couchette/sleeper for each individual train, and tot up the fares to find the overall cost. (The alternative is to use an InterRail pass: see the next section below.)

1. London to Paris by Eurostar
From £39 one-way or £69 return 2nd class.
From £107 one-way or £189 return 1st class.

2. Paris to Munich by sleeper train (per person)	In a seat	In a couchette		In the sleeping-car (standard room)			Deluxe sleeper	
		6-bunk	4-bunk	3-bed	2-bed	1-bed	2-bed	1-bed
Savings fare, one-way from	£27	£45	€69 (£60)	£64	£73	£128	£91	£174
Savings fare, return from	£54	£90	€138 (£120)	£128	£146	£256	£182	£348
Normal fare, one-way	£110	£124	€197 (£171)	£143	£161	£198	£213	£250
Normal fare, return	£186	£212	€394 (£342)	£244	£274	£336	£362	£424
Child under 15 with own berth	£55	£62	?	£71	£80	£98	£106	£124
Child under 6 without own berth	Child under 6 sharing berth travels free							

Savings fare = cheap fare, price varies, limited availability, no refunds or changes to travel plans.

Normal fare = fully flexible, refundable, buy any time.

3. Munich to Budapest by RailJet

Economy class special fares from €39 (£33) one-way, €78 (£66) return.

Economy class full price €105 (£91) one-way, €210 (£182) return.

First class special fares from €69 (£60) one-way, €138 (£120) return.

4. Budapest to Bucharest on the *Ister* (per person)

Booked in the UK	£91 each way in 6-berth couchette, £96 each way in 4-berth couchette.
	£101 each way in 3-bed sleeper, £118 each way in 2-bed sleeper.
Bought at the station in Budapest	Basic fare (seat only) is about €60 (£52) one-way, €120 (£104) return. Add €10 (£9) per night for a couchette; about €26 (£23) for a berth in a 3-bed sleeper; about €39 (£34) for a berth in a 2-bed sleeper.

5. Bucharest to Istanbul on the *Bosfor* (per person)	
Booked in the UK	£76 each way in 6-berth couchette.
	£89 each way in 3-bed sleeper, £102 each way in 2-bed sleeper.
Bought at the station in Bucharest	Basic fare (seat only) is about €45 (£39) one-way, €90 (£79) return 2nd class; about €68 (£59) one-way, €135 (£118) return 1st class. Add €9 (£8) to the 2nd class fare for a 6-berth couchette; €23 (£20) for a berth in a 3-bed sleeper; €35 (£31) for a berth in a 2-bed sleeper. Add €80 (£70) to the 1st class fare for a 1-bed sleeper.
Bought at the station in Istanbul	Basic fare (seat only) is 84 Turkish lira (£39) one-way 2nd class. Add TL20 (£9) for a couchette; TL56 (£25) for a berth in a 3-bed sleeper; TL84 (£37) for a berth in a 2-bed sleeper.

Using an InterRail pass

An InterRail pass is the railpass for European residents, giving unlimited train travel over almost the whole of Europe. It's the most flexible way to make a train journey from London or Paris to Istanbul. It's usually cheaper than normal tickets if you're under 26 years of age, but usually a few pounds more than normal tickets if you're over 26, depending on what point-to-point prices you manage to get for your dates of travel.

- **For a one-way trip to Istanbul**, a 5-days-in-10-days flexi InterRail pass gives a total of 5 days of unlimited second class train travel in all the countries you pass through within an overall period of 10 days, which is plenty to make the journey, even with a day or two stopover in Vienna, Budapest or Bucharest if you want. It costs £149 if you are aged under 26, £233 if you're aged 26–59, or £210 if you're over 60. The price for children aged 4–11 inclusive is £117.

- **For a return trip to Istanbul**, a 10-days-in-22-days pass, costing £224 if you are aged under 26, £336 if you're aged 26–59, £302 if you're over 60, and £168 for children aged 4–11 inclusive, gives a total of 10 days of unlimited second class train travel in all the countries you pass through within an overall period of 22 days. This is enough travelling time to make the outward and return journeys, even with a day or two stopover in Vienna, Budapest or Bucharest if you want, and (depending how much time you allocate to stopovers) you'd get up to 16 days in Turkey: you must complete both your outward and return journeys within the 22-day period covered by the pass. If you plan to be away for longer than 22 days, you'll need either a 1-month continuous InterRail pass, or you could buy one 5-days-in-10-days flexi pass for the outward trip and another 5-days-in-10-days flexi pass to cover your return trip, and spend however long you like in Turkey and the Middle East. The one limiting factor is that you can only buy InterRail passes a maximum of 2 months before their start date.

● **Add the price of a Eurostar ticket:** InterRail passes do not cover Eurostar, so you need to add in this cost. You have two options: you can buy a normal cheap Eurostar ticket, from £39 one-way, £69 return, no refunds, no changes to travel plans allowed; or you can buy a special passholder fare, £57 one-way, £100 return, refunds and change of travel plans allowed. The cheapest place to buy Eurostar tickets is **www.eurostar.com**.

● **Add 3 nights' sleeper or couchette supplement each way:** In addition to the cost of the pass, you'll need to pay a supplement for a couchette or sleeper for each of the three nights from London to Istanbul and Istanbul to London. For a couchette, budget for around £17 per person for the first night between Paris and Munich, then £10 for each of the next two nights between Budapest and Bucharest and Bucharest and Istanbul (but sleeper rather than a couchette is recommended east of Budapest). For a bed in a 3-berth sleeper, budget for £30 per person for the night between Paris and Munich, then £22 per person per night for each of the following two nights Budapest–Bucharest and Bucharest–Istanbul. For a bed in a 2-berth sleeper, budget for £45 per person for the night between Paris and

Munich, then £36 per person per night for each of the following two nights Budapest–Bucharest and Bucharest–Istanbul.

● **InterRail flexi passes and overnight trains:** When using an InterRail flexi pass, overnight sleeper trains leaving after 19:00 count as the following day, as long as the overall 10- or 22-day pass validity period has started. For example, if you plan to leave Paris at 22:43 on 1 January on the sleeper to Munich using a 5-days-in-10-days InterRail, you should ask for a pass which starts its 10-day validity period on 1 January, but as the sleeper train leaves Paris well after 19:00, you would write '2 January' in the first of the five 'free travel day' boxes printed on your pass. This free travel day would then cover both the Paris–Munich sleeper and the Munich–Budapest train next day. You don't need to use up a free travel day for the Eurostar, as Eurostar passholder fares don't require a pass day to be used, and you will probably end up buying a normal (non-passholder) Eurostar ticket anyway as these are usually cheaper. Similarly, travelling westbound, if you intend to leave Istanbul at 22:00 on 1 January on the *Bosfor*, you need a pass dated to start its 10-day validity period on 1 January, but the first date you'd write on it would be 2 January, as you're leaving on a sleeper train after 19:00.

How to buy tickets

Option 1: pre-booking. You cannot buy tickets all the way to Istanbul online; you need to buy tickets or passes by phone. I recommend you use the information given above to itemise, for each leg of the journey, the specific train you want to book, the date on which you want to travel, and the type of accommodation, before you pick up the phone. The best agencies to contact are:

European Rail Ltd (**www.europeanrail.com**). Call 020 7619 1083 (lines open 08:30–18:00 Monday–Friday, 09:00–13:00 Saturday). From overseas call +44 20 7619 1083; tickets can be sent outside the

UK if necessary. They charge a £35 booking fee, but their expertise in making complex bookings such as this can be worth the extra few pounds.

Deutsche Bahn's UK office on 08718 80 80 66 (lines open 09:00–20:00 Monday–Friday, 09:00–13:00 Saturday and Sunday). European Rail use the Deutsche Bahn reservation system too, so you'll be offered the same fares by either agency; but on the plus side the Deutsche Bahn UK office don't charge a booking fee, just a 2 per cent credit card fee. On the down side, you will need to talk them through exactly what train bookings you want. Tickets can be sent to UK or Irish addresses, or (for a fee) overseas addresses.

Option 2: buying tickets as you go. If you like, you can stay flexible and buy tickets as you go. However, I'd still recommend buying the Eurostar ticket in advance at **www.eurostar.com,** because prices rise steeply as departure date approaches, like air fares. I'd suggest pre-booking the Paris–Munich train too, using either **www.raileurope.co.uk** or **www.bahn.de** (check prices on both!) as there are cheap deals to be had if you pre-book. The Munich–Vienna–Budapest train doesn't require a reservation and there are always places available, but again you might find a fare of just €39 if you book in advance, whereas it could cost three times this if you leave it until the day of travel. From Budapest to Bucharest and from Bucharest to Istanbul, buying at the station can actually be cheaper than pre-booking from the UK, as (a) the price is the same whether you buy in advance or buy on the day, and (b) the station in Budapest can sell you a ticket for these journeys using cheaper local tariffs, whereas UK agencies can only sell tickets using the standard international tariff. There are almost always places in the sleeping-car available, even on the day of travel, although of course nothing is absolutely certain if you leave it till the day of departure, so buying as you go is probably a good option only if you have plenty of time and/or are planning to stop over en route anyway.

TURKISH VISAS

UK citizens no longer need a visa for Hungary, Romania or Bulgaria, but they need a tourist visa to visit Turkey. There is no need to get this in advance; it's easy to buy it at the Turkish frontier at Kapikule. Take some pounds sterling or euros with you for the visa – in 2010, the visa costs about £10 or €15, payable in pounds sterling or euros.

Kapikule is almost the only frontier post in Europe where you need to leave the train for passport formalities, rather than staying on board. On arrival at Kapikule at 01:25 eastbound, leave the train with everyone else (remember not to leave any valuables in your compartment) and look for the visa office on the station platform. Don't just follow the other passengers into the passport control office, as most of them will be Turks, Bulgarians or Romanians who don't need a visa! After getting your visa, go to the passport control office next door (where by this time the queues should be very short or gone) to get your passport stamped. The train doesn't leave Kapikule until 03:00, so don't worry, there's plenty of time for this to be done. You'll soon be back in bed!

TRAIN TRAVEL WITHIN TURKEY

Guidebooks often tell you that Turkey has a good bus network and that 'buses are faster than trains', but do you really want to spend 12 hours in a bus? In many cases, you can travel on a comfortable air-conditioned train instead, sleeping in a proper bed in your own room, with a restaurant for your meals and space to move around, passing through fantastic scenery unspoilt by roadside development.

Train travel in Turkey can be a wonderful experience, with the best trains now modern and air-conditioned. Sensible travellers will use a train for long distances (for example, Istanbul to Konya, Ankara, Kars or Pamukkale) then make a short bus trip where necessary to reach places off the rail network, for example Antalya or Goreme.

Much of the rail network was built by the Germans, and the joke goes that the Turks paid them by the mile, hence the twisting and curvaceous nature of Turkish railways! However, after major improvements the best air-conditioned Istanbul–Ankara trains now travel at up to 150km/h and take only 5 hours. The first section of a brand-new high-speed line from Istanbul to Ankara opened in March 2009, and journey time will be reduced to just 3 hours by 2013, beating both buses and flights. Overnight trains with sleeping-cars, some now air-conditioned, provide a comfortable, romantic and time-effective way to travel between major cities.

For a map of Turkish train routes, see **www.turkeytravelplanner.com/ Maps/tcdd_harita.html**. There are no trains to Antalya, Marmaris, Bodrum, Alanya, or to Goreme in Cappadocia, but to reach these places you can use a combination of train+bus.

The Turkish Railways website

You can check train times and fares at **www.tcdd.gov.tr**. Click 'English' top right, then click 'passenger transportation' and 'domestic trains', followed by 'TCDD information screen'. You can now enquire about any given route. However, the newer Turkish version of the TCDD site can sometimes be more useful and informative: in the menu at the top, '*Hizli Tren Saatleri*' means 'high-speed trains' (on the Ankara–Istanbul route), '*Anahat Tren Saatleri*' means 'domestic trains', '*Avrupa Trenleri*' means trains to Europe and '*Ortadoğu Yönlü Trenleri*' means 'trains to the Middle East'. It can help to know that *Pullman* means reclining seats, *yemekli* means 'restaurant car', *yatakli* means 'sleeping-car' and *kuşetli* means 'couchettes' (basic bunks). 'K' and 'V' are simply abbreviations for 'departure' and 'arrival'.

www.turkeytravelplanner.com/trans/Train/tcdd_website_rant.html can help you understand the Turkish parts.

How to buy tickets at the station

It's easy to buy tickets at the station when you get to Turkey. Most major stations have a computerised ticketing and reservation system, so can book any journey in Turkey. It's not usually difficult to get seats or berths on the day of travel or a day or two before, although occasionally sleepers can get full. Alternatively, you can buy tickets in advance either online or via a TCDD-authorised agency as shown below.

How to buy tickets online at the TCDD website

The Turkish Railways (TCDD) website **www.tcdd.gov.tr** has an online booking facility, now available in English. The system will book most long-distance trains within Turkey (but not international trains), including seats, couchettes and sleepers. You print out your reservation details and pick up the tickets at the station in Turkey. Online reservations for Turkish trains open 14 days before departure; you cannot book online further in advance than this.

How to buy tickets from outside Turkey, via an agency

If buying tickets online proves difficult, you can book your Turkish train tickets in advance by emailing (or calling) one of these authorised travel agencies in Istanbul:

> Tur-ISTA Tourism Travel Agency, Divan Yolu Caddesi No. 16/B, 34410 Sultanahmet, Istanbul, Turkey; telephone +90 (212) 527 7085 or 513 7119; fax +90 (212) 519 3792; email erdemir@tur-ista.com. I can personally recommend their service. Their office is near the Sultanahmet tram stop, a short way from the Blue Mosque.

> Viking Turizm, Mete Caddesi No. 24, Taksim, Istanbul, Turkey; telephone +90 (212) 334 2600; fax +90 (212) 334 2660; email info@vikingturizm.com.tr.

If you book with one of these agencies, you will need to pick up your tickets at their offices in Istanbul.

They can't book international trains from Turkey in their capacity as official TCDD agents, but they may be willing to buy tickets for international trains on your behalf as a private transaction, for a booking fee.

Haydarpaşa station

Trains for Asian destinations (i.e. including all Turkish destinations on the Asian side of the Bosphorus) leave from Haydarpaşa station, a ferry ride across the Bosphorus from Sirkeci station where the European trains arrive and depart. Ferries sail to Haydarpaşa station every 10–30 minutes from the Karaköy ferry terminal next to the Galata Bridge on the European side of Istanbul. The fare is TL1.50 (£0.70). The Haydarpaşa ferry terminal is right in front of the station. Haydarpaşa station was built in 1908, a gift from the German Kaiser to the Ottoman Sultan, and named after one of the Sultan's generals. It may be closed in 2013 or 2014, when a new rail tunnel under the Bosphorus is supposed to open, allowing both suburban and long-distance trains to run through from Asian Turkey to the European side of Istanbul.

What are Turkish trains like?

Trains in Turkey have several types of accommodation to choose from:

- Pullman seats. First class reclining seat in a carpeted open-plan saloon.

- First class ordinary seats, usually in 6-seat compartments.

- Second class seats, usually in 8-seat compartments.

- Sleeping-cars (*'yatakli wagon'* in Turkish). Private 1- and 2-bed rooms with washbasin.

- Couchettes (*'kuşet'* in Turkish). Shared 4-bunk compartments (6-berth on some routes).

The best Turkish trains now use modern air-conditioned TVS2000 coaches like these, which are excellent and as good as anything in western Europe. TVS2000 trains run from Istanbul to Ankara, Istanbul to Denizli/Pamukkale, Ankara to Izmir, Ankara to Adana, and Ankara to Erzurum and Kars. Restaurant cars serve very cheap full meals. A three-course meal with a half-bottle of wine costs only about TL11 (£5 or $8). Treat yourself! Brand-new 250km/h high-speed trains are also now operating on the Istanbul–Ankara route.

Sleeping-cars: The best overnight trains in Turkey use modern air-conditioned TVS2000 sleeping-cars and there's usually a TVS2000 restaurant car too.

Sleeper compartments have beds and a washbasin, soap and towels provided. There's even a fridge for your beer, and a shower at the end of the corridor. Compartments convert from a bedroom at night to a private sitting room with armchairs and small table for the daytime part of a journey. Trains with TVS2000 sleeping-cars include the *Ankara Express* from Istanbul to Ankara, the *Pamukkale Express* from Istanbul to Denizli, the *Meram Express* from Istanbul to Konya, the night trains from Ankara to Izmir, the *Curacova Express* from Ankara to Adana, and the *Erzurum Express* from Ankara to Erzurum and Kars. Travelling in these sleepers is like staying in a good hotel, a great way to travel that saves on hotel bills, too.

Couchettes: Couchettes are basic padded bunks, with four bunks per compartment (six bunks in a few trains). Couchettes convert to ordinary seating compartments for the daytime part of a journey. On some trains, couchettes are provided without bedding, but on other trains there are 'covered couchettes' (*örtülü kuşet*), with sheet, blanket and pillow supplied. The best overnight trains, such as those on the Istanbul–Ankara, Istanbul–Konya and Ankara–Izmir routes, now have modern air-conditioned TVS2000 couchette cars. Older trains may have an old type of car.

ISTANBUL TO ANKARA

The first section of the Istanbul–Ankara high-speed line opened in March 2009, and conventional trains from Istanbul to Eskişehir (with modern air-conditioned TVS2000 Pullman seats) now connect with brand-new 250km/h high-speed trains (YHT or *Yüksek Hizli Tren* in Turkish) for the remainder of the journey from Eskişehir to Ankara (see the services marked 'A' in the timetable below; one remaining conventional train with TVS2000 Pullman seats runs direct and is marked 'B'). The rest of the high-speed line is due to be completed by 2013, with direct 250km/h Istanbul–Ankara trains taking just 3 hours.

The best overnight train is the *Ankara Express* (marked 'sleeper' in the timetable below), a rolling hotel with modern air-conditioned TVS2000 sleeping-cars and a TVS2000 restaurant car for breakfast. Other night trains have seats and couchettes.

Trains leave from Haydarpaşa station in Istanbul, on the Asian side of the Bosphorus. Ankara station is in central Ankara, unlike the long-distance bus terminal (2–3 miles outside the city) or the airport (15–20 miles outside).

Istanbul → Ankara

Notes		A	A	B	A	A	cc	Sleeper	cc
Istanbul (Haydarpaşa)	depart	07:10	11:00	12:00	14:00	17:50	22:00	22:30	23:30
Eskişehir	arrive	11:00	14:54	I	17:56	21:42	I	I	I
Eskişehir	depart	11:15	15:10	I	18:10	21:52	I	I	I
Ankara	arrive	12:45	16:40	21:05	19:40	23:22	06:38	07:07	07:23

Ankara → Istanbul

Notes		A	B	A	A	A	cc	Sleeper	cc
Ankara	depart	07:00	08:00	11:10	15:00	18:00	22:00	22:30	23:30
Eskişehir	arrive	08:30	I	12:40	16:29	19:30	I	I	I
Eskişehir	depart	08:40	I	12:55	16:45	19:45	I	I	I
Istanbul (Haydarpaşa)	arrive	12:35	16:46	16:50	20:42	23:38	07:15	08:00	07:30

All trains run daily; check times at www.tcdd.gov.tr.

Note A: brand-new 250km/h high-speed train (*Yüksek Hizli Tren* or YHT) between Eskişehir and Ankara; connecting conventional train with TVS2000 Pullman seats between Istanbul and Eskişehir.

Note B: *Bogazici Express*: the single remaining conventional (non-high-speed) train running direct between Istanbul and Ankara, with TVS2000 reclining Pullman seats.

cc = overnight train with modern TVS2000 air-conditioned 4-berth couchettes and TVS2000 reclining Pullman seats.

sleeper = *Ankara Express.* Excellent modern TVS2000 sleeping-cars (1- and 2-bed rooms) and TVS2000 restaurant car.

Fares and how to buy tickets

Istanbul–Ankara					
by daytime high-speed train		by overnight train			
Economy class	Business class	in a couchette	in the sleeping-car		
		4-bunk	2-bed	1-bed	
TL40 (£17, $27)	TL50 (£21, $33)	TL35 (£15, $23)	TL60 (£25, $40)	TL85 (£35, $57)	

These fares are one-way per person.

Return tickets cost 20 per cent less than two one-way fares.

You can check train times and fares at **www.tcdd.gov.tr**, which now has some English pages. Also see **www.turkeytravelplanner.com**. Buy your ticket at the ticket office in Istanbul or use one of the travel agencies in Istanbul recommended on page 140.

ISTANBUL TO KONYA

Easily the best way to travel between Istanbul and the historic city of Konya is the daily overnight *Meram Express*, with sleeping-car and restaurant car: a wonderful way to travel. There's also the *Içanadolou Mavi Tren* (shown as '*Mavi*' below), also with an air-conditioned sleeping-car and restaurant. Westbound, the *Içanadolou Mavi Tren* can arrive in Konya from Adana running late, so the *Meram Express* is the better choice. TVS2000 cars are modern, soundproofed and smooth-riding.

As an alternative, you could take a daytime train from Istanbul to Ankara (see above) then the overnight *Cukurova Mavi* train from Ankara to Adana (see page 151).

Istanbul → Konya, Adana

		Daily *Meram*	Daily *Mavi*
Istanbul (Haydarpaşa)	depart	19:40	23:50
Konya	arrive	08:39	12:32
Karaman	arrive	–	13:56
Adana	arrive	–	18:40

Adana, Konya → Istanbul

		Daily *Meram*	Daily *Mavi*
Adana	depart	–	14:00
Karaman	depart	–	19:05
Konya	depart	17:05	20:44
Istanbul (Haydarpaşa)	arrive	06:35	08:58

Meram = *Meram Express*, with air-conditioned TVS2000 sleeping-car (1- and 2-bed rooms with washbasin), TVS2000 couchette car (4-bunk compartments), TVS2000 Pullman reclining seats, and TVS2000 restaurant car.

Mavi = *Içanadolou Mavi Tren*, with TVS2000 sleeping-car (1- and 2-bed rooms with washbasin), TVS2000 Pullman reclining seats and a TVS2000 restaurant car, but no couchettes.

Fares

	in a reclining Pullman seat	in a couchette 4-bunk	in the sleeping-car 2-bed	in the sleeping-car 1-bed
Istanbul to Konya	TL28 (£12 or $19)	TL38 (£16 or $25)	TL61 (£25 or $41)	TL78 (£32 or $52)
Istanbul to Adana	TL40 (£17 or $27)	–	TL73 (£30 or $49)	TL90 (£38 or $60)

All fares are one-way per person.

Return tickets cost 20 per cent less than the cost of two one-way fares.

You can check times and fares at **www.tcdd.gov.tr**.

ISTANBUL TO DENIZLI (PAMUKKALE)

Denizli is the place to head for if you want to visit the magnificent natural spa at Pamukkale. The *Pamukkale Express* is the overnight link between Istanbul and Denizli; however, because of major engineering work to rebuild the railway, this train was cancelled for most of 2008 and 2009, and in 2010 it is still not running. The service should resume in 2011; please check locally. The *Pamukkale Express* was re-equipped with ultra-modern, fully air-conditioned, soundproofed and smooth-riding TVS2000 cars in 2005: a sleeping-car with comfortable 1- and 2-bed rooms with washbasin, a couchette car with 4-bunk compartments, Pullman reclining seats, and an elegant restaurant car. Its scheduled departure time is 17:35 daily from Istanbul (Haydarpaşa), arriving at Denizli at 08:20 the next morning; and 17:00 daily from Denizli, arriving in Istanbul at 08:34.

The one-way fare per person is TL28 (£12 or $19) in a Pullman seat, TL38 (£16 or $25) in a couchette, TL61 (£25 or $41) in a 2-bed sleeper compartment, or TL78 (£33 or $52) in a 1-bed sleeper compartment. Return fares cost 20 per cent less than two one-way fares.

ISTANBUL TO ANTALYA, MARMARIS, BODRUM

There are direct buses from Istanbul to Antalya, Marmaris and the Mediterranean coast, but this is a nightmarishly long bus journey, especially if done overnight slumped in a cramped bus seat. A much better, more civilised way is to take the comfortable air-conditioned *Pamukkale Express* (when it is running – see preceding section) overnight from Istanbul to Denizli, which offers modern TVS2000 reclining seats, couchettes (4-bunk), sleeping-car (1- and 2-bed rooms) and a restaurant car for your dinner and breakfast. Then take a bus from Denizli for the last bit to Antalya, Marmaris, Bodrum or Fethiye. See above for train times and fares for the *Pamukkale Express*. Buses run every few hours from Denizli to Antalya, taking a few hours, and buses also run from Denizli to Marmaris, Fethiye and Bodrum.

ISTANBUL TO GORËME (CAPPADOCIA)

Cappadocia is an incredible land of strange rock formations and cave dwellings that should not be missed. Taking the sleeper train from Istanbul to Ankara or Konya, then a relatively short bus ride to Gorëme in Cappadocia is a great way to get there, avoiding a nightmare bus journey of 12 hours and more all the way from Istanbul. It lets you sleep in a comfortable berth on the train, with breakfast in the restaurant car, before taking a bus ride for the last bit. Alternatively, for a really short bus section, take the train to Kayseri just 70 km from Gorëme and get a bus from there.

Istanbul → Gorëme by train+bus

Option 1: Take a train from **Istanbul** (Haydarpaşa station) to **Ankara** as shown on pages 142–4. Take the metro from the station to Ankara's long-distance bus terminal, located a couple of miles out of the city centre. Buses run from **Ankara** to **Gorëme** or **Nevşehir** in Cappadocia every hour or two throughout the day, taking about 3–4 hours.

Option 2: Take the overnight *Meram Express* from **Istanbul** to **Konya** as shown on pages 144–5. Konya, home of the whirling dervishes, is well worth a stop in itself. Buses run several times a day from **Konya** to **Gorëme**, taking about 5 hours.

Option 3: Take a sleeper train from **Istanbul** to **Kayseri** as shown below, page 152, then a bus from **Kayseri** to **Gorëme**. At only 70 km, this is the shortest bus journey (maybe 1½ hours), though this route is longer overall.

ISTANBUL TO IZMIR, by ferry and train via the Sea of Marmara

An enjoyable year-round way from Istanbul to Izmir is across the Sea of Marmara to Bandirma by fast ferry, then on the connecting air-conditioned *6 Eylül Express* to Izmir. Much nicer than 9 hours stuck in a bus! The service runs daily.

Istanbul → Izmir

Travel from **Istanbul** to **Bandirma** by the IDO ferry company's fast SeaCat ferry, which leaves at 07:00 daily from the Yenikapi ferry terminal in Istanbul, arriving at Bandirma at 09:30. Then take the connecting train which leaves **Bandirma** at 09:50, arriving at **Balikesir** at 11:31 and **Izmir** Alsancak station at 15:18. This is the *6 Eylül Express*, which has modern air-conditioned TVS2000 reclining Pullman seats and restaurant car. It is possible that, due to the final stages of engineering work under way to upgrade this line, a bus may replace the train between Çiğli (30 minutes north of Izmir) and Izmir.

Izmir → Istanbul

The *6 Eylül Express* air-conditioned train leaves **Izmir** (Alsancak station) daily at 09:15 (though while engineering work on upgrading the line is in progress a bus may replace the train between Izmir and Çiğli), arriving at **Balikesir** at 13:17 and **Bandirma** at 14:56. The IDO SeaCat ferry leaves **Bandirma** at 15:30 (apart from Monday to Thursday between late September and mid April, when departure is much later, at 18:30), arriving at **Istanbul** Yenikapi ferry terminal at 18:00 (21:00 on the days with 18:30 departure from Bandirma).

Fares

Izmir to Bandirma in a Pullman seat is TL15 (£7 or $10) one-way. A combined ferry and train fare from Istanbul to Izmir is TL32 (about £13 or $22) one-way. You can check ferry times and fares at **www.ido.com.tr** (the system recognises the Istanbul terminal as 'Yenikapi'), and train times and fares at **www.tcdd.gov.tr**.

ISTANBUL TO IZMIR, by train all the way via Eskişehir

Istanbul → Izmir

You leave **Istanbul** Haydarpaşa station at 17:50 by express train with reclining Pullman seats and restaurant car, arriving in **Eskişehir** at 21:42. Depart **Eskişehir** at 22:19 on the *Izmir Mavi Tren* (with seats and sleeping-cars plus restaurant car) overnight to **Izmir** Alsancak station, arriving at 08:49. Both trains can be reserved in Istanbul at Haydarpaşa station.

Izmir → Istanbul

Take a train overnight from **Izmir** (Alsancak station) to **Eskişehir**: the 18:55 departure has seats and couchettes, arriving in Eskişehir at 06:10; or the 18:15 *Mavi Tren* has seats and sleeping-cars, arriving in Eskişehir at 05:04. The 08:40 from **Eskişehir** (first class only with restaurant car) arrives in **Istanbul** at 12:45.

Fares

Istanbul to Eskişehir costs TL20 (£9 or $13) in a Pullman seat. Add to this the fare from Eskişehir to Izmir, which costs TL21 (£9 or $13) in a reclining Pullman seat, TL54 (£24 or $36) in a shared 2-berth sleeper or TL108 (£48 or $72) in a private single-berth sleeper.

ISTANBUL TO IZMIR, by direct ferry

Deniz Lines (**www.denizline.com.tr**) used to run a cruise ferry from Istanbul to Izmir, but this service no longer operates.

ISTANBUL TO EDIRNE

Two trains a day link Istanbul's Sirkeci station with the historic city of Edirne in European Turkey.

The first is a daytime train, which has quite comfortable modernised coaches, with first and second class seats arranged in compartments. It departs Istanbul Sirkeci station daily at 15:20, arriving in Edirne at 21:17; from Edirne it leaves daily at 07:33, arriving in Istanbul at 13:04.

The second is in fact an international train: the combined *Bosfor*, with coaches from Istanbul to Bucharest, and *Balkan Express*, with coaches from Istanbul to Sofia and Belgrade. Local passengers are allowed to use this train, but can only travel in second class seats. It departs Istanbul Sirkeci station daily at 22:00, arriving at Edirne at 02:28. In the other direction it calls at Edirne at 03:20, arriving in Istanbul at 07:50; however it's not uncommon for this train to be running an hour or two late by the time it reaches Edirne.

ISTANBUL TO BURSA

There are direct fast ferries to Bursa from Istanbul's Yenikapi ferry terminal. Departures from Istanbul are at 07:30 (not Sunday), 17:30 (daily), 20:30 (Friday and Sunday only); journey time 2 hours. Departures from Bursa are at 07:30 (daily except Sunday), 18:00 (daily) and 20:30 (Friday and Sunday only). More services are run between June and September. See the IDO ferry company website **www.ido.com.tr** to check ferry times and fares (the system recognises the Istanbul terminal as 'Yenikapi'). You'll also find more frequent ferries between Istanbul (Yenikapi) and Yalova, from where you can reach Bursa by minibus taxi.

ANKARA TO IZMIR

Modern trains link Ankara with Izmir overnight, with comfortable air-conditioned sleeping-cars. You have a choice of two: the *Izmir Mavi Tren*, with modern air-conditioned TVS2000 sleeping-cars (1- and 2-bed compartments), reclining Pullman seats and restaurant car, leaves Ankara daily at 19:50, arriving at Izmir Alsancak station at 09:00 the next morning; and the *Karesi Express*, which has first and second class seats, couchettes (4-bunk) and restaurant car, leaves Ankara daily at 17:50, arriving at Izmir Alsancak station at 08:02 the next morning. Eastbound, the *Izmir Mavi Tren* leaves Izmir Alsancak station at

19.30, arriving in Ankara at 09:29; and the *Karesi Express* departs Izmir at 17:30, arriving in Ankara at 08:35.

Fares

Ankara to Izmir one-way costs TL27 (£11 or $18) in a Pullman reclining seat, TL35 (£15 or $23) in an air-conditioned 4-bunk couchette, TL60 (£25 or $40) for a berth in a 2-bed sleeper, or TL80 (£33 or $53) for a 1-bed sleeper. Return tickets cost 20 per cent less than two one-way fares.

ANKARA TO ADANA

The daily *Cukurova Mavi Tren* has a modern air-conditioned sleeping-car with 1- and 2-bed compartments, reclining Pullman seats and a restaurant car. These are all ultra-modern, fully air-conditioned, soundproofed and smooth-riding TVS2000 cars. The train leaves Ankara at 20:05, arriving in Adana at 07:25 the next morning. From Adana it departs daily at 19:30, arriving in Ankara at 07:35.

Fares

Ankara to Adana one-way costs TL22 (£9 or $15) in a Pullman reclining seat, TL55 (£22 or $37) for a berth in a 2-bed sleeper compartment, or TL72 (£30 or $48) for a 1-bed sleeper compartment. Return tickets cost 20 per cent less than the cost of two one-way fares.

ISTANBUL AND ANKARA TO EASTERN TURKEY

It's a long way to eastern Turkey – but the trains have sleeping-cars, couchettes, and a restaurant car for a comfortable and wonderfully scenic two-night journey (or in the case of the Istanbul–Kars *Doğu Express*, two days, one night), making the train far more comfortable, civilised and enjoyable than a long-distance bus. Most trains now use modern air-conditioned TVS2000 sleeping-cars and reclining seat cars.

Istanbul ➜ Eastern Turkey

		Doğu Express Daily	Güney Express Tue, Thur Fri, Sun	Van Gölü Express Mon, Sat	Trans-Asia Express Wed
Istanbul (Haydarpaşa)	depart	07:05 day 1	18:25 day 1	18:25 day 1	23:55 day 1
Ankara	depart	16:40 day1	04:03 day 2	04:03 day 2	10:25 day 2
Kayseri	arr/dep	23:59 day 1	11:20 day 2	11:20 day 2	17:33 day 2
Sivas	arr/dep	03:51 day 2	15:20 day 2	15:20 day 2	21:42 day 2
Erzurum	arr/dep	14:29 day 2	I	I	I
Kars	arrive	19:32 day 2	I	I	I
Diyarbakir	arr/dep	–	02:55 day 3	I	I
Kurtalan	arrive	–	06:30 day 3	I	I
Elazig	arr/dep	–	–	23:20 day 2	xx:xx day 3
Tatvan	arrive	–	–	–	11:32 day 3

Eastern Turkey ➜ Istanbul

		Trans-Asia Express Sat	Doğu Express Daily	Güney Express Mon, Wed, Fri, Sun	Van Gölü Express Tue, Thur
Tatvan	depart	05:05 day 1	–	–	–
Elazig	arr/dep	xx:xx day 1	–	–	11:30 day 1
Kurtalan	depart	I	–	04:55 day 1	I
Diyarbakir	arr/dep	I	–	08:42 day 1	I
Kars	depart	I	18:00 day 1	I	I
Erzurum	arr/dep	I	23:10 day 1	I	I
Sivas	arr/dep	22:02 day 1	10:13 day 2	19:49 day 1	19:49 day 1
Kayseri	arr/dep	01:47 day 2	14:00 day 2	23:45 day 1	23:45 day 1
Ankara	arrive	09:30 day 2	21:44 day 2	07:50 day 2	07:50 day 2
Istanbul (Haydarpaşa)	arrive	18:34 day 2	07:30 day 3	17:15 day 2	17:15 day 2

xx:xx = exact time not available

Doğu Express: Runs daily, recommended train. Sleeping-car (1- and 2-bed rooms, now a modern air-conditioned TVS2000 type), couchettes (4-berth TVS2000), TVS2000 Pullman seats and restaurant car.

Güney Express: Runs from Istanbul to Diyarbakir and Kurtalan on Tuesday, Thursday, Friday, Sunday, leaving Ankara the following morning. Westbound, runs from Kurtalan and Diyarbakir on Monday, Wednesday, Friday, Sunday. Sleeping-car (1- and 2-bed rooms), Pullman reclining seats, ordinary seats, restaurant car.

Van Gölü Express: Runs from Istanbul to Elazig on Monday and Saturday (departing Ankara the following morning). Westbound, runs from Elazig on Tuesday and Thursday. Sleeping-car (1- and 2-bed rooms), reclining Pullman seats, ordinary seats.

Trans-Asia Express: Carries international passengers only. Runs from Istanbul on Wednesday, departing Ankara on Thursday. Westbound, runs from Tatvan on Saturday. Air-conditioned TVS2000 4-berth couchette cars and restaurant car Istanbul–Ankara–Tatvan–Tehran. See the Iran chapter, pages 102–5.

Fares

Sample fares are given in the table below; fares for other journeys will be broadly similar. Return tickets cost 20 per cent less than two one-way fares. You can check all times and fares at **www.tcdd.gov.tr**.

One-way	in a reclining	in a couchette	in the sleeping-car	
per person	Pullman seat	4-bunk	2-bed	1-bed
Istanbul to Kars (*Doğu Express*)	TL45 (£19 or $30)	TL55 (£23 or $37)	TL75 (£31 or $50)	TL87 (£36 or $58)
Istanbul to Kayseri (*Güney Express*)	TL25 (£10 or $17)	–	TL50 (£21 or $33)	TL62 (£26 or $41)
Istanbul to Elazig (*Van Gölü Express*)	TL41 (£17 or $27)	–	TL66 (£28 or $44)	TL78 (£33 or $52)
Ankara to Kars (*Doğu Express*)	TL39 (£16 or $26)	TL49 (£20 or $33)	TL72 (£30 or $48)	TL89 (£37 or $59)

IZMIR TO EPHESUS AND PAMUKKALE

The station for ancient Ephesus is Selçuk, 78 km by train from Izmir. The ruins at Ephesus are within walking distance of the modern town of Selçuk. Denizli is the station for the magnificent natural springs at Pamukkale. However, major rebuilding work has been in progress for some years on the line to Denizli, and trains are still not operating beyond Nazilli. All train times and fares can be checked at **www.tcdd.gov.tr**.

Izmir ➜ *Selçuk (Ephesus) and Denizli*

		Daily	Daily	Daily	Daily	Daily	Daily
Izmir (Basmane station)	depart	08:10	10:25	14:25	15:30	17:40	19:10
Selçuk for Ephesus	arr/dep	09:29	11:35	15:42	17:00	18:53	20:39
Aydin	arr/dep	10:23	12:27	16:35	18:00	19:46	–
Nazilli	arrive	–	13:12	17:20	18:51	20:30	–
Denizli for Pamukkale	arrive	–	–	–	–	–	–

Denizli and Selçuk (Ephesus) ➜ *Izmir*

		Daily	Daily	Daily	Daily	Daily	Daily
Denizli for Pamukkale	depart	–	–	–	–	–	–
Nazilli	arr/dep	–	05:45	07:00	–	13:25	17:35
Aydin	arr/dep	–	06:31	07:53	10:40	14:13	18:23
Selçuk for Ephesus	arr/dep	06:49	07:27	08:53	11:36	15:10	19:20
Izmir (Basmane)	arrive	08:17	08:38	10:20	12:45	16:25	20:31

All these services have first and second class seats, and are now operated by comfortable modern air-conditioned diesel trains.

The railway to Denizli is temporarily closed due to major rebuilding work, but it may reopen in 2011. In the meantime, change in Nazilli for local buses to Denizli and Pamukkale.

Change in Aydin for buses to Bodrum, Marmaris, Datca.

MOVING ON FROM TURKEY

Istanbul ➜ *Syria, Jordan, Egypt*

Take the daily air-conditioned sleeper train through great scenery from **Istanbul** Haydarpaşa station to **Adana** (see page 117) then a bus to

Aleppo in Syria. Then catch a 160km/h air-conditioned train from **Aleppo** to **Damascus**. From **Damascus** you can catch a bus to **Amman** in Jordan, with onward buses to **Petra** and **Aqaba**, from where a ferry will take you to **Nuweiba** in Egypt. See the Syria, Jordan and Egypt chapters, pages 116, 112, 161, for information about each stage of this great journey.

Istanbul and Ankara ➜ Tehran (Iran)

A weekly express train, the *Trans-Asia Express*, with modern air-conditioned sleeping-car and restaurant car, runs from Istanbul and Ankara to Tabriz and Tehran in Iran. See the Iran chapter, pages 102–5, for full details.

Istanbul and Ankara ➜ Tbilisi (Georgia)

Take a train from **Istanbul** or **Ankara** to **Erzurum** or **Kars** (see page 152), then a bus or *dolmus* (local minibus taxi) to the Georgian border at **Sarp**, followed by another *dolmus* for the 16 km from **Sarp** to **Batumi**, just the other side of the frontier. There is a comfortable daily overnight train from **Batumi** to **Tbilisi**, with Russian-style 2-berth and 4-berth sleepers, leaving around 22:30 and arriving in Tbilisi at 06:45.

Istanbul ➜ Yerevan (Armenia)

The border with Armenia is currently closed, and there is no train service between Turkey and Armenia. However, it's possible to travel from Turkey to Tbilisi in Georgia (see above), then travel from Tbilisi to Yerevan in Armenia by overnight train. The Tbilisi–Yerevan train runs every second day, departing Tbilisi at 16:40 on even-numbered dates (2nd, 4th, 6th etc. of each month) and arriving at Yerevan at 07:35 next day. Returning, it leaves Yerevan at 19:00 on odd-numbered dates, arriving at Tbilisi at 09:15 next morning. It has 2- and 4-berth sleepers.

PART
4

AFRICA

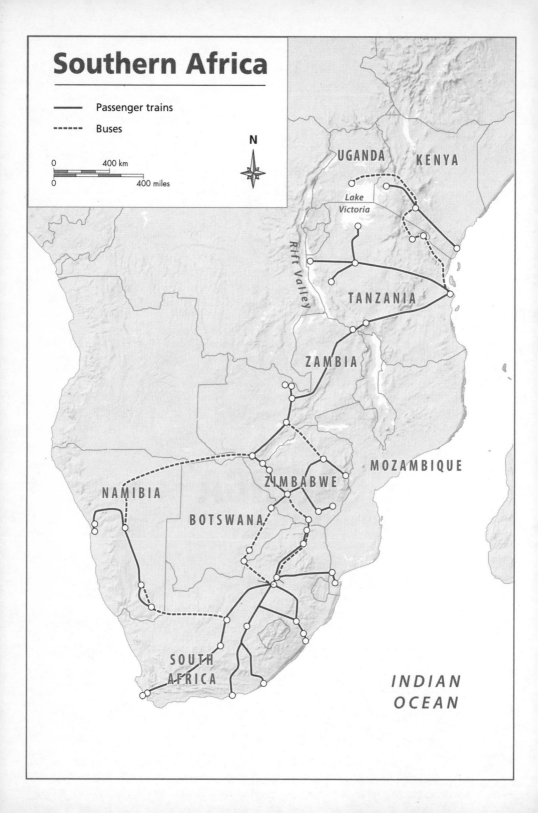

Southern Africa

Passenger trains

Buses

0   400 km

0   400 miles

N

UGANDA   KENYA

Lake
Victoria

Rift Valley

TANZANIA

ZAMBIA

MOZAMBIQUE

ZIMBABWE

NAMIBIA

BOTSWANA

SOUTH
AFRICA

INDIAN
OCEAN

BOTSWANA

Sadly, you won't now find many trains in Botswana. The railway through Botswana was once the main line between South Africa and Zimbabwe, and until recently there was a good air-conditioned sleeper train between Lobatse in the south, Botswana's capital Gaborone and Francistown in the north, even though it no longer crossed the border at either end. However, this train was withdrawn in 2009 and the only passenger train is now a thrice-weekly Zimbabwean train from Francistown in the north across the border to Bulawayo.

Train operator:	Botswana Railway (BR), no official website
Time:	GMT+2
Currency:	£1 = approx. 10.4 Botswanan pula, $1 = approx. 6.7 pula
Tourist information:	**www.gov.bw**
Visas:	UK, US, Canadian, Australian, NZ citizens and citizens of most EU countries do not need a visa to visit Botswana.

EUROPE TO BOTSWANA, without flying
You can travel from Europe to Cape Town in South Africa by passenger-carrying freighter or the occasional cruise. You can then take a train from Cape Town to Johannesburg and a bus to Gaborone in Botswana, see below.

SOUTH AFRICA TO BOTSWANA, by train and bus
There are no trains between Botswana and South Africa, as the daily train to

Mafeking and weekly train to Johannesburg were withdrawn in 1999. However, you can still take a comfortable train from Cape Town to Johannesburg (see the South Africa chapter, page 220), from where there is a bus to Gaborone. The bus leaves Johannesburg daily at 14:30 and arrives in Gaborone at 21:10. In the other direction, the bus leaves Gaborone daily at 06:30, arriving in Johannesburg at 13:00. See **www.intercape.co.za** for fares, times and online booking.

ZIMBABWE TO BOTSWANA, by train

In 1999, the weekly Johannesburg–Gaborone–Bulawayo train was withdrawn and the daily Mafeking–Gaborone–Bulawayo 'blue train' was cut back to run purely within Botswana: Francistown–Gaborone–Lobatse. However, after an absence of more than six years, an international train service between Zimbabwe and Botswana, using modern Zimbabwean coaches, restarted in June 2006, linking Francistown and Bulawayo, three times a week. It leaves Bulawayo at 09:30, Monday, Wednesday and Friday, arriving at Francistown at 15:00. From Francistown it runs on Tuesday, Thursday and Saturday, departing at 09:00 and arriving at Bulawayo at 15:00. The train has standard class coaches with reclining seats. The fare is 25 pula one-way (£3 or $5). For the situation with train connections to Gaborone and Lobatse (near the South African border), see below.

TRAIN TRAVEL WITHIN BOTSWANA
Francistown → *Gaborone* → *Lobatse*

A shock announcement in early 2009 was that Botswana Railways intended to stop all passenger service indefinitely because of mounting losses. The day train had already stopped running in 2006, and the last overnight train between Francistown, Gaborone and Lobatse ran on 1 April 2009. There are now no passenger trains at all on this route.

EGYPT

Egypt is one of the most fabulous countries to visit in the world, and Cairo one of the most fascinating cities. There's no need to book a tour; it's easy to travel round Egypt independently, by train. Egyptian Railways are by far the most comfortable way to travel between Cairo (for the pyramids at Giza), Luxor (for the Valley of the Kings), Aswan, Alexandria, Port Said and Suez. The views from the train can be wonderful, especially on the Cairo–Luxor–Aswan and Cairo–Alexandria routes. You may also get to meet Egyptians on board the trains, a very hospitable people.

Train operator:	Egyptian National Railways, **www.egyptrail.gov.eg**
	Sleeper trains Cairo–Luxor–Aswan: **www.sleepingtrains.com**
Time:	GMT+2 (GMT+3 from last Friday in April to last Thursday in September)
Currency:	£1 = approx. 8.1 Egyptian pounds (LE), $1 = approx. LE5.6
Tourist information:	**www.touregypt.net**
Visas:	UK, EU, US, Canadian, Australian and NZ citizens need a visa to visit Egypt. You can buy this in pounds sterling or US dollars on arrival for stays of up to one month. For more information contact the Egyptian Consulate-General, 2 Lowndes Street, London SW1X 9ET, telephone 020 7235 9719.

UK TO EGYPT, without flying

Adriatica Line's *Espresso Egitto* used to sail weekly from Venice and Piraeus to Alexandria. Michael Palin travelled on it in 1989 and I used it in 1990 – Michael gets everywhere a year or two before I do, and he doesn't have to pay for his own ticket. Sadly, the terrorist problems in Egypt ended this service.

Until 2001, Salamis Lines sailed weekly from Greece to Egypt via Cyprus, but their services have been suspended for some years now because of the problems in Israel, the ship's ultimate destination. However, a new ferry service started in May 2010, linking Venice with Alexandria (for the train to Cairo), and once more you can easily visit Egypt from the UK without flying. London to Cairo takes five nights outward, four nights on the return, including a day in Venice. It remains to be seen if the ferry will survive, but details are shown below.

It is also possible to reach Egypt travelling overland via the Middle East, as outlined on page 164: a route for the adventurous with time to spare.

LONDON TO ALEXANDRIA, by train and ferry, via Venice

A new weekly ferry service started on 20 May 2010 linking Venice in Italy with Alexandria in Egypt, operated by Visemar Lines, **www.visemarline.com**. It sails from Venice on Thursday, taking four nights to reach Alexandria, calling at Tartus in Syria on the way. From Alexandria it sails on Monday direct to Venice, taking three nights. A lunchtime Eurostar from London to Paris will connect with the direct overnight sleeper train from Paris to Venice, as shown in the suggested timetable below; or you could take an earlier Eurostar and stop overnight in Milan or Switzerland. You might also like to stop off for longer in Venice.

London → Egypt

Wednesday: Travel from **London** to **Paris** by Eurostar, leaving St Pancras at 14:02, arriving at Paris Gare du Nord at 17:23. Cross Paris by metro to the Gare de Bercy. Take the overnight sleeper train from **Paris** to **Venice**, departing from the Gare de Bercy at 20:33 and arriving at Venice Santa Lucia at 09:37 on Thursday morning.

Thursday: Embark on the Visemar Lines ferry at **Venice** ferry terminal. There is a 2-hour check-in, and the ferry sails at 16:00. Thursday, Friday and Saturday nights are spent at sea, and it arrives at **Tartus** at 12:00 on Sunday, leaving 6 hours later at 18:00.

Monday: The ferry arrives at **Alexandria** at 14:00.

Egypt ➜ *London*

Monday: Sail from **Alexandria** on the Visemar Lines ferry, departing at 20:00. Remember there is a 2-hour check-in. Monday, Tuesday and Wednesday nights are spent at sea.

Thursday: The ferry arrives at **Venice** ferry terminal at 08:00. Spend the day in Venice, then take the overnight sleeper to **Paris**, departing Venice Santa Lucia at 19:57 and arriving at Paris Gare de Bercy at 08:19 on Friday.

Friday: Take the Eurostar from **Paris** Gare du Nord to **London**. There is a departure at 11:13, arriving at St Pancras at 12:29; remember to allow for the 30-minute check-in.

How much does it cost?

London to Egypt by train+ferry costs around £420 return in total for both train and ferry, depending on what sleeping accommodation you choose on the train and the ferry and on what price you manage to find for the Eurostar and the Paris–Venice sleeper trains. For the ferry alone, fares from Venice to Alexandria start at €290 (around £263) return, including a bed in a shared 4-berth cabin, or €202 (£183) one-way. Two passengers sharing a private 2-berth en suite cabin would pay €416 (£378) return per person. You'll find more information about travelling from London to Venice on **www.seat61.com/Italy.htm** or in the Italy section of my first book, *The Man in Seat 61: A guide to taking the train from the UK through Europe.*

How to buy tickets

Start by booking the ferry. You can book the ferry online at **www.visemarline.com**. To book it by phone in the UK, call Visemar's UK agents, Southern Ferries, on 0844 815 7785. Then book train travel to Venice, by phone with Rail Europe on 0844 848 5848, or online at **www.raileurope.co.uk**. If you book online, split the journey into two bookings, London–Paris and Paris–Venice, otherwise the best fares for each leg will not show up.

LONDON TO CAIRO, via Turkey, Syria and Jordan

An alternative, more adventurous option is to travel overland by train via Istanbul, Syria and Jordan. See the Turkey chapter, pages 127–38, for train travel between London and Istanbul. Then see the Syria and Jordan chapters, pages 116 and 112, for details of the train and bus journey from Istanbul to Damascus and on to Amman. From Amman, a long-distance bus leaves on Saturday, Sunday, Tuesday and Thursday at 14:00, taking 20 hours to reach Cairo, crossing into Israel for part of the journey. It is run by Jordan Express Tourist Transportation (JETT), **www.jett.com.jo**, telephone +962 6 5664146. A better option, and one which avoids Israel, is to take a bus or taxi from Amman or Petra to Aqaba for the ferry to Nuweiba in Egypt, from where buses run to Cairo. See the Jordan chapter, page 114, for details.

TRAIN TRAVEL WITHIN EGYPT

How to check Egyptian train times

Train times for key routes are shown below. Egyptian National Railways now has a website, **www.egyptrail.gov.eg**, and you can use this to check timetables. There is limited train information on the Egyptian national tourist office website **www.touregypt.net**.

How to buy tickets

You cannot book Egyptian trains online, so you'll have to buy tickets either at the station, or through a local travel agency by email, or (if you want the Cairo–Luxor sleeper trains) direct with Abela Egypt by phone or email. There is in fact now an online reservation facility on the Egyptian Railways website (**www.egyptrail.gov.eg**, click 'English' then 'Reservation services'), but as this doesn't accept non-Egyptian credit cards (I've tried!) it isn't any use for non-Egyptians.

Buying tickets at the station: It's easy to buy tickets at the station ticket office when you get to Egypt, although a degree of patience is called for. (The exception is buying tickets for Cairo–Luxor/Aswan where official restrictions apply, see pages 166–7.) Cairo main station has several booking windows, one for each class and group of destinations, so check that you are joining the right queue. You can pay for train tickets in Egyptian pounds, except when booking the deluxe Abela Egypt sleeper, which must be paid for in foreign currency (US dollars, euros or pounds sterling) at the Abela Egypt sleeper office (see below). Except during busy periods, it's normally easy to get first class tickets on the day of travel or the day before. The deluxe overnight sleeper train from Cairo to Luxor and Aswan often has places available if you book a day or two in advance, but at peak tourist times such as Easter it can get fully booked by tour groups, so pre-booking from outside Egypt is recommended if you cannot afford to take a chance.

Buying tickets through a local agency: If you want to book Egyptian train tickets in advance before you leave home, try arranging tickets by email through an Egyptian travel agency. Reputable agencies include Osoris (**www.osoris.com**), Egyptian Travel Service (**www.egyptiants.net**), Safari Egypt (**www.safariegypt. com**) and (in Luxor) Sunrise Tours (**www.sunrisetours-eg.com**). Osoris charges fares about £7 ($10) higher than the normal ticket price, plus a £4 ($5) booking fee if you collect the tickets from their office in Cairo, a £17 ($25) booking fee if you want them delivered to your hotel, £17 ($25) for delivery to the airport to meet your flight, or £14 ($20) to meet you with the tickets at Cairo railway station. They also make a 6 per cent credit-card charge. To book, email them at egypt@osoris.com, call +20 2 302 8561 or fax +20 2 346 4146. Osoris has been recommended by several travellers. (After two bad comments about Egyptlegend (**www.egyptlegend.com/trainreservation.htm**) I no longer suggest them.)

Buying tickets for the Cairo–Luxor–Aswan sleeper train: The best way to book the deluxe sleeper train between Cairo, Luxor and Aswan is direct with the train operator, Abela Egypt, by phone, fax or email. Times and fares are given on Abela Egypt's website, **www.sleepingtrains.com**. You can in theory email your booking request to reservation@sleepingtrains.com, but travellers report that they don't usually get a reply. Instead, fax your request to +202 2574 90 74 (according to reports, the reservation office responds to faxes quickly) or phone the reservation office on +202 2574 94 74 or +202 2574 92 74. They will give you a booking reference and you can pick up the tickets and pay for them (in sterling, US dollars or euros) at the Abela Egypt sleeper reservation office at Cairo station. You must collect them at least 24 hours before departure. If you cannot pick up tickets at least 24 hours in advance, the alternative is to book through a travel agency as recommended above, paying slightly higher fares plus a booking fee.

Learn Arabic numbers

A top tip for train travel in Egypt is to learn how numbers are written in Arabic script. The indicator boards at main stations use Arabic characters for train numbers, departure times and platform numbers, not western-style numerals. If you know what the numbers look like in Arabic, you can recognise them, making it easy to find your train from the departure time, even if you can't read the destination. Similarly, your ticket will show the train number, date of travel, coach number and seat or berth number for your journey in Arabic characters, not western ones. In Arabic, numbers are written left to right, exactly like western numbers, even though Arabic words are written right to left.

0	1	2	3	4	5	6	7	8	9
٠	١	٢	٣	٤	٥	٦	٧	٨	٩

Tourist train-travel restrictions between Cairo, Luxor and Aswan

Since the terrorist attacks in Egypt some years ago, the Egyptian government has put restrictions on which trains foreigners may take between Cairo and Luxor/Aswan, allegedly so that the government can assure tourists' safety. There are no restrictions on other routes, such as Cairo to Alexandria, where you can take any train you like. Details are almost impossible to confirm, but it's reported that as from 1 March 2009 the *only* trains which tourists are officially allowed to use between Cairo and either Luxor or Aswan are the overnight Abela Egypt deluxe sleeper trains, in either the sleeping-cars or the seats cars. You can take a wider selection of trains if you're only travelling between Aswan and Luxor.

These restrictions mean that the ticket offices at Cairo, Luxor and Aswan will not sell you a ticket for any train except the few trains which tourists are allowed to take. Naturally, you may well wish to get around this discrimination, whether you're wanting to travel on a daytime air-conditioned express train along the scenic Nile Valley just for the experience, or to use an ordinary train because the deluxe sleepers are fully booked, or simply to save a few pounds because you're on a very tight budget. One way around the restrictions is to ask your hotel to send someone to buy a ticket for your chosen (restricted) train for a small fee. They may or may not be prepared to do this. The other (and easier) option is simply to board whatever train you like and buy tickets on board, which you can do on payment of a small surcharge (a mere pound or two!). There are no ticket barriers at Cairo, Luxor or Aswan that prevent you from doing this. A seat61 correspondent reported in January 2010: 'At both Aswan and Luxor, but not the smaller stations, there was an airport-style security barrier, where they X-ray selected passengers' baggage. However, there was no ticket check at the barrier. Everyone including the tourist office, police and railway staff said we could go on the ordinary [restricted] trains if we paid the small surcharge for buying a ticket on board, the restriction was only on buying the tickets in advance.'

CAIRO TO ALEXANDRIA

The train service between Alexandria and Cairo is excellent. There are broadly two sorts of train: modern air-conditioned express trains with comfortable first and second class, not dissimilar to European trains, and ordinary trains with very basic non-air-conditioned second and third class (plus air-conditioned second class on some trains). A first class one-way ticket for an air-conditioned express from Cairo to Alexandria costs about LE50, less than £6 or $9!

Cairo → *Alexandria*

		Ord+	Exp	Exp	Turbo	Exp	Ord+	Turbo	Exp	Exp	Ord	Turbo	Exp	Exp	Turbo	Exp
Cairo	depart	05:00	06:00	07:00	08:00	08:15	08:30	09:00	10:00	11:15	10:30	12:00	12:15	13:00	14:00	14:15
Alexandria	arrive	09:55	09:15	09:25	10:25	11:05	11:15	11:25	12:30	14:10	14:40	14:30	15:10	15:30	16:25	17:40

		Ord	Exp	Exp	Ord+	Exp	Exp	Exp	Ord	Turbo	Ord	Turbo	Exp	Ord+	Exp	Exp	Exp
Cairo	depart	12:45	15:00	15:15	15:25	16:00	16:15	17:15	17:15	18:00	18:25	19:00	20:15	20:30	21:00	22:15	23:00
Alexandria	arrive	16:15	17:25	18:10	18:36	18:25	19:25	20:15	21:00	20:30	21:40	21:20	23:10	00:20	23:25	01:10	01:30

Alexandria → *Cairo*

		Ord+	Exp	Turbo	Ord+	Turbo	Exp	Exp	Ord+	Exp	Ord	Exp	Exp	Ord+	Ord	Turbo
Alexandria	depart	05:30	06:15	07:00	07:15	08:00	08:15	09:00	09:30	11:15	11:40	12:00	12:15	12:30	13:30	14:00
Cairo	arrive	09:10	09:35	09:10	10:20	10:25	11:10	11:25	13:25	14:10	14:55	14:30	15:25	16:05	17:40	16:25

		Exp	Exp	Ord	Exp	Exp	Exp	Ord	Exp	Exp	Turbo	Ord+	Exp	Ord	Exp	Ord+	Exp
Alexandria	depart	15:00	15:15	15:45	16:00	17:00	17:15	17:30	18:00	18:15	19:00	19:15	20:00	20:15	21:00	21:45	22:15
Cairo	arrive	17:25	18:10	19:00	18:25	19:30	20:10	20:20	20:30	21:10	21:25	22:50	22:25	23:10	23:25	00:55	00:45

Turbo = extra-fast train, until recently operated by a French gas-turbine 'Turbotrain', but as of December 2007 operated by normal air-conditioned express carriages as the fuel-thirsty Turbotrains are reportedly too expensive to continue to maintain. Air-conditioned first and second class with refreshments. Recommended.

Exp = air-conditioned express, comfortable first and second class with refreshments. Recommended.

Ord = ordinary train, not normally used by tourists. Basic second and third class.

Ord+ = ordinary train with air-conditioned second class as well as basic second and third.

You can check times at **www.egyptrail.gov.eg**.

Cairo–Alexandria is 208 km (129 miles)

Fares

Cairo to Alexandria one-way by Turbotrain costs LE50 (£6 or $9) first class, LE29 (£4 or $6) second class; by air-conditioned express it costs LE40 (£5 or $7) first class, LE19 (£3 or $5) second class. The one-way fare in air-conditioned second class on ordinary trains (where it is available – those marked 'Ord+' in the timetable opposite) is LE16 (£2 or $3); a basic non-air-conditioned second class ticket, which allegedly is not offered to foreigners, costs LE7 (less than £1 or $2). If you have an ISIC student card this gives you a 33 per cent reduction in the fare. Children aged 0–3 travel free, children aged 4–9 travel at half fare, children of 10 and over pay full fare.

CAIRO TO LUXOR AND ASWAN

You can travel between Cairo, Luxor and Aswan on four different types of train (though see the section on pages 166–7 about official travel restrictions). Journey time by express or sleeper train is around 9–10 hours Cairo–Luxor, 12–14 hours Cairo–Aswan. Your options are:

- Overnight deluxe sleeper train (shown as 'sleeper' in the timetable on page 171, recommended). This train, now run by a private company called Abela Egypt, has modern air-conditioned sleeping-cars with 1- and 2-berth rooms, and a bar-lounge car. The fare includes a basic airline-style tray-meal in the evening and breakfast. Room service can serve drinks in your compartment at extra cost. Passengers travelling alone who don't want to pay the single-berth fare can book a berth in a 2-berth compartment and share with another passenger of the same sex. For more information, see **www.sleepingtrains.com**. This is probably the most comfortable and relaxing way to make the journey, as well as saving you time and the cost of a hotel bed. (Note that due to engineering work, these trains are leaving from Giza station, not Cairo.)

- Overnight air-conditioned express train (with seats only). These trains have first and second class seats and some have one coach with

Nefertiti class seats (six to a compartment). If you don't mind sleeping in a seat, which I find not a very nice or comfortable experience, these overnight trains are a much cheaper option than the deluxe sleeper, and you are still not using up a day in travel. Take a fleece or jumper as the air-conditioning can be quite powerful. There are departures pretty much hourly from Cairo from 19:00 to midnight.

- Daytime air-conditioned express trains (shown as 'Exp' in the timetable opposite, recommended). These have comfortable first and second class seats. The journey takes most of the day, but it's a very pleasant ride all along the Nile Valley, so just relax and enjoy the scenery. The trains run along the Nile for much of the journey, past palm trees, feluccas, camels, and fellahin working in the fields. You will see how the Nile makes a small strip of land green either side of the river before the desert resumes.

- Daytime ordinary slow trains, not normally offered to tourists. The non-air-conditioned second and third class are fairly basic and only recommended for the more adventurous visitors. Government restrictions prevent tourists from being sold a ticket for these trains, although you could get on without a ticket and pay the conductor on board. On this route most of these trains have air-conditioned second class as well as non-air-conditioned.

In the timetable below, recommended trains are in **bold type**.

Cairo → *Luxor and Aswan*

Train type		Exp*	Exp	**Exp**	Ord+	Ord+	**Exp**	Ord+	**Exp**	Ord+	Ord+	Exp	slee-per	Exp	slee-per	Exp	Exp	Exp*	Exp
Train number		1902	934	**980**	80	158	**982**	160	**986**	164	1434	988	**84**	88	**86**	886	976	2000	2002
Alexandria	dep	–	22:15	–	–	07:15	–	–	–	11:40	–	–	–	17:00	–	–	–	–	–
Cairo	dep	00:15	01:00	**08:00**	07:30	10:30	**12:00**	12:30	**13:00**	15:30	18:20	19:00	–	20:00	–	21:00	21:15	22:00	23:00
Giza†	dep	00:35	01:20	**08:20**	07:50	10:50	**12:20**	12:50	**13:20**	15:50	18:40	19:20	**20:00**	20:20	**21:10**	21:20	21:35	22:20	23:20
Luxor	arr/dep	09:30	10:10	**17:45**	19:20	21:05	**21:50**	23:25	**22:40**	01:50	03:50	04:10	**05:10**	06:25	**06:10**	06:40	06:35	07:10	08:25
Isna	arr	10:20	–	**18:30**	20:10	–	**22:57**	–	–	02:40	|	05:00	|	07:17	|	07:30	–	08:00	|
Edfu	arr	11:05	–	**19:15**	21:05	–	**23:35**	–	–	03:30	05:20	05:45	|	07:55	|	08:15	–	08:45	09:50
Kom Ombo	arr	11:50	–	**20:10**	22:10	–	**00:25**	–	–	04:25	06:10	06:35	|	08:50	|	09:05	–	09:30	10:40
Aswan	arr	12:40	–	**21:00**	23:05	–	**01:15**	–	–	05:25	06:55	07:20	**08:15**	09:40	**09:30**	09:50	–	10:15	11:25

Aswan and Luxor → *Cairo*

Train type		Exp	**Exp**	Ord+	**Exp**	**Exp**	Exp	Ord+	Ord+	Ord+	Exp	Exp	Exp	Exp*	slee-per	Exp	Exp*	Exp	slee-per
Train number		2003	**987**	157	**981**	**983**	935	81	993	163	887	1903	977	2001	**85**	997	89	989	**87**
Aswan	dep	01:00	–	–	**05:00**	**07:00**	–	09:30	–	13:00	15:00	16:00	–	18:00	**18:30**	20:00	20:15	21:30	**21:20**
Kom Ombo	dep	01:43	–	–	**05:48**	**07:48**	–	10:25	–	13:55	15:42	16:48	–	18:43	|	20:43	21:01	22:20	|
Edfu	dep	02:35	–	–	**06:45**	**08:40**	–	11:23	–	14:50	16:30	17:40	–	19:32	|	21:37	21:58	23:15	|
Isna	dep	|	–	–	**07:35**	**09:25**	–	12:10	–	15:40	17:15	18:25	–	20:17	|	22:22	22:46	00:02	|
Luxor	arr/dep	04:15	**06:00**	07:30	**08:30**	**10:30**	13:00	13:15	14:30	16:45	19:10	19:20	20:00	21:10	**21:40**	23:15	23:45	00:55	**00:50**
Giza†	arr	13:20	**15:30**	17:55	**18:05**	**20:50**	22:15	00:45	01:55	02:45	03:50	04:15	05:30	06:00	**06:45**	08:20	09:05	09:45	**09:30**
Cairo	arr	13:35	**15:45**	18:10	**18:20**	**21:05**	22:30	01:00	02:10	03:00	04:05	04:30	05:45	06:15	–	08:35	09:20	10:00	–
Alexandria	arr	–	–	22:30	–	–	01:30	–	–	06:45	–	–	–	–	–	–	–	12:30	–

Exp = express train with air-conditioned first and second class seats with refreshments.

Exp* = also has Nefertiti class with 6-seat compartments.

Ord+ = ordinary train, not normally used by tourists, air-conditioned second class and basic second and third class.

Sleeper = deluxe sleeper train run by Abela Egypt, with sleeping-cars and lounge car.

† Giza station is a fair way from the Pyramids, but if you're staying out that way it can be a more convenient stop than going into Cairo city centre. Note that the deluxe sleeper trains currently start from and finish at Giza, while engineering work on the line is in progress.

Cairo to Luxor is 671 km (419 miles). Cairo to Aswan is 879 km (549 miles).

Fares

	Deluxe sleeper (sharing 2-berth)	Deluxe sleeper (sole occupancy)	Seat on overnight sleeper train***	1st class air-con express	2nd class air-con express	2nd class non-AC ordinary train
Cairo to Luxor	$60 (£34)**	$80 (£45)**	LE170 (£21/$30)***	LE90 (£11/$17)*	LE46 (£6/$9)*	LE40 (£5/$8)*
Cairo to Aswan	$60 (£34)**	$80 (£45)**	LE170 (£21/$30)***	LE109 (£13/$20)*	LE55 (£7/$11)*	LE50 (£6/$9)*
Luxor to Aswan	$13 (£7)****	–	–	LE47 (£6/$9)	LE28 (£3/$5)*	LE10 (£1/$2)*

Fares are one-way, per person. Prices are the same in either direction.

* Not sold to tourists.

** Fare must be paid in foreign currency. Includes evening meal and breakfast.

*** As from March 2009, this is the only seats option officially permitted for tourists.

**** Daytime journey, using sleepers in daytime mode.

If you have an ISIC student card, this gives you a 33 per cent reduction.

Children aged 0–3 travel free, children aged 4–9 travel at half fare, children of 10 and over pay full fare. On the deluxe Abela Egypt sleeper train, children aged 4–9 pay £30 ($45) one-way for Cairo–Luxor or Cairo–Aswan.

You can check train times and fares at **www.egyptrail.gov.eg**. For advice on how to buy tickets, see above, pages 164–6.

CAIRO OR ALEXANDRIA TO PORT SAID

Cairo, Alexandria → Port Said

		Ord+	Exp	Exp	Ord+	Ord+	Ord+
Cairo	depart	06:15	–	13:45	14:40	–	19:45
Alexandria	depart	I	04:30	I	I	15:30	I
Port Said	arrive	10:15	11:10	18:00	19:05	22:10	23:50

Port Said → Alexandria, Cairo

		Ord+	Ord+	Exp	Ord+	Ord+	Exp	Ord+
Port Said	depart	05:30	07:25	09:30	13:00	17:30	18:25	18:15
Alexandria	arrive	I	13:30	I	I	I	00:35	I
Cairo	arrive	09:45	–	13:35	17:10	21:35	–	00:50

Ord+ = ordinary train, with second class air-conditioned and third class non-air-conditioned.

Exp = express train, with air-conditioned first and second class.

Fares

Cairo to Port Said one-way in second class costs LE20 (£2.50 or $4).

CAIRO TO SUEZ

Cairo → Suez

		Ord	Ord+	Ord	Ord	Ord	Ord	Ord
Cairo (main station)	depart	–	05:10	–	–	–	–	–
Cairo (Ain Shams station)	depart	06:30	I	09:20	13:10	16:15	18:45	21:45
Suez	arrive	08:40	09:50	11:35	15:20	18:30	21:00	00:00

Suez → *Cairo*

		Ord	Ord	Ord	Ord+	Ord	Ord	Ord
Suez	depart	06:00	10:10	13:10	15:25	15:50	19:00	21:25
Cairo (Ain Shams station)	arrive	08:15	12:15	15:25	I	18:05	21:10	23:35
Cairo (main station)	arrive	–	–	–	20:05	–	–	–

Ord = ordinary train, with non-air-conditioned second class and third class.

Ord+ = ordinary train, with air-conditioned second class and non-air-conditioned third class.

Fares

Cairo to Suez one-way in second class costs about LE7 (less than £1).

CAIRO OR ALEXANDRIA TO EL ALAMEIN AND MERSA MATRUH

Cairo, Alexandria → *Mersa Matruh*

		Ord	Note A	Ord	Note B
Cairo	depart	–	06:40	–	23:00
Alexandria	depart	06:40	I	13:30	I
El Alamein	arrive	09:24	11:45	17:17	I
Mersa Matruh	arrive	12:05	14:15	20:20	06:00

Mersa Matruh → *Alexandria, Cairo*

		Ord	Note A	Ord	Note C
Mersa Matruh	depart	07:05	13:35	15:45	23:00
El Alamein	depart	10:24	16:20	18:30	I
Alexandria	arrive	13:30	I	21:15	I
Cairo	arrive	–	21:35	–	06:00

Ord = ordinary train, with second and third class seats, basic seating, not air-conditioned.

Note A: Express train with air-conditioned first and second class seats, runs June–September only. At other periods, travel via Alexandria.

Note B: Sleeper train. Runs 15 June–15 September on Monday, Wednesday, Saturday. For information see **www.sleepingtrains.com**.

Note C: Sleeper train. Runs 15 June–15 September on Tuesday, Thursday, Sunday. Fare £30 ($43) per person in 2-berth sleeper, £40 ($60) in single-berth sleeper. For information see **www.sleepingtrains.com**.

OTHER DESTINATIONS IN EGYPT

Abu Simbel

There are no trains to Abu Simbel, but a bus service operates from Aswan (275 km away). It departs Aswan at 07:00, arriving Abu Simbel at 10:00. It leaves Abu Simbel at 13:00 arriving back in Aswan at 16:00. There are also many tourist day tours, most leaving Aswan very early – for example, 04:00 – for about LE55 (£7 or $10).

Sharm el Sheik (Sinai)

There are no trains to Sharm el Sheik, but there are buses to and from Cairo, most run by the East Delta Bus Co., some by the Super Jet Bus Co. (neither company has a website, but try **www.ask-aladdin.com** for bus times). Sharm el Sheik to Cairo (485 km) takes about 7 hours by bus, and there are about six or seven buses daily including an overnight bus. The fare is around LE60 (£8 or $11). Sharm el Sheik is on the far side of the Gulf of Suez from the Nile Valley, so for Luxor either you need to return to Cairo by bus, then travel by train from Cairo to Luxor, or you can cross by ferry from Sharm el Sheik to Hurghada, spend the night there, then continue to Luxor by bus. There is a three-times-weekly fast ferry from Sharm el Sheik to Hurghada, plus a three-times-weekly slow ferry.

Hurghada

There are no trains to Hurghada but there are buses from both Cairo and Luxor, run by Super Jet or El Gouna bus companies (no website, but try **www.ask-aladdin.com** for bus times). Hurghada to Cairo (500 km) takes about 7 hours by bus with three or four departures daily, fare around LE55 (£7 or $10). Hurghada to Luxor (255 km) takes 4 hours by bus, with two departures daily (around 06:00 and 12:00 from Luxor, 05:00 and 17:00 from Hurghada). There is a three-times-weekly fast ferry from Hurghada to Sharm el Sheik, plus a three-times-weekly slow ferry.

Siwa Oasis

There are no trains to Siwa. A daily bus links Siwa with Alexandria (590 km), departing Alexandria at 08:30, returning from Siwa at 08:00. There's now a daily overnight bus to Siwa from the Turgoman garage in Cairo, leaving at 18:45 and arriving around 05:45 the next morning. The fare is around LE60 (£8 or $11). It's run by the West Delta Bus Co.

MOVING ON FROM EGYPT

There are no international trains from Egypt, but buses run to Libya, there's a ferry to Jordan and a Nile steamer from Aswan to Sudan.

Cairo → Amman (Jordan), Damascus (Syria) and Istanbul (Turkey)

There is a daily direct bus from Cairo to Amman, run by JETT of Jordan and taking 19 hours, exact times northbound not known – note that this crosses Israel and you may be refused entry to Syria later on if you have any sign of a visit to Israel in your passport. Alternatively, if you want to avoid Israel:

Take a bus from **Cairo** to **Nuweiba** on the Red Sea. A bus run by the Shark el Delta Bus Co. leaves Cairo main bus station at around 08:00, taking about 6 hours to reach Nuweiba.

Take the daily fast catamaran (departing 15:30, crossing 1 hour) or the daily conventional ferry (departing 14:00, crossing 3–4 hours) from **Nuweiba** to **Aqaba** in southern Jordan. The fare is about US$60 (£42) for the ferry or $90 (£62) for the fast catamaran. You must check in at least 2 hours before departure, and pay your fare in US dollars cash. There may also be an Egyptian exit tax to pay, about £7 ($10).

You will probably need to spend the night in Aqaba. There are regular buses and service taxis from **Aqaba** to **Petra** and **Amman**, costing around 3 or 4 Jordanian dinar (about £3); see the Jordan chapter, page 114. For trains and buses onwards to **Damascus**, see the Jordan chapter. For trains from Damascus to **Aleppo** and **Istanbul**, see the Syria chapter, page 116.

Cairo → Tripoli (Libya) and Tunisia

If you have a Libyan visa, there are buses you can take from Egypt into Libya. However, at present the Libyan government will not grant visas for independent travel to Libya, only for people on tours organised by a recognised Libyan travel agency. There are buses onward from Libya into Tunisia, but it's not possible to travel on to Morocco overland, as the Algerian/Moroccan border is closed and Algeria has security problems which make it a no-go zone for westerners.

Aswan → Wadi Halfa (Sudan) and Khartoum

A weekly Nile steamer links Aswan with Wadi Halfa in the Sudan, with a twice-monthly train connection for Khartoum; see the Sudan chapter, page 233, for details.

ETHIOPIA

It may not be the first place you'd think of for a holiday, but believe it or not it does have a train service, and an international one at that. The railway originally started in the capital Addis Ababa, but trains are currently running only from Dire Dawa in Ethiopia across the border to Djibouti.

Train operator:	Chemin de Fer Djibouti Ethiopien (CFDE), no official website
Time:	GMT+3
Currency:	£1 = approx. 20 Ethiopian birr, £1 = approx. 262 Djibouti francs
Tourist information:	http://tourismethiopia.org
Visas:	You will need a visa to enter Ethiopia, see **www.ethioembassy.org.uk/consular/Visa.htm**. To enter Djibouti you must obtain a visa at the Djibouti embassy in Addis Ababa, as visas cannot be issued at the frontier or in Dire Dawa.

ADDIS ABABA TO DIRE DAWA AND DJIBOUTI

There is currently no passenger train service between Addis Ababa and Dire Dawa: there have been no trains for several years, and the line is cut in several places around Addis. In theory there is a plan to restore the railway, but work on this is slow and may indeed have come to a standstill. However, a train still links Dire Dawa and Djibouti three times a week.

Buses link Addis Ababa with Dire Dawa several times daily, journey time 10½ hours, no known website. Addis Ababa to Dire Dawa is 473 km.

Dire Dawa ➜ *Djibouti*

The train departs from Dire Dawa at 06:00 on Tuesday, Thursday and Saturday, and arrives at Djibouti in the late evening, crossing the border at Alisabet. It makes the return journey from Djibouti on Wednesday, Friday and Sunday, departing at 06:00. Total journey time is up to 20 hours. Dire Dawa to Djibouti is 311 km.

The train has first, second and third class. Third class means travelling in a goods wagon. First class seats have padding, second class seats are hard. The train runs on metre-gauge tracks.

Fares and how to buy tickets

Dire Dawa to Djibouti costs 93 birr (£4.60) in first class, 76 birr (£3.80) in second class, 63 birr (£3.10) in third class.

Djibouti to Dire Dawa costs DJF4,900 (£18.50) in first class, DJF3,600 (£13.70) in second class, DJF2,800 (£10.70) in third class.

Children under 4 travel free, children over 4 but under 10 travel at half price.

Remember to get a visa for Djibouti in Addis Ababa, as Djibouti visas cannot be issued at the frontier or in Dire Dawa.

Yes, it is a lot more expensive in one direction than the other! Buy tickets at the station, but check the day before as departures can be cancelled or deferred, perhaps by up to 24 hours.

KENYA

If you are willing to brave Kenya's cities (see **www.fco.gov.uk** for advice on personal security), Kenya Railways provides the classic and enjoyable way to travel between Nairobi and Mombasa. Indeed, spotting big game from the Nairobi–Mombasa night express has always been one of Kenya's great travel experiences, so make sure you factor the train journey into your itinerary. You'll also find a weekly sleeper train from Nairobi to Kisumu on Lake Victoria, though at present there is no onward train service into Uganda.

Train operator:	Kenya Railways, no official website, but see **www.eastafricashuttles.com/train.htm**
Time:	GMT+3
Currency:	£1 = approx. 119 shillings, $1 = approx. 77 shillings
Visas:	UK, EU, US, Canadian, Australian and NZ citizens need a visa to visit Kenya. You can get them in London from the Kenyan Embassy, 45 Portland Place, London W1B 1AS, telephone 020 7636 2371/5.
Travel advice:	Kenya has a serious crime problem in the cities. Check the travel advice at **www.fco.gov.uk**.

EUROPE TO KENYA, without flying

There is no easy way to travel from Europe to Kenya without flying. Travelling overland would mean an expedition rather than straightforward travel, and there appear to be few or no passenger-carrying freighters between Europe and Kenya.

TRAIN TRAVEL WITHIN KENYA

Kenya Railways operate two classic sleeper trains, the Nairobi–Mombasa *Jambo Kenya Deluxe* and the Nairobi–Kisumu *Port Florence Express*. Originally daily, the Nairobi–Mombasa train now runs only three times a week as they have only one operational trainset. The Nairobi–Kisumu train is currently running only once weekly in each direction, reduced from three times a week due to a number of operational problems.

Both the Nairobi–Mombasa *Jambo Kenya Deluxe* and the Nairobi–Kisumu *Port Florence Express* have first class sleepers (2-berth), second class sleepers (4-berth) and third class seats, with restaurant car complete with white-gloved waiters serving full meals, snacks, drinks and beer. Advance reservation is required.

First class converts from seats to sleeping berths at night with full bedding, with two berths per compartment plus washbasin. The first class fare includes dinner and breakfast in the restaurant car. Second class converts to bunks at night, four bunks per compartment plus washbasin. Third class consists of basic seats.

Although it is comfortable (and in spite of the 'deluxe' in the train name), don't expect western standards: the Nairobi–Mombasa train is high on faded grandeur with the emphasis on 'faded' in its British-built 1950s carriages! Treat the journey as an adventure: the electricity in your compartment may or may not work, and the various fittings may or may not be broken. Clean bedding is provided, but take your own insect repellent, mineral water and toilet paper.

Nairobi → Mombasa

The *Jambo Kenya Deluxe* leaves **Nairobi** at 19:00 on Monday, Wednesday and Friday, calling at **Makindu** 23:15, **Mtito Andei** 01:11, **Voi** 04:00, and arrives at **Mombasa** at 08:25 according to the timetable – but you should be prepared for an actual arrival around 11:00. The train can run late, sometimes hours late, so relax, play safe and don't plan any tight connections at the other end! Nairobi to Mombasa is 530 km (329 miles).

Mombasa → *Nairobi*

The *Jambo Kenya Deluxe* leaves **Mombasa** at 19:00 on Tuesday, Thursday and Sunday, calling at **Voi** 23:20, **Mtito Andei** 01:50, **Makindu** 03:50, and arrives at **Nairobi** at 09:00 according to the timetable – but you should be prepared for an actual arrival around 11:00. Relax and enjoy the journey: look out for impala, giraffe, ostrich and other game whilst taking breakfast in the restaurant car.

Nairobi → *Kisumu*

The *Port Florence Express* leaves **Nairobi** at 18:30 on Friday, calling at **Naivasha** 22:30, **Nakuru** 01:05, and is scheduled to arrive at **Kisumu** at 07:45 – though you should expect delays and an actual arrival time of 10:00–11:00. Don't plan any tight connections! This train was reduced from three times weekly to once weekly in 2010, but may resume thrice-weekly operation at some point in the future.

Kisumu → *Nairobi*

The *Port Florence Express* leaves **Kisumu** at 19:00 on Sunday, calling at **Nakuru** 02:55, **Naivasha** 04:55, and arrives at **Nairobi** at 08:00 according to the timetable, but probably 10:00–11:00 in practice.

Fares

Nairobi to Mombasa one-way costs about 3,660 shillings (£30 or $48) per person for a berth in a first class 2-bed compartment, including dinner and breakfast in the restaurant car; or about 2,640 shillings (£22 or $35) per person in a second class 4-bunk compartment, including breakfast. Children under 3 travel free; for a child aged 3–11 the fare is 2,225 shillings (£19 or $29) in first class, 1,715 shillings (£15 or $23) in second class.

Nairobi to Kisumu one-way costs about 2,550 shillings (£22 or $33) per person for a berth in a first class 2-bed compartment, including dinner and breakfast in the restaurant car; or about 1,750 shillings (£15 or $23) per person in a second class 4-bunk compartment, including breakfast. Children under 3 travel free; for a child aged 3–11 the fare is 1,555 shillings (£13 or $20) in first class, 1,155 shillings (£10 or $15) in second class.

How to buy tickets

You can book these trains when you get to Kenya at the station reservation office at Nairobi, or at Mombasa for the *Jambo Kenya Deluxe*. Or you can make a booking in advance from outside Kenya, through one of several travel agencies:

> East Africa Shuttles, **www.eastafricashuttles.com/train.htm**. You can email your booking request to info@eastafricashuttles.com.

> Kuja Safaris, **www.kujasafaris.com**, email info@kujasafaris.com, telephone +254 020 313371. Kuja Safaris charge a booking fee of about £3/$5 on top of the normal ticket-office price, but may waive this if you also choose to book hotels, safaris or tours through them.

> For Nairobi–Mombasa you could also try **www.kenyasafaripackages. com/train.htm** or **www.wilddreamliners.com** who can book this train.

MOVING ON FROM KENYA

There are no international trains from Kenya to Tanzania, and the railway from Nairobi to Kampala is non-operational, at least as far as passenger trains are concerned. But there are bus services as follows:

Nairobi ➜ Kampala (Uganda)

Three main reputable bus companies ply this route: Akamba Bus Company, Regional Bus Company, Kampala Coaches. Akamba offer two overnight buses (departing 19:30 and 21:30) and an air-conditioned daytime bus departing Nairobi at 07:15 and arriving at Kampala at 20:00. Eastbound, the day bus departs Kampala 07:00 and arrives at Nairobi 20:00. See **www.akambabus.com** for details.

Mombasa → Dar es Salaam (Tanzania)

A daily bus leaves **Mombasa** at 08:00, arriving in **Dar es Salaam** at 18:00. Northbound, it leaves Dar es Salaam at 08:00, arriving at Mombasa 17:30. The fare is 1,600 Kenyan shillings (£13 or $21) or 19,000 Tanzanian shillings (£9 or $14). See **www.scandinaviagroup.com** for details. It's reported that this service may no longer be running, though there may be alternative bus operators on this route; please check locally.

Nairobi → Arusha (Tanzania) and Dar es Salaam

Akamba Bus Company runs a daily bus, departing **Nairobi** at 06:30 and arriving in **Dar es Salaam** at 21:00. The fare is in the region of 3,200 Kenyan shillings (£27 or $42) or 38,000 Tanzanian shillings ((£18 or $27). See **www.akambabus.com**.

For onward train travel from Dar es Salaam to Zambia, Zimbabwe and South Africa, see the Tanzania and Zambia chapter, page 235, and the Zimbabwe and South Africa chapters, pages 251 and 213.

MOROCCO

Morocco has to be the most exotic place most easily reached from the UK without flying. Just 48 comfortable hours after leaving London's St Pancras station you can be on board a ferry sailing into Tangier, having spent a pleasant morning in Madrid and a night in Algeciras across the bay from the Rock of Gibraltar. Once in Morocco you'll find a cheap and comfortable network of air-conditioned trains, whisking you between Tangier, Rabat, Casablanca, Fez, Meknès and Marrakech. All of these cities are well worth visiting, although 'Casa' (as it's usually known locally) is more famous for its name than its urban beauty. Marrakech is a must-see, but don't miss Fez which is in many ways the more historic and interesting (and certainly less heavily touristed) city. If you do visit Marrakech, why not hire a car for a few days and explore the country south of the city? The road over the Tizi n Tichka pass is one of the most spectacular I have ever driven, and don't miss the mud-built town of Ait ben Haddou, often used as a film set.

Train operator:	Office Nationale des Chemins de Fer Maroccains (ONCFM), **www.oncf.ma**
Ferries to Morocco:	**www.trasmediterranea.es** (Spain–Tangier) **www.comanav.ma** (France–Tangier) **www.frs.es** (Gibraltar–Tangier)
Time:	GMT. Since 2008, Morocco has used GMT+1 from early June until Ramadan.
Currency:	£1 = approx 12 dirhams, $1 = approx. 8.1 dirhams
Tourist information:	**www.tourism-in-morocco.com**
Visas:	UK, EU, US, Canadian, Australian and NZ citizens do not need a visa to visit Morocco.

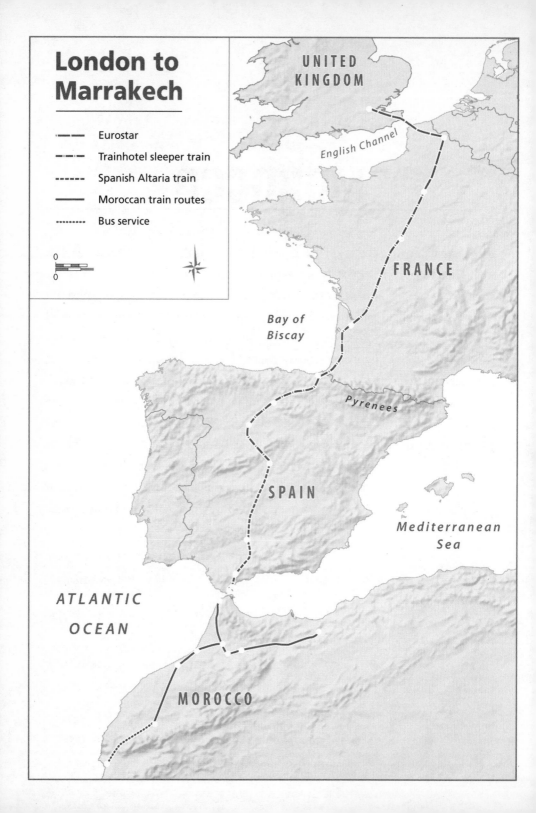

London to Marrakech

Eurostar

Trainhotel sleeper train

Spanish Altaria train

Moroccan train routes

Bus service

UNITED KINGDOM

English Channel

FRANCE

Bay of Biscay

Pyrenees

SPAIN

Mediterranean Sea

ATLANTIC OCEAN

MOROCCO

LONDON TO MOROCCO, without flying

It's easy to travel from the UK to Morocco without flying, in comfort and safety, using scheduled train and ferry services. And what a journey! Take Eurostar to Paris, grab a beer in a Parisian café and board the excellent trainhotel sleeper train to Madrid. Enjoy a meal with wine in the restaurant car and a nightcap in the bar before retiring to your sleeper for the night as the train speeds south across France, then wake up to breakfast as the sun rises over distant Spanish mountains. Spend a day in Madrid, visit the Prado Museum or soak up the atmosphere in the Plaza Santa Ana before taking an afternoon express across Andalusia to Algeciras on the Straits of Gibraltar. Next morning, take the ferry from Europe to Africa, the Rock of Gibraltar close on the port beam and the African coast getting slowly nearer. Once in Morocco, let the real Marrakech Express speed you south towards the incredible High Atlas mountains.

London ➜ *Morocco*

Day 1: Travel from **London** to **Paris** by Eurostar, leaving London St Pancras at 14:02 and arriving in Paris Gare du Nord at 17:23. By all means book an earlier Eurostar if you'd like to spend some time in Paris or if it has cheaper seats available. There are left-luggage lockers at both Paris Nord and Paris Austerlitz.

Cross Paris by metro to the Gare d'Austerlitz: you want metro line M5, direction Place d'Italie.

Day 1, evening: Travel from **Paris** to **Madrid** overnight on the excellent Elipsos trainhotel, leaving Paris Gare d'Austerlitz at 19:45 and arriving next morning at Madrid Chamartin station at 09:10. The Paris–Madrid trainhotel normally runs daily, but it does not run on Tuesday or Wednesday nights from mid-October until mid-March. The trainhotel is a special articulated sleeper train with 4-berth tourist class sleepers, 1- and 2-berth first class sleepers, and 1- and 2-berth *gran clase* sleepers with private shower and toilet. The trainhotel has an elegant restaurant car and a vibrant café-bar. There's a virtual tour at **www.elipsos.com**.

Day 2: Spend some time enjoying Madrid. There are left-luggage lockers at both Madrid Chamartin where you arrive and Madrid Atocha from where you depart. You can take the metro from Chamartin into the city centre (see **www.metromadrid.es**) or take a suburban train free of charge to Atocha (show your trainhotel ticket) and deposit your bags there. In the late afternoon, make your way by metro to Madrid's Atocha station, or simply walk there from the city centre which takes about 25 minutes.

Travel from **Madrid** to **Algeciras** (the Spanish town across the bay from Gibraltar) on the early evening Altaria air-conditioned 125mph train, leaving Madrid Atocha station at 15:05 and arriving in Algeciras at 20:39. It's a scenic ride, though the last part will be after dark. Altaria trains have first class (*preferente*) and second class (*turista*) and a café-bar with full-length wooden bar and barstools. The *preferente* fare includes a complimentary aperitif of sherry or cava, then an airline-style hot meal with choice of wines, followed by coffee and chocolate. *Preferente* passengers may also use the Sala Club (first class lounge) in Madrid Atocha station, with complimentary coffee, juices and free beer.

Spend the night in Algeciras – easily the nicest place to stay is the historic 4-star but relatively inexpensive Hotel Reina Cristina, set in its own grounds 10 minutes' walk from both the railway station and the ferry terminal.

Day 3: Travel from **Algeciras** to **Tangier** by ferry. In Algeciras, the modern ferry passenger terminal is only a 10-minute (800-metre) walk from the station straight ahead of you. You can sail on either a leisurely ship taking 1 hour 30 minutes or a fast ferry taking around 1 hour. There is a range of departures throughout the day, operated by a variety of ferry companies (see page 194 for details of their websites). The fast ferries are more modern and quicker, but you'll be sealed in except for a windy observation deck at the rear which may or may not be open. The conventional ships are older and slower, but their open decks allow you to enjoy the crossing and take photographs in the open air. There's usually a Comarit ship leaving either at 07:00, arriving in Tangier at 07:30/06:30, or at 09:00, arriving in Tangier at 09:30/08:30

(arrival times vary as Spanish time is normally an hour ahead of Moroccan time, but 2 hours at certain times of year).

Whichever you choose, the ferry sails out of Algeciras harbour in a wide arc to starboard with the Rock of Gibraltar to port, then sails across the Straits of Gibraltar. It's a scenic trip, and you can see for yourself just how narrow the straits between Europe and Africa really are between the two famous 'Pillars of Hercules'!

As from May 2010, the ferries arrive at Tanger Port Med, a new port some 45 km east of Tangier itself (note that in French the town name is spelled Tanger). Buses link Tangier Port Med with Tangier town in about 30 minutes, and a rail link is due to open at some point. For onward travel from Tangier southwards, see the section 'Train travel within Morocco', page 196.

An alternative, if you'd prefer to spend the night in Madrid instead of in Algeciras, on day 2, stay the night in a hotel in Madrid, then on the morning of day 3 take the 09:05 Altaria train from Madrid Atocha station to Algeciras, arriving at 14:45. An afternoon ferry from Algeciras will get you to Tangier in the evening on day 3. Although a half day slower overall, this option gives you a full day and evening in Madrid, and the morning Altaria train to Algeciras will show you the wonderful mountain scenery in southern Spain in daylight.

Morocco ➜ *London*

For train connections from Marrakech, Casablanca, Rabat, Fez, Meknès to Tangier, see the section 'Train travel within Morocco', page 196.

Day 1, evening: Take a bus from Tangier town to **Tangier Port Med** then a ferry to **Algeciras**. On most days there are Comarit ships which sail from Tangier Port Med at 18:00, arriving in Algeciras at 20:30/21:30, and at 20:00, arriving in Algeciras at 22:30/23:30 (Spain is sometimes an hour ahead of Morocco, sometimes 2 hours, depending on the time of year). It's a 1 hour 30 minute crossing by ship or around 1 hour by fast seacat. Spend the night in Algeciras.

Day 2: Travel from **Algeciras** to **Madrid** by high-speed Altaria train. You leave Algeciras at 08:24 and arrive in Madrid Atocha at 13:57. Altaria trains have air-conditioned second class (*turista*), first class (*preferente*) and a café-bar. The *preferente* fare includes an at-seat meal with aperitif and selection of wines. Make your way by metro or suburban train to Madrid Chamartin.

As an alternative, if you'd prefer a day and night in Madrid: on day 1, leave Tangier Port Med on a ferry around 10:00 or 11:00, arriving in Algeciras at lunchtime, then take the afternoon Altaria train from Algeciras (departing at 16:50) to Madrid (arriving Madrid Atocha at 22:50), and spend the night in Madrid.

Day 2, evening: Travel from **Madrid** to **Paris** on the excellent overnight trainhotel, leaving Madrid Chamartin at 19:00 and arriving in Paris Gare d'Austerlitz at 08:32 next morning. The Madrid–Paris trainhotel normally runs daily, but it does not run on Monday or Tuesday nights from mid-October to mid-March. Sleepers, bar, restaurant are available. Trainhotel passengers in *preferente* and *gran clase* sleepers may use the Sala Club (first class lounge) at Madrid Chamartin near platform 14, with complimentary tea, coffee, juices and free beer. On arrival in Paris, take the metro to the Gare du Nord: Metro line 5 links Paris Austerlitz and Paris Nord; just follow the signs 'M5 direction Bobigny Pablo Picasso'.

Day 3, morning: Travel from Paris to London by Eurostar, leaving Paris Gare du Nord at 11:13 and arriving in London at 12:29.

Why not see Gibraltar on the way?

Buses (bus M-120) link Algeciras bus station (across the road from the railway station) with La Linea, the frontier with Gibraltar, every 30–45 minutes, taking about 45 minutes, fare about €2.05 (£1.85). The bus operator website, for checking times and fares, is **www.ctmcg.com**. You then walk 250 metres from La Linea across the frontier into Gibraltar town centre (about 10 minutes). The walk takes you across Gibraltar airport's main runway, but don't worry, they stop the cars and pedestrians when a plane comes in to land! Alternatively, a taxi from Algeciras railway station all the way to Gibraltar costs around €24 (£22).

A fast ferry occasionally operates between Gibraltar and Tangier, see **www.frs.es,** but it only runs on a handful of dates, so as a general rule you will need to use the regular Algeciras–Tangier ferries and make the Gibraltar excursion a round trip from Algeciras.

Can I stop off on the way?

Of course. The Eurostar, the trainhotel and the Altaria train are ticketed as three separate journeys, so feel free to book each leg of the journey on whatever dates you like, spending however long you like in Paris or Madrid on the way. The Altaria trains between Madrid and Algeciras all stop at Ronda, a wonderful town to visit. There are left-luggage facilities in Madrid.

How much does it cost?

You can't buy a 'London to Morocco' ticket: the cost is the sum of the tickets for each part of the journey.

1. London to Paris by Eurostar

London to Paris starts at £39 one-way, £69 return in standard class, £99 one-way, £189 return in first class.

2. Paris to Madrid by trainhotel (per person)	First class reclining seat	Tourist class sleeper	First class sleeper ***			Gran clase sleeper ****	
		4-berth	2-berth	1-berth	2-berth	1-berth
Special one-way fare*	–	£67	£101 or £159*	–	£146 or £197*	–
Special return fare*	–	£134	£202 or £318*	–	£292 or £393*	–
Normal one-way fare	£134	£148	£245	£372	£301	£440
Normal return fare	£189	£208	£344	£522	£423	£617
Railpass holders one-way	£44	£67	£101	£152	£146	£189
Child/senior/ youth one-way**	£95	£104	£172	£261	£212	£312
Child 4–11 (inclusive) sharing a bed	£56 each way. You must occupy the whole compartment.					

* Special fares: In tourist class the £67 fare (£83 in summer) is called 'Prems'; it must be booked at least 14 days in advance, and is non-refundable, non-changeable. In first class (*preferente*) and *gran clase* 2 people must travel together and either the lower (Mini à Deux) or higher (Duo) price will be available on a given date. Mini is non-refundable, non-changeable, limited availability. Duo is refundable, exchangeable, usually available.

** Child = 4–11 years old; Youth = 12–25 years old; Senior = anyone over 60.

*** Fare includes breakfast.

**** Fare includes evening meal with wine in the restaurant and breakfast.

Children under 4 go free, as long as the parents have sole use of a compartment.

Note: 10–22 per cent higher fares apply mid-June to mid-September and at Easter (e.g. £67 becomes £83).

3. Madrid to Algeciras by Altaria train

Second class (*turista*):
Cheap 'Web' fare booked in advance at **www.renfe.es**: €24 (£22) one-way.
Cheap 'Estrella' fare if you book in advance: €37 (£34) one-way.
Normal flexible fare: €61 (£56) one-way, €98 (£90) return.

First class (*preferente*), at-seat meal and drinks included.
Cheap 'Estrella' fare if you book in advance: €57 (£52) one-way.
Normal flexible fare €95 (£87) one-way, €152 (£140) return.

Check fares and book online at **www.renfe.es**.

4. Algeciras to Tangier Med Port by ferry

€20 (£18) one-way, €40 (£36) return. You can check ferry times and fares at
www.trasmediterranea.es, **www.balearia.com**, **www.comarit.com** or **www.euroferrys.com**.

How to buy tickets

The easiest and cheapest way to book your London–Morocco train journey is online, and instructions are given below. If you prefer to book by phone you can book the train travel all the way from London to Algeciras through Spanish Rail UK (www.spanish-rail.co.uk) on 020 7224 0345 (lines open 09:30–17:30 Monday to Friday), or Rail Europe on 0844 848 5 848 (lines open 09:00–21:00 Monday to Friday, 09:00–18:00 Saturday, closed on Sunday).

To book online:

- Book the London–Paris Eurostar and the Paris–Madrid trainhotel at either **www.raileurope.co.uk** (UK residents) or **www.voyages-sncf.com** (residents of any country). Remember that on your return journey your Eurostar departure from Paris will be the day after your departure from Madrid, and make sure, too, that you allow for the 30-minute Eurostar check-in time when arranging the connection.

- Book the train from Madrid to Algeciras and back. There are two ways to do this. Option 1, painless but usually more expensive, is to stay with **www.raileurope.co.uk**, click 'continue shopping' and book it along with your London–Paris–Madrid tickets as one transaction. Remember that the outward date will be the day after your departure from London. If the system refuses to book a return, try booking as two one-ways. However, **www.raileurope.co.uk** can only sell the normal flexible fare between Madrid and Algeciras, it can't sell the cheap 'Web' or 'Estrella' fares. So option 2 is to book the Madrid–Algeciras and Algeciras–Madrid trains using the Spanish Railways website **www.renfe.es**, looking for these cheap deals.

Tickets for the ferry can easily be bought at the ferry terminal when you get to Algeciras, as there are always places available, no pre-booking necessary. Just turn up and buy your ticket at the ticket offices at the entrance to the passenger terminal, then go inside the terminal and upstairs to the check-in windows. To check ferry times and fares, see **www.trasmediterranea.es** (ship and fast ferry), **www.comarit.com** (ship) or **www.euroferrys.com** (ship and fast ferry, also bookable through **www.trasmediterranea.es**) or **www.balearia.com** (fast ferry).

Using a railpass

If you simply want to travel to and from Morocco, just buy normal tickets as a railpass is unlikely to save any money. In fact, it will probably cost a lot more. For example, if you have a railpass you have to pay a £67 supplement to travel on the Paris–Madrid trainhotel in a 4-berth sleeper, but you can find a £67 special fare if you book in advance without a railpass, so why bother with the pass? However, if you want to make other trips in France, Spain or Morocco, a railpass may become worthwhile; here are the factors relating to this particular journey you'll need to take into account:

- You'll need a global InterRail pass, which gives unlimited travel in most of Europe, including France and Spain. You can check prices and buy an InterRail pass online at **www.raileurope.co.uk** or by telephone through Rail Europe on 0844 848 5 848.

- You will need to add at least £69 return for the Eurostar from London to Paris as railpasses do not cover Eurostar.

- You will need to budget for supplements: railpass-holder supplement for the Paris–Madrid trainhotel is £67 one-way in a 4-berth sleeper, £101 in a 2-bed sleeper. The supplement for the Altaria train Madrid–Algeciras is around £10 one-way.

London ➜ Morocco, via South of France

If you prefer a longer sea voyage, there are regular passenger ships from Sète in the south of France to Tangier, run by Comanav (Compagnie Maroccaine de Navigation). See **www.southernferries.co.uk/ comanav_ferries.htm** or call 0844 815 7785 for sailing dates and fares. It's easy to get from London to Sète by train: use **www.raileurope.co.uk** to find train times and prices, or call Rail Europe on 0844 848 5 848.

THE CONTINENTAL HOTEL, TANGIER

Easily the most interesting place to stay in Tangier is the Continental Hotel, whatever your budget. As you walk into town from the ferry, you'll easily spot it on your right high up on the edge of the medina overlooking the port. Opened in 1888 and used by many famous people, including (allegedly) Winston Churchill and Queen Victoria's son Prince Alfred, it's now a travellers' favourite, with classic Moroccan décor and an atmosphere straight out of Agatha Christie. In spite of all this history, it's cheap: a single room with shower and toilet costs around 460 dirhams (£38) per night, including a light breakfast; a double room with shower and toilet around 560 dirhams (£47), including breakfast. Ask for a room on the first floor with a balcony overlooking the port and new town. Rooms are small and fairly basic, but have clean en suite showers and toilets. The hotel is handy for the port, well located inside the old medina walls and a stone's throw from the old town centre, Petit Socco and Grand Socco. The hotel has a good and cheap restaurant, too. Rooms can't be booked online and they don't accept credit cards, but email them at hcontinental@iam.net.ma, or hcontinental@menara.ma, or just turn up. The address is 36, Dar Baroud (Medina), Tangier; telephone +212 39 93 10 24.

THINGS TO SEE IN TANGIER

Tangier sometimes gets a bad press from travellers who are hassled by a few touts at the port, who then hurry through without seeing it and tell everyone else to do the same. This is very short-sighted, as Tangier is the intriguing and atmospheric city where Europe meets Africa. Indeed, fans of the film *Casablanca* will find it a far more plausible setting for Rick, Elsa, Captain Renault and Major Strasser than the big and unremarkable city to the south. Tangier was an international zone from 1923 until its incorporation with Morocco in 1956, and it really was awash with spies from both sides in the Second World War. It retains a faint air of mystery and intrigue even today, although I've always felt very safe there! It's a wonderful and fascinating place to spend a day or two, so make sure you include it in your itinerary. Be sure to see the medina (old town), kasbah (fort), the Petit Socco (small square) and Grand Socco (large square), the English Church, and Tangier American Legation museum (the first bit of overseas territory ever acquired by the United States, see **www.legation.org**). For more information on Tangier, see **http://en.wikipedia.org/wiki/Tangier**.

TRAIN TRAVEL WITHIN MOROCCO

The trains in Morocco are some of the best in Africa, and they're the ideal choice for getting around between cities. Fast, modern, air-conditioned *trains rapides climatisés* link Tangier, Rabat, Casablanca, Marrakech, Meknès, Fez and Oujda: see the route map on page 186. Regular trains link Casablanca airport with the city centre. Agadir and Essaouira have no railway station, but are linked to Marrakech by connecting bus.

On board the trains

The long-distance *rapides climatisés* have first and second class air-conditioned smooth-riding coaches, with a trolley service of inexpensive tea, coffee, sandwiches and snacks. Second class cars have plastic padded seats and seats are unreservable, so cannot 'sell out'. First class cars have comfortable fabric seats and carpets, and all seats are reservable, so can sell out at busy times.

A popular way to travel from Tangier to Marrakech is to take the direct overnight train, sleeping in a couchette and saving a night in a hotel. One couchette car is attached to this train, with eleven first class 4-berth compartments, each berth provided with pillow, sheet and light blanket. The car is air-conditioned, although it may be a while before the air-con kicks in if the car has been standing in the sidings all day! The compartment doors lock securely, and it is a safe, comfortable and time-effective way to travel. As there is only one couchette car, berths can sometimes get sold out, so book ahead if you can. However, it's not impossible to find berths available even if you book at the station on the day of travel, so give it a try.

How to check train times and fares

You can easily check Moroccan train times and fares at the Moroccan Railways (ONCF) website, **www.oncf.ma**, which has an English language button at top left. Fares are very cheap by European standards.

How to buy tickets

There is no easy way to book trains from outside Morocco, and you don't generally need to book in advance anyway. Just buy your ticket at the station on the day, or perhaps the day before. In second class, seat reservation isn't possible, you just buy a ticket and hop on, so the train can never be 'full'. Seats can be reserved in first class up to a month in advance. In Morocco, you can also book by phone on 090 20 30 40, but this number is not accessible from overseas.

Sleeping-berths (4-berth couchettes) on the convenient Tangier–Marrakech overnight train can be reserved up to two months in advance. These can sometimes get fully booked, so book as soon as you reach Morocco if you can, but it's reportedly sometimes possible to find berths available on the day of travel. One seat61 correspondent suggests arranging couchette tickets on this train through local travel agency Travel Link (**www.travellink.ma**; 83 Rue de la Liberté (next to the El Minza Hotel), Tangier; telephone +212 39 93 58 77; email nait@travellink.ma), though reports about this agency have been mixed. Travel Link charge a hefty 500 dirham (£41) booking fee on top of the ticket cost, but it could be worth it if catching this train the day you arrive in Tangier is mission-critical.

Tangier's new station

The old station in Tangier near the port and medina was closed a few years ago (it's now the police station!), but an impressive new Tanger Ville station has now been completed just inland from the far end of the sea front. Walking from the port, the medina or the Continental Hotel to the new station takes around 30–35 minutes, so take a *petit taxi* as this only costs 20 dirhams or so (about £1.70).

TAKING THE TRAIN SOUTH FROM TANGIER

Here is the complete train timetable from Tangier to the rest of Morocco. Tangier is on a branch line from a junction station called Sidi Kacem, located on the main line linking Fez, Meknès, Sidi Kacem, Rabat, Casablanca and Marrakech. Most trains run Tangier–Sidi Kacem–Casablanca, so you must change at Sidi Kacem for Meknès and Fez. However, a couple of trains run Tangier–Sidi Kacem–Fez, and on these you change at Sidi Kacem for Casablanca. Trains now run every hour or so on the main line between Casablanca, Rabat, Meknès and Fez; see **www.oncf.ma** for a complete timetable. Look for the 'Les horaires dans la poche' link at the bottom of the ONCF home page to print out a complete pocket timetable to take with you.

Tangier → Marrakech and Fez

	Notes	A	A	A	A	A	A	X
Tangier (Ville)	depart	07:35	08:25	10:40	11:35	13:35	17:35	21:35
Meknès	arrive	I	12:19	14:19	I	I	21:09m	01:55k
Fès (Fez)	arrive	I	13:00	15:00	I	I	21:50m	02:20k
Rabat (Ville)	arrive	11:09	–	–	15:09	17:09	21:09	03:09
Casablanca (Voyageurs)	arrive	12:20	–	–	16:20	18:20	22:20	04:30
Marrakech	arrive	16:05c	–	–	20:05c	22:05c	–	08:05

Marrakech and Fez → Tangier

	Notes	X	A	A	A	A	A	A
Marrakech	depart	21:00	–	07:00c	–	09:00c	–	13:00c
Casablanca (Voyageurs)	depart	00:45	07:45	11:45	–	13:45	–	17:45
Rabat (Ville)	depart	01:57	08:47	12:47	–	14:47	–	18:47
Fès (Fez)	depart	01:45k	07:10m	I	13:05	I	17:05	I
Meknès	depart	02:20k	07:50m	I	13:42	I	17:42	I
Tangier (Ville)	arrive	07:00	12:30	16:30	17:25	18:30	21:25	22:25

Note A: Air-conditioned rapide, first and second class, refreshment trolley.

Note X: Direct overnight train Tangier–Marrakech with couchette car. The couchette car has 4-bunk first class compartments, bedding provided. Seats also available.

c = change trains at Casablanca.

k = change trains at Sidi Kacem.

m = change trains at Mechra bel Ksiri.

No letter next to the arrival or departure time = direct train.

This timetable shows all trains to and from Tangier, but there are lots of other trains on the main line linking Marrakech, Casablanca, Rabat, Meknès and Fez. You can check train times at **www.oncf.ma**.

Fares

Tangier to Fez one-way by air-conditioned rapide costs 97 dirhams (£8 or $12) in second class, 145 dirhams (£12 or $18) in first class. Tangier to Marrakech one-way costs 190 dirhams (£16 or $24) in second class, 290 dirhams (£24 or $36) in first class; for a first class (4-bunk) couchette on the overnight direct train the fare is 350 dirhams (£29 or $44). Children aged 0–3 travel free, children aged 4–10 travel at half fare, children aged 11 and over pay the adult fare.

BUS CONNECTIONS TO AGADIR AND ESSAOUIRA

Buses from Marrakech to Agadir and Essaouira are run by Supratours, a subsidiary of ONCF, the Moroccan railways, and depart from the Supratours terminal next to Marrakech railway station. You can check bus times at **www.oncf.ma**. Marrakech to Essaouira costs about 65 dirhams (£5 or $7), Marrakech to Agadir about 95 dirhams (£8 or $12). Luggage must be checked in, and a small fee is payable for this in addition to your fare. You can buy combined train+bus tickets from any Moroccan railway station to Agadir and Essaouira via Marrakech – ask for a *billet rail et route*.

Marrakech → *Agadir*

Marrakech	depart	00:30	05:00	09:00	10:45	12:45	14:30	15:00	17:00	19:00	22:30
Agadir	arrive	04:59	08:59	13:59	15:29	16:59	18:59	19:59	21:59	23:29	02:59

Agadir → *Marrakech*

Agadir	depart	04:00	06:00	07:00	08:00	08:15	10:00	13:15	14:00	15:30	19:30	23:30
Marrakech	arrive	08:29	09:59	12:29	12:29	12:59	14:29	18:29	18:29	12:29	00:29	03:59

Marrakech → *Essaouira*

Marrakech	depart	08:30	10:45	14:45	17:00	19:00
Essaouira	arrive	11:29	13:44	17:44	19:59	21:59

Essaouira → *Marrakech*

Essaouira	depart	06:45	09:30	11:45	15:15	18:30
Marrakech	arrive	09:29	11:59	14:29	18:29	21:29

MOZAMBIQUE

There are several railway services in Mozambique, one of them allowing for international travel to or from South Africa.

Train operator:	Caminhos de Ferro do Moçambique (CFM), **www.cfmnet.co.mz**
Time:	GMT+2
Currency:	£1 = approx. 50 meticals, $1 = approx. 33 meticals
Tourist information:	**www.turismomocambique.co.mz**
Visas:	UK citizens and most other nationalities need a visa for Mozambique, see **www.mozambiquehighcommission.org.uk**.

SOUTH AFRICA TO MOZAMBIQUE, by train

You can travel between Johannesburg or Pretoria in South Africa and Maputo in Mozambique by train – a real adventure, although the South African overnight train currently lacks any sleeping-cars; it just has seats.

Johannesburg and Pretoria ➜ *Maputo*

Travel from **Johannesburg** or **Pretoria** to **Komatipoort** by train, leaving Johannesburg Park Station daily except Saturdays at 18:00 or Pretoria at 19:40, calling at Nelspruit (for Kruger Park) at 04:15 and arriving in Komatipoort at 06:30 next morning. This train is the *Komati*, run by Shosholoza Meyl, **www.shosholozameyl.co.za**. It runs daily except Saturdays, with economy seats only; there are no sleepers.

Take a bus across the border from **Komatipoort** to **Ressano Garcia**. It's only a few kilometres. The CFM train used to cross the border, but this proved too difficult for the customs authorities, so now you must walk across or use a local bus.

Travel from **Ressano Garcia** to **Maputo** by train, leaving Ressano Garcia at 12:10 Monday to Friday or 12:30 on Saturday and Sunday, arriving in Maputo at 16:40 Monday to Friday or 17:20 Saturday and Sunday. This train is run by CFM, the Caminhos de Ferro do Moçambique. It runs daily with third class seats only. See **www.cfmnet.co.mz**.

Johannesburg to Komatipoort is 530 km (331 miles). Ressano Garcia to Maputo is 88 km (55 miles).

Maputo ➜ *Pretoria and Johannesburg*

Travel from **Maputo** to **Ressano Garcia** by CFM train (third class seats only), leaving Maputo at 07:45 Monday to Friday or 08:00 on Saturday and Sunday, arriving at Ressano Garcia at 11:20 Monday to Friday or 11:35 on Saturday and Sunday.

Take a local bus across the border from **Ressano Garcia** to **Komatipoort**.

Travel by train from **Komatipoort** to **Pretoria** or **Johannesburg** on the *Komati* (economy seats only, no sleepers), leaving Komatipoort daily except Saturday at 18:00, calling at Nelspruit (for Kruger Park) at 20:40 and arriving in Pretoria at 04:50 and Johannesburg Park Station at 06:16 next morning.

How much does it cost?

Johannesburg to Komatipoort costs RS170 (about £16 or $24). Ressano Garcia to Maputo costs MT15 (about 30p or 45¢).

How to buy tickets

You can buy tickets for the South African train at the station on the day. If you want to book in advance and are in South Africa, you can call Shosholoza Meyl reservations on 086 000 8888 or book in person at any station reservation office. Bookings open 90 days before departure; you can't book before reservations open. Reservations are computerised, so any reservation office can book any journey in South Africa. When booking by phone, you will be given a booking reference number, which you quote at the station when you pick up and pay for your tickets. To book from overseas, telephone +27 11 7744 555.

For the Mozambique train, you simply buy tickets at the station, either at Ressano Garcia or Maputo.

OTHER TRAIN ROUTES IN MOZAMBIQUE

Besides the line to Maputo in the south, there are also various rail lines leading inland from Beira. However, service is suspended due to line rebuilding. There are a couple of other lines out of Maputo: see **www.cfmnet.co.mz** for details.

NAMIBIA

A network of overnight passenger trains called 'Starline' links the Namibian capital Windhoek with major towns, and it's possible to travel between Windhoek and Johannesburg or Cape Town in South Africa by a combination of bus and train. Finally, Namibia is also home to a tourist train, the *Desert Express*.

Train operator:	Transnamib, **www.transnamib.com.na** (click 'Products' then 'Passenger services')
Time:	GMT+1 (GMT+2 from first Sunday in September to first Sunday in April)
Currency:	£1 = approx. 11 Namibian dollars
Tourist information:	**www.namibiatourism.com.na**
Visas:	UK, US, Canadian, Australian and NZ citizens do not need a visa for stays of up to 90 days, but must have a return ticket or evidence of ability to return out of Namibia. Most EU citizens do not require a visa.

EUROPE TO NAMIBIA, without flying

There are no regular passenger ships between Europe and Namibia, but you may be able to find an occasional freighter from Europe which carries a handful of passengers. The best place to start looking for a passage by freighter is with **www.strandtravelltd.co.uk**, telephone +44 (0)20 7921 4340.

SOUTH AFRICA TO NAMIBIA

It's possible to travel between Namibia and South Africa by train with only one relatively short section now, sadly, involving a bus. Here's how:

Cape Town or Johannesburg ➔ Windhoek

Travel from **Cape Town** to **Kimberley** by Shosholoza Meyl *Trans-Karoo* passenger train, departing Cape Town 12:30 on Wednesday, Friday and Sunday, arriving in Kimberley at 06:45 next day. This is a comfortable and safe tourist class train, with 2-berth and 4-berth sleepers and restaurant car. As you leave Cape Town you get great views of Table Mountain, pass through Stellenbosch and Paarl wine country, then into the veldt up the Hex River pass, with great scenery!

Or from **Johannesburg** travel to **Kimberley** on the *Trans-Karoo* (the same train as from Cape Town, travelling in the opposite direction), which departs Johannesburg at 10:30 on Wednesday, Friday and Sunday, arriving at Kimberley at 19:07 the same day.

Stay a day or two in Kimberley (visit the mining museum!).

From **Kimberley** travel by bus to **Keetmanshoop**: sadly things have degenerated so there's now only a bus link, no longer a train. The bus is run by InterCape, and runs on Friday and Sunday at 11:40, arriving at Upington at 16:30 the same day; you then need to switch buses, departing Upington 18:30 and arriving at Keetmanshoop at 00:25 the same night. Stay overnight at Keetmanshoop.

The following day take the overnight StarLine passenger train from **Keetmanshoop** to **Windhoek**. This leaves Keetmanshoop daily except Saturday at 18:50, arriving in Windhoek at 07:00 next day. The train is modern and air-conditioned, with reclining seats in business class and economy class, also basic 6-berth sleepers on Tuesday, Thursday and Sunday. Note that a train used to run from Upington to Keetmanshoop twice a week to connect with this overnight train to Windhoek (and is still shown as running in the un-updated 2006 timetable on the StarLine website), but this train now only runs from Karasburg (just inside the Namibian frontier) to Keetmanshoop, so you may as well switch from bus to train at Keetmanshoop.

Windhoek → Cape Town or Johannesburg

Travel from **Windhoek** to **Keetmanshoop** by StarLine passenger train. The train leaves Windhoek at 19:40 daily except Saturday, arriving at Keetmanshoop at 07:00 next morning. The train is modern and air-conditioned, with reclining seats in business class and economy class, also basic 6-bunk sleepers on Monday, Wednesday and Friday. Spend the day in Keetmanshoop.

Go by bus from **Keetmanshoop** to **Kimberley**, as sadly there's now only a bus link (see the note above about the now discontinued Keetmanshoop–Upington train service). The bus is run by InterCape, and departs Keetmanshoop on Wednesday and Friday at 23:15; you need to switch buses at Upington (arrive 06:15, depart 07:30), and you arrive at Kimberley at 12:40 on the Thursday or Saturday. Stay overnight at Kimberley.

Take the Shosholoza Meyl *Trans-Karoo* passenger train from **Kimberley**: either to **Cape Town**, departing Kimberley at 19:07 on Wednesday, Friday and Sunday, arriving Cape Town at 12:41 the next day; or to **Johannesburg**, departing Kimberley at 06:45 on Monday, Thursday and Saturday, arriving at Johannesburg at 15:18 the same day.

Fares and how to buy tickets

The fare from Cape Town to Kimberley one-way is around R210 (£19 or US$29) including sleeper. Johannesburg to Kimberley costs around R110 (£8 or US$15). For more information about Shosholoza Meyl trains, fares and how to book tickets, see the South Africa chapter, page 219.

Kimberley–Keetmanshoop by InterCape bus costs around R390–R500 (£36–£46 or US$54–US$69). You can check times and fares and book online at **www.intercape.co.za**.

For fares and booking information for Keetmanshoop–Windhoek see the next section, 'Train travel within Namibia'.

TRAIN TRAVEL WITHIN NAMIBIA

Regular passenger trains run by TransNamib and marketed as 'StarLine' link Windhoek with Swakopmund, Walvis Bay and Keetmanshoop, and run between Keetmanshoop and Karasburg. The trains that used to operate between Windhoek and Tsumeb and between Windhoek and Gobabis have been cancelled indefinitely as of January 2009. TransNamib also operate a weekly tourist-orientated train between Windhoek and Swakopmund, the *Desert Express*.

StarLine trains have business class and economy class reclining airline-style seats in relatively modern, air-conditioned cars, complete with TV entertainment (but don't expect too much of the latter!). There are vending machines but no restaurant or buffet car, so take your own food and drink. These passenger trains also include freight wagons.

There are generally no sleepers on these StarLine trains, just seats, with one exception: the Windhoek–Keetmanshoop train has a basic sleeping car attached on every second departure, theoretically Tuesday, Thursday and Sunday from Keetmanshoop, Monday, Wednesday and Friday from Windhoek. This sleeper has 6-bunk couchette-style compartments in both economy and business class; prices are the same as for a seat. No bedding is provided, so bring your own as it can get cold in the desert.

Windhoek → Swakopmund and Walvis Bay
StarLine passenger train runs daily except Saturday, departing Windhoek 19:55 and arriving next day at Swakopmund 05:20 and at Walvis Bay 07:15.

Walvis Bay and Swakopmund → Windhoek
Runs daily except Saturday; departs Walvis Bay 19:00, Swakopmund 20:45, arrives at Windhoek 07:00 next day.

Windhoek → Keetmanshoop
Runs daily except Saturday, departing Windhoek 19:40 and arriving at Keetmanshoop at 07:00 next day.

Keetmanshoop ➜ Windhoek

Runs daily except Saturday, departing Keetmanshoop 18:50 and arriving at Windhoek at 07:00 next day.

Keetmanshoop ➜ Karasburg

Runs on Wednesday and Saturday, departing Keetmanshoop 08:50 and arriving at Karasburg at 14:30.

The train makes the return journey on Sunday and Thursday, departing Karasburg at 11:20 and arriving at Keetmanshoop at 16:30.

Fares and how to buy tickets

Windhoek–Walvis Bay one-way in economy class costs around N\$80 (£7 or US\$10), Windhoek–Keetmanshoop around N\$87 (£8 or US\$12). Business class costs N\$20 (£2 or US\$3) extra. However, fares vary from N\$80 to N\$130 (£7 to £12 or US\$10 to US\$18) according to time of year and peak/off-peak. Children under 2 travel free, children aged 2 and up but under 12 go for half fare.

To pre-book tickets you can telephone central reservations at Windhoek on +264 (0) 61 298 2032, or email paxservices@transnamib.com.na.

The Desert Express

This is a weekly tourist-orientated train between Windhoek and Swakopmund, operated by TransNamib. The train has sleepers with en suite shower/toilet, a restaurant, bar and lounge. See **www.desertexpress.com.na** for more details.

The *Desert Express* runs from Windhoek on Friday, leaving at 12:00 (13:00 in summer), and arrives at Swakopmund at 10:00 next day.

It leaves Swakopmund at 15:00 on Saturday, arriving at Windhoek at 10:30 the next day.

The fare per person one-way is N\$1,850 (£168 or US\$252) for a berth in a shared compartment, N\$2,400 (£218 or US\$327) for single occupancy.

You can book via the dedicated website, **www.desertexpress.com.na**.

MOVING ON FROM NAMIBIA

For the connection by train+bus from Namibia to South Africa, see pages 204–6.

There are buses, but no trains, between Namibia and Zambia or Zimbabwe. These are operated by the South African company InterCape, **www.intercape.co.za**; the fares are in rand and are bookable online.

Windhoek → *Victoria Falls (Zimbabwe) or Livingstone (Zambia)*

A bus leaves Windhoek at 16:15 on Monday and Friday, and arrives next day at Livingstone at 13:00, or Victoria Falls at 14:00.

In the other direction the bus leaves Victoria Falls at 11:00 on Wednesday and Sunday, or Livingstone at 12:00, and arrives at Windhoek at 06:45 next day.

The fare is R455–R580 (£41–£53 or US$62–US$79).

SENEGAL AND MALI

The two- or three-day train journey from Dakar in Senegal to Bamako in Mali used to be one of West Africa's great rail adventures. Sadly, the train is currently suspended due to the condition of the track, although a train service of sorts still operates within Mali at the eastern end of the route. However, work is in hand to reinstate the service from Dakar, so it may soon be possible once more to get from the Senegalese coast to Bamako in central Mali, the jumping-off point for a bus or river steamer for Timbuktu.

Train operator:	Transrail (a Canadian consortium which has taken over the Senegalese and Malian railways)
Time:	GMT all year round
Currency:	£1 = approx. 748 Senegal CFA francs (both Senegal and Mali), $1 = approx. 500 francs
Visas:	UK, US and some EU citizens do not need a visa for Senegal (though Australians and some eastern EU nationalities do). UK citizens and all western nationalities need a visa for Mali. Mali has no embassy in London, but there is an embassy in Brussels.
Travel advice:	Check travel advice at **www.fco.gov.uk**.

EUROPE TO SENEGAL, without flying

There are no regular passenger ships between Europe and Senegal, but you may be able to find an occasional freighter from Europe which carries a handful of passengers. The best place to start looking for a passage by freighter is with Strand Travel, **www.strandtravelltd.co.uk**, telephone +44 (0)20 7921 4340.

TRAIN TRAVEL WITHIN SENEGAL AND MALI

There used to be a weekly train (originally twice-weekly) from Dakar in Senegal to Bamako in Mali, a two-night, two-day journey. Sadly, the tracks deteriorated and the train finally stopped running completely in summer 2009. It's not clear whether it will be reinstated at some time in the future, although in summer 2010 reports suggest a train may resume running from Dakar in 2011. A train still runs within Mali, between Kayes and Bamako, three times a week.

Dakar → Bamako

	See note A (running)	Express (cancelled)
Dakar	–	10:00 Sat
Thies	–	12:15 Sat
Diourbel	–	15.28 Sat
Guinguineo	–	16:56 Sat
Kaffrine	–	18:40 Sat
Tambacounda	–	03:25 Sun
Kidira (frontier)	–	08:20 Sun
Kayes	07:15 Tue, Thur, Sun	13:35 Sun
Diamou	xx:xx Tue, Thur, Sun	16:40 Sun
Kati	xx:xx Tue, Thur, Sun	07:12 Mon
Bamako	22:00 Tue, Thur, Sun	08:15 Mon

Bamako → *Dakar*

	Express (cancelled)	See note B (running)
Bamako	09:15 Wed	07:15 Mon, Wed, Sat
Kati	10:25 Wed	xx:xx Mon, Wed, Sat
Diamou	00:55 Thur	xx:xx Mon, Wed, Sat
Kayes	03:45 Thur	22:00 Mon, Wed, Sat
Kidira (frontier)	08:25 Thur	–
Tambacounda	13:00 Thur	–
Kaffrine	21:05 Thur	–
Guinguineo	22:55 Thur	–
Diourbel	00:12 Fri	–
Thies	03:35 Fri	–
Dakar	05:55 Fri	–

Note A: This train is still running in 2010. Runs three times a week, on Tuesday, Thursday, Sunday. It's composed of second-hand Indian carriages.

Note B: This train is still running in 2010. It runs on Monday, Wednesday, Saturday only. It's composed of second-hand Indian carriages.

xx:xx = exact times not known.

The fare between Kayes and Bamako is CFA7,000 (about £9.50 or $14) in first class.

SOUTH AFRICA

Contrary to what you may have heard and to what many middle-class South Africans may tell you, taking a long-distance passenger train is a remarkably safe, civilised and enjoyable way to travel between cities in South Africa. In fact, you'd be crazy not to consider it. You'll find several different types of train, from the famous, luxurious (and expensive) *Blue Train* to the comfortable and much cheaper Shosholoza Meyl 'Premier Classe' service to the incredibly cheap yet still comfortable Shosholoza Meyl tourist class trains. Whichever type of train you take, the Cape Town to Johannesburg route has to be one of the world's great train rides, from beneath Cape Town's Table Mountain, past the diamond mines at Kimberley to the country's economic hub at Johannesburg.

Train operator:	Shosholoza Meyl, **www.shosholozameyl.co.za** Premier Classe train, Cape Town–Johannesburg: **www.premierclasse.co.za** Luxury *Blue Train*, Cape Town–Pretoria: **www.bluetrain.co.za**
Time:	GMT+2
Currency:	£1 = approx. 11 rand, $1 = approx 7.3 rand
Tourist information:	**www.southafrica.net**, **www.safrica.info**
Visas:	UK, EU, US, Canadian, Australian and NZ citizens do not need a visa to visit South Africa.

EUROPE TO SOUTH AFRICA, without flying

Freight ships with limited passenger places, plus an occasional cruise liner link the UK with Cape Town. Start your search with Strand Travel (**www.strandtravelltd.co.uk**, telephone +44 (0)20 7921 4340) and www.cruisepeople.co.uk, two UK agencies which book both cruise liners and freighters. Cunard have occasional sailings from Southampton to Cape Town, see **www.cunard.com**. The St Helena steamship also has very occasional sailings from the UK to Cape Town, see **www.rms-st-helena.com**.

TRAIN TRAVEL WITHIN SOUTH AFRICA

There are several completely different train services in South Africa:

- **The *Blue Train*:** A world-famous luxury train from Cape Town to Pretoria once or twice a week. The *Blue Train* costs from R10,930 (£920 or $1,380) one-way, including meals, wine and even cigars.

- **Premier Classe trains:** An affordable twice-a-week deluxe service between Cape Town and Johannesburg, also now between Durban and Johannesburg, and Johannesburg and Hoedspruit for Kruger National Park. Cape Town–Jo'burg costs around R1,500 (£136 or $200) per person, including all meals and a private sleeper. It's highly recommended by travellers, who give Premier Classe rave reviews.

- **Shosholoza Meyl passenger trains:** South Africa's cheap, safe and comfortable long-distance tourist class trains are also highly recommended by travellers. The three-times-a-week Cape Town to Johannesburg train passes exactly the same wonderful scenery as the expensive *Blue Train*, but costs only R280–R560 rand (£25–£51 or $38–$77), including a bed in a 2- or 4-berth sleeper. Other routes include Cape Town to Durban (weekly), Johannesburg to Durban (daily except Tuesday), and Johannesburg to Port Elizabeth (daily except Saturday). Shosholoza Meyl also run economy class trains on various routes, with basic seats and a refreshment car.

- **Metro suburban trains:** Suburban ('Metro') trains around Johannesburg and Pretoria are not safe, which is why some South Africans will mistakenly tell you that all South African trains are unsafe. However, those around Cape Town can be used if you're careful, to reach Stellenbosch, Paarl and Simonstown.

- **Cruise trains:** There are several 'cruise' trains run by companies like Rovos Rail or Shongololo, aimed at tourists and charging western-style prices.

Each of these train services is described in more detail below.

Security

People who tell you that 'trains in South Africa are unsafe' may well never have been on one, and are probably confusing the civilised and safe Shosholoza Meyl trains with the suburban Metro trains around the big cities which they see adversely reported on South African TV. Shosholoza Meyl tourist class trains are perfectly safe to travel on, and can even be recommended for families and women travelling alone. Sleeping compartments have both a normal lock and a security lock which cannot be opened from the outside, and the train manager and his assistants do a good job looking after their passengers. It goes without saying that the high-end Premier Classe and *Blue Train* services are very safe, too. Having said that, you should take advice before walking into Johannesburg city centre. Johannesburg station (Park Station) itself is relatively safe and well patrolled with security guards and CCTV, but surrounding streets may not be, so arrange a car to pick you up at the station entrance.

THE *BLUE TRAIN*

It's the most famous train in South Africa, and one of the most famous luxury trains in the world. South Africa's *Blue Train* links Cape Town with Pretoria once or twice a week, year round. The luxury-level fares mean it's now aimed squarely at foreign visitors. However, the *Blue Train* is definitely the most fabulous way to travel between these two cities, and if you do choose to splurge, you will not be disappointed!

The train runs four or five times a month in each direction (it was two or three times a week before the collision in late 2005 which damaged one of the two sets of coaches used to run the service). Northbound it departs Cape Town at 08:50, arriving at Pretoria at 12:30 next day; southbound it leaves Pretoria at 08:50, arriving at Cape Town at 12:00 next day. The northbound journey includes a one-hour stop at the nineteenth-century health resort of Matjiesfontein in the heart of the Karoo. The southbound trip includes a stop at Kimberley for a tour of the Kimberley 'big hole' mining museum. The train no longer serves Johannesburg in either direction, as few tourists want to go there because of its security problems. The *Blue Train* rolling stock is also used to run irregular rail cruises, usually monthly from Pretoria to Victoria Falls, and also on a couple of other scenic routes within South Africa.

For more information, including details of departure dates, see **www.bluetrain.co.za**.

A bit of history

A fast train called the *Union Express* northbound and the *Union Limited* southbound was introduced in 1923 to link the Union Castle steamers arriving at Cape Town from Southampton with the goldfields of Jo'burg and the Transvaal capital at Pretoria. The original wooden coaches were replaced in 1937 with steel coaches built in Birmingham and painted a smart blue. Before long, the train became known colloquially as 'that blue train', and its name was changed officially to 'the *Blue Train*' in 1946. Two new sets of coaches were built for the *Blue Train* in 1972, and both of these were beautifully refurbished in 1997. You travel in these same trainsets today. The *Blue Train* is still run by the South African Railways ('Spoornet'), but it is now a separate business unit, due for privatisation.

On board the Blue Train

The *Blue Train* offers two types of room: deluxe compartments have either a double bed or two single beds and en suite shower or small bath; luxury compartments cost a bit more, but are almost identical except for having a full-size bath (yes, really) and a video. The train has a dining car and two lounge cars (one smoking, one non-smoking) and one of the two trainsets has an observation car at the rear, allowing you to look back along the line.

Meals and drinks (and even Montecristo Havana cigars!) are included in the fare, and there is an extensive list of South African wines available. You probably won't be able to drink £800-worth before you reach Pretoria, but you can have a damn good try.

How much does it cost?

The table shows prices for 2011.

Cape Town to Pretoria or vice versa, (meals and drinks included)	Low season (1 Jan to 31 Aug and 16 Nov to 31 Dec)	High season (1 Sept to 15 Nov)
Luxury suite, per person sharing	R11,805 (£1,073)	R14,685 (£1,335)
Luxury suite, per person sole occupancy	R17,705 (£1,610)	R21,830 (£1,985)
Deluxe suite, per person sharing	R10,930 (£994)	R13,485 (£1,226)
Deluxe suite, per person sole occupancy	R16,390 (£1,490)	R20,215 (£1,838)

How to buy tickets

For more information about travelling on the *Blue Train*, to check specific departure dates and to make reservations by email, see **www.bluetrain.co.za**. UK flight booking companies such as Travelbag or Trailfinders (**www.trailfinders.com**) can also organise the *Blue Train* for you.

If you'd rather travel on the *Blue Train* as part of an organised tour with other travellers, try Great Rail Journeys (**www.greatrail.com**), who offer escorted tours to South Africa which include the *Blue Train*.

PREMIER CLASSE TRAINS

This is an affordable deluxe service on key routes, aimed at both overseas visitors and South Africans themselves. If you can't afford the famous *Blue Train*, but still want safe, civilised deluxe travel at ground level through superb South African scenery that you can't see from 30,000 feet, take a Premier Classe train. Premier Classe started out in 1998 as a service from Cape Town to Johannesburg, originally running once a week attached to the regular Shosholoza Meyl *Trans-Karoo* train. In 2006 it was made into a completely separate train and increased to twice a week. In October 2008 they introduced a twice-weekly Durban–Johannesburg train, then in July 2009 they added a weekly overnight train from Jo'burg to Hoedspruit in the Kruger National Park – easily the best way to reach the Kruger game reserve.

Premier Classe trains are hotels on rails. They use standard South African Railways (Spoornet) sleeping-cars (in fact, the same 1960s–1970s type used by the Shosholoza Meyl tourist class trains) which have been refurbished to deluxe standards, but you are given twice the normal amount of space per passenger: solo passengers get sole occupancy of what would have been a 2-berth coupé; two passengers get sole use of what would have been a 4-berth compartment, i.e. there are no upper berths. The sleeping-cars aren't air-conditioned – a big advantage for photographers as the windows open! There's a deluxe Premier Classe restaurant car serving 3- to 5-course meals and a Premier Classe lounge car with armchairs, sofas and a bar. The fare includes all your meals and complimentary tea/coffee, although alcoholic drinks cost extra. Premier Classe passengers can use the luxury *Blue Train* VIP lounges at Cape Town and Johannesburg stations.

You can even take a car by Premier Classe: cars can be transported on these trains between Cape Town or Durban and Jo'burg, and between Cape Town and Port Elizabeth.

Timetables and fares are given below (pages 220–7). All information can be checked at **www.premierclasse.co.za**. Premier Classe is now a division of the new Passenger Rail Authority of South Africa (PRASA, **www.sarcc.co.za**).

SHOSHOLOZA MEYL TRAINS

South Africa's 'normal' long-distance passenger trains are perhaps the best-kept travel secret of all. Shosholoza Meyl – which means 'a pleasant experience' – was originally part of Spoornet (South African Railways) but it's now a division of the new Passenger Rail Authority of South Africa (PRASA, **www.sarcc.co.za**). Since 2006 its services have been divided into 'tourist class' with sleepers and restaurant car aimed at the middle classes, and 'economy class' with basic seats aimed at less affluent South Africans. Shosholoza Meyl trains are a great way to travel, as they let you see South Africa cheaply and comfortably at ground level, without having to fly or spend whole days and nights in a bus seat. The website is **www.shosholozameyl.co.za**.

Tourist class

The sleeping-cars have 4-berth rooms known as 'compartments' and smaller 2-berth rooms known as 'coupés'. The berths convert to seating for daytime use. There's a cut-away 3-D picture of the tourist class coach layout at **www.shosholozameyl.co.za**. Each compartment has basic leatherette bench seats which convert to bunks at night, and a washbasin with hot and cold water. Bedding is provided for a small extra charge (R20, about £1.80) and expertly made up for you in the evening by the train attendant. Each sleeping-car has a hot shower at the end of the corridor, with lockable shower cubicle and changing area – bring your own soap and towel. The coaches are not air-conditioned, so the windows open for a superb view of the countryside. A metal/mesh screen is provided for use at night to allow cool air in. Two passengers travelling together will normally be booked into a 2-berth coupé; a solo traveller will normally be booked into a 4-berth compartment with passengers of the same sex. The price is the same. If as a solo traveller you pay for two tickets (quite affordable, given the fare) you can have sole occupancy of a coupé. The whole train is non-smoking.

There's a restaurant car serving snacks, drinks and affordable complete meals. Catering used to be sub-contracted to caterers such as BJ's, the South African equivalent of Wimpy, but is now back in-house. A 'farmhouse breakfast' (their equivalent of full English) hits the spot in the morning, and beer and a wine list is available for something to go with your lunch or dinner. The food is not expensive, even by South African standards. Restaurant-car staff also come down the train to sell tea and coffee to you at your seat.

Economy class

Economy trains have basic 'sitter class' seating, which does not convert to berths. It's fine for daytime journeys, but not generally recommended for visitors on overnight trips unless you're prepared to rough it. They normally also have a restaurant or buffet car.

Timetables are given route by route below; for fares and how to buy tickets, see pages 228–31.

CAPE TOWN TO JOHANNESBURG, PRETORIA

Cape Town → Johannesburg, Pretoria

Days of running		Wed, Fri, Sun	Daily	Tue and Sat	Once or twice weekly
Type of train		Shosholoza Meyl tourist class	Shosholoza Meyl economy class	Premier Classe train	*Blue Train*
Cape Town	depart	12:30 day 1	10:00 day 1	09:05 Tue, Sat	08:50 day 1
Belleville	arr/dep	13:00 day 1	10:35 day 1	I	I
Wellington	arr/dep	13:59 day 1	11:36 day 1	I	I
Worcester	arr/dep	15:50 day 1	13:30 day 1	I	I
Matjiesfontein	arr/dep	17:55 day 1	15:36 day 1	I	I
Beaufort West	arr/dep	22:00 day 1	19:50 day 1	18:45 Tue, Sat	I
De Aar	arr/dep	02:40 day 2	23:45 day 1	22:35 Tue, Sat	I
Kimberley	arr/dep	06:45 day 2	03:46 day 2	03:00 Wed, Sun	I
Klerksdorp	arr/dep	11:30 day 2	08:26 day 2	I	I
Johannesburg	arrive	15:18 day 2	12:16 day 2	11:03 Wed, Sun	I
Pretoria	arrive	*	*	*	12:30 day 2

Pretoria, Johannesburg ➔ *Cape Town*

Days of running		Wed, Fri, Sun	Daily	Thur and Sun	Once or twice weekly
Type of train		Shosholoza Meyl tourist class	Shosholoza Meyl economy class	Premier Classe train	*Blue Train*
Pretoria	depart	*	*	*	08:50 day 1
Johannesburg	depart	10:30 day 1	12:30 day 1	15:00 Thur, Sun		
Klerksdorp	depart	14:15 day 1	16:25 day 1				
Kimberley	arr/dep	19:07 day 1	21:20 day 1	23:03 Thur, Sun		
De Aar	arr/dep	23:05 day 1	01:35 day 2	02:45 Fri, Mon		
Beaufort West	arr/dep	03:40 day 2	06:00 day 2	07:20 Fri, Mon		
Matjiesfontein	arr/dep	07:08 day 2	09:43 day 2				
Worcester	arr/dep	09:40 day 2	12:05 day 2				
Wellington	arr/dep	11:14 day 2	13:54 day 2				
Belleville	arr/dep	12:15 day 2	15:00 day 2				
Cape Town	arrive	12:40 day 2	15:30 day 2	16:16 Fri, Mon	12:00 day 2

Shosholoza Meyl tourist class train: 2- and 4-berth sleepers (convert to seating for daytime use), restaurant car.

Shosholoza Meyl economy class train: economy class seats only; OK for daytime trips but not recommended for overnight sections.

Premier Classe train: deluxe 1- and 2-berth sleepers, restaurant car, lounge.

The *Blue Train*: luxury sleeper train with suites, restaurant and lounges.

* Shosholoza Meyl and Premier Classe no longer run through-trains to/from Pretoria – since May 2006 they start/finish their journey at Johannesburg. Remember that Johannesburg city centre isn't safe for visitors, although the station itself has security and is well patrolled and secure. Be very careful if you walk outside the station. It's recommended that you pre-book a car or taxi to pick you up at Jo'burg station when you arrive, and when leaving again take a taxi or car to the station entrance. Pretoria is a safer city to use as a base when visiting the Jo'burg area.

CAPE TOWN TO DURBAN

Cape Town → *Durban*

Days of running		Wednesday	Monday
Type of train		Shosholoza Meyl tourist class train	Shosholoza Meyl economy class train
Cape Town	depart	18:00 Wed	18:50 Mon
Belleville	arr/dep	18:30 Wed	19:20 Mon
Worcester	arr/dep	21:20 Wed	22:15 Mon
Beaufort West	arr/dep	04:00 Thur	04:30 Tue
De Aar	arr/dep	08:30 Thur	08:40 Tue
Kimberley	arr/dep	12:25 Thur	12:45 Tue
Bloemfontein	arr/dep	15:35 Thur	15:59 Tue
Kroonstad	arrive	18:30 Thur	19:06 Tue
Ladysmith	arrive	01:43 Fri	02:05 Wed
Pietermaritzburg	arrive	04:59 Fri	05:55 Wed
Durban	arrive	07:45 Fri	08:10 Wed

Durban ➜ *Cape Town*

Days of running		Friday	Wednesday
Type of train		Shosholoza Meyl tourist class train	Shosholoza Meyl economy class train
Durban	depart	18:00 Fri	18:30 Wed
Pietermaritzburg	arr/dep	20:36 Fri	21:00 Wed
Ladysmith	arr/dep	23:55 Fri	01:00 Thur
Kroonstad	arr/dep	06:45 Sat	08:19 Thur
Bloemfontein	arr/dep	09:55 Sat	11:45 Thur
Kimberley	arr/dep	13:05 Sat	15:15 Thur
De Aar	arr/dep	17:05 Sat	19:40 Thur
Beaufort West	arrive	22:10 Sat	23:50 Thur
Worcester	arrive	04:25 Sun	05:45 Fri
Belleville	arrive	07:15 Sun	08:17 Fri
Cape Town	arrive	07:40 Sun	08:45 Fri

Shosholoza Meyl tourist class train: 2- and 4-berth sleepers (convert to seating for daytime use), restaurant car.

Shosholoza Meyl economy class train: economy class seats only; OK for daytime trips but not recommended for overnight sections.

JOHANNESBURG TO DURBAN

Johannesburg → Durban

Days of running		Tue and Fri	Daily except Tue
Type of train		Premier Classe	Shosholoza Meyl tourist and economy class train
Johannesburg	depart	18:20 day 1	18:30 day 1
Ladysmith	arr/dep	02:20 day 2	01:31 day 2
Pietermaritzburg	arr/dep	05:40 day 2	04:58 day 2
Durban	arrive	08:30 day 2	07:21 day 2

Durban → Johannesburg

Days of running		Wed and Sun	Daily except Tue
Type of train		Premier Classe	Shosholoza Meyl tourist and economy class train
Durban	depart	17:30 day 1	19:15 day 1
Pietermaritzburg	arr/dep	20:08 day 1	21:36 day 1
Ladysmith	arr/dep	23:28 day 1	00:42 day 2
Johannesburg	arrive	06:20 day 2	07:44 day 2

Premier Classe: deluxe 1- and 2-berth sleepers, restaurant car, lounge.

Shosholoza Meyl tourist class train: 2- and 4-berth sleepers (convert to seating for daytime use), restaurant car.

Shosholoza Meyl economy class train: economy class seats only; OK for daytime trips but not recommended for overnight sections.

JOHANNESBURG TO PORT ELIZABETH

Johannesburg ➜ *Port Elizabeth*

Days of running		Daily except Sat
Type of train		Shosholoza Meyl tourist and economy class train
Johannesburg	depart	13:15 day 1
Kroonstad	arr/dep	17:22 day 1
Bloemfontein	arr/dep	20:30 day 1
Nouport	arr/dep	02:35 day 2
Port Elizabeth	arrive	09:15 day 2

Port Elizabeth ➜ *Johannesburg*

Days of running		Daily except Sat
Type of train		Shosholoza Meyl tourist and economy class train
Port Elizabeth	depart	15:00 day 1
Nouport	arr/dep	22:29 day 1
Bloemfontein	arr/dep	04:46 day 2
Kroonstad	arr/dep	07:52 day 2
Johannesburg	arrive	11:35 day 2

Shosholoza Meyl tourist class train: 2- and 4-berth sleepers (convert to seating for daytime use), restaurant car.

Shosholoza Meyl economy class train: economy class seats only; OK for daytime trips but not recommended for overnight sections.

JOHANNESBURG TO EAST LONDON

Johannesburg → *East London*

Days of running		Daily except Sat
Type of train		Shosholoza Meyl economy class train Note A
Johannesburg	depart	14:20 day 1
Kroonstad	arr/dep	18:32 day 1
Bloemfontein	arr/dep	21:35 day 1
East London	arrive	10:20 day 2

East London → *Johannesburg*

Days of running		Daily except Sat
Type of train		Shosholoza Meyl economy class train Note A
East London	depart	14:15 day 1
Bloemfontein	arr/dep	04:08 day 2
Kroonstad	arr/dep	07:12 day 2
Johannesburg	arrive	10:50 day 2

Note A: This train is the *Amatola*, with economy class seats and 3- and 6-berth sleepers.

JOHANNESBURG TO HOEDSPRUIT (KRUGER PARK) AND KOMATIPOORT

Johannesburg → *Hoedspruit, Komatipoort*

Days of running		Thursday	Daily except Sat
Type of train		Premier Classe	Shosholoza Meyl economy class train Note A
Johannesburg	depart	17:45 Thursday	18:10 day 1
Pretoria	arr/dep	19:25 Thursday	19:40 day 1
Nelspruit	arr/dep	05:11 Friday	04:15 day 2
Hoedspruit (Kruger Park)	arrive	10:03 Friday	I
Kaapmuiden	arr/dep	–	05:15 day 2
Komatipoort	arrive	–	06:38 day 2

Komatipoort, Hoedspruit → *Johannesburg*

Days of running		Sunday	Daily except Sat
Type of train		Premier Classe	Shosholoza Meyl economy class train Note A
Komatipoort	depart	–	18:10 day 1
Kaapmuiden	arr/dep	–	19:40 day 1
Hoedspruit (Kruger Park)	depart	14:00 Sunday	I
Nelspruit	arr/dep	19:25 Sunday	20:40 day 1
Pretoria	arr/dep	06:30 Monday	04:50 day 2
Johannesburg	arrive	07:55 Monday	06:16 day 2

Premier Classe: deluxe 1- and 2-berth sleepers, restaurant car, lounge.

Note A: Runs daily except Saturday. This train is the *Komati*, with economy class seats only (it used to have sleepers, but no longer does). For onward connection to and from Maputo in Mozambique, see Mozambique chapter, page 202.

JOHANNESBURG AND PRETORIA TO MESSINA

A Shosholoza economy class train, the *Bosvelder*, runs daily except Saturday on this route. The train has economy seats only, so this overnight journey is one for those prepared to rough it.

From Johannesburg the train departs at 19:00, calling at Pretoria 20:56, and arriving at Louis Trichardt (Makhado) at 07:59 next morning, and Messina (Musina) at 11:15.

From Messina it departs at 15:25, calling at Louis Trichardt at 18:15, and arriving at Pretoria at 04:25 next morning, and Johannesburg at 05:44.

Messina is 12 km from the Zimbabwean frontier at Beitbridge (the other side of the Limpopo River), from where it is possible to get to Bulawayo or Harare; see the Zimbabwe chapter, page 252.

FARES

Fares for both Premier Classe and Shosholoza Meyl trains vary by month, so, for example, Cape Town to Jo'burg in tourist class is only R280 in August, R350–R380 in September–October, R280 in November, R560 in December and January. The fares shown below for Shosholoza Meyl trains represent roughly the middle of the price range.

For Shosholoza Meyl tourist class trains the fare includes a sleeper berth in a 2-, 3-, 4- or 6-berth sleeper compartment. Couples can request berths in a 2-berth compartment, though this can't be guaranteed. Bedding (sheets, blankets, pillow, made up for you by the train attendant) is an extra R25 (£2) or so per person, paid on the train.

The Premier Classe fares include a sleeper berth in a private 1- or 2-bed compartment (no extra charge for bedding), and all meals.

Cape Town to Johannesburg costs around R1,380–R2,480 (£125–£225 or $189–$340) each way per person in Premier Classe, depending on the season, including all meals and private sleeper. By tourist class train it costs around R350 (£32 or $48).

Cape Town to Kimberley one-way by tourist class train costs around R210 (£15 or $29).

Cape Town to Durban one-way by tourist class train costs around R415 (£38 or $57).

Durban to Johannesburg by Premier Classe costs around R750–R1,100 (£68–£100 or $103–$151) one-way per person with dinner, breakfast and private sleeper. By tourist class train it costs around R155 (£14 or $21).

Cape Town to Port Elizabeth by Premier Classe costs around R1,250 (£114 or $172) one-way per person with dinner, breakfast and private sleeper.

Johannesburg to Kimberley one-way by tourist class train costs around R110 (£10 or $15).

Johannesburg to Hoedspruit (Kruger Park) by Premier Classe costs around R980 (£89 or $134) one-way per person including dinner, breakfast and private sleeper.

The fares on Shosholoza Meyl economy class trains are very low: as an example, Cape Town to Johannesburg in a seat in the daily economy class train (not generally recommended for overseas visitors!) costs around R170 (£15 or $23), as does Johannesburg to Komatipoort.

On tourist class trains, all children under the age of 10, including infants and babies, travel at half fare, children of 10 or over pay full fare. On economy class and Premier Classe trains, children under 5 travel free, children aged 5 and up but under 10 travel at half fare, children of 10 and over pay full fare.

Return tickets are twice the one-way fare. There may be further reductions for students and seniors in off-peak periods, so ask when booking.

You can check fares for Premier Classe trains at **www.premierclasse.co.za**. You may be able to check Shosholoza Meyl fares (if they've uploaded them, which they usually haven't) at **www.shosholozameyl.co.za**.

Cars can be transported on Premier Classe trains between Cape Town or Durban and Jo'burg, at R1,100 (£100) per car to/from Durban or R1,780–R3,700 (£162–£336) per car to/from Cape Town. They can also be transported on Shosholoza Meyl trains: contact **www.shosholozameyl.co.za** for details.

Pets are not allowed on board, except guide dogs.

HOW TO BUY TICKETS

You cannot book Premier Classe tickets online, only by phone or email. Call +27 11 774 4555 or +27 12 334 8039 (lines open Monday–Friday, 09:00–16:30, GMT+2) or email your request to info_premierclasse@transnet.net. There is more information at the Premier Classe website, **www.premierclasse.co.za**. You can also book through a tour agency: **www.satravelbooking.co.za**.

For Shosholoza Meyl trains an online booking system does now seem to have been implemented at **www.shosholozameyl.co.za**, but as yet neither I nor any other seat61 correspondent has been able to get it to work. By all means try, but if you don't succeed, book by phone as follows:

> **From outside South Africa:** Call the Shosholoza Meyl reservations service on +27 11 774 4555. Bookings open 90 days before departure; you can't book before reservations open. You will be given a reference number, and can pick up your tickets at any station reservation office when you get to South Africa. Your ticket will not show your coach or berth number, but a passenger list showing which berth is allocated to which passenger is posted in a glass case at the station about an hour before departure. You may also be able to book by email, as there are contact details including email addresses for reservations staff, at **www.shosholozameyl.co.za**.

> **If you're in South Africa:** Call Shosholoza Meyl reservations on 086 000 8888 or book in person at any station reservation office. Bookings open 90 days before departure; you can't book before reservations open. Reservations are computerised, so any reservation office can book any journey in South Africa. When booking by phone, you will be given a booking reference number, which you quote at the station when you pick up and pay for your tickets. Your ticket will not show your coach or berth number, but a passenger list showing which berth is allocated to which passenger is posted in a glass case at the station about an hour before departure.

You should reserve as many days in advance as you can, rather than leaving it to the last minute – some trains, such as the *Trans-Karoo* from Cape Town to Johannesburg, regularly leave with all sleeper class berths fully booked.

SUBURBAN 'METRO' TRAINS

Metro trains around Johannesburg and Pretoria

Although long-distance Shosholoza Meyl trains are perfectly safe, Metro Rail suburban trains around Johannesburg and Pretoria are a different matter. Unless you are particularly foolhardy or adventurous, they are probably best avoided completely.

Metro trains around Cape Town

Metro Rail suburban trains around Cape Town are less of a problem and, providing you take care, leave your valuables at your hotel and don't travel after dark, they can be a good way to get from central Cape Town to the seaside town of Simonstown (a scenic run along the coast), or to the wine regions at Stellenbosch or Paarl. Indeed, there is a new initiative to encourage tourists to use the Cape Town–Simonstown train service to tour the coast. Two classes are available, first (Metro Plus) and third. Outside the rush hours, there is a train from Cape Town to Simonstown or Stellenbosch every hour or so, taking about an hour. Make sure you sit in a carriage with other travellers. To reach the wineries, bicycles can be hired in Stellenbosch for about £4 a day.

CRUISE TRAINS

Several companies run all-inclusive tours using special 'cruise' trains. Rovos Rail (**www.rovos.co.za**) runs a cruise train to a regular schedule from Cape Town to Pretoria and on to Victoria Falls. The train consists of beautifully restored South African coaches with all the usual tourist facilities – lounge, restaurant, private sleeping compartments and showers. Meals are included in the tour price. For times, dates of running and prices, see **www.rovos.co.za** or call +27 12 315 8242.

Another cruise train operating on various routes in Southern Africa and into neighbouring countries is Shongololo, **www.shongololo.com**, telephone +27 11 483 0657. Also try **www.jbtours.co.za**.

BUSES IN SOUTH AFRICA

The trains don't go everywhere in South Africa, and there are times when you might need to take a bus. There are several long-distance bus operators. Useful internet addresses are:

TransLux, **www.translux.co.za**, telephone +27 (011) 774 3333.

Greyhound, **www.greyhound.co.za**, telephone 083 915 9000

InterCape, **www.intercape.co.za**, telephone 0861 287 287, or from outside South Africa +27 21 380 4400.

MOVING ON FROM SOUTH AFRICA

See the route map on page 158. Unfortunately, there are now no international trains (other than occasional tourist cruise trains) from South Africa to Namibia, Botswana or Zimbabwe, but for information on international travel by a combination of train and bus from South Africa to Zimbabwe, see the Zimbabwe chapter, page 252. For onward travel to Zambia and Tanzania, see page 236. For travel to Namibia, see the Namibia chapter, pages 204–6. For travel to Botswana, see the Botswana chapter, pages 159–60. It is possible to reach Maputo in southern Mozambique by train: see the Mozambique chapter, page 202, and Johannesburg–Komatipoort timetable, page 227.

SUDAN

Sudan may not be the most popular destination, but the journey from Cairo to Khartoum by Egyptian train, Nile steamer and weekly Sudanese train is one of Africa's classic routes.

Train operator:	Sudan Railways Corporation, no official website
Time:	GMT+3
Currency:	£1 = approx 3.6 Sudanese pounds, $1 = approx. 2.3 Sudanese pounds
Tourist information:	**www.sudan.net/tourism.shtml**
Visas:	UK citizens and most other nationalities need a visa to visit Sudan, see **www.sudan-embassy.co.uk**.

EGYPT TO SUDAN, by train and steamer

It's possible to travel up the Nile from Cairo to Khartoum in Sudan by a combination of train, river steamer and train. For travel between Europe and Egypt, see pages 161–4.

Cairo, Aswan ➔ Wadi Halfa ➔ Khartoum

Travel by train from **Cairo** to **Aswan** – see the Egypt chapter, pages 169–72, for details.

A weekly Nile steamer, run by Nile Valley River Transport, sails every Monday at 12:00 from **Aswan High Dam** (El Sadd el Ali) to **Wadi Halfa** in Sudan, arriving on Tuesday. The first class fare (with cabin) is about LE131 (£16 or $24), meal included, the second class fare (deck place) is around LE78 (£10 or $15). Call (202) 578 9256 for information and reservations. You'll need to spend at least one night in Wadi Halfa.

A weekly train connects with the Nile steamer, leaving **Wadi Halfa** at 20:45 every Thursday (earlier reports have said Wednesday, please check locally), arriving at Atbara at 02:00 on Saturday morning and **Khartoum** (Bahri station) at 12:30 on Saturday. It has first class sleepers, first, second and third class seats. The train is slow, old and basic, but should get you there give or take the odd breakdown. It's not air-conditioned, so bring plenty of water: it can get very hot as the train crosses the desert. The Wadi Halfa–Khartoum first class fare is reportedly around £26 or $40.

Khartoum → Wadi Halfa → Aswan, Cairo

Travel from **Khartoum** to **Wadi Halfa** by train. The weekly train leaves Khartoum Bahri station at 08:40 on Monday, Atbara 19:00 on Monday, arriving at **Wadi Halfa** at 22:45 on Tuesday. Spend the night in Wadi Halfa.

Travel from **Wadi Halfa** to **Aswan High Dam** (El Sadd el Ali) by ferry, sailing from Wadi Halfa on Wednesday around 16:00, arriving in Aswan at lunchtime on Thursday. The northbound ferry fare is around £12 or $20 in first class. Don't forget the Sudan exit tax when leaving Sudan.

Travel from **Aswan** to **Cairo** by overnight air-conditioned sleeper train; see the Egypt chapter, pages 169–72.

Note: The Wadi Halfa to Khartoum train was reported as cancelled in summer 2010, while the tracks were repaired. Please check locally whether this train has resumed running.

TANZANIA AND ZAMBIA

You'll find three different rail networks in Tanzania and Zambia. Tanzanian Railways runs trains from Dar es Salaam northwest to Kigoma and Mwanza, although the service to Moshi and Arusha remains suspended; the famous TAZARA railway heads southwest to link Dar with Mbeya and Kapiri Mposhi in Zambia; and Railway Systems of Zambia operates trains within Zambia between Kitwe, Kapiri Mposhi and Livingstone, which is just across the border from Victoria Falls in Zimbabwe. TAZARA in particular provides an epic journey across Africa, offering insights into the Dark Continent which you simply won't get at 35,000 feet.

Train operators:	Tanzania Railways Corporation (TRC), **www.trctz.com** Tanzania and Zambia Railway Authority (TAZARA), **www.tazarasite.com** Railway Systems of Zambia, no website
Time:	GMT+2
Currency:	£1 = approx. 2,100 Tanzanian shillings = approx. 7,150 Zambian kwacha
Tourist information:	**www.tanzaniatouristboard.com**, **www.zambiatourism.com**
Visas:	UK, EU, US, Canadian, Australian and NZ citizens need a visa to visit both Tanzania and Zambia. Tanzanian and Zambian tourist visas can be bought at airports and border points, but it may be better to obtain them in advance from the relevant embassy. UK residents see **www.tanzania-online.gov.uk** and **www.zambia.embassyhomepage.com**.

EUROPE TO TANZANIA OR ZAMBIA, without flying

There appear to be few or no passenger-carrying freighters between Europe and Tanzania, although you can travel by freighter or the occasional cruise ship from Europe to Cape Town in South Africa, then make your way by train to Johannesburg, bus to Bulawayo, train to Victoria Falls and onward by bus and train to Lusaka in Zambia and ultimately Dar es Salaam in Tanzania. See the Southern African train routes map on page 158, and contact an agency such as Strand Travel (**www.strandtravelltd.co.uk**, telephone +44 (0)20 7921 4340) to ask about sea travel to South Africa.

DAR ES SALAAM TO KIGOMA, MWANZA, MPANDA, MOSHI, ARUSHA (TANZANIAN RAILWAYS)

See the route map on page 158. The Tanzanian Railways network serves northern Tanzania. Trains aren't running on the route from Dar es Salaam to Moshi or Arusha at the moment, but here's what is running to northern Tanzania. The Tanzanian Railways station in Dar es Salaam is about 8 km from the TAZARA station used by the trains serving the route through southern Tanzania into Zambia.

Dar es Salaam → Kigoma and Mwanza

Km	Classes		1, 2, 3	1, 2, 3
0	Dar es Salaam	depart	17:00 Tue, Fri, Sun	17:00 Tue, Fri
465	Dodoma	arr/dep	08:10 Wed, Sat, Mon	08:10 Wed, Sat
840	Tabora	arrive	18:25 Wed, Sat, Mon	18:25 Wed, Sat
840	Tabora	depart	20:10 Wed, Sat, Mon	21:30 Wed, Sat
1,256	Kigoma	arrive	07:25 Thur, Sun, Tue	l
1,220	Mwanza	arrive	–	07:35 Thur, Sun

Kigoma and Mwanza ➜ Dar es Salaam

Classes		1, 2, 3	1, 2, 3
Mwanza	depart	–	18:00 Thur, Sun
Kigoma	depart	17:00 Tue, Thur, Sun	I
Tabora	arrive	04:30 Wed, Fri, Mon	04:00 Fri, Mon
Tabora	depart	07:25 Wed, Fri, Mon	07:25 Fri, Mon
Dodoma	arr/dep	18:40 Wed, Fri, Mon	18:40 Fri, Mon
Dar es Salaam	arrive	08:50 Thur, Sat, Tue	08:50 Sat, Tue

On these trains first class consists of 2-berth sleepers; second class converts to 6-berth sleeper compartments for overnight use; third class is simple seating.

Change at Tabora for Mpanda: a train departs Tabora on Monday, Wednesday and Friday at 21:00, arriving in Mpanda at 10:30 next day.

In the other direction, a train leaves Mpanda on Tuesday, Thursday and Saturday at 13:00, arriving in Tabora at 02:45 next day, where you change trains for Dar es Salaam.

There's a route map at the official Tanzanian Railways Corporation website, **www.trctz.com/networkmain.htm**.

The one-way fare per person from Dar es Salaam to Kigoma is 54,900 shillings (£26 or $39) in a first-class sleeper, or 39,700 shillings (£19 or $28) in a second class sleeper.

ZANZIBAR

There is a range of ferries daily between Dar es Salaam and the island of Zanzibar, journey time 1 hour 30 minutes by fast ferry or up to 3 hours by ship. The cost is around £37/$55 economy class or £43/$65 first class. See **www.explorerkenya.com** and look for the small 'ferry service to Zanzibar' link.

DAR ES SALAAM TO KAPIRI MPOSHI (TAZARA)

The Tanzania and Zambia Railway Authority (TAZARA) runs trains between Dar es Salaam, Mbeya and Kapiri Mposhi, taking two nights. See the route map

on page 158. The trains have sleeping-cars and a restaurant car, and the journey
is a great adventure. The line is 1,860 km long and was only opened in 1976,
built with Chinese funding and assistance.

The times shown here reflect the new timetable introduced in October 2008
and still in force in 2010. There are no longer any additional local trains Dar es
Salaam–Mbeya or Kapiri Mposhi–Nakonde, just the two trains shown here –
one train per week an express, the other now an ordinary train. There are two
trainsets, used for either service, one named the *Kilimanjaro*, the other the
Mukuba Express (*mukuba* means 'copper' in the Bemba language). There are two
official TAZARA websites: **www.tazara.co.tz** has been 'under construction' for
several years, but there is basic information at **www.tazarasite.com**. Please
double-check exact times locally.

In Dar es Salaam these trains arrive at and depart from the TAZARA
station, which is about 8 km from the Tanzanian Railways station. In Kapiri
Mposhi they arrive at and depart from the 'new' station, which is about 2 km
from the 'old' Zambian Railways station used by the trains on the
Livingstone–Lusaka–Kitwe route.

Dar es Salaam → Mbeya → Kapiri Mposhi

Km			*Mukuba* or *Kilimanjaro* express service 1S, 2S, 2, 3, M or R	*Mukuba* or *Kilimanjaro* ordinary train 1S, 2S, 2, 3, R
0	Dar es Salaam	depart	15:50 Tuesday	13:50 Friday
849	Mbeya	arrive	13:08 Wednesday	14:10 Saturday
		depart	13:23 Wednesday	14:40 Saturday
969	Tunduma (frontier)	arrive	17:02 Wednesday	18:38 Saturday
		depart	17:17 Wednesday	18:53 Saturday
970	Nakonde	arrive	16:22 Wednesday	17:58 Saturday
		depart	16:47 Wednesday	18:18 Saturday
1852	Kapiri Mposhi (New)	arrive	09:26 Thursday	13:37 Sunday

Kapiri Mposhi → *Mbeya* → *Dar es Salaam*

		Mukuba or *Kilimanjaro* express service 1S, 2S, 2, 3, M or R	*Mukuba* or *Kilimanjaro* ordinary train 1S, 2S, 2, 3, R
Kapiri Mposhi (New)	depart	16:00 Tuesday	14:00 Friday
Nakonde	arrive	08:39 Wednesday	09:13 Saturday
	depart	09:09 Wednesday	09:23 Saturday
Tunduma (frontier)	arrive	10:14 Wednesday	10:30 Saturday
	depart	10:29 Wednesday	10:45 Saturday
Mbeya	arrive	14:13 Wednesday	14:32 Saturday
	depart	14:28 Wednesday	15:00 Saturday
Dar es Salaam	arrive	12:35 Thursday	15:46 Sunday

1S = first class 4-berth sleepers

2S = second class 6-berth sleepers

2 = second class seats

3 = third class seats

M = meal at seat service

R = restaurant car

Fares

One-way fare per person, travelling on express train. Ordinary train fares are around 20 per cent less.	
Dar es Salaam to Kapiri Mposhi	72,600 Tanzanian shillings (£35 or $52) in 1st class sleeper
Dar es Salaam to Mbeya	37,000 Tanzanian shillings (£18 or $26) in 1st class sleeper
Kapiri Mposhi to Dar es Salaam	237,000 Zambian kwacha (£33 or $50) in 1st class sleeper 198,000 kwacha (£28 or $42) in 2nd class sleeper 171,600 kwacha (£24 or $36) in 2nd class seat 145,200 kwacha (£20 or $30) in 3rd class seat
Kapiri Mposhi to Mbeya	118,800 Zambian kwacha (£17 or $26) in 1st class sleeper 86,600 kwacha (£12 or $18) in 2nd class sleeper 79,100 kwacha (£11 or $17) in 2nd class seat 71,400 kwacha (£10 or $15) in 3rd class seat

On TAZARA trains children under 7 travel free, children 7 and over but under 15 pay half fare.

The sleepers are single sex, so men and women will be in separate compartments unless your party books the complete compartment.

How to buy tickets

You cannot buy tickets online. You can either buy them at the station, or you can try booking by phone, calling the Kapiri (Zambia) booking office on +260 21 1220646 for eastbound journeys or the Dar es Salaam office on +255 22 26 2191 for westbound journeys.

Alternatively, to buy tickets from outside the country, try contacting a local travel agency. For arranging train tickets starting in Dar es Salaam, **www.inihotours.co.tz** has been suggested as one option; another suggested option is Sykes Travel Ltd (**www.sykestravel.com**, telephone +255 22 2115542, email **abe@sykestravel.com**).

KITWE TO KAPIRI MPOSHI TO LUSAKA TO LIVINGSTONE (Railway Systems of Zambia)

A concession called Railway Systems of Zambia has taken over from Zambia Railways, running passenger trains between Livingstone, Lusaka, Kapiri Mposhi (change for TAZARA trains to Dar es Salaam in Tanzania) and Kitwe. See the route map on page 158. Note that these trains use the 'old' Zambian Railways station in Kapiri Mposhi, which is about 2 km from the 'new' station used by the TAZARA trains.

Until 2006, there were four classes of accommodation on these trains: sleeper class with 2-berth and 4-berth compartments, first and second class upholstered reclining seat, and economy class with basic hard seats. However, handing the line over to a concession has meant the withdrawal of all sleepers, and from 2006 the train has had economy class seats only, using ex-South African economy seats cars.

Livingstone → *Lusaka* → *Kitwe*

km			Note A
0	Livingstone	depart	20:00 Mon, Fri
467	Lusaka	arrive	13:20 Tue, Sat
		depart	14:20 Tue, Sat
652	Kapiri Mposhi	arr/dep	21:30 Tue, Sat
785	Ndola	arr/dep	02:50 Wed, Sun
851	Kitwe	arrive	06:00 Wed, Sun

Kitwe → *Lusaka* → *Livingstone*

		Note A
Kitwe	depart	08:45 Mon, Fri
Ndola	arr/dep	11:30 Mon, Fri
Kapiri Mposhi	arr/dep	16:42 Mon, Fri
Lusaka	arrive	23:50 Mon, Fri
	depart	00:30 Tue, Sat
Livingstone	arrive	18:45 Tue, Sat

Note A: Economy class seats only. No sleepers or first class. Run by Railway Systems of Zambia using South African passenger coaches.

Fares

The one-way fare per person in economy class (the only one available) is around 30,000 Zambian kwacha (£4 or $6) for Livingstone–Lusaka, 43,000 kwacha (£6 or $9) for Livingstone–Kapiri Mposhi, 13,000 kwacha (£2 or $3) for Lusaka–Kapiri Mposhi. Children under 6 travel free, children over 6 but under 14 pay half fare. Just buy tickets at the station.

MOVING ON FROM TANZANIA OR ZAMBIA

From Tanzania there are buses to Kenya, running from Dar es Salaam to Nairobi, and possibly to Mombasa: see the Kenya chapter page 184 for details.

From Zambia you can get to Zimbabwe, either by crossing from Livingstone to Victoria Falls as described below or by bus from Lusaka to Harare. There is also a twice-a-week bus service from Livingstone to Windhoek (Namibia): see the Namibia chapter, page 209, or **www.intercape.co.za**.

Livingstone to Victoria Falls

Victoria Falls (Zimbabwe) and Livingstone (Zambia) are about 13 km apart either side of the Zim/Zam border across the Zambezi River. Although they are linked by a railway line there are currently no passenger trains between the two places – other than irregular steam specials. However, you can take a taxi from Livingstone the few miles to the frontier, walk through the Zambian border post, and walk across the famous road/rail bridge spanning the Zambezi River gorge (resisting the urge to bungee-jump) to the Zimbabwean border post. Once you have passed through Zimbabwe customs it's an easy walk between the border post and central Victoria Falls. For trains between Victoria Falls and Bulawayo (for buses to South Africa), see the Zimbabwe chapter, page 253.

TUNISIA

Tunisia has a good rail network, with fast, comfortable air-conditioned trains linking Tunis with Sousse, Sfax, Gabès and Tozeur. There is also a branch line to Mahdia and the popular holiday resort of Monastir. If you'd rather not fly to Tunisia that's no problem, as comfortable cruise ferries sail to Tunisia from Marseilles or Genoa every few days. It can take as little as 48 hours to go from London to Marseilles by Eurostar and high-speed TGV, then Marseilles to Tunis by cruise ferry.

Train operator:	Société Nationale des Chemins de Fer Tunisiens (SNCFT), **www.sncft.com.tn**
Ferries to Tunisia:	Marseille–Tunis, Genoa–Tunis: SNCM, **www.sncm.fr**; Compagnie Tunisienne de Navigation (CTN), **www.ctn.com.tn** Genoa–Tunis: Grandi Navi Veloci, **www.gnv.it**
Time:	GMT+1
Currency:	£1 = approx. 2.1 dinars, $1 = approx. 1.4 dinars
Tourist information:	**www.cometotunisia.co.uk**
Visas:	UK, most EU, US and Canadian citizens do not need a visa to visit Tunisia. Australian and NZ citizens require a visa.

LONDON TO TUNISIA, by train and ferry

You don't need to fly to reach Tunisia. Take Eurostar and a high-speed TGV from London to Marseilles, then a comfortable cruise ferry to Tunis, and you can step ashore in Tunisia just 48 hours after leaving St Pancras. Here's how.

London ➜ Tunis, via Marseilles

Day 1: Travel from **London** to **Marseilles** by train, leaving London St Pancras by Eurostar at 14:04 (14:34 on Sunday), changing at Lille Europe (arrive 16:24, depart 17:54) on to a direct TGV to Marseilles, arriving at Marseille St Charles at 22:46 (22:21 on Sunday). Alternative trains are available if you'd like to leave London earlier and spend an afternoon or evening in Marseilles.

It's a very scenic trip, as south of Lyon the TGV runs along the Rhône Valley, crossing and re-crossing the River Rhône, flying at ground level through the hills of Provence over some impressive viaducts to reach Marseilles. Watch out for a dramatic viaduct over the Rhône just before Avignon, with views of the famous 'Palais des Papes' in the distance (though if you can spot anyone dancing 'sur le pont d'Avignon' you've got better eyesight than me). You'll catch a glimpse of Marseilles harbour with its Château d'If of Count of Monte Cristo fame to your right just before arriving at Marseille St Charles station. Spend the night in a hotel.

Day 2: Sail from **Marseilles** to **Tunis** by cruise ferry, usually leaving in the morning or at lunchtime and arriving in Tunis the following morning (day 3). Two ferry companies, the French SNCM and the Tunisian CTN (Compagnie Tunisienne de Navigation), sail from Marseilles to Tunis several times a week all year round. Sailing times and dates vary, so see **www.sncm.fr** for actual times and fares for both SNCM and CTN ferries for your dates of travel. CTN also have their own website, **www.ctn.com.tn**, although without online booking. Both French SNCM and Tunisian CTN ships are modern and comfortable with a full range of restaurants, bars, cinema and cabins. Make sure you're on deck as the ship sails out of the port of Marseilles, past the fishing boats in the Vieux Port and the infamous Château d'If, with great views of the city. Twenty-four hours later you've crossed the Mediterranean, and the ship sails into the Bay of Tunis, past the ruins of the ancient city of Carthage on Byrsa Hill, with a real sense of arrival that airline passengers will never know.

Day 3: The ferry arrives at Tunis international ferry terminal at La Goulette, about 6 miles (10 km) from Tunis city centre. You can either take a taxi (10–15 dinars, £5–£7, but insist that the driver uses the meter), or walk to the nearby La Goulette station on the Tunis–Marsa 'TGM' light railway and take a train two stops to the Tunis Marine station at the end of the line, journey time about 15 minutes. There are banks in La Goulette for local currency to buy a ticket.

Tunis ➔ *London, via Marseilles*

Day 1: Sail from **Tunis** to **Marseilles** by cruise ferry. Ferries sail several times a week, usually at around 11:00 or 12:30, arriving in Marseilles the following day (day 2) at 08:30, 10:30 or occasionally 14:00. Sailing times and dates vary, so see **www.sncm.fr** for times and fares for both SNCM and CTN ferries. Tunis international ferry terminal is at La Goulette, 6 miles (10 km) from the city centre; you can get there by taxi or by light railway plus a short walk.

Day 2: Travel by train from **Marseilles** to **London**. Allow at least 3 hours to make a connection in Marseilles between the scheduled arrival of the ferry and the departure of your train. If the ferry arrives 08:00–09:30, there's a 13:39 TGV high-speed train from Marseilles; change at Lille (arrive 18:37, depart 19:35) on to Eurostar, arriving London St Pancras at 19:56, still on day 2. If your ferry arrives 09:30–11:00, there's a 15:28 TGV to Paris arriving Paris Gare de Lyon at 18:41; change trains and stations in Paris and take the Eurostar leaving Paris Gare du Nord at 20:13, arriving London 21:36. If your ferry is due to arrive any later than 11:00, then you should plan to spend the night in a hotel and travel the next day (day 3). This advice takes into account the fact that ferries can sometimes arrive late.

How much does it cost?

The fare from London to Marseilles starts at £68 one-way or £119 return by Eurostar+TGV high-speed train.

From Marseilles to Tunis, a ferry ticket starts at £141 single, £281 return, including a berth in a 4-berth cabin. You can check fares for different cabin types and dates at **www.sncm.fr**.

How to buy tickets

Book the ferry first, either online at **www.sncm.fr** or by phone through SNCM's and CTN's UK agent, Southern Ferries (www.southernferries.co.uk), on 0844 815 7785. Make a note of the sailing dates and times.

Then book the train from London to Marseilles. You can book online at either **www.raileurope.co.uk** or **www.voyages-sncf.com,** but a top tip is to break the journey down into two separate bookings, one from London to Lille or Paris and back, the other from Lille or Paris to Marseilles and back (this allows you to mix and match classes and fare types on each leg, and it often results in a cheaper total fare). If you book this way, you can still pay for all the tickets together, by adding each ticket to the website's 'shopping basket'. If you prefer to book by phone you can call Rail Europe on 0844 848 5848 (lines open 09:00–21:00 Monday to Friday, 09:00–18:00 Saturday), or you can book through any European rail-appointed travel agent such as Ffestiniog Travel (01766 772050).

London ➜ Tunis, via Genoa

It's also possible to travel from London to Tunisia via Genoa in Italy. In fact, the ferry from Genoa may be a bit cheaper than from Marseilles, but the train from London to Genoa is usually more expensive and less convenient than London to Marseilles. If you'd like to go via Genoa, SNCM (French) and CTN (Tunisian) provide a joint ferry service from Genoa to Tunis once or twice a week, with fares starting at about £85 single, £155 return; visit **www.sncm.fr** to check fares and sailing dates for both companies.

Grandi Navi Veloci (Italian) also sail from Genoa to Tunis two or three times a week; see **www.gnv.it** to check fares and sailing dates.

For details of train times and fares between London and Genoa, and how to buy tickets, see **www.seat61.com/Italy.htm** or my first book, *The Man in Seat 61: A guide to taking the train from the UK through Europe.*

TRAIN TRAVEL WITHIN TUNISIA

Tunisian trains have three classes of accommodation: second class, first class and *classe confort*, although new railcars delivered in 2008 have just one class, called 'Express'. Second class is perfectly adequate, first class very comfortable. *Classe confort* is very similar to first class, but with even more space. The overnight trains have no sleeping berths, just seats. You can double-check times at the official SNCFT website, **www.sncft.com.tn** (in French, as the English version is 'under construction').

Tunis → Sousse, Sfax, Tozeur, Gabès

	Daily	Daily	Daily	Daily	Daily	Daily	Daily	Daily	Daily	Daily	Daily	Mon-Fri	Daily	Daily	Daily	Daily	Daily	Daily
Classes	2	C,1,2	E	E	C,1,2	C,1,2	E		C,1,2	C,1,2	C,1,2	C,1,2	C,1,2	C,1,2	C,1,2	C,1,2	C,1,2	C,1,2
Tunis	–	06:00	07:05	08:00	08:40	09:40	11:20	12:05	12:35	13:05	13:25	15:40	16:30	17:35	18:00	18:45	20:50	22:20
Sousse (Kalaâ Séghira)*	–			09:37			12:45		14:22	14:49		17:36	18:07		19:45	20:41		
Sousse (Ville)	x	08:07	08:36		10:50	11:41		13:58			15:15	17:43		19:27		20:48	22:55	00:25
Monastir	x		–		11:30			–	15:07		–	–		–		–		
Mahdia	x		–		–			–	16:00		–	–		–		–		
El Jem	–	09:00	–		–	12:36	13:23	–	–	15:38	–	–		–	20:31	–	23:48	01:18
Sfax	–	10:00	–	11:00	–	13:27	14:00	–	–	16:33	–	–	19:35	–	21:20	–	00:40	02:15
Gafsa	–		–	–	–	16:34	–	–	–		–	–		–	–	–	03:47	
Metlaoui	–		–	–	–	17:11	–	–	–		–	–		–	–	–	04:24	
Tozeur	–		–	–	–	17:59	–	–	–		–	–		–	–	–	05:12	
Gabès	–	12:06	–	–	–	–	–	–	–	18:33	–	–	21:25	–	–	–	–	04:15

Gabès, Tozeur, Sfax, Sousse → Tunis

	Mon–Fri	Daily	Mon–Fri	Daily	Daily	Daily	Daily	Daily	Daily	Daily	Daily	Daily	Daily	Daily	Daily	Daily	Daily	Daily
Classes	C,1,2	2	C,1,2	C,1,2	C,1,2	C,1,2	E	C,1,2	C,1,2	C,1,2	C,1,2	E	C,1,2	C,1,2	C,1,2	C,1,2	C,1,2	C,1,2
Gabès	–	–	–	–	05:00	–	–	–	–	11:15	–	–	–	–	–	16:10	00:05	–
Tozeur	–	–	–	–	|	–	–	–	06:30	|	–	–	–	–	–	|	|	20:30
Metlaoui	–	–	–	–	|	–	–	–	07:21	|	–	–	–	–	–	|	|	21:21
Gafsa	–	–	–	–	|	–	–	–	08:00	|	–	–	–	–	–	|	|	22:00
Sfax	–	–	–	05:25	06:53	–	–	–	11:20	13:30	–	14:55	16:30	–	–	18:22	02:10	01:15
El Jem	–	–	–	06:15	|	–	–	–	12:07	14:21	–	15:37	|	–	–	19:15	02:57	02:08
Mahdia	–	x	–	|	|	–	–	–	|	|	–	|	|	16:58	–	|	|	|
Monastir	–	x	–	|	|	–	–	11:45	|	|	–	|	|	18:00	–	|	|	|
Sousse (Ville)	05:10	x	06:15	07:23	|	08:45	09:30	12:35	13:15	|	15:30	|	|	|	18:05	20:22	04:04	03:15
Sousse (Kalaâ Séghira)	05:18	–	|	|	08:17	|	|	|	|	|	15:07	|	16:17	17:54	18:30	|	|	|
Tunis	07:20	–	08:09	09:15	09:53	10:38	11:00	14:35	1506	16:50	17:24	17:35	19:30	20:20	19:57	22:15	05:54	05:07

* Sousse Kalaâ Séghira station is 8 km west of Sousse and is easily reached from the town centre by *louage* (shared taxi).

x = regular electric trains link Sousse (Sousse Bab Jedid station, 500 m from Sousse Ville) with Monastir and Mahdia every hour or so throughout the day.

C,1,2 = first and second class plus *classe confort*.

E = express class in new fast railcar.

Tunis to Bizerte

Tunis to Bizerte by train is 98 km, journey time 1 hour 35 minutes, second class only. There are departures from Tunis at 05:55 (Mon–Fri only), 11:55, 14:30 (Fri and Sat only), 16:10 (daily except Fri and Sat), 18:25. Departures from Bizerte are at 05:40 (Mon–Fri only), 08:20, 14:15, 18:35. See **www.sncft.com.tn**.

Tunis to Kalaâ Kasbah

Trains leave Tunis at 06:02 and 14:15, arriving at Kalaâ Kasbah at 11:05 and 19:11 respectively. Returning, trains leave Kalaâ Kasbah at 05:45 and 12:45, arriving at Tunis at 10:32 and 17:35 respectively. See **www.sncft.com.tn**.

Tunis to Carthage and Marsa

There is a light railway (run by SMLT) linking Tunis centre, La Goulette (for the ferry terminal to Marseilles and Genoa), Carthage (for the ancient ruins and Byrsa Hill) and Marsa Plage. Departures are at frequent intervals from 04:00 to 00:50 and the fare is about 0.7 dinar (£0.35).

Kairouan

Kairouan is one of Tunisia's most historic cities. There is no railway station at Kairouan, but regular SNTRI buses run from Sousse to Kairouan taking 1½ hours, and from Tunis to Kairouan every hour taking 2½ hours. There are also shared taxis (*louages*) from Sousse to Kairouan about every 30 minutes throughout the day.

Fares and how to buy tickets

Tunisian Railways has an official website at **www.sncft.com.tn**. You can book online within three days of departure, but it's easy to book Tunisian rail tickets at the station in Tunis – bookings only open three days in advance, so don't worry about pre-booking before you get to Tunisia.

Approximate one-way fare	Classe confort	1st class	2nd class
Tunis to Sousse	10.5 dinar (£5 or $10)	9.8 dinar (£4.70 or $9)	7.3 dinar (£3.50 or $7)
Tunis to Sfax	17 dinar (£8 or $16)	16 dinar (£7 or $12)	11.9 dinar (£5.50 or $9)
Tunis to Gabès	25 dinar (£12 or $24)	23.5 dinar (£11 or $22)	17.4 dinar (£8 or $16)
Tunis to Monastir	–	–	7 dinar (£3.50 or $7)

Children aged 0–3 travel free, children aged 4–9 travel at 75 per cent of the adult fare, children aged 10 and over pay full fare.

10-day return tickets are 15 per cent less than the cost of two one-way tickets.

Railpasses – 'Carte Bleue'

Tunisian Railways offers an excellent 'Carte Bleue' railpass for 7, 15 or 21 days, valid for unlimited travel in first, second or *classe confort* class. Prices for a 7-day pass are around 19.5 dinar (£10) second class, 27.3 dinar (£13) first class, 29.3 dinar (£14) *classe confort*. Prices for a 15-day pass are twice the 7-day price; 21-day prices are three times the 7-day price. Although the pass gives you unlimited travel, you still need to pay a small air-conditioning supplement for travel on any air-conditioned train, which means almost all the long-distance ones – in second class the supplement is 0.7 dinar (£0.35) for up to 100 km, 0.9 dinar (£0.45) for 101–160 km, 1.4 dinar (£0.70) for 161–300 km and 1.8 dinar (£0.90) for over 300 km. Just pay this supplement at the ticket office before making each journey using the pass. Railpasses can be bought at Tunisian railway stations – in theory you need a passport-sized photo to buy these passes, but it is reported that showing your passport may be sufficient.

The Lézard Rouge *tourist train*

A privately run tourist train called the *Lézard Rouge* runs from Metlaoui to the Gorges de Selja, a 40-minute, 43-km ride through spectacular scenery. It runs from 1 May to 30 September, daily except Saturday, departing Metlaoui at 10:00 on Tuesday, Thursday and Sunday, or 10:30 on Monday, Wednesday and Friday, arriving at Gorges de Selja 40 minutes later, then departing after a 20-minute stop and arriving at Metlaoui 45 minutes later, total trip length around 1 hour 45 minutes. The fare is 20 dinars (£10) for adults, 12.50 dinars (£6.50) for children under 10, children under 4 travel free. You can confirm this information, but currently only in French, at **www.sncft.com.tn** – click 'Français' to select their French language version, then look for 'tourisme' then 'trains touristiques'.

ZIMBABWE

Zimbabwe, or 'Zim' as it is known locally, has had its trials and tribulations in recent years. However, it's a rewarding country to visit, with friendly local people, the famous Victoria Falls and other beautiful national parks to see such as Hwange or Matobo, where Cecil Rhodes is buried. There's no better way to reach Victoria Falls than on the overnight train from Bulawayo, which still uses British-built sleeping-cars dating from the 1950s. The carriages may have become somewhat ropey, and your compartment lights may or may not work, but taking this classic train to the Falls is an adventure no traveller should miss. There is also an overnight train between Bulawayo and Harare and on several other routes.

Train operator:	National Railways of Zimbabwe, no official website but there is some information on **www.planet.nu/sunshinecity/nrz/railinfo.html**
Time:	GMT+2
Currency:	Zimbabwean dollars are no longer in use. US$ are commonly used.
Tourist information:	**www.zimbabwetourism.co.zw**
Visas:	Most nationalities now need a visa to visit Zimbabwe, but UK, US, Canadian, Australian and some EU citizens can buy a visa at the point of entry for about £35.

EUROPE TO ZIMBABWE, without flying

You can travel by passenger-carrying freighter or the occasional cruise ship from Europe to Cape Town in South Africa, then make your way by train to Johannesburg and bus to Bulawayo or Harare. See the African train routes

map on page 158, and contact an agency such as Strand Travel
(**www.strandtravelltd.co.uk**, telephone +44 (0)20 7921 4340) to ask about sea
travel to South Africa.

SOUTH AFRICA TO ZIMBABWE, by train or bus

Whatever you may read in your guidebook, there are unfortunately no direct
scheduled trains now from South Africa to Zimbabwe, and have not been for
some years. If your guidebook is a few years old, it may mention weekly trains
from Johannesburg to Harare and Bulawayo, but for political reasons (in fact,
exorbitant haulage charges imposed by the National Railways of Zimbabwe)
these were suspended in 1999. Similarly, the daily train that used to link
Mafeking and Bulawayo via Gaborone was first cut back to run purely within
Botswana, and was then withdrawn completely in 2009. In 2007, National
Railways of Zimbabwe were allegedly considering reinstating a
Harare–Johannesburg train some time before 2010, but nothing has come of
this. So there are now several less-than-brilliant choices for overland travel from
South Africa to Zimbabwe (see the route map on page 158).

Johannesburg ➔ *Bulawayo by bus*

Two companies run modern buses overnight from Johannesburg/
Pretoria to Bulawayo, with departures most nights. The journey takes
about 13 hours from Pretoria. Visit **www.greyhound.co.za** and
www.translux.co.za for details. Although neither as civilised nor as
comfortable as a train, this is probably the simplest overland option.

Johannesburg ➔ *Bulawayo, by train or train+bus*

You can take the overnight Shosholoza Meyl economy train (see the
South Africa chapter, page 228), with seats but now no sleepers, from
Johannesburg or Pretoria to Messina. Messina is 12 km short of the
frontier at Beitbridge, from where you can take irregular African buses

to both Harare and Bulawayo. Alternatively, a train links Beitbridge and Bulawayo twice a week, leaving Beitbridge at 21:00 on Monday and Friday and arriving in Bulawayo at 08:45 next morning. In the other direction, it leaves Bulawayo at 18:30 on Thursday and Sunday, arriving in Beitbridge at 10:00 next morning. The train has first and second class sleepers and economy class seats.

South Africa ➔ *Zimbabwe by cruise train*

If you have the money, there are several tourist 'cruise' trains. The *Blue Train* (**www.bluetrain.co.za**) operates from Pretoria to Victoria Falls about once a month. However, you can reckon on a one-way fare exceeding £500. Rovos Rail (**www.rovos.co.za**) also operates on this route. Check that these trains are still operating – National Railways of Zimbabwe's high haulage rates have hit these companies, too.

BULAWAYO TO VICTORIA FALLS

This classic overnight train is *the* way to reach Victoria Falls from Bulawayo, even though (given Zimbabwe's economic situation) it's now getting very down-at-heel. It's an experience in itself, a piece of history with British-built coaches, some with wood-panelled interiors, dating from 1952 and 1958. The train might just receive new coaches at some point, as it was reported way back in 2006 that 64 new long-distance coaches were due to be delivered from China, but there's no sign of them yet, even in 2010.

The service now runs five days a week (it used to be daily, but was cut back in May 2009): it departs Bulawayo at 20:00 on Tuesday, Thursday, Friday, Saturday and Sunday, calling at Dete 01:29, Hwange 03:04, and arriving at Victoria Falls at 07:00 according to the timetable, but in practice more likely around 09:00 or even later. From Victoria Falls it departs at 18:30 on Monday, Wednesday, Friday, Saturday and Sunday, calling at Hwange 22:22, Dete 00:50, and arriving at Bulawayo at 07:00 – though, as with the outward journey, you should not expect to make Bulawayo before 09:00 in practice.

Fares

Fares are incredibly cheap, even judged at the very poor official exchange rate. The one-way first class sleeper fare from Bulawayo to Victoria Falls is about £5 or $8 at the prevailing official rate of exchange. A second class sleeper ticket costs about £3 ($5).

How to buy tickets

You can buy tickets at Bulawayo station reservation office or the Victoria Falls reservation window, up to 30 days before departure. Reservations are not fully computerised, and can only be made for trains leaving from that station – reservations for your return journey will need to be made when you reach your destination. Your ticket will not show your coach or berth number – this will be shown on a passenger list posted in a glass case on the platform about an hour before the train departs. Although the train appears to be well used, it's a long train with plenty of berths available, and there is unlikely to be a problem getting a place even for travel on the same day.

What's the train like?

There are three classes on the Bulawayo–Victoria Falls train:

> **First class sleepers**, which have 2-berth rooms (known as coupés) and 4-berth rooms (known as compartments). These have leatherette bench seats convertible to bunks, and each room has a washbasin with (cold) water. Full bedding used to be provided, but this is no longer the case, so perhaps buy a cheap blanket or two before boarding if you can. The windows open for a clear view of the countryside, and at night there is a metal/mesh screen to allow cool air in whilst keeping you secure. The carriage lights may not work, so a torch is handy!

> **Second class sleepers**, which are identical to first class sleepers except that there are 3 berths per coupé and 6 berths per compartment.

> **Economy class seats**: basic seating, which does not convert to bunks.

In first class, two passengers travelling together will normally be booked into a 2-berth coupé, whereas a solo traveller will be booked into a 4-berth compartment with passengers of the same sex. If as a solo traveller you pay for two tickets (perfectly affordable, given the fare) you can have sole occupancy of a coupé.

The sleeping-cars are all British-built, the ones with wood-panelled interiors in Gloucester in 1952, the ones with the less attractive Formica interiors in Birmingham in 1958. Although they now carry National Railways of Zimbabwe insignia, they are still painted in the original 'Rhodesia Railways' colours, and windows and mirrors are etched with the 'RR' logo. The coaches were in OK condition when I travelled myself in 2001, but admittedly have been let go a bit lately, given Zimbabwe's economic circumstances.

Things to do in Victoria Falls . . .

- Visit the park to see the Falls from the Zimbabwe side. The park entrance fee is about £15 – take some waterproof clothing!

- Walk across the frontier into Zambia to see the Zambian part of the Falls. Between the Zimbabwean and Zambian frontier posts you cross the famous steel bridge that carries the road and railway across the Zambezi to link the Zimbabwean and Zambian sides of the river. Remember to have US$10 on you in cash, as this is the cost of a Zambian one-day visa. Sterling is also accepted, but not Zimbabwe dollars or South African rand. If you pass any warthogs on the way, give them a wide berth.

- Arrange a day trip to Chobe game reserve in Botswana. There are many operators offering similar trips. A 45-minute minibus transfer takes you from your hotel to the Botswana frontier. A 3-hour game drive in the Chobe National Park is followed by a 3-hour river trip with lunch. Animals include lion, impala, antelope, elephant, hippo, warthog, crocodile, mongoose, and even tortoise.

- Take afternoon tea at the Victoria Falls Hotel, the poshest hotel in town. Staying there will cost you around £150 per night. Afternoon tea (complete with cucumber sandwiches) will cost you closer to £10. The hotel is right next to the railway station.

- Go on an afternoon river cruise on the Zambezi. Many operators offer similar trips for the going rate of about £15, which includes plentiful wine or beer. You will probably see hippo and crocodile.

- For those interested, there are a whole range of adventure activities available such as white-water rafting down the Zambezi, or, for the completely insane, bungee-jumping off the Zambezi bridge.

. . . and in Bulawayo

Bulawayo is a pleasant town, with very wide open streets and relatively little traffic. There is an excellent railway museum, which features Cecil Rhodes's private railway coach. You should not miss a day trip to the Matobo National Park, some 25 miles south of Bulawayo. Day tours generally visit the Whovi game reserve in the morning (famous for its rhinos), then the haunting hills of the main park in the afternoon. Cecil Rhodes is buried in a breathtaking spot in Matobo, on a rocky outcrop known as 'the view of the world'.

BULAWAYO TO HARARE

A train links Bulawayo and Harare three times a week (cut back in May 2009 from its previous daily service). It runs from Bulawayo to Harare on Monday, Thursday and Saturday, and from Harare to Bulawayo on Tuesday, Friday and Sunday. In either direction it departs at 21:00, arriving at its destination at 08:00 next day.

How to buy tickets

The only way to buy tickets is at Bulawayo and Harare station reservation offices, up to 30 days before departure. Reservations are not fully computerised, and can only be made for trains leaving from that station – reservations for your return journey will need to be made when you reach your destination. Your ticket will not show your coach or berth number – this will be shown on a passenger list posted in a glass case on the platform about an hour before the train departs. Fares are not expensive – in the region of £20/US$35 or less one-way in sleeper class.

What is the Bulawayo–Harare train like?

Unlike the Bulawayo–Victoria Falls train, this train received new coaches a few years ago. There are three classes of accommodation on board:

> **Sleeper class:** 2-berth rooms (known as coupés) and 4-berth rooms (known as compartments). These have leatherette bench seats convertible to bunks, and each room has a washbasin. Full bedding is provided, included in the fare. There is a hot shower available at the end of the sleeping-car corridor. The sleeping-car is not air-conditioned, but the windows open for a superb view of the countryside, and at night a metal/mesh screen can be used to allow cool air in but still keep you safe and secure.

> **Standard class:** comfortable airline-style seating (does not convert to sleeping berths).

> **Economy class:** basic seating (does not convert to berths).

In sleeper class, two passengers travelling together will normally be booked into a 2-berth coupé, whereas a solo traveller will be booked into a 4-berth compartment with passengers of the same sex. If as a solo passenger you pay for two tickets, you can have sole occupancy of a coupé.

MOVING ON FROM ZIMBABWE

For the various possible routes from Zimbabwe to South Africa, see pages 252–3. You can also get to Botswana, Namibia, Zambia and Tanzania without needing to get on a plane.

Zimbabwe to Botswana, by train

The daily Bulawayo–Francistown–Gaborone–Mafeking train was cut back to run purely within Botswana in 1999 and was finally withdrawn completely in 2009. However, a new Bulawayo–Francistown train service started in June 2006, running three times a week with modern Zimbabwean coaches complete with TV entertainment. See the Botswana chapter, page 160, for train times and days of running. However, there are now no trains south of Francistown.

Zimbabwe to Zambia and Tanzania, by train

There are now no scheduled passenger trains across the famous Zambezi bridge from Victoria Falls (Zimbabwe) to Livingstone (Zambia). But you can walk across the bridge from Victoria Falls to the Zambian border post and take a taxi the few miles on to Livingstone. Trains run from Livingstone to Lusaka and Kapiri Mposhi, where you can change trains on to the TAZARA line to Dar es Salaam. See the Tanzania and Zambia chapter, page 242, for train times, fares and days of running.

Namibia to Zimbabwe, by bus

A bus links Victoria Falls with Windhoek three times a week: see the Namibia chapter, page 209, or **www.intercape.co.za**.

PART
5
ASIA

BANGLADESH

Watching the news, you could be forgiven for thinking Bangladesh to be not so much a country as a disaster zone. But you'd be surprised. It is a fascinating country with a rich and varied history and at present fairly few tourists. Bangladesh has a largely British-built rail network linking most major towns and cities, including Dhaka and Chittagong. The network is divided into two halves, eastern and western, by the great rivers which divide the country itself. The western network is largely broad-gauge, the eastern network largely metre-gauge. Unfortunately, connections between these two networks are often poor. There is a railway route map at **www.railway.gov.bd**.

Train operator:	Bangladesh Railways (BR), **www.railway.gov.bd**
Time:	GMT+6
Currency:	£1 = approx. 105 taka, $1 = approx. 69 taka
Visas:	UK citizens and most other western nationalities need a visa for Bangladesh, see **www.bhclondon.org.uk**.

DHAKA TO CHITTAGONG, by train

There is a good train service between the capital city, Dhaka, and Bangladesh's second city, Chittagong. Dhaka and Chittagong are both in the eastern half of the country on the metre-gauge train network, linked by fast daytime InterCity trains and two good overnight trains with sleeping-cars. The high-quality InterCity trains are very popular and often leave full, so make reservations at the station as soon as you can. Here is a timetable of the best trains, which you can check at **www.railway.gov.bd**:

Dhaka → Chittagong

Train number		704 InterCity	4 Express	722 InterCity	702 InterCity	2 Mail	742 InterCity*
Days of running		Daily	Daily	not Sun	not Fri	Daily	Daily
Dhaka	depart	07:40	08:20	15:00	16:20	22:30	23:00
Chittagong	arrive	14:30	18:45	21:45	22:15	07:20	06:15

Chittagong → Dhaka

Train number		701 InterCity	721 InterCity	3 Express	703 InterCity	1 Mail	741 InterCity*
Days of running		not Fri	not Sun	Daily	Daily	Daily	Daily
Chittagong	depart	07:00	07:15	10:10	15:00	22:30	23:00
Dhaka	arrive	12:45	13:55	19:40	21:35	07:25	05:55

InterCity = fast quality train, fully air-conditioned, restaurant car, recommended. Air-conditioned (AC) class seats, first and second class seats.

InterCity* = *Turna Express*. Fast quality train, with air-conditioned 2-berth sleepers, AC class and first class seats. Recommended.

Express = slower than InterCity trains. AC class seats, first and second class seats.

Mail = *Chittagong Mail/Dhaka Mail*. AC class 2-berth sleepers, first class 4-berth sleepers, first, second and third class seats.

not Sunday = daily except Sunday; **not Friday** = daily except Friday.

Fares

Dhaka to Chittagong one-way costs 660 taka (£6 or $9) per person in a 2-berth AC class sleeper, or 455 taka (£4 or $6) in a 4-berth first class sleeper. For a seat the one-way fare is 430 taka (£4 or $6) in AC class, 290 taka (£3 or $5) in first class, 150 taka (£1.50 or $2) in second class.

Children under 3 travel free, children aged 3 to 9 pay half fare. Children of 10 and over pay the adult fare.

You can check fares at **www.railway.gov.bd**.

COX'S BAZAAR

There is no train service to Cox's Bazaar (Bangladesh's prime beach resort), but you can take a train from Dhaka to Chittagong then a bus on from Chittagong. Bus information is not available.

TRAVEL BETWEEN BANGLADESH AND INDIA

Dhaka to Calcutta by direct train

A new train service started on 14 April 2008 between Dhaka and Calcutta (Kolkata). Called the *Maitree Express* (*maitree* meaning 'friendship'), it is run by the Indian and Bangladeshi railways. The distance via the somewhat roundabout route is 538 km (120 km in India, 418 km in Bangladesh), and it's routed via the border points at Gede and Darshana. Train services from Calcutta to Dhaka were suspended following the India–Pakistan war in 1965 and this is a major step forward.

The *Maitree Express* runs twice a week in either direction. From Dhaka it departs Cantonment station every Tuesday and Sunday at 08:30 Bangladeshi time, stops at the Bangladesh border point of Darshana 14:15–15:20, stops at the Indian border point at Gede 14:00–16:00 (Indian time), and arrives at Calcutta Chitpur station at 18:45 – remember that Indian time is always GMT+5½, Bangladeshi time is GMT+6 (they adopted daylight saving time in 2009, but dropped it for 2010).

From Calcutta it departs Chitpur station at 07:10 Indian time on Wednesday and Saturday, stops at Gede 09:25–11:25, stops at Darshana 11:35–13:25 (Bangladeshi time), and arrives at Dhaka Cantonment station at 18:00.

Westbound, immigration controls take place at Dhaka Cantonment station. Eastbound, customs and immigration checks take place at Darshana just inside the Bangladeshi border.

The train has three classes of accommodation: air-conditioned seats, non-air-conditioned seats, and sleepers. Which class is best? AC seats and non-AC seats are in fact identical, and similar in layout and appearance to Indian AC chair class. The only difference is that AC seats are air-conditioned with sealed windows, non-AC seats have opening windows. Sleepers are in compartments with berths for lying down and more room (yes, even though it's a daytime train!).

A one-way ticket Dhaka to Calcutta costs around £6/$8 in a non-air-conditioned seat, £9/$14 in an air-conditioned seat, or £15/$23 in an air-conditioned first class sleeper.

Tickets go on sale 10 days before departure, and sales close at 3pm the day before departure. In Dhaka, buy tickets at Dhaka Kamalapur station ticket office. In Calcutta, buy tickets at the Fairlie Place reservation centre at the Foreign Tourist Reservation Counter, open 10:00–17:00 Monday–Saturday, 10:00–14:00 Sunday. Passports and visas must be shown when booking. Only one-way tickets can be booked.

Bangladesh to Calcutta by train+bus

There are two train links to Calcutta (Sealdah station) from the Bangladesh/India frontier, one from Gede and one from Bangaon. Gede is a 1-km walk across the frontier from the Bangladesh railway station of Darshana, served by trains from Khulna in the south or from further north, but not from Dhaka. Bangaon is a short walk across the frontier from Benapol station in Bangladesh, served by a daily train from Khulna (but again, not from Dhaka). Please confirm that foreigners are permitted to cross at your chosen border point.

Dhaka to Calcutta by bus

Direct air-conditioned long-distance buses link Dhaka with Calcutta several times daily, taking 8 or 9 hours. The bus fare is about £7–£8 ($10–$12) one-way. I know of no websites giving information on these.

BURMA (MYANMAR)

There are significant human rights issues in Burma, and for that reason you may decide not to go; see the section below. However, if you do decide to go, you'll find a fascinating country which is easy and safe to visit, with friendly and honest people. Paradoxically, the lack of mass tourism due to the boycott of the regime has preserved Burma from the westernisation affecting some other Asian countries, making it one of the most interesting places to visit now, before it's too late.

Train operator:	Myanmar Railways (MR), no official website but try **www.yangonow.com/eng/transportation/train/fare.html** or **www.gomoasia.com/train.htm**
Time:	GMT+6½
Currency:	US$ widely accepted, and foreigners must pay hotel bills and train fares in US$ (£1 = approx. $1.50). Credit cards and travellers' cheques are NOT accepted in Burma.
Visas:	UK citizens and most other nationalities need a visa to visit Burma (Myanmar), obtainable from the Embassy of the Union of Myanmar, 19a Charles Street, London W1X 8ER, visa section open 10:00–13:00 Monday–Friday, visa fee £14. Call 020 7629 4486 or 24-hour visa information line (premium rates) 0891 600306. Fax 020 7629 4169.

SHOULD YOU VISIT BURMA?

Burma is not noted for the attractiveness of its regime – to put it mildly. There are arguments for and against visiting Burma which will not be repeated here, but they are well explained in guidebooks such as the Lonely Planet Guide to

Myanmar and you should consider them carefully before deciding whether to go. You might also want to look at **www.burmacampaign.org.uk**, which tells tourists not to go.

IS IT 'MYANMAR' OR 'BURMA'?

'Myanmar' is the Burmese-language name for Burma, and always was, even in colonial times. 'Burma' is the English-language name for Myanmar, and still is. The Burmese government switched to using the Burmese-language name for the country in 1948, and in 1989 also switched to using the Burmese-language names for a number of places around the country. In this book, the familiar English-language name is used first, with the Burmese name in brackets, for example 'Rangoon (Yangon)' or 'Moulmein (Mawlamyine)'.

INTERNATIONAL TRAVEL TO AND FROM BURMA

There are no international trains or ferries from Burma, and it can be difficult to enter Burma overland from either India or Thailand because the borders are closed to foreigners and foreigners are not permitted in most border areas.

TRAIN TRAVEL WITHIN BURMA

Train travel in Burma is a real experience. It's not fast or modern, but you'll find the journeys as much of an adventure as the destinations. On the premier Rangoon to Mandalay route, the express trains are in fact reasonably clean, comfortable and even speedy, at least for Burma. On other routes, don't expect western standards! Trains are often wonderfully slow, grubby, and their fittings, such as lights and seats, are usually not in the best state of repair. But best of all, the glass panes and metal shutters over the windows are normally secured out of the way, giving you a clear and unobstructed view of the countryside and villages of 'real' Burma as it trundles past, with nothing between you and it.

What are the trains like?

Burmese trains have three classes: upper class, first class and ordinary class. There were sleeping-cars on all the main Rangoon–Mandalay trains until

September 2006 when all Rangoon–Mandalay trains were re-timed to run by day. Now on this route there are sleepers (private compartments for four people) only on trains 29 and 30. The best Rangoon–Mandalay trains have restaurant cars, with 4-seat tables, serving meals, drinks and snacks.

Upper class has comfortable reclining seats, sometimes two abreast on each side of the aisle, sometimes one on one side of the aisle and two abreast on the other. The seats normally all face the direction of travel, but can be rotated to face each other (for example, to make a group of four seats) if required. Upper class on the main Rangoon–Mandalay express trains is relatively clean and comfortable, with fresh seat covers and curtains at the window. Upper class on secondary trains is much grubbier but still quite comfortable, although you will find your seat recline mechanism in various states of repair.

First class has basic wooden seats, almost identical to ordinary class, but with a padded leatherette seat bottom. For the first half hour, this padding seems to make the extra cost worthwhile. After that, you wonder whether the ordinary class wooden seats would be less sweaty in the heat! First class is only available on certain trains.

Ordinary class has basic wooden seats and is quite bearable for many journeys, such as Mandalay to Pyin Oo Lwin or Hsipaw. The seats are numbered on the back (in Burmese numerals) and every passenger has a specific seat number written on their ticket, so there's no overcrowding or scrum for seats. Just watch out for the local produce stacked all over the floor!

Fares

Foreigners pay higher fares than Burmese citizens, and must pay in US dollars. Children under 3 years old travel free, children over 3 but under 10 pay half fare. Although the Myanmar Railways has no official website, you can check train times and fares on several travel agency websites – try **www.myanmarventure.com/train/index.html**, **www.yangonow.com/eng/transportation/train/fare.html** or **www.gomoasia.com/train.htm**.

How to buy train tickets in Burma

It's easy to buy a ticket at station ticket offices. There are hardly ever any signs in English, but don't worry: just ask at the first available ticket window and, as a foreigner, you may well be invited inside the ticket office and told to sit down while someone is called to help you. You will need the names, nationality and passport number of each passenger as these will be written on your ticket.

Bookings for upper class open 3 days in advance, ordinary class bookings open just one day in advance. You cannot buy tickets before bookings open, and at some smaller stations you may be told to come back and buy a ticket just before departure. It's good practice to buy your ticket at least the day before travel, but if necessary it's not usually difficult for a foreigner to secure a seat on the day of departure, unless you want a sleeper. All passengers get a reserved seat, even in ordinary class, and the coach and seat numbers will be written on the ticket. Reservations are not computerised, but based on hand-written reservation lists, so bookings can only be made at the station where your journey will start. Sleepers are in short supply, as only a few trains have sleepers and there's normally just one sleeping-car per train, so book as soon as you can.

To buy train tickets in Rangoon, go to the advance booking office, which is not in the station but in Bogyoke Aung San road on the south side of the tracks, opposite the Sakura Tower and diagonally opposite the Traders Hotel. It is open daily 06:00–10:00 and 13:00–16:00. It looks more like a farmyard than a reservations office! Walk off the main road, 30 metres down the track into the booking hall proper, and you'll see a row of about ten ticket windows. The window for booking trains from Rangoon to Mandalay is the first one on the left. You can also book train tickets through your hotel or through the Rangoon MTT office at the Sule Paya. In Mandalay, the ticket office is on the first floor of the station, above the tracks.

How to buy train tickets from outside Burma

You can book trains from outside Burma by email through a number of travel agencies. Your tickets can be sent to your hotel and paid for when you get to Burma. A small fee is charged for this service. If you want to be sure of a sleeper on a Rangoon–Mandalay train just days after you arrive in Rangoon, using an agency can be a good idea.

A recommended agency is Sanay Travel, website **www.yangonow.com/eng/ transportation/train/fare.html**. Just email your booking request to info@yangonow.com, quoting your journey details (from, to, date, train number or departure time), passenger details for each passenger (name, address, phone number, passport number, passport expiry date, nationality) and your hotel in Rangoon. Sanay Travel respond promptly to emails and are very helpful. They charge a $10 (£7) fee plus the cost of the ticket.

RANGOON (YANGON) TO MANDALAY

The Rangoon to Mandalay express trains are a comfortable and (in fact) relatively fast and punctual option for travel between these cities. A bit bumpy in places, perhaps, but much more comfortable than cramped buses and far more of a real Burmese travel experience than a flight. In fact, the train ride is a highly recommended experience! The timetable below shows the all-new timetable introduced in September 2006 (changed again in November 2006 and still in force now), which rescheduled most Rangoon–Mandalay trains to run by day rather than overnight.

Rangoon (Yangon) → *Mandalay*

Train number		31	5	3	11	1	7	29
Classes		U,O	U,1,O,R	U,1,O	U,O	U,1,O	U,O	S,U,O
Rangoon (Yangon)	depart	03:15	05:00	05:30	06:00	04:00	12:00	12:45
Pegu (Bago)			05:05	06:51	07:21	07:50	06:11	13:50	I
Taungoo		09:27	11:28	12:19	12:38	xx:xx	18:23	19:00
Pyinmana (Naypyitaw)		11:45	13:48	14:36	15:13	xx:xx	20:43	21:05
Thazi		–	16:56	18:03	18:38	xx:xx	–	00:03
Mandalay	arrive	–	20:10	21:30	22:00	06:40	–	03:00

Mandalay → Rangoon (Yangon)

Train number		32	30	8	6	4	12	2
Classes		U, O	S, U, O	U, O	U,1,O,R	U,1,O	U,1,O	U,1,O
Mandalay	depart	–	21:45	–	05:00	05:30	06:00	19:15
Thazi		–	01:13	–	07:48	08:20	09:33	23:44
Pyinmana		05:00	04:11	13:45	11:01	11:52	12:47	04:32
Taungoo		07:00	06:18	15:45	13:18	14:13	15:03	08:12
Pegu (Bago)		11:37	I	20:13	17:52	19:12	19:22	16:22
Rangoon (Yangon)	arrive	13:45	13:00	22:15	20:10	21:30	21:30	19:33

xx:xx = exact time not available

S = sleeping-car

U = upper class seats

1 = first class seats

O = ordinary class seats

R = restaurant car

Rangoon–Mandalay is 622 km (388 miles). All the trains shown here run daily. Trains 29 and 30 are known as the 'Chinese trains', using the newest Chinese coaches, better than other trains.

Fares

One-way per person, in US$	Upper class sleeper	Upper class seat	First class seat	Ordinary seat
Rangoon to Mandalay (train 29 or 30)	$40 (£26)	$35 (£24)	?	$15 (£10)
Rangoon to Mandalay (other trains)	$33 (£22)	$30 (£20)	?	$11 (£7)
Rangoon to Thazi	$33 (£22)	$25 (£17)	?	$9 (£6)
Rangoon to Pyinmana	$27 (£18)	$20 (£13)	?	$7 (£5)
Rangoon to Pegu (Bago)	–	$5 (£3)	?	$2 (£1)

Foreigners must pay fares in US dollars.

Children under 3 travel free, children over 3 but under 10 pay half fare.

About the journey

Contrary to what you might read in your guidebook, the Rangoon to Mandalay express trains are comfortable, fairly fast and reasonably punctual. Trains are available for boarding at Rangoon in good time (normally at the platform right ahead of you when you enter the station), and they generally depart promptly with whistles blown, flags waved and a long low hoot from the locomotive.

The train trundles out of Rangoon at just 15mph with the local children trying to hang on to the outside, accelerating to 40–45mph once clear of the city, clickety-clacking past small villages of palm-thatched cottages built on stilts, ox carts trundling slowly along dusty roads, and occasional white or gold stupas. Burmese children love to wave at trains, especially if they see a western face at the window, and will smile broadly when you wave back. You'll be travelling along a railway originally built by the British – look out for the old-fashioned semaphore signals and mock-Tudor signal boxes at Pegu (Bago).

Even when night falls, you'll see the palm trees silhouetted in the moonlight, and the smell of the village cooking fires will drift into your sleeper compartment through the open window. Make sure you have a jumper or fleece handy if you travel overnight, as it can get very cold a few hours after dark. The track is not the best in the world and in places it will put your carriage suspension through its paces, but you stand a good chance of arriving at the other end within 5 or 10 minutes of the advertised time. However, delays of 30–60 minutes or more are not uncommon, so make allowances.

RANGOON (YANGON) TO BAGAN (PAGAN)

Bagan, where 800-year-old temples and stupas litter a huge plain as far as the eye can see, should not be missed. There is a new direct overnight train from Rangoon to Bagan, introduced in early 2010, or you can take an express train from Rangoon to Thazi (see the section above), then a bus or taxi to Bagan; or take an express train from Rangoon to Mandalay, visit Mandalay, then travel to Bagan using the express ferry down the Irrawaddy – a wonderful river journey.

If you want to use the direct train, here is the timetable. Train 61 leaves Rangoon at 16:00 daily, arriving in Bagan next day at 08:00. Train 62 leaves

Bagan daily at 16:30, arriving in Rangoon next day at 08:00. Trains 61 and 62 have an upper class sleeper, upper class seats and first class seats. The one-way fare from Rangoon to Bagan is $50 (£33) in an upper class sleeper, $40 (£27) in an upper class seat or $30 (£20) in a first class seat.

Bagan station is a modern pagoda-style station in the middle of nowhere about 5 km southeast of the Nyaung Oo township, roughly 9 km from Old Bagan. It's possibly one of the few stations in the world further from the town it serves than the airport!

RANGOON (YANGON) OR MANDALAY TO INLE LAKE

Inle Lake is one of the most beautiful places in Burma, and it attracts many visitors. The usual base for exploring the lake is Nyaungshwe, at its north end. Trains and buses don't go directly to Nyaungshwe, but go (from Thazi) to the junction town of Shwenyaung 11 km away. The bus is faster (4–5 hours on bad roads), but a scenic trip on the 'Slow Train from Thazi' is a wonderful experience which should not be missed: stock up on mineral water and beer, then recline in your upper class armchair (you may have no choice – the recline mechanism may be broken . . .), and gaze through wide-open windows at the wonderful scenery passing by at just 15–20mph.

Rangoon (Yangon) ➔ *Inle Lake*

Take an express train from **Rangoon** (or from Mandalay) to **Thazi**; see the Rangoon–Mandalay section, pages 269–71, for details. Stay the night in Thazi: there are guesthouses at the end of the station approach on the main street.

Next morning take the Slow Train from **Thazi** to **Shwenyaung**; you should have no difficulty buying a ticket at Thazi ticket office when you get there. Train 143 departs at 05:00, arriving at Shwenyaung at 13:48; train 141 departs at 08:00, arriving at Shwenyaung at 17:15 (both call at Kalaw on the way, at 11:14 and 14:19 respectively). Accommodation is upper class seats and ordinary class seats only.

The journey is wonderfully scenic: after crossing the plain from Thazi, the train enters the hills and climbs up a steep mountainside on a series of switchbacks, reversing several times and backing up the slope to gain height. In several places, the train loops around and doubles back on itself. Look out for the very English mock-Tudor station building at the old British hill station of Kalaw.

From **Shwenyaung** there are plenty of local taxis and buses to **Nyaungshwe**: journey time around 25 minutes.

Inle Lake ➜ *Rangoon (Yangon)*

Travel from **Nyaungshwe** to **Shwenyaung** by local taxi or public pick-up. Make sure you turn up at Shwenyaung station 30–40 minutes before the departure of the Slow Train to Thazi and you're unlikely to have any difficulty getting an upper class ticket (in Nyaungshwe, there are lots of travel agencies who can arrange just about anything *except* train tickets!).

Take one of the two daily trains from **Shwenyaung** to **Thazi**: train 142 leaves at 08:30, arriving at Thazi at 18:00; train 144 leaves at 10:11, arriving at Thazi at 20:10. Both have upper class and ordinary class seats only, and call at Kalaw on the way (at 11:56 and 14:03 respectively).

In Thazi, the Red Star restaurant, where the station approach joins the main road, is a good choice for a meal while you change trains. A deluxe waiting room for foreigners is also available at Thazi station for $1 (£0.70) per person. However, depending on your final destination, you'll probably need to spend the night in Thazi.

Travel onwards by express train from **Thazi** to **Rangoon** or **Mandalay**; see the Rangoon–Mandalay section, pages 269–71, for details. You can buy your ticket when you get to Thazi.

Fares

For fares between Rangoon and Thazi, see page 270. Thazi to Shwenyaung costs $7 (£5) for an upper class seat, or $3 (£2) for an ordinary class seat.

RANGOON (YANGON) TO MOULMEIN (MAWLAMYINE)

Moulmein is not on every visitor's itinerary, but if you have the time it's well worth a visit for its colonial buildings and historic mosques. Although Rudyard Kipling wrote the 'Road to Mandalay', Moulmein was the only Burmese city which he actually visited, and the main pagoda on the ridge overlooking the city is the setting for his poem 'Burma Girl'. You can now (since 2006) travel from Rangoon to Moulmein by direct daytime train, and there are three departures daily in either direction.

The train follows the Rangoon–Mandalay main line as far as Pegu (Bago), where it branches off and heads across the plains to the broad Sittung River, which it crosses via a huge and heavily guarded road/rail bridge. The scenery becomes more interesting on the other side – look out for primitive brickworks on the left in several locations, with brick kilns and bricks drying in the sun, and of course you'll see lots of stupas, especially on the mountain ridge to the east. Historically, the railway from Rangoon ended at Moatama (Martaban), which was the ferry terminal for ferries across the Thanlwin River to Moulmein itself. A new road+rail bridge has now been built, opened to road traffic in February 2005 and to trains in April 2006. Trains now rumble slowly across the bridge into a brand-new station behind the hill on which Moulmein pagoda stands. The Moatama–Moulmein ferry service has been discontinued. Expect an arrival generally around 30–60 minutes late.

Rangoon (Yangon) → *Moulmein (Mawlamyine)*

Train number		35	89	175
Classes		U,O	U,O	U,O
Rangoon (Yangon)	depart	06:30	07:15	02:00
Pegu (Bago)		I	11:39	03:51
Kyaikto		11:19	14:49	06:43
Martaban (Moatama)	arrive	I	19:49	I
Moulmein (Mawlamyine)	arrive	15:23	20:25	11:30

Moulmein (Mawlamyine) → *Rangoon (Yangon)*

Train number		36	90	176
Classes		U,O	U,O	U,O
Moulmein (Mawlamyine)	depart	06:00	08:15	11:20
Martaban (Moatama)	depart	I	08:50	I
Kyaikto		11:03	13:31	16:00
Pegu (Bago)		I	16:21	18:55
Rangoon (Yangon)	arrive	16:35	19:15	21:00

U = upper class seats

O = ordinary class

There are no sleepers on train 175, just seats.

Fares

Rangoon to Moulmein one-way costs $17 (£11) in an upper class seat, or $6 (£4) in an ordinary class seat. Pegu (Bago) to Moulmein one-way costs $11 (£7) in an upper class seat, or $5 (£3) in an ordinary class seat.

RANGOON (YANGON) TO PROME (PYAY)

Three trains a day link Rangoon with Prome, all with upper class, first class and ordinary class seats only.

From Rangoon there are departures at 07:00 (train 63), arriving at Prome at 18:00; 11:00 (train 75), arriving at 22:15; and a faster train at 13:00 (train 71), arriving at 21:30.

From Prome there are departures at 02:00 (train 76), arriving at Rangoon at 13:40; 06:15 (train 64), arriving at 17:30; and a faster train at 23:30 (train 72), which arrives at Rangoon at 07:50 next day.

Note that trains 63, 64, 75 and 76 use Rangoon Kyemyindine station, not Rangoon main station. Kyemyindine station is a few stops northwest of Rangoon main station on the city's circular train line.

The fare for Rangoon to Prome is $15 (£10) in an upper class seat, or $6 (£4) in an ordinary class seat.

MANDALAY TO PYIN OO LWIN (MAYMO), HSIPAW (THIBAW), LASHIO

Pyin Oo Lwin, also known as Maymyo after its founder Colonel May, is well worth a visit for its colonial buildings, botanic gardens and a ride in the miniature stagecoaches that are used as taxis. Many visitors also head off to the market towns of Shan state such as Hsipaw. The train ride from Mandalay up into the hills is a wonderful experience. South of Hsipaw, the train crosses the famous Gokteik viaduct, which is a historic landmark in its own right.

Two trains a day in either direction link Mandalay and Pyin Oo Lwin. The recommended option is train 131, the one through-train a day from Mandalay to Lashio, with first class and ordinary class seats only; this departs Mandalay at 04:35, arriving at Pyin Oo Lwin at 08:21 where it makes a 30-minute stop, then calling at Gokteik 11:32, Kyaukme 13:50, Hsipaw (Thibaw) 15:26, and arriving at Lashio at 19:45. In the opposite direction (train 132) it departs Lashio at 05:00, calling at Hsipaw 09:40, Kyaukme 11:25, Gokteik 13:25, arriving at Pyin Oo Lwin at 16:05; it then leaves Pyin Oo Lwin at 17:40, arriving at Mandalay at 22:40.

It's an early start from Mandalay, but this train ride is easily the best way to reach the old British hill station of Pyin Oo Lwin and the Shan state towns of Hsipaw and Lashio. Leaving Mandalay heading south, the train soon turns northeast across the plains. It's still dark at this time, but traders with torches and fires flock to the train when it calls at wayside stations. At dawn, the train reaches the foot of the mountains and starts climbing. It gains height using a series of zig-zags, stopping and reversing up the steep gradient twice to reach the plateau at the top of the escarpment. Soon after reaching the plateau, the train arrives at Pyin Oo Lwin.

After Pyin Oo Lwin the train snakes its way through pleasant countryside to the highlight of the trip, the crossing of a spectacular valley on the dramatic Gokteik viaduct, just after Gokteik station. The Gokteik viaduct was built in 1901 by an American firm of contractors who won the tender with a design allegedly far more advanced than any of the other bids. When built, it had the highest span of any bridge in the British Empire, and was the only American-built bridge in the Empire, too. Rumour has it that the Burmese government did no maintenance on the bridge whilst a British insurance policy was still in force, but you'll be relieved to hear that the bridge was renovated in the 1990s. The train passes over at walking pace, but you may be prevented from taking photographs as the Burmese consider the bridge to be of strategic importance. Don't lean out of the window and look downwards if you suffer from vertigo! Expect an arrival at the other end around 15–60 minutes late.

The other Mandalay–Pyin Oo Lwin service has ordinary class seats only: train 133 leaves Mandalay daily at 14:45, arriving at Pyin Oo Lwin at 19:30; in the other direction, train 134 departs Pyin Oo Lwin at 05:00, arriving in Mandalay at 09:45.

There may also be a second daily train between Pyin Oo Lwin and Lashio: train 137 (first and ordinary class seats) departing at 05:30 and arriving at Hsipaw at 13:14 and Lashio at 17:25. In the return direction, train 138 leaves Lashio at 06:30 and Hsipaw at 11:30, arriving at Pyin Oo Lwin at 18:50. However, according to one report, trains 137 and 138 may no longer be running as of 2009; you'd need to check locally.

Mandalay to Pyin Oo Lwin one-way costs \$4 (£3) in a first class seat, or \$2 (£1) in an ordinary class seat. Mandalay to Hsipaw costs \$9 (£6) in a first class seat, or \$3 (£2) in an ordinary class seat.

MANDALAY TO MYITKYINA

Mandalay → Myitkyina

Train number		43	55	57	41
Classes		S,U,O	U,O	Lux	S,U,O
Mandalay	depart	08:30	13:50	16:40	17:45
Sagaing		09:43	I	I	18:35
Shwebo		13:33	17:10	19:51	22:10
Kawlin		20:31	22:24	01:02	00:31
Myitkyina	arrive	17:30	12:00	14:40	19:30

Myitkyina → Mandalay

Train number		56	42	58	44
Classes		U,O	S,U,O	Lux	S,U,O
Myitkyina	depart	07:00	08:45	13:50	22:30
Kawlin		21:43	00:51	03:18	16:25
Shwebo		01:42	06:10	07:53	22:35
Sagaing		I	09:12	I	01:58
Mandalay	arrive	04:55	10:10	11:10	03:10

All trains take one night.

S = sleeping-car

U = upper class seats

O = ordinary class seats

Lux = privately run *Malika–Mandalar Express*. Runs 4 times a week: from Mandalay on Mon, Wed, Fri, Sun. Days of operation on return journey not known. Sleeping-cars only, higher fares charged.

MANDALAY TO BAGAN (PAGAN), by train

The river journey aboard the Mandalay–Bagan express ferry service (see the next section below) is the recommended way to get from Mandalay to Bagan, but if you prefer to go by train there are two departures a day: from Mandalay at 09:50 (ordinary class seats only) and 22:00 (upper class and ordinary class seats only), arriving at Bagan (Nyaung Oo township) at 19:55 and 04:50 respectively; and from Bagan (Nyaung Oo) at 04:00 (ordinary class seats only) and 07:00 (upper class and ordinary class seats), arriving at Mandalay at 14:20 and 13:40 respectively. Mandalay to Bagan is just 179 km, making this a very slow train journey, even though the line was only built in 1996! Bagan station is a modern pagoda-style station in the middle of nowhere, about 5 km southeast of the Nyaung Oo township, 9 km from Old Bagan.

IRRAWADDY RIVER STEAMERS

Taking a river steamer along the Irrawaddy is one of the most enjoyable ways to travel. In particular, the Mandalay–Bagan express ferry is recommended as the best way to travel between these two places, as it will show you slices of Burmese life both on the river and along its banks. There now appear to be three ferries, a twice-weekly slow ferry mainly for locals, the original daily express ferry used by tourists, and a new twice weekly express ferry also aimed at tourists.

Ferry tickets can be booked through your hotel or via a travel agency, through the MTT (government tourist information) offices in major towns (for example, the MTT office at Mandalay station or in Rangoon near the Sule Paya) or at Inland Water Transport (IWT) offices.

Mandalay → Bagan → Prome (Pyay) → Rangoon (Yongan)

		Note A	Note C	Note B	Daily
Mandalay (Gawwein jetty)	depart	07:00 day 1	07:30 day 1	05:00 day 1	–
Bagan (Nyaung Oo)	arr/dep				09:25 day 2	–
Bagan (Old Bagan)	arrive	17:30 day 1	12:30 day 1			–
Prome (Pyay)	arrive	–	–	18:30 day 3	–
Prome (Pyay)	depart	–	–	–	06:00 day 1
Rangoon (Yangon)	arrive	–	–	–	06:00 day 3

Note A: Mandalay–Bagan express ferry, recommended. Now runs daily. Fare $25 (£17).

Note B: Slow ferry. Runs only on Wednesday and Sunday. Please double-check times locally.

Note C: New faster Mandalay–Bagan express ferry. Runs only on Wednesday and Saturday. See **www.travelmyanmar.com/malika_river_cruise_2.html**. Fare $26 (£17) (lower deck) or $35 (£23) (upper deck).

Rangoon (Yongan) → *Prome (Pyay)* → *Bagan* → *Mandalay*

		Daily	Note E	Note D	Note F
Rangoon (Yangon)	depart	18:30 day 1	–	–	–
Prome (Pyay)	arrive	16:40 day 4	–	–	–
Prome (Pyay)	depart	–	05:30 day 1	–	–
Bagan (Old Bagan)	depart	–	|	–	–
Bagan (Nyaung Oo)	arr/dep	–	14:15 day 3	05:30 day 1	xx:xx day 1
Mandalay (Gawwein jetty)	arrive	–	12:30 day 5	18:30 day 1	xx:xx day 1

xx:xx = times not known, please check locally.

Note D: Bagan–Mandalay express ferry, highly recommended, now runs daily, fare $25 (£17).

Note E: Slow ferry. Runs only on Wednesday and Saturday. Please double-check times locally.

Note F: New faster Mandalay–Bagan express ferry, runs only on Thursday and Sunday. Fare $26 (£17) (lower deck) or $35 (£23) (upper deck).

CAMBODIA

Cambodia has little in the way of trains – in fact its last train, a weekly one from Phnom Penh to Battambang, has now disappeared – but it's nevertheless a fascinating country to visit. The Angkor Wat temples at Siem Reap are a world-class attraction. You can easily travel between Cambodia and neighbouring countries by bus; this chapter will tell you how.

Train operator:	Chemin de Fer du Cambodge (CFC), no known website
Time:	GMT+7
Currency:	£1 = approx. 6,416 riel, $1 = approx. 4,165 riel
Visas:	Visas are required by UK, EU, US, Australian and most other western nationals, but they can be bought at the frontier points at Poiphet and Bavet/Moc Bai, at a cost of about £15/$25. You save time and hassle by buying an e-visa at **http://evisa.mfaic.gov.kh/e-visa/vindex.aspx**. Cambodian embassy in London: **www.cambodianembassy.org.uk**.

EUROPE TO CAMBODIA, without flying

If you have the time, you can reach Cambodia overland from London, taking trains as far as Saigon, then a bus from Saigon to Phnom Penh. See the Vietnam chapter, page 426, for more information on the London–Saigon journey. See page 285 for details of the bus service between Saigon and Phnom Penh.

TRAIN TRAVEL WITHIN CAMBODIA

There are now no passenger trains within Cambodia, the last remaining weekly Phnom Penh to Battambang train having been withdrawn in January 2009.

However, there are plans to revive the railway. A 30-year concession has been granted to a company called Toll Royal Railway (**www.tollroyalrailway.com**), and it's possible that trains will be running again by 2013, perhaps even direct from Phnom Penh to Bangkok.

BANGKOK TO PHNOM PENH, by train and bus

Since the war in Cambodia, the railway line between Bangkok and Phnom Penh has only been running between Bangkok and Aranyaprathet on the Thai side of the Thai/Cambodian border (and until 2009 within Cambodia between Battambang and Phnom Penh). Train service across the border between Aranyaprathet and Battambang has been suspended for some years, although there is talk of restoring the complete Phnom Penh–Bangkok rail link sometime in the future. In the meantime, a trip from Bangkok to Phnom Penh can be made over two days; here's how.

Bangkok → Phnom Penh

Day 1: Take the daily 05:55 train from **Bangkok** (the main Hualamphong station), arriving in **Aranyaprathet** at 11:35. Aranyaprathet is just a few kilometres from the Cambodian frontier. There's also a 13:05 train from Bangkok, arriving in Aranyaprathet at 17:35, but this is too late to move on from the frontier and you will have to spend the night at Poiphet. These trains are third class only, but they are clean, spacious and it's a pleasant and enjoyable ride, clickety-clacking along with a breeze blowing through the open window. The fare is only 58 baht (£1.20 or $1.80).

At **Aranyaprathet**, take a tuk-tuk (about 40–60 baht (about £1)) or motorcycle (50 baht) or wait for the bus (about 10 baht (20p)) from the station to the Cambodian border at **Poiphet** (15 km). The border is open 07:00–20:00, and visas can be bought there. Don't get sidetracked into a travel agency; make sure the tuk-tuk driver takes you to the official border post to buy your Cambodian visa (or buy an e-visa beforehand). Be careful with your valuables when crossing the border, as there may be pickpockets around.

Take a Cambodian taxi, bus or pick-up truck from **Poiphet** to **Sisophon** (48 km) and **Battambang** (112 km). You will need to spend the night in Battambang.

Day 2: Take a bus from **Battambang** to **Phnom Penh**. Buses run many times daily between 06:30 and 12:45, journey time 5½ hours, fare around 14,000 riel (£2 or $3).

You may prefer to travel via Siem Reap to see the temples at Angkor Wat. If so, see the Bangkok–Siem Reap and Siem Reap–Phnom Penh sections below.

Phnom Penh → Bangkok

Day 1: Take a morning bus from **Phnom Penh** to **Battambang**. Buses run many times daily between 06:30 and 12:45, journey time 5½ hours, fare around 14,000 riel (£2 or $3). You will need to spend the night at Battambang.

Day 2: Take a taxi, bus or pick-up truck from **Battambang** via **Sisophon** to **Poiphet** on the Thai frontier (48 km from Sisophon, 112 km from Battambang).

After passing through customs into Thailand, take a bus (10 baht (20p)) or tuk-tuk (40–60 baht (around £1)) the 15 km from **Poiphet** to the railway station at **Aranyaprathet**.

Two reliable trains a day run from **Aranyaprathet** to **Bangkok**. You should be able to make the 13:55 departure from Aranyaprathet, arriving in Bangkok at 19:55. If not, the other train leaves Aranyaprathet at 06:40, arriving in Bangkok at 12:05. Both trains are third class only, but they are clean and it's a very pleasant ride. The fare is only 58 baht (£1.20 or $1.80).

BANGKOK TO PHNOM PENH, via Siem Reap (for Angkor Wat)

Bangkok → Siem Reap (for Angkor Wat) → Phnom Penh

Travel by train from **Bangkok** to **Aranyaprathet**, and then on to **Poiphet** by tuk-tuk, motorcycle or bus, as described in the Bangkok–Phnom Penh section above.

Take a share taxi from **Poiphet** to **Siem Reap**. The journey usually takes around 2–3 hours now that the highway has been improved, and it costs about £20/$30 for the whole car or £6/$9 for the front seat, depending on your bargaining powers. There are also buses, some quite basic, from Poiphet to Siem Reap, fare around £2/$3, journey time around 5 hours.

Spend a day or two in Siem Reap, seeing the temples. When you're ready to move on to Phnom Penh, there are two options, boat or bus. There's a daily boat along the river from **Siem Reap** to **Phnom Penh** departing 07:00 and arriving 13:30 (distance 251 km, fare £17/$25). Alternatively, there are buses at various times throughout the day from 06:30 until about 12:30 (journey time 6 hours, fare around £7/$10, distance 314 km). Buses are run by several operators. Some buses are double-decker, and some have a WC and refreshments.

Phnom Penh → Siem Reap (for Angkor Wat) → Bangkok

There are two options for travel from **Phnom Penh** to **Siem Reap**: bus or boat. The daily boat along the river from Phnom Penh to Siem Reap departs at 07:00 and arrives at 13:30 (fare around £17/$25). Alternatively, there are buses at various times throughout the day from 06:30 until about 14:00 (journey time 6 hours, fare around £7/$10). Buses are run by several operators. Some buses are double-decker, and some have a WC and refreshments.

Spend a day or two in Siem Reap. When you are ready to move on, take a share taxi from **Siem Reap** to the Thai frontier at **Poiphet**. The journey usually takes under 3 hours, and it costs about £20/$30 for the whole car or £6/$9 for the front seat.

After passing through customs into Thailand, take a bus or tuk-tuk from **Poiphet** to the railway station at **Aranyaprathet**, and the train from **Aranyaprathet** to **Bangkok** as described in the Phnom Penh–Bangkok section, page 283.

PHNOM PENH TO SAIGON (HO CHI MINH CITY) (VIETNAM)

There is no railway (yet) between Saigon and Phnom Penh. However, there's a daily bus service that departs Phnom Penh at 06:30 and arrives at Bavet (on the Cambodian side of the frontier) at 11:00. You have to change buses at the frontier, making your way on foot from Bavet to Moc Bai on the Vietnamese side. The Vietnamese bus leaves Moc Bai at 12:00 and arrives at Saigon at 14:00 (total distance around 250 km). The fare is about £8/$12. Visas can be bought at the frontier.

From Saigon the bus leaves at 06:00, arriving at Moc Bai at 08:00; you cross the frontier on foot, then the Cambodian bus departs Bavet at 09:00, arriving in Phnom Penh at 13:30.

Other buses are also available – in fact, several daily buses run by various different companies. For instance, you could try **www.bigpond.com.kh/users/capitol/opentour.htm**, which offers an 08:00 bus from Phnom Penh to Saigon.

Alternatively, a number of local tour operators run a river boat+bus service from Saigon to Phnom Penh – a very enjoyable way to travel between the two cities. Try **www.bigpond.com.kh/users/capitol/opentour.htm**.

CHINA

China has one of the biggest and busiest rail networks in the world, and trains link almost every town and city. The Chinese Railways are actively building more lines, many of them high-speed, and even Lhasa in Tibet is now linked to the rest of the network, over a high-altitude railway only completed in 2006. Chinese trains are a safe, comfortable and cheap way to travel around China, and a Chinese train journey in itself is an experience not to be missed.

Train operator:	Chinese Railways
	Train times in English: **www.chinahighlights.com/china-trains/**
	Map of Chinese railways: **www.johomaps.com/as/china/chinarail.html**
	Official sites (in Chinese only): **www.china-mor.gov.cn** and **www.tielu.org**
	Kowloon–Canton Railway Corporation (local trains in Hong Kong plus through trains HK to Beijing and Shanghai): **www.kcrc.com**
Time:	GMT+8
Currency:	£1 = approx. 9.9 yuan (renminbi, RMB) = approx. 11.9 Hong Kong dollars
	$1 = approx. 6.8 yuan = approx. 7.7 Hong Kong dollars
Tourist information:	**www.cnto.org.uk** (UK), **www.cnto.org** (US), **www.cnto.org.au** (Aus)
Visas:	UK citizens and most other nationalities need a visa for China. In the UK, Chinese visa issuing has been outsourced to **www.visaforchina.org.uk**.

EUROPE TO CHINA BY TRANS-SIBERIAN RAILWAY

You can reach China from the UK in less than ten days, from around £800 one-way. First, take Eurostar and connecting trains to Moscow (around 48 hours). Then take one of two direct weekly trains from Moscow to Beijing, taking six nights. For details, see the chapter on the Trans-Siberian, page 33.

TRAIN TRAVEL WITHIN CHINA

Online train timetables for China

- For online train timetables in English between any two major Chinese cities, you can use the journey planner at either **www.chinatravelguide.com/ctgwiki/Special:CNTrainSearch? method=1** or **www.chinahighlights.com**. These are the best online timetables in English that I've seen, and they also give fares, shown in US dollars or RMB.

- There is an excellent free downloadable Quick Reference timetable in English for train times between the biggest cities at **www.chinatt.org**. This is produced by Chinese Railways expert Duncan Peattie.

- The official Chinese Railways websites are only in Chinese, **www.china-mor.gov.cn** (Chinese Ministry of Railways) and **www.tielu.org**.

- You can find maps of Chinese train routes at **www.johomaps.com/ as/china/chinarail.html** and **www.nordling.nu/schaefer/china map.gif**, and a map of the Beijing metro (showing the location of Beijing Main (Zhan) and Beijing West (Xi) mainline stations) at **www.johomaps.com/as/china/beijing/beijingmetro.html**.

Printed train timetables for China

As well as his free summary timetable (see above), Duncan Peattie produces an excellent English translation of the whole Chinese Railways national timetable, available by email from mail@chinatt.org. This costs about £9 ($14 or €11) in pdf format, or £15–£18 ($23–$27 or €17–€21) in printed format (including postage). It covers all trains in the national timetable between some 850 stations. For more information, see **www.chinatt.org**.

Classes of seat and sleeper

Chinese trains generally have 4 classes, although not all trains have all classes – for example, the best Beijing–Shanghai trains are soft sleeper only.

Soft sleeper: Most western travellers choose soft sleeper, a comfortable, civilised and affordable way to travel. Soft sleepers are spacious 4-berth compartments with two upper and two lower berths by night, converting to two sofas for daytime use. All necessary bedding is provided. There's a table with tablecloth, and usually a vacuum flask of hot water for making tea (or drinking chocolate or cuppa soups if you've brought some). The compartment door locks securely, and a smartly dressed attendant looks after each car. The best trains even feature individual TV screens and power sockets for laptops and mobiles.

Hard sleeper: If you're on a tight budget, there's no reason why you shouldn't go hard sleeper, as many western backpackers do. Hard sleeper consists of open-plan carriages with a broad aisle on one side of the car, bays of 6 bunks (upper, middle and lower) on the other side. In spite of the name, hard sleeper bunks are reasonably well padded, and bedding is supplied. Newer trains even have power sockets for laptops and mobiles.

Soft seat and **hard seat:** Equivalent to first and second class on a European train. Short-distance daytime trains often only have hard class seats, though some intercity trains also have soft class seats. The new C, D and G category high-speed trains are usually described as having first and second or sometimes business and economy class. In Chinese terms these are first-class soft seat and normal soft seat, this allows the Chinese ministry of railways to get around government limits on the price of normal soft and hard class train fares.

Deluxe soft sleeper: In addition to the four normal classes, a handful of trains also have deluxe soft sleepers, for instance on the Beijing–Hong Kong, Beijing–Shanghai and Beijing–Xian routes. These are 2-berth compartments with private toilet. There are only a few of these 2-berth compartments available, often booked by government officials, so by all means ask for one but don't bang your head against a brick wall trying to get one – be prepared to travel in normal 4-berth soft class if necessary. Sharing a 4-berth really isn't a problem; it's the norm in China, and you might even meet some real Chinese people this way.

Restaurant cars, toilets, smoking

Most long-distance trains have a restaurant car, with waiter service of drinks, snacks and meals. The best trains on key routes such as Beijing–Shanghai have menus in both Chinese and English.

Chinese trains generally have both western and 'squat' toilets, but it's always a good idea to take your own supply of toilet paper. The toilets on the modern D and Z category trains are immaculate, so no worries there!

Smoking is not permitted in the sleeping-car compartments or corridors on Chinese trains, but is allowed in the vestibules between carriages and in the restaurant cars.

Categories of train

Chinese train numbers usually start with a letter, which indicates the category of train. The better the category of train, the faster it is likely to be, and the more modern and comfortable the carriages are likely to be. Slightly higher fares are charged for the better train categories.

C and D trains (modern high-speed daytime and sleeper trains): These are top-quality high-speed trains with ultra-modern air-conditioned coaches and streamlined power-cars at each end. Some are 200–300km/h daytime electric trains; a few D trains are top-quality 200km/h sleeper trains.

Z trains (high-quality express sleeper trains): Before the introduction of C and D trains these were the top-quality sleeper trains; the Z trains are now the second best, but still with very modern air-conditioned coaches.

T trains: Trains with a 'T' in their number are the next best category, described as 'extra fast'.

K trains: Trains with a 'K' in their number are 'fast'.

Finding and boarding your train

Always arrive at the station in plenty of time before the departure of your train. In major cities, especially Beijing, stations can be large and busy, and it may take a while to find your train. At major stations such as in Beijing or Shanghai there are security checks (including airline-style X-ray luggage checks) to go through before boarding. Departure indicators may be in Chinese, but you can easily find your train if you know the train number and departure time.

Boarding trains in Beijing

There are two major stations in Beijing: Beijing Main (metro Beijing Zhan) and Beijing West (also called Beijing Xi or Xizhan, metro Junshibowuguan). Trans-Siberian trains to Moscow and Ulan Bator use Beijing Main, as do a handful of trains to Shanghai. The direct train to Hong Kong and trains to Xian, Guangzhou and Tibet all use Beijing's newer West station. The daytime and overnight D category high-speed trains from Beijing to Shanghai now use the little-known Beijing South station. Trains to the Great Wall at Badaling use the even smaller Beijing North station.

- Both Beijing Main and West stations are large and busy, and some people find them confusing. So arrive in plenty of time for your train!

- When you reach the station, you must first go through airport-style security controls into the departure area.

- For soft sleeper travel, you must then find the appropriate waiting lounge for your train. There are a number of different waiting lounges, and the electronic message boards show which is the right one for each specific train. Tickets are checked on entering the lounge, so you can be sure you are in the right place.

- Inside the lounge, the electronic message boards show the trains departing from that lounge over the next 24 hours. Trains are usually allocated between lounges so there is 30 minutes or more between each departure from that lounge. Most trains will be shown as 'on time', but the most immediate departures are shown as 'waiting'. Once a train is ready for boarding (normally about 30 minutes before departure) it is shown as 'check in', meaning you can proceed through ticket control to the platform. About 5 minutes before departure the barrier is closed and the train is shown as 'check out'.

HOW TO BUY TICKETS

Buying tickets at the station

It's easy to buy tickets yourself at the station, but remember to take your passport with you. In big cities such as Beijing or Shanghai you should look for the special ticket window for foreigners. In Shanghai, the English-speaking ticket window at the main station used to be window 43, though this has reportedly now changed to window 10 on the ground floor of the main ticket office to the southeast of the main station. (For particular advice on buying tickets in Beijing, see the next section below.)

Reservations for the best D- or Z-category express trains open 10–20 days before departure, but reservations for other trains only open 5–10 days before departure. You cannot buy tickets before reservations open. If the train you want starts its journey somewhere else and calls at your boarding station already well into its journey, tickets may only be available 2 days before departure. The exact rules vary by city and by train.

Chinese Railways doesn't have a central reservation system, only local computer reservation systems based in each city that aren't linked to each other. So a station can generally only sell you a ticket for a journey starting at that station, not for journeys starting elsewhere. For example, the ticket office at Shanghai can sell you a Shanghai–Beijing ticket but cannot sell you a Beijing–Xian ticket. At major cities you can sometimes buy a return ticket for key routes – for example, in Beijing you can buy a ticket from Beijing to

Shanghai and also from Shanghai back to Beijing. But in most cases you'll need to book your return journey when you get to your destination.

Tickets are best booked at least 2–3 days in advance, and around peak periods (the Spring Festival, May Day, National Day on 1 October) they should be booked as soon as reservations open.

Buying tickets in Beijing

You can buy tickets at Beijing Main station (metro Beijing Zhan), or Beijing West station (called Beijing Xi or Xizhan; metro Junshibowuguan, sometimes called 'Military Museum'). At Beijing Main station, the ticketing office for foreigners is on the northwest corner of the first floor, accessed via the soft seat waiting room. It is open 05:30–07:30, 08:00–18:30, 19:00–23:00. Only domestic Chinese tickets are sold, not international tickets. At Beijing West station, ticket window 1 in the main hall is marked 'English speaking', open 24 hours. Service here is reported as 'fluent and efficient'. Alternatively, you can buy train tickets at BTG Travel and Tours, on Fwai Dajie between the New Otani and Gloria Plaza hotels, open 08:00–20:00. For advice on how to buy Trans-Siberian tickets from Beijing to Ulan Bator or Moscow, see the chapter on the Trans-Siberian railway, page 50. For advice on how to buy tickets from Beijing to Hanoi, see the Vietnam chapter, page 440.

How to buy tickets from outside China

There are several ways to arrange Chinese train tickets from outside China. Just remember that reservations for the best D- and Z-category express trains open 20 days in advance, but for most other trains bookings only open 5–10 days before departure. Even an agency cannot positively confirm your booking before reservations open and they buy your ticket!

Your cheapest and easiest option may well be to ask your hotel to arrange train tickets for you (having first booked the hotel, of course). Many hotels will do this for a small fee, perhaps RMB50 (£5).

Alternatively you can book through train ticket agencies such as **www.chinatripadvisor.com**, **www.chinatraintickets.net** or **www.china-train-ticket.com**. Tickets cannot be posted abroad, but can be delivered to your hotel in China to be picked up when you get there. This will cost more than you'd pay at the ticket office (you'll find comparison fares for several journeys in the route-by-route sections below), but if you really need to be on a particular train on a particular date, it can be worth booking ahead, especially at peak periods, such as around the time of the Spring Festival, 1 May, or 1 October. All these agencies are reputable, and chinatripadvisor has been recommended by at least one seat61 correspondent.

Buying tickets for departures from Hong Kong

You can book departures from Hong Kong to Beijing and Shanghai by email at the official (cheap!) ticket office price through KCRC (Kowloon Canton Railway Corporation) Customer Services. Visit their website at **www.mtr.com.hk** (click 'customer site' then 'intercity passenger services' then 'more information'. Note that the online booking system on their intercity trains home page is only for the Hong Kong–Guangzhou intercity trains; for the Beijing and Shanghai through trains you'll need to email their customer services department. When looking up times and fares on their website, remember that Hong Kong is shown as 'Hung Hom'). You will be given a reference number and can then pick up and pay for tickets at Hong Kong's Hung Hom station in Kowloon. Note that Hong Kong ticket office does not accept credit cards, only cash. However, there is an ATM just round the corner from the station.

BEIJING TO SHANGHAI

The best way to travel between Beijing and Shanghai is by train. Choose between a high-speed daytime train or a time-effective overnight sleeper.

Beijing → Shanghai

Train number		D29	D31	D321 S	D307 S	D301 S	D305 S	T103 S	T109 S
Beijing (Main)	depart	–	–	–	–	–	–	22:09	22:15
Beijing (South)	depart	07:47	11:05	21:21	21:36	21:41	21:46	I	I
Shanghai (Hongqiao station)	arrive	18:52*	21:23*	07:15	07:25	07:30	07:35	11:09*	11:39*

Shanghai → Beijing

Train number		D30	D32	D306 S	D302 S	D314 S	D322 S	T104 S	T110 S
Shanghai (Hongqiao station)	depart	07:19*	10:31*	21:30	21:35	21:40	21:38	21:58*	22:04*
Beijing (South)	arrive	18:18	20:48	07:24	07:29	07:34	07:45	I	I
Beijing (Main)	arrive	–	–	–	–	–	–	11:17	11:23

* These trains use Shanghai main station, not Hongqiao.

S = sleeper train, arriving next day after departure

All trains shown here run daily.

Beijing–Shanghai is 1,454 km (909 miles).

Which train should you take?

Trains D301–D322 are the top-quality sleeper trains: immaculate brand-new 200km/h sleeper trains introduced in December 2008, with 4-berth soft sleepers and bar-restaurant car. Fully air-conditioned, each sleeper berth even has its own TV screen and there are power sockets for laptops or mobiles. Expect these trains to be very punctual. There were originally no 2-berth sleepers on this train, but one report suggests that there now are some 2-berth deluxe soft sleepers with private toilet on at least one of these D trains. Trains D29, D30, D31 and D32 are the recommended daytime trains in either direction: new D-category 200–250km/h express electric trains, introduced in April 2007, with first and second class seats and bar-restaurant car. First class seats are two abreast each side of the aisle, second class seats are three abreast one side, two abreast the other. Fares for these trains are RMB540 (£54 or $79) for a first class ticket, and RMB450 (£45 or $66) for second class.

Trains T109 and T110 have deluxe 2-berth compartments with private toilet and washroom as well as normal soft and hard sleepers.

Trains T103 and T104 have soft and hard sleepers. If you are on a tight budget and want to save money, travel hard sleeper on one of these slower T-category trains. Hard sleeper is still a comfortable and safe way to travel.

Fares

Beijing–Shanghai one-way per person	T-category sleeper train		D-cat sleeper train	Deluxe sleeper (only T109/110)	D-category daytime train	
	Hard sleeper	Soft sleeper	Soft sleeper		First class seat	Second class seat
Bought at reservations office in China	RMB350 (£35 or $52)	RMB500 (£51 or $74)	RMB730 (£74 or $107)	RMB921 (£93 $135)	?	RMB327 (£33 or $48)
Booked in advance at www.chinatripadvisor.com	$65 (£44)	$95 (£64)	$128 (£86)	$165 (£111)	$81 (£54)	$69 (£46)
Booked in advance at www.china-train-ticket.com	$100 (£67)	$130 (£87)	?	$195 (£131)	?	?

Children under 120 cm tall travel free, children 120–140 cm tall travel for half fare, children over 140 cm tall pay full fare.

At Shanghai station there are reportedly now some self-service ticket machines with an English-language facility, able to sell tickets for these trains.

BEIJING TO XIAN

The best way to travel between Beijing and Xian is by train, using a time-effective sleeper train. The superb Z-category trains Z19 and Z20 have top-quality air-conditioned sleeping-cars, far superior to any flight – and you save time over flying, too. These trains are soft class only (no hard class) with 4-berth soft class sleepers, restaurant car (with menu in Chinese and English, beer a reasonable RMB15 (£1.50), and the crispy fried prawns are recommended!) and bar. It is reported that the on-board staff are helpful and speak some English, and the berths are even fitted with small TV screens.

If you are set on having a 2-berth sleeper, you'll need to travel in train T44/T43.

The Terracotta Warriors are 40–45 minutes from Xian station by bus 306 or 307, fare about RMB7 (70p). Minibuses and taxis are also available.

Beijing → Xian

Train number		T41	T231	T43**	Z19*	
Beijing (West)	depart	16:43	16:55	20:36	21:18	day 1
Xian	arrive	05:22	06:42	08:42	08:19	day 2

Xian → Beijing

Train number		T232	T42	Z20*	T44**	
Xian	depart	20:40	18:42	20:16	20:34	day 1
Beijing (West)	arrive	09:06	06:22	07:17	07:40	day 2

* Recommended trains, with 4-berth soft class sleepers, restaurant car and bar. There are now no 2-berth sleepers on this train.

** Trains T44 and T43 have 2-berth deluxe sleepers with private toilet, as well as normal 4-berth soft sleepers, hard class sleepers and restaurant car.

Beijing–Xian is 1,200 km (750 miles).

All trains shown are daily. Other trains are also available; only the best options are shown here.

Fares

Beijing–Xian one-way per person	Hard sleeper	Soft sleeper	Deluxe soft sleeper
Bought at reservations office in China	RMB275 (£28 or $40)	RMB420 (£42 or $62)	RMB750 (£76 or $110)
Booked in advance at www.chinatripadvisor.com	$50 (£34)	$80 (£54)	$135 (£90)
Booked in advance at www.china-train-ticket.com	$105 (£70)	$130 (£87)	$175 (£117)

Children under 120 cm tall travel free, children 120–140 cm tall travel for half fare, children over 140 cm tall pay full fare.

BEIJING TO BADALING FOR THE GREAT WALL OF CHINA

If you're spending a few days in Beijing, you'll probably want to visit the Great

Wall of China. Badaling is the most-visited section of rebuilt Great Wall, an easy day trip north of Beijing. Most people go there on a one-day bus tour, but this often gives only 30 rushed minutes to see the Wall. It can be better to visit the Wall independently, taking a comfortable train from Beijing up into the mountains to Badaling, exploring and taking photographs at your leisure for an hour or two, then returning by train at a time to suit you. These trains are modern and air-conditioned with soft and hard seats plus buffet car.

Beijing → Badaling

Train number		Y563	Y567	Y571	Y575	Y579
Beijing (North)	depart	07:26	09:33	11:08	13:19	15:01
Badaling (for Great Wall)	arrive	08:25	10:42	12:15	14:28	16:10

Badaling → Beijing

Train number		Y568	Y572	Y576	Y580	Y584
Badaling (for Great Wall)	depart	09:25	11:42	13:10	15:22	17:08
Beijing (North)	arrive	10:47	12:59	14:29	16:28	18:30

Beijing North station is at metro stop Xizhimen on metro lines 2 and 4. On exiting the metro follow signs in English to Beijing North Station. Buying tickets is easy: just write the train number (for example 'Y567') on a bit of paper, plus the date you want to go, and buy at any of Beijing's station ticket offices (Main, West or North stations). The fare is around RMB14 (£1.50 or $2) each way hard seat (second class), or around RMB30 (£3 or $4) in soft seat (first class).

For the first 20 minutes of the journey, the train negotiates the Beijing suburbs, then it accelerates to around 80mph for a brief sprint to its first station stop. After stopping briefly at this station, the train starts climbing at slow speed into the mountains to Badaling. You start to see parts of the Great Wall as soon as you leave the station stop, so have your camera ready! Two hours at the Wall is plenty, so taking the 09:33 from Beijing out and the 13:10 from Badaling back, or the 11:08 out and 15:22 back, or the 13:19 out and 17:08 back, all work fine.

On arrival at Badaling station, leave the station and turn left and walk up the hill, following everyone else. The Great Wall ticket office is about 800 metres away on the right – you can't miss it. Entrance fee is around RMB40 (£4 or $6). Signs are in English, so no guide is required.

BEIJING TO TIANJIN

High-speed 350km/h C-category trains (sometimes known as 'Hexie' trains) link Beijing South station and Tianjin every 10–20 minutes, taking just 30 minutes for the 120-km journey. Simply use **www.chinatravelguide.com** to find specific train times. The fare is around RMB58 (£6 or $9) in a second class seat, RMB69 (£7 or $10) in a first class seat. It's easy enough to buy tickets at the station on the day of travel.

BEIJING TO GUANGZHOU (CANTON) AND HONG KONG

You can easily travel from Beijing to Guangzhou or Hong Kong by train, in a comfortable sleeper. There are two departures daily to Guangzhou, and a direct train to Hong Kong every other day, all with 2-berth deluxe soft sleepers with private toilet, normal 4-berth soft sleepers, hard sleepers and restaurant car. (There are also daily air-conditioned trains every few hours between Guangzhou and Hong Kong, so Beijing–Hong Kong with a change of trains at Guangzhou is an option; see **www.mtr.com.hk** for times, fares and online booking.) The station in Hong Kong is in Kowloon and called Hung Hom. It can help to know that the Chinese refer to Hong Kong/Kowloon as 'Jiulong'.

Departing from Beijing for Hong Kong, you should arrive at Beijing West station 90 minutes before departure for passport control and exit formalities. Departing from Hong Kong, you should arrive at Kowloon's Hung Hom station 45 minutes before departure for passport control and exit formalities.

Beijing → Guangzhou and Hong Kong

		Every 2 days*	Daily	Daily
Train number		T97	T15	T201
Beijing (West)	depart	13:08 day 1	11:00 day 1	18:16 day 1
Guangzhou (main)	arrive	I	07:35 day 2	15:01 day 2
Hong Kong (Hung Hom)	arrive	12:56 day 2	–	–

Guangzhou and Hong Kong → Beijing

		Every 2 days*	Daily	Daily
Train number		T98	T16	T202
Hong Kong (Hung Hom)	depart	15:15 day1	–	–
Guangzhou	depart	I	16:48 day 1	09:48 day 1
Beijing (West)	arrive	14:51 day 2	13:18 day 2	06:34 day 2

* Trains T97 and T98 run on even-numbered dates (2nd, 4th, 6th etc.) in some months and odd-numbered dates in others. You can check days of running, times and fares at **www.mtr.com.hk** (click 'customer site' then 'intercity passenger services' then 'more information' and remember that Hong Kong is shown as either 'Kowloon' or 'Hung Hom').

Fares

Hong Kong–Beijing one-way per person	Hard sleeper	Soft sleeper	Deluxe soft sleeper
Bought at reservations office in Hong Kong	HK$587 (£50 or $75)	HK$934 (£80 or $120)	HK$1,191 (£103 or $155)
Booked in advance at www.chinatripadvisor.com	$95 (£63)	$155 (£103)	$199 (£133)

Beijing–Hong Kong one-way per person	Hard sleeper	Soft sleeper	Deluxe soft sleeper
Bought at reservations office in Beijing	RMB507 (£50 or $75)	RMB822 (£80 or $120)	RMB1,200 (£120 or $175)
Booked in advance at www.chinatripadvisor.com	$95 (£63)	$155 (£103)	$199 (£133)
Booked in advance at www.china-train-ticket.com	$160 (£107)	$230 (£154)	$280 (£188)

Beijing–Guangzhou one-way per person	Hard sleeper	Soft sleeper	Deluxe soft sleeper
Bought at reservations office in China	RMB460 (£46 or $68)	RMB705 (£71 or $104)	?
Booked in advance at www.chinatripadvisor.com	?	?	?

Children under 120 cm tall travel free, children 120–140 cm tall travel for half fare, children over 140 cm tall pay full fare.

How to buy tickets

If your journey starts in Hong Kong, you can book tickets by email at **www.mtr.com.hk** (click 'customer site' then 'intercity passenger services') and pick up tickets at the booking office, or just buy them at the station reservations office. If your journey starts in Beijing or Guangzhou, see the advice on buying tickets above. Be warned, the Beijing–Hong Kong through-train is very popular and gets booked up very rapidly.

HONG KONG: Kowloon to Victoria Island Star Ferry

Regular Star Ferries shuttle between Kowloon (including Hung Hom railway station) and Hong Kong Victoria Island, see **www.starferry.com.hk**. The Star Ferry from Kowloon Hung Hom pier to Victoria Central area pier costs HK$6.30 (50p), runs every 20 minutes and takes 15 minutes for the journey.

HONG KONG TO GUANGZHOU (CANTON)

Air-conditioned intercity trains run every few hours between Guangzhou (Canton) and Hong Kong. See **www.mtr.com.hk** for times, fares and online booking.

HONG KONG TO MACAU

There are fast ferry services (jetfoils) from Hong Kong to Macau: see **www.turbocat.com**. These run every 15 minutes throughout the day, and every few hours at night, journey time 55 minutes. Fares start from HK$134 (£12 or US$18) in economy class. The jetfoils depart from the Hong Kong Macau Ferry Terminal, Shun Tak Centre, 200 Connaught Road Central.

HONG KONG TO SHANGHAI

A direct train runs between Hong Kong and Shanghai every other day, with 2-berth deluxe soft sleepers with private toilet, normal 4-berth soft sleepers, hard sleepers and restaurant car. From Hong Kong (train T100) it departs at 15:15, arriving at Shanghai at 11:15 next day. From Shanghai (train T99) it departs at 17:09, arriving at Hong Kong Hung Hom station at 13:05 next day. Departures fall on odd-numbered dates (1st, 3rd, 5th etc.) in some months and on even-numbered dates in others; you can check times, fares and days of running at **www.mtr.com.hk** (click 'customer site' then 'intercity passenger services' then 'more information' and remember that Hong Kong is shown as 'Hung Hom' or 'Kowloon').

Departing from Shanghai, you should arrive at Shanghai station 90 minutes before departure for passport control and exit formalities. Departing from Hong Kong, you should arrive at Kowloon's Hung Hom station 45 minutes before departure for passport control and exit formalities.

Fares

Hong Kong–Shanghai one-way per person	Hard sleeper	Soft sleeper	Deluxe soft sleeper
Bought at reservations office in Hong Kong	HK$519 (£45 or $67)	HK$825 (£71 or $107)	HK$1,039 (£90 or $135)

Shanghai–Hong Kong one-way per person	Hard sleeper	Soft sleeper	Deluxe soft sleeper
Bought at reservations office in Shanghai	RMB408 (£41 or $62)	RMB627 (£63 or $95)	RMB1,040 (£100 or $135)
Booked in advance at www.chinatripadvisor.com	$92 (£61)	$145 (£97)	$175 (£117)

How to buy tickets

If your journey starts in Hong Kong, you can book tickets by email at **www.mtr.com.hk** (click 'customer site' then 'intercity passenger services') and pick up tickets at the booking office, or just buy them at the station reservations office. If your journey starts in Shanghai, buy at the ticket office (there's an English-speaking window) or pre-book through an agency; see pages 292–3.

SHANGHAI TO XIAN

Two trains a day link Shanghai and Xian (there are more trains that run between Shanghai and Xian en route to other places, but two that operate specifically between these two cities). A high-quality Z-category train (train Z92 Shanghai–Xian, train Z94 Xian–Shanghai), with modern air-conditioned soft sleepers (4-berth), hard sleepers and restaurant car, departs Shanghai daily at 19:58, arriving at Xian at 09:49 next day; and eastbound departs Xian daily at 17:00, arriving at Shanghai at 06:53 next day. This is the recommended option.

A slower T-category train, also air-conditioned, with soft and hard sleepers and restaurant car (train T138), leaves Shanghai daily at 15:53, arriving at Xian at 07:58 next day; eastbound train T140 departs Xian daily at 19:50, arriving at Shanghai at 12:12 next day.

Shanghai to Xian one-way costs around £42/$63 per person in soft sleeper class or £27/$40 in hard sleeper when bought at the Shanghai reservations office; or around £53/$79 in soft sleeper, £37/$55 in hard sleeper when booked through **www.chinatripadvisor.com**.

TRAINS TO LHASA AND TIBET

The first regular passenger trains started running over the new railway to Lhasa in Tibet on 1 July 2006. The Qinghai–Tibet Railway is the highest in the world, climbing from 2,829 metres above sea level at Golmud (Geermu) to 3,641 metres at Lhasa, much of it built on permafrost. Its highest point is in the Tanggula Pass, at 5,072 metres (16,640 feet) above sea level. Because of the lack of oxygen at that altitude, all passenger coaches have extra oxygen pumped into them, and oxygen is available to passengers through tubes if they have problems. Before the railway into Tibet was built, travellers could take a train as far as Golmud (which the railway reached in 1984) but then faced a gruelling 48-hour bus journey to Lhasa. Now you can travel from Beijing, Shanghai, Guangzhou or Xian to Lhasa by direct air-conditioned train.

There are several trains a day to Lhasa, including a daily express from Beijing (a two-night, two-day journey) running via Xian, and other trains running every second day from Shanghai and Guangzhou (formerly called Canton, near Hong Kong). These are modern air-conditioned Chinese Railways trains, with soft and hard class sleepers, soft and hard class seats and a restaurant car.

Beijing, Shanghai, Guangzhou, Xian → Lhasa (Tibet)

		Daily	Every 2 days*	Every 2 days*	Every 2 days*	Every 2 days*
Train number		T27	T222/223	T22/23	T264	T164
Beijing (West)	depart	21:30 day 1	–	–	–	–
Shanghai	depart	|	–	–	–	19:52 day 1
Guangzhou	depart	|	–	–	12:19 day 1	|
Chongqing	depart	|	19:42 day 1	–	|	|
Xian	depart	08:42 day 2	06:27 day 2	–	09:45 day 2	10:12 day 2
Chengdu	depart	|	|	18:18 day 1	|	|
Lanzhou	depart	15:21 day 2	13:48 day 2	13:48 day 2	16:19 day 2	16:46 day 2
Xining	depart	18:08 day 2	16:49 day 2	16:49 day 2	19:05 day 2	19:40 day 2
Golmud (Geermu)	depart	03:42 day 3	04:18 day 3	04:18 day 3	04:42 day 3	05:48 day 3
Lhasa	arrive	18:38 day 3	17:21 day 3	18:28 day 3	18:58 day 3	20:48 day 3

Lhasa (Tibet) → Beijing, Shanghai, Guangzhou, Xian

		Daily	Every 2 days*	Every 2 days*	Every 2 days*	Every 2 days*
Train number		T28	T224/221	T24/21	T266	T166
Lhasa	depart	09:20 day 1	09:05 day 1	09:05 day 1	12:25 day 1	09:50 day 1
Golmud (Geermu)	arrive	23:45 day 1	23:15 day 1	23:15 day 1	01:27 day 2	00:36 day 2
Xining	arrive	09:59 day 2	11:10 day 2	11:10 day 2	10:54 day 2	10:26 day 2
Lanzhou	arrive	12:34 day 2	14:20 day 2	14:20 day 2	13:26 day 2	13:01 day 2
Chengdu	arrive	|	|	09:55 day 3	|	|
Xian	arrive	20:22 day 2	22:57 day 2	–	21:30 day 2	20:50 day 2
Chongqing	arrive	|	09:55 day 3	–	|	|
Guangzhou	arrive	|	–	–	18:58 day 3	|
Shanghai	arrive	|	–	–	–	11:15 day 3
Beijing (West)	arrive	07:34 day 3	–	–	–	–

All trains are air-conditioned with extra oxygen available, and have soft class and hard class sleepers and seats, and restaurant car. The soft sleepers have 4-berth compartments, complete with personal LCD televisions, occasionally showing English-language movies.

xx:xx = the train stops, but exact time not known.

* = runs every second day, on odd-numbered dates in some months and even-numbered dates in others. The only way to double-check which days the non-daily trains run is to look at the pdf timetable at **www.chinatt.org/download.htm**.

Another train (not shown here) runs daily between Xining and Lhasa, extended to Lanzhou on alternate days. Many other trains link Beijing, Xian, Lanzhou and Xining.

Beijing–Lhasa is 4,064 km (2,540 miles), of which 1,110 km (693 miles) are over the newly built Qinghai–Tibet railway.

Fares

One-way fare per person (approx.)	Hard sleeper	Soft sleeper
Beijing to Lhasa, bought at reservations office in Beijing	RMB813 (£82 or $120)	RMB1,262 (£127 or $186)
Beijing to Lhasa, booked in advance at www.chinatraintickets.net	$240 (£160)	$310 (£207)
Shanghai to Lhasa, bought at the station reservations office	RMB850 (£86 or $125)	RMB1,350 (£136 or $199)
Guangzhou to Lhasa, bought at the station reservations office	RMB1,000 (£101 or $147)	RMB1,500 (£152 or $221)
Chengdu to Lhasa, bought at the station	RMB704 (£71 or $104)	RMB1,112 (£112 or $164)
Xining to Lhasa, bought at the station	RMB523 (£53 or $77)	RMB810 (£82 or $119)

How to buy tickets

Bookings open ten days in advance. In the first months of operation of the new line, tickets were reported as selling out almost as soon as bookings opened, with no sign of demand diminishing. However, it's become easier to get tickets, and you can now arrange tickets, tours and Tibet permits through **www.china traintickets.net** or **www.chinahighlights.com**. Alternatively, you can try buying tickets yourself at the station, arranging a permit separately (see page 306).

Getting a permit for Tibet

In addition to a normal Chinese visa, foreigners require a special permit to enter Tibet, although there is talk of discontinuing this requirement, so please check. The only way to get a permit is through a Chinese travel agency, for example **www.chinatraintickets.net** or **www.chinahighlights.com**, who can arrange both trains and tailor-made tours. The permit is valid to enter Tibet and reach Lhasa, though a further permit is required to travel any further. There's a good article about Tibet permits at **http://kekexili.typepad.com/life_on_the_ tibetan_plate/2007/02/travel_in_tibet.html**.

Deluxe tourist trains to Lhasa

Deluxe tourist trains, a joint venture between Chinese Railways (Qinghai-Tibet Rail Corporation) and a Canadian company called RailPartners, were due to start running from Beijing to Lhasa in spring 2009, later postponed to spring 2010 because of the recession; see **www.tangulaluxurytrains.com**. The launch may well have been postponed again or even cancelled – certainly their website is no longer working as I write this. The trains, to be marketed as Tangula Luxury Trains, were to have luxurious sleeping-cars (featuring double beds, private shower and toilet), restaurant. cars and lounge-observation cars. Exact dates, times and fares have not been announced, but it is intended the Beijing–Lhasa train should run year-round, with about 75 departures a year.

LHASA (TIBET) TO KATHMANDU (NEPAL)

If you want to travel from Lhasa through the Himalayas to Kathmandu in Nepal (for bus and train on to Delhi or Varanasi), the only way this can be done legally at present is with an organised tour. The cheapest tours cost about £270/$400 and take eight days (seven nights) for the 955-km journey. Try **www.heiantreks.com**, who normally run Lhasa–Kathmandu overland tours twice a week, **www.trekkingtibet.com** (recommended by one seat61 correspondent), **www.visitnepal.com/getaway** (weekly, £300/$450) or **www.richatours.com**; or do a Google search for other agencies. In 2005, there were reports of a new twice-weekly bus service from Kathmandu to Lhasa but apparently this service folded soon after it started.

BEIJING TO HANOI AND SAIGON (VIETNAM)

There's a comfortable twice-weekly soft sleeper train with restaurant car from Beijing to Hanoi, taking two nights and one day. For train times and fares, see the Vietnam chapter, pages 438–9. You can book this train in Beijing at the reservations office, or in advance from outside China with **www.chinatripadvisor.com**.

HONG KONG TO HANOI AND SAIGON (VIETNAM)

You can travel overland by train+bus from Hong Kong to Hanoi in Vietnam, quite cheaply and comfortably. You take an intercity train from Hong Kong to Guangzhou, the overnight sleeper train from Guangzhou to Nanning, a connecting train to Pinxiang then a bus to the border and on to Hanoi. For details of how to do this, see the Vietnam chapter, pages 441–3.

INDIA

Without a shadow of a doubt, the best way to see India is not on a plane at 35,000 feet, but at ground level on the incredible Indian railway system. In fact, no visit to India is complete without experiencing the bustle of Indian railway stations and a comfortable journey on an Indian express train with the tea seller's welcome cry of 'Chai, chai, garam chai' ringing down the aisle. You can safely forget media images of overcrowded suburban trains with people sitting on the roof. On a long-distance express train in an AC chair car or an AC1 or AC2 sleeper, all seats and berths are reserved and it's a safe, cheap and civilised way to get around India. Even long distances such as Bombay to Delhi, Delhi to Varanasi or Delhi to Udaipur can be covered more time-effectively than flying, using overnight AC sleeper trains, city centre to city centre, saving a hotel bill into the bargain.

Train operator:	Indian Railways, **www.indianrail.gov.in** (for train times and fares; go to **www.cleartrip.com** or **www.makemytrip.com** for online booking) UK IndRail pass agency: **www.indiarail.co.uk**
Time zone:	GMT+5½ all year round
Currency:	£1 = approx. 68 rupees, $1 = approx. 44 rupees
Tourist information:	**www.incredibleindia.org**
Visas:	UK citizens and most other western nationalities need a visa to visit India. Information and application form are available at **www.hcilondon.net**. Apply by post or in person to the Indian High Commission, India House, Aldwych, London WC2B 4NA, telephone 020 7836 8484.

EUROPE TO INDIA, overland

It's possible to travel overland from the UK to India via Turkey, Iran and Pakistan, although there are some security concerns and visa issues along the way at the moment, making it more of an expedition than a straightforward way to travel. For details, see page 90.

TRAIN TRAVEL WITHIN INDIA

The Indian Railways network

With 63,000 km (39,000 miles) of rail routes and 6,800 stations, the railway network in India is the third biggest in the world after Russia and China, and the second biggest in the world in terms of passenger kilometres. Indian Railways is also the world's biggest employer, with over 1.5 million staff. The trains in India go almost everywhere, and it's generally safe to assume that you can travel between any two Indian cities or major towns by train. For an Indian railways route map see **www.indianrail.gov.in** and look for 'maps'.

There's currently no railway to Kashmir, although a line to Srinagar and beyond is under construction: part is now open but the rest is unlikely to open until 2016. The line heads through tough terrain, and will feature the highest railway bridge in the world.

Incidentally, Khajuraho (often visited by tourists for its temples) now has a station, with an overnight train three times a week from Delhi's Nizamuddin station at 21:35 on Tuesday, Friday and Sunday. It returns from Khajuraho at 18:15 on Monday, Wednesday and Saturday.

In fact there are so many routes, trains and destinations, it's impossible to list them all here. But to give you an idea of what's available, the table below shows a selection of trains from Delhi to key tourist destinations. The various classes of accommodation are described in detail on page 320; the generally recommended option for western travellers would be AC2 for overnight travel, CC for daytime.

Delhi to	Train times	Classes	Fare in AC2	Remarks
Agra	New Delhi depart 06:15 Agra arrive 08:12 (same day)	XC, CC	Rs390 (£6/$9)	Shatabdi Express – quality train, breakfast included
Bombay (Mumbai)	New Delhi depart 16:30 Bombay Central arrive 08:35 (next day)	AC1, AC2, AC3, CC	Rs2,200 (£32/$50)	Rajdhani Express – quality sleeper train, meals included
Calcutta (Kolkata)	New Delhi depart 17:00 Calcutta Howrah arrive 09:55 (next day)	AC1, AC2, AC3, CC	Rs2,270 (£33/$52)	Rajdhani Express – quality sleeper train, meals included
Jaisalmer	Delhi depart 17:30 Jaisalmer arrive 11:45 (next day)	AC2, AC3, SL	Rs1,390 (£20/$32)	Delhi–Jaisalmer Express
Madras (Chennai)	New Delhi depart 22:30 Madras arrive 07:10 (2 nights later)	AC1, AC2, AC3, SL,2	Rs2,280 (£34/$52)	Tamil Nadu Express
Simla	Delhi Sarai Rohilla depart 05:40 Simla arrive 17:20 (same day)	CC, 2	Rs490 (£7/$11)	By broad-gauge train to Kalka, then by Toy Train
Udaipur	New Delhi depart 19:05 Udaipur arrive 07:20 (next day)	AC1, AC2, AC3, SL	Rs1,200 (£18/$27)	Mewar Express
Varanasi	New Delhi depart 18:45 Varanasi Jn arrive 07:30 (next day)	AC1, AC2, AC3, SL,2	Rs1,272 (£19/$29)	Shiv Ganga Express

XC = air-conditioned executive chair class.

CC = air-conditioned chair class.

AC1 = air-conditioned first class (2- and 4-berth sleeper compartments).

AC2 = air-conditioned 2-tier (2- and 4-berth sleeper bays).

AC3 = air-conditioned 3-tier (2- and 6-berth sleeper bays).

SL = sleeper class (non-air-conditioned, 2- and 6-berth sleeper bays).

2 = second class seats, unreserved, non-air-conditioned.

HOW TO FIND OUT INDIAN TRAIN TIMES

You can check train times and fares for any journey in India at **www.indianrail.gov.in**, the official Indian Railways website. This is an amazing site, but a little bewildering. In fact, it's a good training course for your travels in India! There are some tips for using **www.indianrail.gov.in** below. You can also use the privately run Indian train website **www.cleartrip.com**, which many people find easier to use.

Tips for using www.indianrail.gov.in

- Look for 'Trains Between Imp. Stations' at the top of their home page. This will give you train times and fares between all the most important places in India.

- If you can't find a train between your chosen destinations, it may be because www.indianrail.gov.in can only find direct trains. If there isn't a direct train you'll need to guess at a likely interchange station and make separate enquiries for both sections of the journey. For example, for Varanasi to Jaisalmer, try asking for Varanasi to Delhi and then Delhi to Jaisalmer, or Varanasi to Jaipur then Jaipur to Jaisalmer. For journeys to Simla the interchange station is Kalka; for trips to Darjeeling it is New Jalpaiguri.

- City names: Bombay appears as Mumbai, Madras as Chennai, Calcutta as Kolkata. Delhi is still Delhi, at least for now. Forgive me if I stick to the familiar English names!

- The main city-centre station in Delhi is New Delhi, so look for 'New Delhi' as well as 'Delhi'. Delhi Junction station is in central old Delhi. H. Nizamudin and Sarai Rohilla stations are secondary Delhi stations, further from the city centre and best reached by taxi.

- There are several stations in Bombay, but the most important (and impressive) is the magnificent colonial Victoria Terminus, now renamed 'CST'. So start by looking for trains from 'Mumbai CST'. If you don't see any suitable trains, try Bombay Central ('Mumbai BCT'), then finally Dadar which is a little way out of the centre.

- The main station in Calcutta is across the river in Howrah, often just shown as 'Howrah'. Trains from Calcutta to New Jalpaiguri (the railhead for Darjeeling) use Calcutta Sealdah station, often just shown as 'Sealdah'.

- In Agra the main station for fast trains is Agra Cantonment ('AGRA CANTT'), which is an autorickshaw or taxi ride from the Taj Mahal, although Agra Fort is nearer the town centre.

- Goa isn't a town or city, it's a region. The main stations in Goa are Magdaon and Vasco da Gama, so use these when you check for train times.

- If the system shows a train running overnight, make sure it isn't actually two or more nights. The journey from Bombay to Calcutta or from Delhi to Madras is about 36 hours, i.e. typically two nights. On the other hand, travelling on a fast train, Bombay to Delhi or Calcutta to Delhi takes just one night.

- There are eight different classes on Indian Railways, but not all of them are available on every train. For overnight journeys, most visitors choose AC2 (second class 2-tier air-conditioned, shown as '2A') or if they can afford it, AC1 (first class air-conditioned, shown as '1A'), although more adventurous backpackers might choose sleeper class ('SL'). AC3 (shown as '3A') is also fine. For daytime journeys, air-conditioned chair car ('CC') is a good choice where it's available.

- Rajdhani Express trains are excellent extra-fast air-conditioned long-distance trains linking Delhi with regional capitals such as Bombay, Calcutta, etc. These are the best trains to take. The Delhi–Bombay and Delhi–Calcutta Rajdhani Expresses leave in the early evening and arrive in the morning, so actually save time compared with flying. Meals are included in the fare, served at your seat. The Delhi–Bombay Rajdhani uses brand-new German-designed coaches. Highly recommended, these trains beat flying, hands-down!

● Shatabdi Express trains are excellent fast daytime trains running on routes such as Delhi–Agra and Delhi–Jaipur with air-conditioned chair class and executive air-conditioned chair class. Refreshments are included in the fare. Again, these are the best trains to take – highly recommended.

FARES

You can check train fares at **www.indianrail.gov.in** or at **www.cleartrip.com**. The table below shows some sample one-way fares in rupees, including reservation and fast train charges, which will give you an idea of how much Indian train travel costs, and how the fares for different classes compare. For a full description of the various classes, see page 320.

All fares shown are in rupees (source: www.indianrail.gov.in)	AC1	AC Exec chair car	AC2	First class	AC chair car	AC3	Sleeper class
Delhi to Agra (by Shatabdi Express)	–	755 (£11)	–	–	390 (£6)	–	–
Delhi to Agra (by ordinary express)	–	–	495 (£7)	–	–	311 (£5)	121 (£1.75)
Delhi to Udaipur	2,263 (£33)	–	1,200 (£18)	863 (£13)	–	–	284 (£4)
Delhi to Varanasi	2,395 (£35)	–	1,272 (£19)	–	–	826 (£12)	313 (£5)
Delhi to Bombay (by Rajdhani Express)	4,120 (£61)	–	2,200 (£32)	–	–	1,470 (£22)	–

All fares shown are in rupees	AC1	AC Exec chair car	AC2	First class	AC chair car	AC3	Sleeper class
Delhi to Bombay (by ordinary express)	3,373 (£50)	–	1,775 (£26)	–	–	1,140 (£17)	425 (£6)
Delhi to Calcutta (by Rajdhani Express)	4,215 (£62)	–	2,250 (£33)	–	–	1,510 (£22)	–
Delhi to Calcutta (by ordinary express)	3,443 (£51)	–	1,811 (£27)	–	–	1,163 (£17)	433 (£6)

Shatabdi Express = premier daytime train, special fare payable, meals included.

Rajdhani Express = premier overnight train, special fare payable, meals included.

Children aged 0–4 travel free, children aged 5–11 travel at half fare, children aged 12 and over pay full fare.

HOW TO BUY TICKETS IN INDIA

Do you need a reservation?

Yes, you do. You need to make a seat or berth reservation for all long-distance journeys on Indian trains, you cannot simply turn up and hop on. Bookings open 90 days before departure – this was originally 60 days, but it was extended to 90 days experimentally and made permanent in 2008. Some short-distance intercity trains may open for bookings later than this. Reservations are now completely computerised. Indeed, according to an Indian professor with whom I once shared a compartment, computerisation saved him 50 per cent of his travel costs as he had always had to pay the same again in bribes to get a reservation! Indian trains are usually very busy, and they often get booked out days or even weeks ahead. You should make reservations as far in advance as possible – you may see TV screens in the reservation offices in major cities showing berth availability on the main trains from that city over the next few weeks. However, a special 'tourist quota' gives foreigners (and IndRail passholders; see page 323) preferential treatment.

The tourist quota

Many important trains (but not all trains) have a special quota of seats or berths available for foreign tourists and IndRail passholders. This is very useful: a train which is fully booked for Indian travellers may still have a few 'tourist quota' berths available within a day or two of departure so that foreign travellers can travel around at short notice. However, it's not foolproof. Even using this special quota, you may have to wait a day or so before there is a berth available to your chosen destination in your chosen class. There is a tourist quota on perhaps 200 trains a day out of a total of 9,000 trains, and the quota might be just two places, seldom more than twelve places, spread over each class. Tickets issued against the tourist quota must be paid for in US dollars, pounds sterling, or rupees backed by an exchange certificate proving they have been obtained from a bank or bureau de change in exchange for foreign currency. Rupees backed by an ATM receipt and foreign bank card are usually sufficient.

'Reservation Against Cancellation' (RAC) and 'Waitlisted' (WL) places

Indian Railways has a unique system: after a train becomes fully booked, a certain number of places in each class are sold as 'Reservation Against Cancellation' (RAC). After all the RAC places have been sold, further prospective passengers are 'Waitlisted' (WL). If you hold an RAC ticket, as and when a passenger with a confirmed reservation cancels before the departure of the train, you will be promoted to that confirmed seat or berth on the train (shown as 'CNF' meaning 'confirmed'), and your name will be shown against a specific seat or berth on the reservation list on the day of travel at the boarding station (so remember to check it!). A waitlisted passenger will then be promoted to RAC in your place. Even if nobody cancels, if you hold an RAC ticket you are allowed to board the train and travel. You will normally be given a place to sit (but not a berth) in a carriage of the relevant class, for example two RAC passengers might have to share a two-seat space that would normally convert into a berth for one person. If one of the confirmed passengers fails to show up for the train, the on-board staff will allocate the spare berth to the first RAC passenger (and the second RAC passenger may then find himself with a berth to himself, solving two RAC passengers' problems!). Obviously, if there are no no-shows, the RAC passengers will have to sit up all night, or perhaps take turns using the berth to snooze. However, if you're offered an RAC place, do take it, as you'll usually end up with a confirmed berth on the train. Indeed, you've a good chance of getting on the train even with a low-number waitlisted ticket. You can confirm the current status of your booking at **www.indianrail.gov.in/pnr_stat.html** by entering the 'PNR' number on your ticket, but remember that things can change even on the day of departure. When the reservation chart is produced on the day of departure, unsold tickets in various special quotas may be released, and WL passengers promoted to RAC and RAC passengers promoted to CNF (confirmed). What a system!

'Tatkal' places

To allow travel at short notice on trains that had always become fully booked weeks before departure, Indian Railways introduced a system called 'Tatkal', which means 'immediate' in Hindi. A number of tickets on key trains are held back and released at 08:00 two days before departure (originally 72 hours before, but as from August 2009 only two days), then sold with a 75–300 rupees (£1–£5) extra Tatkal charge. If there's a tourist quota place available then the Tatkal system may be irrelevant for you, but if you can't get a tourist quota place, a Tatkal place may be useful.

Tourist reservation bureaux

The main stations in big cities and tourist centres such as New Delhi, Bombay, Calcutta, Agra, Jaipur and Varanasi have an International Tourist Bureau where foreign travellers can book trains away from the crowds and queues at the normal booking office. There is also a 24-hour rail booking office at Delhi International Airport. For a list of stations with an International Tourist Bureau, and opening times, visit **www.indianrail.gov.in** and select 'Information' then 'International Tourist'. Ignore anyone telling you the reservations office is closed, but their travel agency across the street can sell you a ticket!

HOW TO BUY TICKETS FROM OUTSIDE INDIA

Buying tickets online

Indian trains often get fully booked weeks in advance, so it's worth booking before you get to India if you have limited time or need to be on a particular train soon after your arrival. The official online ticket sales website is **www.irctc.co.in**; however, as of summer 2010 it no longer accepts non-Indian credit cards (other than Amex), so overseas visitors should use a privately run website: **www.cleartrip.com**. Cleartrip.com charges a fee on top of the regular ticket price, but this fee is only 20 rupees (about 30p or $0.50), and it is far easier to use than irctc.co.in. It happily accepts international credit cards and issues you with an 'e-ticket', so there are no worries about ticket delivery. Many seat61 correspondents have praised cleartrip.com, saying that it is far easier to use than irctc.co.in, and the time and hassle saved were worth the small fee.

Buying tickets via an IndRail pass agency

Alternatively, the hassle-free way of booking an Indian train journey in advance from outside India, or indeed booking a complete itinerary by rail around India, is to buy an IndRail pass from the official IndRail pass agency in your home country, complete with any train reservations you need. Even a single Indian train journey can be arranged this way: you use a half-day pass for any journey lasting less than 12 hours, costing £17 ($26) in AC2 or £38 ($57) in AC1; or a one-day pass for any journey lasting less than 24 hours, costing £28 ($43) in AC2 or £63 ($95) in AC1. There are IndRail pass agencies in the UK, Australia, Germany, Finland, Malaysia, South Africa and some other countries; see the IndRail pass section, page 323.

TIPS FOR TRAIN TRAVEL IN INDIA

Checking your reservation

Your train, coach and berth number will be printed on your ticket. Reservation lists for each long-distance train are posted on the notice board at each station about 2 hours before departure, showing the name, age and sex of each passenger reserved in each berth in each coach – the age and sex help the ticket inspector identify that the right passenger is in the right berth. The reservation list for each coach will also be pasted on the train itself, next to the entrance door. Check to see that your name is listed. The system is very efficient, and the days of finding your reserved berth already occupied by several passengers are long gone.

Food and drink on Indian trains

There are no restaurant or buffet cars on Indian Railways, but on long-distance trains an attendant will appear in your coach and ask you if you would like to order food. He will note down your order (usually a choice of 'veg' or 'non-veg') on a bit of paper. An hour or so later he will reappear with some rice and curry in small foil containers from the kitchen car. It is not expensive – you can reckon on £1–£2 per meal. Attendants also regularly pass down each car selling soft drinks, snacks, or excellent hot sweet Indian tea (*garam chai*) for a few rupees. On the premier Rajdhani Express trains (linking Delhi with Bombay, Calcutta, etc.) and the premier daytime Shatabdi Express trains (linking Delhi with Jaipur and Agra etc.) food, served at your seat, is included in the fare.

Cleanliness, toilets and crowding

The efficient reservation system means that you can safely forget any pictures you've seen of overcrowded Indian trains with people sitting on the roof or hanging on the side. These photos show suburban trains, or basic unreserved second class on long-distance ones. On fast long-distance trains in AC1, AC2, AC3, or AC chair class, all passengers have an assigned seat or sleeping berth so there's no overcrowding. Don't expect pristine western standards anywhere in India, but you'll find AC1, AC2, AC3 and AC chair class fairly clean by Indian standards, with both western-style and squat toilets usually kept in a reasonably sanitary condition by the sleeper attendant. Remember to take your own toilet paper.

Sleeper class, on the other hand, gets much grubbier than the AC classes and unreserved passengers may sometimes enter the coaches, making it crowded.

Second class unreserved can be incredibly crowded. Toilets in sleeper class or basic non-AC second class seats can leave a lot to be desired.

Security on Indian trains

Indian trains are safe to travel on, even for families or women travelling alone, and you are unlikely to have any problems at all. Having said that, theft of luggage is not unheard of, so for peace of mind take along a bicycle lock or medium-sized padlock to secure your bags. In the sleeping-cars, there are wire hoops hanging down underneath the seats to which you can secure your luggage. As in any busy place, pickpockets operate at the major stations, for example Delhi and New Delhi, so take care.

Do Indian trains run on time?

Generally, Indian Railways are very efficient, but Indian trains do run late, and sometimes it's hours rather than minutes. Rather than listen to hearsay, why not go to **www.erail.in** and see how late yesterday's Delhi–Jaisalmer Express arrived, or last Thursday's Bombay–Delhi Rajdhani Express? At www.erail.in, select the origin and destination that interests you, and bring up the train list. Now find the train that you want and click on it. Now select a date and click the 'train running status' button. It will show you a table of scheduled times and actual times at each station. Data are only held for the last few days, not weeks or months ago.

Alternatively, these examples from my own travels may give you a feel for the likely delay: Delhi–Varanasi overnight express spot on time, Bombay–Calcutta Mail 1½ hours late, Madras–Bombay Chennai Express 40 minutes late, Calcutta–Delhi Rajdhani Express spot on time (Rajdhani Expresses get priority and are pretty punctual), Delhi–Agra Shatabdi Express spot on time (Shatabdi Expresses also get priority and are pretty punctual), Jaisalmer–Delhi Express 2 hours late starting and 3 hours late arriving, Delhi–Kalka–Simla Himalayan Queen spot on time, Varanasi–Agra–Jaipur Marudhar Express 50 minutes late, Delhi–Madras Grand Trunk Express 1½ hours late.

Recharging mobiles and cameras

These days, people seem unable to go anywhere without an array of electrical gadgetry. You'll find shaver sockets in most AC1/2/3 sleeper cars, which can be used to recharge cameras and mobiles, though you won't generally find specific power sockets for this purpose on Indian trains. One tip is to invest in a Power Monkey universal backup battery, which will give you up to 96 hours' phone stand-by when your phone battery dies, and can also be used for recharging PDAs, iPods and some cameras whilst on the move.

THE EIGHT CLASSES ON INDIAN TRAINS

Remarkably, there are eight different classes of accommodation on Indian trains, although only some of these classes will be available on any particular train. These are the classes, in roughly descending order of cost:

Air-conditioned first class (AC1/1A)

Spacious, carpeted and lockable 4-berth and 2-berth compartments with washbasin. All necessary bedding is provided, and berths convert to seats for daytime use. AC1 is a very comfortable and civilised way to travel, although usually rather grubbier than the first class you'd expect in Europe. AC1 is only found on the most important long-distance trains and it costs about twice the price of AC2. In AC1, you'll be mixing with bank managers and army officers. You cannot specify that you want berths in a 2-berth rather than a 4-berth compartment when you book. Specific berth numbers are only allocated closer to the departure date and are shown on reservation lists at the station before departure and on the coach side. Couples are normally given preference for the 2-berth coupés; families and passengers travelling alone are normally allocated berths in one of the 4-berth compartments; but of course this can't be guaranteed.

AC executive chair class

AC executive chair class is found only on the most important Shatabdi Express trains, for example Delhi to Agra. It is available to holders of an AC1 IndRail pass. It consists of fabric-covered reclining seats in an open-plan coach.

Air-conditioned 2-tier (AC2/2A)

AC2 provides seats by day which convert to bunks at night. AC2 coaches are not divided into separate compartments, but are open-plan, with berths arranged in bays of four (two upper, two lower) on one side of the aisle, and in bays of two along the coach side above and below the windows on the other side of the aisle. Each bay is curtained off for privacy, and an attendant distributes pillows, sheets and blankets in the evening. AC2 is found on almost all long-distance express trains, and it is the way the Indian middle classes travel. It's relatively clean and uncrowded, and a sound choice for most visitors to India.

Air-conditioned 3-tier (AC3/3A)

AC3 is very similar to AC2, but it has three tiers of bunks – upper, middle and lower – arranged in bays of six on one side of the aisle, and bays of two (upper and lower) along the coach side on the other side of the aisle. It's therefore more crowded than AC 2-tier, and it lacks the privacy curtains and individual berth lights found in AC2. As in AC2, an attendant distributes pillows, sheets and blankets in the evening. Berths convert to seats for daytime use. It's still a good choice for western travellers.

First class

Classic 'first class' without air-conditioning has now virtually disappeared, as Indian Railways have progressively phased it out in favour of AC2. It consists of non-air-conditioned coaches with lockable 4-berth and 2-berth compartments. Bedding is not included in the fare, but may be available for a small extra charge if booked in advance. It is generally grubbier than AC1, AC2 or AC3 as it is not sealed against the dirt.

AC chair class (CC)

AC chair cars are comfortable air-conditioned seating cars with seats in open-plan coaches. AC chair class is found on a number of 'intercity' daytime trains (for example Delhi–Jaipur, Delhi–Agra, Delhi–Kalka for Simla), and is available to holders of an AC2 class IndRail pass. It's a good choice for daytime travel.

Sleeper class (SL)

Sleeper class is the way most of the Indian population travels long-distance, and the majority of cars on a long-distance train will be sleeper class. It consists of open-plan berths with upper, middle and lower bunks arranged in bays of six on one side of the aisle, and along the coach wall in bays of two (upper and lower) on the other side of the aisle. Bedding is not provided, so bring a sleeping bag. Sleeper class is found on almost all long-distance trains except for the premier Rajdhani Express services. Sleeper class can be quite crowded (although in theory all berths must be reserved, so it can't get overcrowded), and it's fairly grubby and basic. On the other hand, you get a better view of the countryside than in AC coaches, where the windows are sealed, tinted and sometimes dirty. In summer, there are fans on the ceiling and a breeze from the windows. In winter, wrap up warm at night and take a sleeping bag and fleece, as it can get cold. Sleeper class is used by the more adventurous backpackers who are prepared to take the rough with the smooth.

Unreserved second class

Open-plan seats cars with wooden or padded plastic seats. Not recommended for long-distance overnight journeys (you'll see the huge scrum of Indians all trying to bag a seat), but quite acceptable for daytime journeys of up to a few hours.

INDRAIL PASSES

Should you buy an IndRail pass or normal tickets?

Indian trains are very busy and often get booked up weeks in advance. Foreign visitors can make use of the special tourist quota, but even so, you may find the train you want fully booked. The great benefit of an IndRail pass is that you can ask the UK IndRail pass agency to pre-book some or all of your trains before you get to India, saving time, hassle and possible disappointment. If you have limited time in India, this is a very good way to get all your train travel pre-booked before you leave home. If, on the other hand, you intend to stay flexible and make reservations as you go, you can still do this with an IndRail pass (and passholders qualify for places from the tourist quota), but there is little advantage in having one and ordinary tickets may be cheaper.

What types of IndRail pass are there?

IndRail passes come in three classes: AC1, AC2 and second class. You can buy one for any time period from a half-day to 90 days. You can use a half-day or one-day pass to book a single one-off train trip or you can arrange a complete pre-booked itinerary all round India using a longer period pass or a combination of passes.

Will an IndRail pass cost more than normal tickets?

An IndRail pass will very likely cost more than buying normal point-to-point tickets, depending on the exact journeys you want to do, but probably not that much more. A normal ticket from Delhi to Varanasi costs 1,272 rupees (£19) in AC2 class, whereas a one-day AC2 IndRail pass costs $43, about £28. A trip to Delhi, Varanasi, Agra, Jaipur, Jaisalmer and Simla, all booked in advance from the UK using a 15-day AC2 pass, costs $185 (£123), whereas normal point-to-point tickets would have been about £118.

Which class of pass?

There are eight different classes on Indian trains, but IndRail passes come in just three types: AC1, AC2 and second class (AC = air-conditioned). With an AC1 IndRail pass, you can travel in AC1 and AC executive chair classes, or in cheaper accommodation where there is no AC1 available. With an AC2 IndRail pass, you can travel in AC2, ordinary first class sleepers and AC chair cars. With a second class pass, you can only travel in sleeper class and unreserved second class. AC1 is most comfortable, but it's found only on the most important long-distance trains and a handful of shorter-distance ones, so an AC1 pass is not worth it unless you're sure you are going to use trains which have AC1 or executive chair class. For most people, an AC2 pass is the best bet. With an AC2 pass, you will be booked in an AC2 sleeper where available, or an AC chair car on a daytime journey where one is available, unless you specifically ask for ordinary (non-air-conditioned) first class. Travelling in sleeper class is an experience, but a second class pass (which allows travel in sleeper class as well as second class seats) is probably only for the more adventurous (or extremely budget-conscious) traveller.

Suggested itineraries

India is vast, and many first-time visitors wonder where to start. One strategy is to tour only a small area, for example Rajasthan or the beaches of Goa. But I'd suggest using the excellent Indian train network to see an amazing cross-section of India, picking one example of each totally different type of place: one big city, one Himalayan hill station, one or two princely cities in Rajasthan, unmissable Agra (for the Taj Mahal) and perhaps Varanasi, the classic Hindu holy city on the Ganges. This way, you'll get to see just how varied India is, with overnight trains minimising the number of daytime hours spent travelling and cutting your hotel costs at the same time. Here's just one suggested itinerary that covers some of northern India's most unmissable cities, and easily fills two to three weeks, depending on the pace you want to set.

Sample itinerary 1

Delhi: spend 1–3 days in the city.

Take the Shiv Ganga Express leaving New Delhi at 18:45, arriving at Varanasi Junction at 07:30 next morning. AC1, AC2, AC3, sleeper class.

Varanasi: stay 2–3 days. This is the unmissable Hindu holy city on the Ganges. Make sure you stay in a local Indian riverside hotel such as the Hotel Alka. Western chain hotels are all in the new town, away from the action.

Take the Marudhar Express from Varanasi Junction at 17:20 (18:15 on some days), arriving at Agra Fort at 05:55 next morning. AC2, AC3, sleeper class.

Agra: stay 2 days, including a visit to the fantastic royal city of Fatephur Sikhri, some 30 km away by bus or car. Agra may be the most touristy place in India, but the Taj is well worth the tourist tout hassle. The fort and 'baby Taj' are also worth a visit.

Take the Marudhar Express from Agra at 06:15, arriving at Jaipur at 11:30 the same day. AC2, AC3, sleeper class.

Jaipur: stay 2–3 days. The 'Pink City' is one of the most wonderful princely cities in Rajasthan, and indeed in India.

Take the Delhi–Jaisalmer Express leaving Jaipur at 23:57, arriving at Jaisalmer at 11:30 next morning. AC2, AC3, sleeper class. On the day of departure from Jaipur, negotiate a rate to keep your hotel room until you leave for the station.

Jaisalmer: stay 2–3 days. This is Rajasthan's fairytale city, in the desert close to the Pakistan border. It has no airport, so only those who make the effort get to see it!

Take the Jaisalmer–Delhi Express leaving Jaisalmer at 16:45 and arriving at New Delhi at 11:05 next morning. Spend the day and overnight in Delhi.

An early start! Take the Himalayan Queen leaving Delhi Sarai Rohilla at 05:40, arriving at Kalka at 11:10. AC chair class and second class seats. Change on to the train leaving Kalka at 12:10, arriving at Simla at 17:20. This journey to Simla by narrow-gauge 'Toy Train' is a delight.

Simla: stay 2–3 days. Cool relaxation and colonial charm in this Himalayan hill station from the days of the Raj. The ideal final destination for your trip!

Take the Shivalik Deluxe (AC chair class, meal included) leaving Simla at 17:40, arriving at Kalka at 22:20. Change on to the mainline Kalka Mail leaving Kalka at 23:55 and arriving at Delhi (this time old Delhi station) at 06:15 next morning. AC1, AC2, AC3, sleeper class.

You can make this itinerary on either a 15-day or a 21-day IndRail pass, depending on how long you stay in each place. As you can see from the classes available on each train, an AC2 pass would be the best option: you would get little practical benefit from paying the extra for an AC1 pass.

Alternatively, how about a round trip from Calcutta:

Sample itinerary 2

Calcutta

Overnight sleeper train from Calcutta to New Jalpaiguri, then the famous Darjeeling Toy Train.

Darjeeling

Varanasi

Overnight sleeper train from Varanasi to Agra.

Agra

Daytime train from Agra to Jaipur.

Jaipur

Overnight sleeper train from Jaipur to **Calcutta**.

You can find train times for this itinerary (or any other you choose) using **www.indianrail.gov.in** or **www.cleartrip.com**.

IndRail pass prices

A 7-day AC2 pass costs $135 (about £90), a 15-day pass $185 (about £125), a 21-day pass $198 (about £132). The pass gives unlimited travel within that period, including all reservations, sleeper berths and bedding; there are no supplements or surcharges to pay. To check IndRail pass prices, see **www.indiarail.co.uk** or call SD Enterprises on 020 8903 3411, open 09:30–17:30 Monday–Friday, 09:30–14:00 Saturday.

How to buy an IndRail pass in the UK

You can buy an IndRail pass, complete with any required train reservations, from the UK IndRail agency, SD Enterprises of Wembley. Call 020 8903 3411 or see **www.indiarail.co.uk**. I can personally recommend SD Enterprises as an excellent and long-established family firm, who know their subject and go out of their way to advise and help their clients. If you can, visit them in person, as it is an experience in itself. You may even get to see Dr Dandpani's video on visiting India.

How to buy an IndRail pass in other countries

For a list of IndRail pass agencies in other countries, go to **www.indianrail.gov.in**, click 'Information' then 'International Tourist'. There are IndRail agencies in Malaysia, Finland, Germany and South Africa, but surprisingly not currently in the USA, Canada, Australia or New Zealand. If you're from one of these countries, try contacting the UK agency (SD Enterprises, **www.indiarail.co.uk**). In fact, although they are the UK agency, they are normally happy to arrange passes (4-day and longer) and reservations for people from overseas – but not one-day or half-day passes, which they sell only to people living in the UK.

CRUISE TRAINS

India now has several 'cruise trains' aimed at western tourists and running inclusive tours, with luxury accommodation, meals and tours included.

The Palace on Wheels

The 'Palace on Wheels' is India's first and most celebrated 'cruise train', and was voted the world's fourth-best luxury train by *Condé Nast Traveller* magazine. Prices range from around £157 ($244) for a simple two-day trip from Delhi to Agra to see the Taj Mahal, or up to £930 ($1,441) to £1,195 ($1,853) for a twelve-day tour around key cities in Rajasthan such as Jaisalmer, Jaipur, Udaipur and Jodhpur, with all meals, off-train tours and on-board accommodation included. All suites feature private shower and spotlessly clean toilet, TV and CD player, and the train's two elegant restaurant cars offer both Indian and international cuisine. See **www.palaceonwheels.com** to browse itineraries and prices.

Other cruise trains

The Palace on Wheels is no longer the only cruise train in India. A number have sprung up, though prices are sky-high. Be warned that most of these companies misleadingly quote a rate per night, not for the whole tour!

- *Indian Maharaja*, **www.theindianmaharaja.com**. Offers eight-day (seven-night) 'land cruises' between Delhi and Bombay in either direction on various dates between October and April, with stopovers and tours at Agra, Jaipur, Udaipur and the Ellora and Ajanta Caves, starting at around £2,642 ($4,095) per person for two people sharing, or from £3,374 ($5,229) for single occupancy.

- *Royal Rajasthan on Wheels*, **www.royalrajasthanonwheels.com**. Offers eight-day (seven-night) itineraries with weekly departures from Delhi back to Delhi, stopping at Jodhpur, Udaipur, Ranthambore National Park, Jaipur, Khajuraho and Varanasi. From around £2,665 ($4,130) per person for two people sharing, or £3,726 ($5,775) single occupancy for the least expensive suites.

- *Deccan Odyssey*, **www.deccan-odyssey-india.com**. A luxury train offering weekly departures from Bombay for a week-long tour to Goa, Pune, and the caves at Ajanta and Ellora.

- *Golden Chariot*, **www.deccan-odyssey-india.com/golden-chariot**. A luxury train offering weekly departures from Bangalore for a week-long tour to Goa and southern India.

- *Maharaja's Express*, **www.maharajas-express.com**. Runs various six- or seven-night tours from Delhi back to Delhi or between Delhi and Bombay, via places such as Agra, Jaipur, Varanasi, Lucknow. From £4,129 ($6,400) per person. This train is a joint venture between Cox & Kings India Ltd and Indian Railway Catering and Tourism Corporation (IRCTC).

These trains can also be booked in the UK through SD Enterprises.

INDONESIA

You'll find a good and fairly comprehensive train network on Java, including a train service between Java's capital, Jakarta, and its second city, Surabaya.

Train operator:	PT Kereta Api, **www.kereta-api.co.id**
Time:	Jakarta GMT+7, central Indonesia and Bali GMT+8, east Indonesia GMT+9
Currency:	£1 = approx. 13,425 rupiah, $1 = approx. 9,300 rupiah
Tourist information:	**www.indonesia-tourism.com**
Visas:	UK citizens and most other western nationals need a visa for Indonesia. It can be obtained on arrival at all major airports and some seaports, including Belawan. See **www.indonesianembassy.org.uk**.

FERRIES TO INDONESIA

Penang (Malaysia)–Medan (Indonesia)

A daily ferry operates from Penang in Malaysia to Belawan (the port of Medan) in Indonesia (Sumatra, the northwesternmost island), sailing at 09:00 and arriving at 13:00. Returning, it sails from Belawan (Medan) at 10:30 and arrives at Penang at 14:30. The fare is about 90 Malaysian ringgit (£18 or $27). For more information, see **www.langkawi-ferry.com**.

TRAIN TRAVEL WITHIN INDONESIA

Sumatra

There are a few train services in Sumatra, but no system covering the whole island. From Medan to Panjang (for the twice-daily ferry to Merak on Java) you will need a bus to Padang (730 km, 28 hours, twice daily), another from Padang to Palembang (900 km, one bus daily), then a train from Palembang (Kertapati station) to Panjang (daily, 8 hours by daytime train). The train arrives at Tanjungkarang station, with a bus connection for the final 2-hour leg to Palembang ferry. Alternatively, you can take a train from Medan to Kisaran, bus to Tanjungbalai, then ferry to Batam and again from Batam to Palembang (three weekly).

Java

A train system links most main cities in Java, including Jakarta and Surabaya via several different routes. Bookings are computerised and can be made up to 30 days in advance. For train times and fares on Java, see **www.kereta-api.co.id**. Here are some hints for using this system:

- There used to be an English button at bottom right, but the current incarnation of **www.kereta-api.co.id** seems not to have an English version.

- The main stations in Jakarta are Jakarta Kota (often written as 'Jakartakota'), which is closer to the old colonial city centre, and Jakarta Gambir (often written just as 'Gambir'), closer to the centre of the modern city.

- There are two main stations in Surabaya: Surabaya Gubeng and Surabaya Pasarturi. Gubeng is more central, Pasarturi is slightly to the north.

- Indonesian trains have three classes: executive (*eksecutif*), business (*bisnis*) and economy (*ekonomi*). Executive is spacious and air-conditioned; seat reservation is compulsory. Business class is not air-conditioned; seat reservation is compulsory. Economy is not air-conditioned, it can be crowded, and seat reservation is not possible, except on a handful of very long-distance trains.

> • Trains are often identified by name rather than number. Trains with 'Argo' in the name are the best services, and are executive class only.

JAKARTA TO SURABAYA

Lots of trains link Jakarta with Surabaya, via at least two major routes, but the best Jakarta–Surabaya train is the Argo Bromo Anggrek service, which is executive class only, modern and air-conditioned, snacks and mineral water included in the fare. It has comfortable reclining seats with footrests. There is both a daytime service (trains 1 and 2) and a time-effective overnight service (trains 3 and 4). However, the night trains no longer have sleepers, just seats.

Train 2 departs Jakarta at 09:30, arriving at Surabaya at 19:58. Train 4 departs Jakarta at 21:30, arriving at Surabaya at 07:57 next morning.

Train 1 leaves Surabaya at 08:00, arriving at Jakarta at 18:37. Train 3 departs Surabaya at 20:00, and arrives at Jakarta at 06:31 next morning.

The one-way fare is about 200,000 rupiah (£15 or $22). Total distance is 725 km.

JAKARTA TO BANDUNG

There is a train to Bandung every hour or two from Jakarta Gambir station, with executive and business class seats, taking about 3 hours for the 173-km journey, fare about 175,000 rupiah (£13 or $20). See **www.kereta-api.co.id** for more details.

BANDUNG TO SURABAYA

There are two recommended trains on this route (a 696-km journey), one daytime, one overnight; both are air-conditioned. Daytime trains 5 and 6 are the *Argo Wilis*: train 6 departs Bandung at 07:00, arriving in Surabaya at 19:53; train 5 departs Surabaya at 07:30, arriving in Bandung at 10:56.

Train 38 leaves Bandung at 19:00, arriving at Surabaya at 08:20 next morning. Train 37 departs Surabaya at 18:00, and arrives at Bandung at 07:10 next morning.

JAPAN

Japan is justly famous for its *shinkansen* or 'bullet trains' linking all the major cities including Tokyo, Kyoto (Japan's historic capital and not to be missed), Osaka (Japan's second city), Himeji (for a visit to Japan's best-preserved traditional castle) and Hiroshima (where the 'Atomic Bomb Dome', museum and Peace Park are must-sees). Japanese National Railways provide the ideal way to get around and explore the country, and the trains are not only fast, they are incredibly efficient, with an average delay measured in seconds! In addition to the standard-gauge *shinkansen* lines, you'll find efficient narrow-gauge lines linking other towns and cities, such as Nagasaki, Nikko and Nara. The temples at Nikko can be seen as a day trip from Tokyo, and the Great Hall of the Buddha (the world's largest wooden building, housing the world's largest bronze Buddha) at Nara is an easy day trip by train from Kyoto.

Train operator:	There are six main regional railway companies, known collectively as Japan Railways (JR), plus many local railway operators. Japan train times: **www.hyperdia.com** (the English button is upper left) Japan rail map: **www.railkey.com/tickets/popups/Japan_map_en.pdf** Tokyo metro website (with map): **www.tokyometro.jp**
Time:	GMT+9
Currency:	£1 = approx. 130 yen, $1 = approx. 90 yen
Tourist information:	**www.jnto.go.jp** or **www.seejapan.co.uk**
Visas:	UK, EU, US, Canadian, Australian and NZ citizens do not require a visa to visit Japan.

EUROPE TO JAPAN BY TRANS-SIBERIAN RAILWAY

You can reach Japan from London without flying in just two weeks, by Trans-Siberian Railway.

First, travel from London to Moscow by daily trains in around 48 hours (two nights). You then have a choice.

Option 1 is to take the *Rossiya*, which runs every second day from Moscow to Vladivostok, taking seven days. From Vladivostok you take the 1993-built ferry *Eastern Dream*, which operates once a week all year to Sakaiminato in Japan, taking 36 hours (two nights).

Option 2 is to travel from Moscow to Beijing on one of two weekly Trans-Siberian trains, taking six days. From Beijing, take an overnight train to Shanghai, from where there are two weekly ships to either Osaka or Kobe in Japan.

The route via Vladivostok requires fewer visas, so is a bit easier to organise, but the route via Beijing is the more interesting option. See the chapter on the Trans-Siberian Railway, page 33, for more information on both these routes.

TRAIN TRAVEL WITHIN JAPAN

Everyone has heard of the 'bullet train' lines, known in Japan as *shinkansen*. These are high-speed lines, built to standard gauge (4' 8½"). The first *shinkansen* opened in 1964, and there are now a whole range of *shinkansen* lines linking all the most important cities in Japan, including Niigata, Tokyo, Kyoto, Osaka, Hiroshima and Hakata.

An extensive network of original 3' 6" gauge lines remains, covering the whole of Japan and taking you to almost every city and town of any size.

There are some impressive sleeping-car trains, too – for example Tokyo–Nagasaki and Tokyo–Sapporo. These run on the original narrow-gauge lines, but they can save time compared with daytime travel, even using *shinkansen*.

Travelling by train in Japan is easy, as the stations have signs and departure boards in English as well as Japanese. Japanese trains are very clean and modern, and are amazingly punctual.

Two classes of seating are provided, ordinary class and 'green car' (first class). Green cars are indicated by a green 'clover' symbol next to the entrance door.

How to check train times and fares

Japanese trains link pretty much every city and major town, plus many smaller places.

You can check train times and fares for any train journey in Japan at **www.hyperdia.com** (the English button is upper left). Another useful resource for Japanese train travel is **www.japanrail.com**.

Rail fares in Japan are expensive, and if you are an overseas visitor a Japan Rail Pass can be the cheapest way to travel even if you are only planning one return trip from (say) Tokyo to Hiroshima. See the 'Japan Rail Pass' section below.

In Japan, children aged 0 to 5 travel free, children aged 6 to 11 travel at half fare, children aged 12 and over pay full fare.

A sample selection of train services and fares is shown in the table below.

Sample journey times, train frequency and fares

Journey	Distance	Time by Nozomi	Time by Hikari	One-way fare	Train frequency
Tokyo to Kyoto	513 km	2 hours 18 mins	2 hours 49 mins	¥13,720 (£105)	Every 5–10 minutes, direct
Tokyo to Shin-Osaka	552 km	2 hours 18 mins	2 hours 33 mins	¥14,250 (£110)	Every 5–10 minutes, direct
Tokyo to Hiroshima	894 km	4 hours 8 mins	5 hours 2 mins	¥18,620 (£143)	Every 10–20 minutes, direct
Tokyo to Nagasaki	1,328 km	7 hours 14 mins	8 hours 21 mins	¥24,980 (£192)	Every hour or better, change at Hakata
Kyoto to Hiroshima	380 km	1 hour 36 mins	1 hour 59 mins	¥11,290 (£86)	Every 10–20 minutes, direct
Hiroshima to Nagasaki	434 km	3 hours 10 mins	3 hours 25 mins	¥12,090 (£93)	Every hour or better, change at Hakata

Nozomi = extra-fast train with very few stops. Cannot be used with a Japan Rail Pass.

Hikari = next fastest train. Can be used with a Japan Rail Pass.

RAIL PASSES FOR JAPAN

Even if you are only planning one return intercity journey, a Japan Rail Pass can save you money compared with a normal ticket. For example, the normal return fare from Tokyo to Kyoto is ¥27,440 or about £211, and from Tokyo to Hiroshima ¥37,240 or about £286, whereas a Japan Rail Pass costs around £284 for 7 days' unlimited travel. A rail pass will therefore save you money even for one return journey between Tokyo and destinations beyond Osaka. You can use **www.hyperdia.com** to check point-to-point fares for the journeys you intend to make, then compare these with the Japan Rail Pass prices at **www.internationalrail.com**.

There are two varieties of rail pass available: countrywide or regional.

The Japan Rail Pass

Japan Rail Passes covering the whole of Japan are available for 7, 14 or 21 consecutive days' unlimited travel on the national Japan Railways (JR) network, in a choice of ordinary class or green (first) class. You can use any JR train service, both high-speed *shinkansen* and ordinary slower narrow-gauge trains, except for the very fastest Nozomi Expresses on the Tokyo–Osaka–Hakata *shinkansen*. (This is not a problem, as you can use the Hikari Expresses on this route, which are only slightly slower.) A green class rail pass is great if you can afford it, but standard class on Japanese trains is perfectly adequate; there's no real need to pay more. You can use overnight sleeping-car trains too with a Japan Rail Pass, if you pay the rather large sleeper supplement. Tokyo to Nagasaki by sleeping-car costs ¥10,000 (about £77) one-way for a basic 'B' category bunk in addition to your pass. The Japan Rail Pass does not cover lines that are run by private rail operators. To buy a pass in the UK, see **www.internationalrail.com** or call them on 0871 231 0790.

The Japan East Rail Pass, Japan West (Sanyo) Rail Pass, Japan West (Kansai) Rail Pass

There are also three other Japan Rail Passes covering smaller areas. The Japan East Pass covers Tokyo, Nagano, Niigata, Sendai, Morioka, Misawa and Akita.

The Sanyo area pass covers an area including Osaka, Himeji, Okayama, Hiroshima and Hakata. The Kansai area rail pass covers Kyoto, Osaka, Kobe, Nara and Himeji and costs only around £15 a day – a pretty good deal. See **www.internationalrail.com** for more information or call them on 0871 231 0790.

How does a Japan Rail Pass work?

When you buy a Japan Rail Pass in the UK, you will be given a voucher which needs to be exchanged for the rail pass itself in Japan any time within the following three months. Vouchers can be exchanged at all the most important Japan Railways stations, including Tokyo and its international airports.

Train reservations can be made in Japan at any ticket office once you have your rail pass, but they cannot be made from outside Japan before you get there. However, except at the busiest peak times you are unlikely to have any problem getting reservations on the trains you want. Good websites for further Japan Rail Pass information are **www.japantravel.co.uk/jrp.htm** and **www.japanrailpass.net**.

LAOS

Laos now boasts its own railway, as the main line from Bangkok has been extended across the Friendship Bridge over the Mekong to Thanaleng, just south of the Laotian capital Vientiane. You can now easily travel from Bangkok to Laos by train.

Train operator:	There are no trains in Laos, other than the short link across the Friendship Bridge from Thailand. Buses link Laos with Vietnam.
Time:	GMT+7
Currency:	£1 = approx. 12,998 new kip, $1 = approx. 8,430 new kip
Tourist information:	**www.tourismlaos.org**
Visas:	UK, EU, US and Australian citizens require a visa to visit Laos. A 30-day 'visa on arrival' is available when entering by road or train via the Friendship Bridge near Nong Khai and several other border points, also when arriving at Vientiane or Luang Prabang airports. Laos has no embassy in London, but the Laotian embassy in Paris grants visas, see **www.laoparis.com**.

EUROPE TO LAOS, overland

If you have the time, it's possible to reach Laos overland from the UK, using the twice-weekly Trans-Siberian train from Moscow to Beijing, then the twice-weekly Beijing–Hanoi soft sleeper train. See the Trans-Siberian and Vietnam chapters for details. The whole journey will take about two weeks.

From Hanoi, you have a choice of routes to Laos. The direct route involves a long and arduous 24-hour bus journey from Hanoi to Vientiane; see below.

The more comfortable option means going the long way round and taking several days, by train from Hanoi to Saigon (see the Vietnam chapter, page 428), then bus from Saigon to Phnom Penh and Phnom Penh to Bangkok (see the Cambodia chapter, pages 285 and 283), then train from Bangkok to Nong Khai for Vientiane, see below.

HANOI TO VIENTIANE, by bus

You can take a bus from Hanoi to Vientiane, but bear in mind that it's a 24-hour ride – a night and a day. A few years ago, reports from travellers said that this was a rough ride on poor roads through mountainous areas, but offset by spectacular scenery so well worth doing. Latest reports suggest that things have improved, with better roads and a more modern bus with sleeper bunks, at least on three days a week, and the same wonderful scenery. An older bus, still with sleeper bunks, operates on the other days.

The modern bus leaves Hanoi at 19:00 on Tuesday, Thursday and Saturday, arriving in Vientiane at 19:00 the following day. In the other direction, the modern bus leaves Vientiane at 19:00 on Tuesday, Thursday and Saturday, arriving in Hanoi 24 hours later at 19:00. The older bus runs on the other days of the week in each direction, to the same schedule.

The modern bus has sleeper bunks and a toilet. The older bus also has sleeper bunks but no on-board toilet. Are the bunks long enough to sleep in? Almost, though taller travellers may need to curl up!

The fare is 550,000 Vietnamese dong (around £20 or $30), whichever bus you use. The bus company has no website, so just buy tickets at the bus station or via your guesthouse or a local travel agency when you get to Hanoi or Vientiane. In Hanoi, you can buy tickets for this bus at the Nuoc Ngam (Southern) Bus Station on Giai Phong Street. The ticket office phone number in Vientiane is (020) 98112233. Or simply ask for a bus ticket at any travel agency or guesthouse in Vientiane or Hanoi.

There are also buses from Hue and Danang in Vietnam to the border, for onward buses to Vientiane.

BANGKOK TO VIENTIANE, by train

It's easy to travel from Bangkok to Vientiane (or vice versa) by train, using the daily overnight sleeper train direct from Bangkok to Nong Khai and a special connecting local train to the new international rail terminal at Thanaleng in Laos, some 13 km outside Vientiane. The train uses the new rail link over the Friendship Bridge across the Mekong River into Laos, opened on 5 March 2009. You can then take a local bus or tuk-tuk to central Vientiane. It's safe, cheap and comfortable. Alternatively, you can still travel between Bangkok and Vientiane the old way, using any of the Bangkok–Nong Khai trains, then making your own way by bus or taxi between Nong Khai and Vientiane. This section explains both options.

Bangkok → Nong Khai, Thanaleng (for Vientiane)

Km	Train number		133	77	69
	Classes		2,3	DRC	1,S
0	Bangkok (Hualamphong)	depart	20:45	18:30	20:00
22	Don Muang	depart	21:31	19:13	20:50
71	Ayutthaya	depart	22:17	19:47	21:41
624	Nong Khai	arrive	09:45	05:05	08:25
624	Nong Khai (Thailand)	depart	–	–	09:00c
630	Thanaleng (Laos)	arrive	–	–	09:15c
643	Vientiane	arrive	Note A	Note A	Note B

(Vientiane), Thanaleng, Nong Khai → Bangkok

Train number		76	70	134
Classes		DRC	1,S,3	s,2,3
Vientiane	depart	Note A	Note B	Note A
Thanaleng (Laos)	depart	I	17:00c	I
Nong Khai (Thailand)	arrive	I	17:15c	I
Nong Khai	depart	06:00	18:20	19:05
Ayutthaya	arrive	15:30	04:23	05:34
Don Muang	arrive	16:12	05:22	06:26
Bangkok (Hualamphong)	arrive	17:10	06:25	07:30

c = change trains at Nong Khai. The Nong Khai to Thanaleng train is a separate train with third class seats. You've a couple of hours to change trains in Nong Khai and buy onward tickets, which is easy.

Note A: see option 2 below.

Note B: see option 1 below.

Classes: 1 = first class sleeper. S = second class sleeper (air-conditioned). s = second class sleeper (non-air-conditioned). 2 = second class seats. 3 = third class seats. DRC = Diesel Railcar express with second class air-conditioned seats, meals included. Most western travellers use cheap and comfortable second class sleepers, although others are happy to pay more for first class 2-berth sleepers.

OPTION 1: Vientiane via train to Thanaleng

The easier option is to take the overnight train (train 69 northbound, train 70 southbound) between Bangkok and Nong Khai, and the connecting local train across the Friendship Bridge between Nong Khai and Thanaleng in Laos, just outside Vientiane. An extension of the railway to the suburbs of Vientiane is planned. The new Thanaleng station is pretty much in the middle of nowhere, so pre-arrange a taxi transfer into Vientiane if you can, perhaps by booking a hotel then asking them to arrange a taxi. If you can't, you'll no doubt find a taxi or bus into town, and Thai baht are normally readily accepted.

'Visas on arrival' for Laos are now issued at Thanaleng station, costing $35 (£23) + 1 baht (2p) entry fee.

OPTION 2: *Vientiane by road from Nong Khai*

The other way to travel from Bangkok to Vientiane (or vice versa) is to take any train from Bangkok to Nong Khai, overnight train 69 (train 70 southbound) being the best choice. Nong Khai is just a few kilometres from the Friendship Bridge over the Mekong River into Laos. You then use road transport across the Friendship Bridge into Laos like this: (1) Take a local tuk-tuk taxi from Nong Khai railway station to the Nong Khai bus station. (2) A shuttle bus runs from the bus station across the Friendship Bridge to Laos every 20 minutes throughout the day, fare about 30 baht (65p). It stops at the Thai border post for exit formalities 5 minutes after leaving the bus station, then crosses the Friendship Bridge to arrive at Laotian customs and immigration some 10 minutes later. (You can obtain a 30-day 'visa on arrival' for Laos at this border point.) (3) You now remove your luggage from the bus luggage hold and go through Laotian customs. (4) Take another tuk-tuk to your chosen hotel.

When travelling southbound, leave central Vientiane at least 3 hours before the departure time of your train from Nong Khai for Bangkok, to allow time for border formalities and the various bus/taxi journeys.

Fares

One-way fare per person (in Thai baht)	1st class sleeper air-conditioned express train	2nd class sleeper air-conditioned express train	2nd class seat air-conditioned fast railcar	2nd class seat ordinary train	3rd class seat ordinary train
Bangkok to Nong Khai or vice versa	1,217 (£26, $37)	778 (£16, $23)	498 (£10, $15)	388 (£8, $11)	258 (£5, $8)
Nong Khai to Thanaleng or vice versa	–	20 baht (40p) for a seat		–	–

Children aged 0–3 and less than 100 cm in height travel free; children aged 4–11 and under 150 cm travel at half fare; children of 12 years old and upwards (or over 150 cm tall) pay full fare.

The sleeper fares shown here are for a lower bunk; an upper bunk is 50–100 baht (£1–£2) less in second class. Non-air-conditioned second class sleepers (available on a few trains) cost 160–200 baht (£3–£4) less than the air-conditioned variety. You can check fares at **www.railway.co.th** (but do this by selecting 'timetables', as the fares shown at the bottom of each timetable page include the air-conditioning supplement, sleeper and special express supplements. If you select the 'fares' option, the fares shown don't include those supplements).

How to buy tickets

You can buy your Bangkok–Nong Khai or Nong Khai–Bangkok sleeper ticket at the station reservations office or online using the new Thai Railways online booking service (see the Thailand chapter, pages 406–7). The new online service can now book second class air-conditioned sleepers on trains 69 and 70, but it won't book first class sleepers or tickets for any of the other Bangkok–Nong Khai trains, at least not yet. Online booking opens 60 days before travel, and closes three days before travel (in other words, if you need to travel within the next three days forget about online booking – you'll need to buy tickets at the station). You print out your ticket in pdf format (so make sure any internet café you use has a printer!). Alternatively, you can buy tickets through an agency such as Traveller2000, **www.traveller2000.com**.

If you are taking the train on from Nong Khai you should buy your Nong Khai–Thanaleng ticket for 20 baht when you arrive at Nong Khai station. There's plenty of time to do this, as the train has a 2-hour layover in Nong Khai before the connecting train heads to Thanaleng.

You can't buy through-tickets from Bangkok to Thanaleng, at least not yet; you have to buy a ticket from Bangkok to Nong Khai, then buy the onward ticket from Nong Khai to Thanaleng at the station when you get to Nong Khai. It is, however, now possible to buy tickets all the way to Bangkok at Thanaleng station ticket office, even on the day of travel. You must buy your tickets in Thai baht only, in cash at Thanaleng station. There is no currency exchange or ATM there, so get hold of some baht before leaving central Vientiane.

MALAYSIA AND SINGAPORE

Singapore, Malaysia and Thailand make up one of the world's most popular regions for train travel, judged by the number of people using those pages on the seat61 website. An old narrow-gauge colonial railway winds its way up the Malay Peninsula from Singapore all the way to Bangkok, an epic 1,946-km (1,249-mile) journey that can set you back as little as £40 ($60) for the two-night trip, including comfy sleepers for both nights. Air-conditioned Malaysian trains link Singapore with Kuala Lumpur and Penang, both great cities to visit, and for the more adventurous there's the 'Jungle Line' across the peninsula to Khota Bharu.

Train operator:	Keratapi Tanah Melayu (KTM), **www.ktmb.com.my** Singapore metro: **www.smrt.com.sg**
Time:	GMT+8
Currency:	£1 = approx. 4.8 ringgit (RM) = approx. 2.0 Singapore dollars (S$) $1 = approx. 3.3 ringgit = approx. 1.4 Singapore dollars
Tourist information:	**www.tourism.gov.my** and **www.visitsingapore.com**
Visas:	UK, EU, US, Canadian, Australian and NZ citizens do not need a visa to visit Malaysia or Singapore.

EUROPE TO MALAYSIA AND SINGAPORE, overland

If you have the time, it's possible to reach Malaysia and Singapore overland from the UK, using the twice-weekly Trans-Siberian train from Moscow to Beijing in China, then the twice-weekly Beijing–Hanoi sleeper train, then daily trains onwards to Saigon. See the Trans-Siberian and Vietnam chapters for

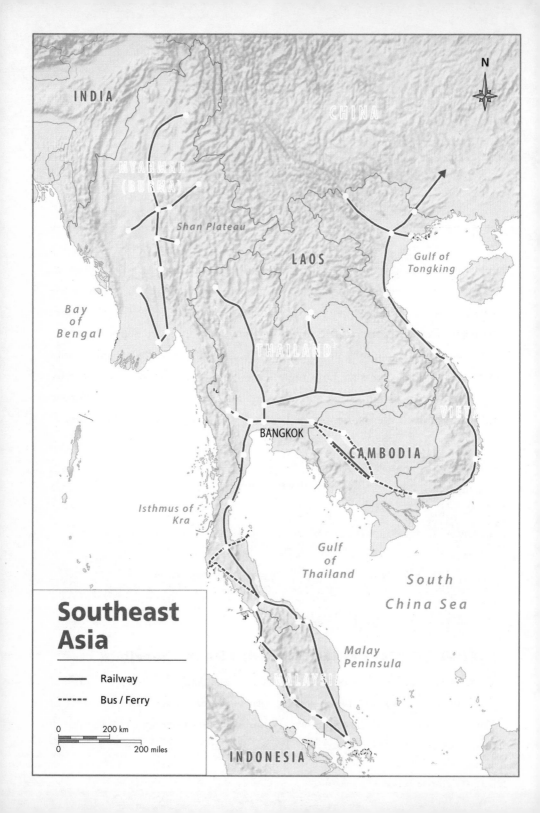

N

INDIA

CHINA

MYANMAR
(BURMA)

Shan Plateau

LAOS

Bay
of
Bengal

THAILAND

Gulf of
Tongking

BANGKOK

CAMBODIA

VIET

Isthmus of
Kra

Gulf
of
Thailand

South

China Sea

Malay
Peninsula

MALAYSIA

INDONESIA

Southeast
Asia

——— Railway

------ Bus / Ferry

0   200 km

0   200 miles

details. The whole journey will take about two weeks. From Saigon, take a bus to Phnom Penh and another bus and train onwards to Bangkok; see the Cambodia chapter. See pages 348–51 for the two-day train ride from Bangkok to Singapore.

TRAIN TRAVEL WITHIN MALAYSIA AND SINGAPORE

The principal railway line in Malaysia runs along the west coast from Singapore to Kuala Lumpur and Butterworth (the mainland connection point for Penang), then on to the Thai border and Bangkok. Taking the train is the ideal way to travel between Singapore, Kuala Lumpur and Penang, or indeed to travel all the way between Singapore and Bangkok. Another line, the so-called 'Jungle Line', runs along the east side of the country, linking Singapore with Khota Bharu on the northeast coast of Malaysia, near the border with Thailand. Both routes are described in detail below. There are also separate sections later in the chapter giving advice on fares and how to buy tickets. A detailed map of train routes in Malaysia can be found on the Malaysian Railways website, **www.ktmb.com.my**, where you should also go to check train times and fares.

What are Malaysian trains like?

Daytime express trains between Singapore and Kuala Lumpur are modern and air-conditioned. They have first and second class seats, marketed as 'Premier' and 'Superior'. The trains have a refreshment trolley and buffet car, but these offer a very limited selection of drinks and snacks, so it's a good idea to bring your own food and drink along. First class (Premier) seats are quite luxurious, although now somewhat worn. They recline and can be rotated to face each other or the direction of travel. Second class (Superior) seats are also very comfortable, although they do not recline and cannot be rotated.

There are overnight trains between Singapore and Kuala Lumpur, Kuala Lumpur and Butterworth (for Penang), Singapore and Tumpat (the line for Khota Bharu), and Kuala Lumpur and Tumpat. These overnight trains have sleepers as well as second class and third (economy) class seats. There is a 360-degree virtual tour of each of the three types of sleeper at **www.ktmb.com.my**.

Second class sleeping-cars, marketed as 'Superior Night', run on all the overnight trains within Malaysia. They are a great way to travel, and are safe, comfortable, cheap and fun too. They are open-plan, with upper and lower berths arranged along the coach on either side of a central aisle. Each bunk has curtains for privacy. Upper berths are cheaper than lower berths, but they are much narrower, so ask for a lower berth if possible. All necessary bedding is provided, with blankets and fresh clean sheets. The Butterworth (Penang)–Bangkok sleepers have a similar layout, but are provided by SRT, the Thai Railways.

First class sleeping-cars, marketed as 'Premier Night Standard', have private air-conditioned 2-berth compartments with washbasin. These sleepers only operate on trains 20 and 21 between Kuala Lumpur and Padang Besar (just before the Thai border), on trains 22 and 23 between Kuala Lumpur and Butterworth (for Penang), and on trains 28 and 29 between Kuala Lumpur and Tumpat on the Jungle Line; *not* on the night trains between Singapore and Kuala Lumpur or Singapore and Tumpat. All necessary bedding, towels and toiletries are provided. Passengers travelling alone can either pay for both berths to gain sole occupancy, or book one berth in a 2-bed compartment and share with another civilised sleeper passenger of the same sex.

A deluxe sleeping-car, marketed as 'Premier Night Deluxe', is available on the Singapore–Kuala Lumpur overnight train (trains 24 and 25), with 1- or 2-bed private rooms with en suite toilet and shower. Two armchairs face each other over a table. At night, the seat converts to a lower berth and an upper bed folds out from the wall. A simple packed meal, served in your compartment, is included in the fare. All necessary bedding, towels and toiletries are provided. There's even a TV in the room (which may or may not work!), and the private toilet/shower room comes complete with electric hairdryer. It's fully carpeted, but expect the carpet to be grubby!

Passengers with first class tickets (seat or sleeper) can use the VIP First Class Lounge at Singapore station and Kuala Lumpur station. To find the lounge at Kuala Lumpur Sentral, go to the escalators down to the platform but instead take the lift to level 3. The lounge has seats, a TV and washrooms.

Singapore station

At the time I write this, trains from Singapore still leave from the faded colonial grandeur of the magnificent and historic art-deco station in Keppel Road, sometimes called Tanjong Pagar. The railway was extended across the causeway from Johor Bahru on to Singapore Island in 1924, initially to a temporary station until the present station was opened to passengers in 1932. The letters 'F M S R' on the front of the building stand for 'Federated Malay States Railway', the railway's original name when Singapore and Malaysia were both part of British Malaya. The station has Asian-style food stalls, kiosks selling snacks, drinks, mineral water, and a currency exchange kiosk, but there are no luggage lockers and no cash-point (ATM). There is a VIP lounge for first class passengers. The closest MRT (metro) station to Singapore mainline station is Tanjong Pagar, but it's a fair walk from there and not very well signposted, so check a map before you set off. For a Singapore MRT metro map and information, see **www.smrt.com.sg**.

However, things are about to change. The station and the railway itself (along with the land they stand on) belong to the Malaysian government, even though they are within Singapore territory. The Singapore government has been trying for years to buy or sequestrate the land so the station can be closed and the land built over. Sadly, it's now reported that the Malaysian government has capitulated and the historic Singapore station will be closed by July 2011, with trains transferred to a new station at Woodlands, just on the Singapore side of the causeway to Malaysia. Malaysian and Singaporean customs and passport control will be co-located here, which will at least save journey time as the train will no longer need to stop for border control on the way. It's planned to preserve the old station building, rather than demolish it.

At present, when leaving Singapore you should arrive at the station at least 30 minutes before your train's departure time, to allow for clearance of Malaysian customs. In practice, you usually file quickly through Malaysian passport control and on to the train. About 20–30 minutes after leaving Singapore station, the train stops at the Woodlands train checkpoint just before the causeway across to Malaysia. Here, you need to leave the train (but can leave your luggage on board), enter this building, pass quickly through the Singaporean passport/immigration/customs control, then re-board the train. When trains are transferred to the new station at Woodlands, you will no doubt also need to arrive in similarly good time, to clear both Singapore exit and Malaysian border formalities.

Kuala Lumpur station

Long-distance trains now serve Kuala Lumpur's shiny new Sentral station, complete with VIP lounge for first class passengers and left luggage office. They no longer use the famous Moorish-style railway station built by the British in 1911. However, suburban trains still stop there.

Kuala Lumpur Sentral–Kuala Lumpur Airport fast rail link

Malaysian Railways operates the new 'KLIA Ekspres' train service between Kuala Lumpur International Airport (KLIA) and Kuala Lumpur Sentral station. It runs every 15 minutes between 05:00 and 01:00 and takes 28 minutes non-stop. The fare is about RM35 (£7) one-way, RM65 (£13) return. See **www.kliaekspres.com** for more information.

SINGAPORE–KUALA LUMPUR–PENANG–BANGKOK

The train trip from Singapore to Bangkok is 1,946 km or 1,249 miles and involves two or three separate train rides, depending on where you want to stop off and change trains. I'd recommend stopping off at Kuala Lumpur and Penang, both fascinating cities. So stage 1 is to take a train from Singapore to Kuala Lumpur, with a choice of two modern air-conditioned daytime trains or an overnight sleeper train. Stage 2 is from KL to Butterworth (which is linked by frequent ferry to Penang, see page 364), again with a choice of two daytime trains or an overnight sleeper. Stage 3 is to take the 'International Express' (*Ekspress Antarabangsa*) leaving Butterworth at lunchtime and arriving in Bangkok next morning. It's entirely up to you whether you do this journey all in one go in around 48 hours or stop off and see places on the way, as each train is booked and ticketed separately. (For advice on how to book, see page 359.)

Besides the Butterworth–Penang ferry, there are bus or ferry connections from pretty much every stop on the line to places well worth a stopover or side trip: see page 364 for connecting services within Malaysia, and the Thailand chapter, page 401, for connections from the stations in Thailand.

The timetable below shows all the trains available between Singapore, Kuala Lumpur, Butterworth and Hat Yai, but there are many more trains between Hat Yai, Surat Thani, Chumphon, Hua Hin and Bangkok – see page 418. There are also now several additional shuttle trains between Kuala Lumpur and Ipoh. (For the privately run luxury Singapore–Bangkok Eastern and Oriental Express, see page 367.)

If you are looking to travel in first class, you should bear in mind that first class accommodation isn't available for the entire Singapore–Bangkok route, whatever combination of trains you choose. The *Ekspress Senandung Langkawi* (trains 20 and 21) has first-class sleepers that run only between Kuala Lumpur and Padang Besar (on the Malaysian side of the frontier with Thailand), so between Padang Besar and Hat Yai you would need to transfer to a second class seat. The International Express (trains 35 and 36) has a Thai Railways first-class sleeping-car that runs only between Bangkok and Hat Yai, so for the journey between Hat Yai and Butterworth you would need to use a second class sleeper (in daytime mode). This works going south, as both legs can be reserved in Bangkok, but is problematic going north, as Hat Yai to Bangkok berths cannot be reserved at Malaysian railway stations, and may be full if you just turn up and approach the sleeper attendant at Hat Yai. Second class sleepers are clean and comfortable; I'd advise sticking with those.

Singapore → *Kuala Lumpur* → *Penang* → *Bangkok*

Train number (see notes below)		10	2	20	22	12	170	36	24
Classes		1,2	1,2	F,S,2,3	F,S,2	1,2	2,3	S	L,S
Days of running		Daily	Daily	Daily	Daily	Daily	Daily	Daily	Daily
Singapore (Keppel Road station**)	depart	–	08:00	–	–	13:00	–	–	22:30
Johor Bahru	depart	–	09:02	–	–	14:03	–	–	23:43
Gemas	arr/dep	–	12:08	–	–	17:28	–	–	03:12
Tampin	arr/dep	–	12:57	–	–	18:18	–	–	04:14
Kuala Lumpur (KL Sentral)	arrive		14:54			20:16	–	–	06:30
	depart	08:05	14:54	21:15*	22:00				
Ipoh	arr/dep	11:01	17:55	00:36	00:59	–	–	–	–
Butterworth (for Penang)	arrive	14:55	21:15	05:03*	04:58	–	–	–	–
	depart	–	–	05:03*	–	–	–	13:45	–
Alor Setar	arr/dep	–	–	07:01	–	–	–	17:07	–
Arau	arr/dep	–	–	07:41	–	–	–	17:41	–
Padang Besar (Thai frontier)	arrive	–	–	08:20	–	–	–	18:14	–
Hat Yai (Thai time)	arrive	–	–	10:12	–	–	–	18:20	–
	depart	–	–	–	–	–	14:35	18:45	–
Surat Thani	arrive	–	–	–	–	–	20:02	23:17	–
Chumphon	arrive	–	–	–	–	–	–	02:32	–
Hua Hin	arrive	–	–	–	–	–	–	05:47	–
Nakhon Pathom	arrive	–	–	–	–	–	–	08:20	–
Bangkok (Hualamphong Station)	arrive	–	–	–	–	–	–	09:55	–

Bangkok → Penang → Kuala Lumpur → Singapore

Train number (see notes below)		35	41	21	23	13	1	11	25
Classes		S	2	F,S,2,3	F,S,2	1,2	1,2	1,2	L,S
Days of running		Daily	Daily	Daily	Daily	Daily	Daily	Daily	Daily
Bangkok (Hualamphong Station)	depart	14:45	–	–	–	–	–	–	–
Nakon Pathom	depart	16:09	–	–	–	–	–	–	–
Hua Hin	depart	18:24	–	–	–	–	–	–	–
Chumphon	depart	22:00	–	–	–	–	–	–	–
Surat Thani	depart	00:50	08:20	–	–	–	–	–	–
Hat Yai	arrive	06:57	12:44	–	–	–	–	–	–
	depart	06:50	–	17:00*	–	–	–	–	–
Padang Besar (Malaysian frontier) (Malaysian time)	depart	07:55	–	17:55	–	–	–	–	–
Arau	arr/dep	10:40	–	19:06	–	–	–	–	–
Alor Setar	arr/dep	11:27	–	19:47	–	–	–	–	–
Butterworth (for Penang)	arrive	13:51	–	20:39*	–	–	–	–	–
	depart	–	–	20:39*	23:00	–	08:00	15:30	–
Ipoh	arr/dep	–	–	02:09	03:33	–	11:25	19:08	–
Kuala Lumpur (KL Sentral)	arrive	–	–	05:36	06:35	–	14:06	22:05	–
	depart	–	–	–	–	09:00	14:06	–	23:00
Tampin	arr/dep	–	–	–	–	11:14	16:14	–	01:10
Gemas	arr/dep	–	–	–	–	12:04	17:02	–	01:59
Johor Bahru	arrive	–	–	–	–	15:30	19:59	–	05:41
Singapore (Keppel Road station**)	arrive	–	–	–	–	16:41	21:10	–	07:00

All times are shown in local time (remember that Thailand is 1 hour behind Malaysian time). Please check times before you travel at **www.ktmb.com.my**; they are subject to change.

Classes: L = deluxe sleeper (Premier Night Deluxe); **F** = first class sleeper (Premier Night Standard); **S** = second class sleeper (Superior Night); **1** = first class seats (Premier); **2** = second class seats (Superior); **3** = third class seats (Economy). For descriptions see pages 345–6.

* This train doesn't call at Butterworth; the time shown is the stop at Bukit Mertajam, a small station about 18 km from Butterworth by bus or taxi.

** See page 347. Keppel Road station will reportedly close by July 2011, and trains will be transferred to a new station at Woodlands, near the causeway to Malaysia.

Trains 1 and 2: *Ekspress Rakyat.* Malaysia's premier express, running Singapore–Kuala Lumpur–Butterworth (Penang) every day. First and second class seats with buffet car serving snacks and light meals, refreshment trolley, all fully air-conditioned.

Trains 10 and 11: *Ekspress Sinaran Utara.* Daily. First and second class, air-conditioned with refreshments available.

Trains 12 and 13: *Ekspress Sinaran Selatan.* Daily. First and second class, air-conditioned with refreshments available.

Trains 20 and 21: *Ekspress Senandung Langkawi.* Kuala Lumpur–Hat Yai daily, not calling at Butterworth. Most of this train runs only between Kuala Lumpur and Padang Besar on the Thai frontier, but one second class sleeping-car (Malaysian) and one second class seats car run direct to/from Hat Yai in Thailand.

Trains 22 and 23: *Ekspress Senandung Mutiara.* Daily Kuala Lumpur–Butterworth (Penang) overnight train. First class sleepers (1- and 2-bed compartments), second class sleepers, second class seats, all air-conditioned.

Trains 24 and 25: *Ekspress Senandung Sutera.* Daily Singapore–Kuala Lumpur overnight sleeper train. Deluxe 1- and 2-berth sleepers with private shower and toilet, second class sleepers, all air-conditioned.

Trains 35 and 36: International Express (*Ekspress Antarabangsa*). Butterworth (Penang)–Bangkok daily. Check the exact times locally, as there is a small discrepancy between Thai and Malay railway websites. The International Express consists of clean and comfortable air-conditioned second class sleepers direct between Butterworth and Bangkok. Between Hat Yai and Bangkok, it also has a restaurant car, a first class sleeping-car (2-bed compartments) and additional second class sleepers. This train is provided by State Railways of Thailand.

Train 41: Hat Yai–Surat Thani fast air-conditioned railcar with second class reclining seats. This train actually comes from Bangkok, but it's not recommended for Bangkok passengers as it has no sleepers.

Train 170: Rapid train, second and third class, not air-conditioned.

Security concerns in southern Thailand

If crossing into Thailand, you'll probably be aware of the security concerns in southern Thailand, particularly at the eastern end of the frontier around Yala and Sungai Kolok, where (like many parts of the world now) there might be a risk of being in the wrong place at the wrong time if you were to hang around for any length of time. Bombs have gone off outside bars and police stations, and the eastern Sungai Kolok–Yala–Hat Yai rail line has been affected on a number of occasions. However, at the time of writing they aren't targeting western travellers, and the western end of the frontier (through which the main Singapore–Kuala Lumpur–Penang–Bangkok rail route passes) isn't as badly affected as the eastern Sungai Kolok end. I'm no security expert, but no one has yet told me of any problems experienced in passing through the area non-stop on board a train using the Singapore–KL–Penang–Bangkok main line via Padang Besar. However, travellers should always take advice and be aware of the current situation. I certainly don't claim to offer current security advice.

THE JUNGLE LINE: SINGAPORE OR KUALA LUMPUR TO KHOTA BHARU

Most people use the main line from Singapore, which heads up the west coast of Malaysia to KL, Penang and on to Bangkok. But there's an alternative route up the east coast, through amazing jungle scenery to Khota Bharu. It's worth making the effort to travel the stretch from Gemas to Khota Bharu (Wakaf Bharu station) by daytime third class slow train, as the scenery is superb, and the direct trains from Singapore and KL travel at night. In Gemas, there's a fair hotel just outside the station, and there will be plenty of hotels with rooms to spare in Khota Bharu, even if it's late at night when you arrive.

Wakaf Bharu is the station for Khota Bharu, about 5 km away. Buses and taxis are available; a bus will cost RM1 (20p), a taxi RM10 (£2).

If you're heading for the Perhentian Islands, you can get off the train at either Tanah Merah or Wakaf Bharu and take a taxi to the port at Kuala Besut or Tok Bali.

It's possible to travel to Bangkok via the Jungle Line, too, taking a bus or taxi from Khota Bharu to the frontier, then walking across the border into Thailand to Sungai Kolok railway station, for a train to Bangkok – see page 367 (but see also the note above about security).

Singapore and Kuala Lumpur → Wakaf Bharu (Khota Bharu) and Tumpat

		Intercity trains			Local 'shuttle' trains				
Train number (see notes below)		14	28	26	82	90	84	86	92
Classes		2	F,S,2,3	S,2,3	3	3	3	3	3
Days of running		Daily	Daily	Daily	Daily	Daily	Daily	Daily	Daily
Singapore	depart	04:30	–	18:00	–	–	–	–	–
Johor Bahru	depart	05:33	–	19:07	–	–	–	–	–
Kuala Lumpur	depart	I	20:30	I	–	–	–	–	–
Tampin (for Malacca)	depart	I	22:48	I	–	–	–	–	–
Gemas	depart	09:17	23:44	22:44	–	03:10	–	–	13:45
Kuala Lipis	arr/dep	13:35	04:15	03:25	05:20	07:45	–	15:25	18:26
Gua Musang	arr/dep	15:18	05:49	05:03	07:00	–	–	17:14	–
Tanah Merah	arrive	18:01	08:38	07:51	11:06	–	16:12	21:16	–
Wakaf Bharu (for Khota Bharu)	arrive	18:45	09:21	08:44	12:15	–	17:25	22:29	–
Tumpat	arrive	19:27	09:40	09:01	12:35	–	17:45	22:48	–

Tumpat and Wakaf Bharu (Khota Bharu) → *Kuala Lumpur and Singapore*

		Intercity trains			Local 'shuttle' trains					
Train number (see below)		15	29	27	91	81	83	93	85	91
Classes		2	F,S,2,3	S,2,3	3	3	3	3	3	3
Days of running		Daily	Daily	Daily	Daily	Daily	Daily	Daily	Daily	Daily
Tumpat	depart	07:00	18:45	20:30	–	03:50	10:10	–	15:30	–
Wakaf Bharu (for Khota Bharu)	depart	07:16	19:02	20:47	–	04:08	10:29	–	15:47	–
Tanah Merah	depart	07:59	19:45	21:32	–	04:56	11:20	–	16:33	–
Gua Musang	arr/dep	10:51	22:34	00:24	–	08:39	–	–	20:28	–
Kuala Lipis	arr/dep	12:33	00:14	02:15	08:15	10:30	–	18:50	22:05	–
Gemas	arrive	17:04	04:32	06:28	12:36	–	–	22:50	–	–
Tampin (for Malacca)	arrive	I	05:49	I	–	–	–	–	–	–
Kuala Lumpur	arrive	I	07:55	I	–	–	–	–	–	–
Johor Bahru	arrive	20:56	–	09:52	–	–	–	–	–	–
Singapore	arrive	22:02	–	11:00	–	–	–	–	–	–

Classes: F = first class sleeper (Premier Night Standard); **S** = second class sleeper (Superior Night); **2** = second class seats (Superior); **3** = third class seats (Economy). For descriptions see page 345.

Trains 14 and 15: *Ekspress Sinaran Timur.* Daily. Second class seats, air-conditioned. No first class.

Trains 26 and 27: *Ekspress Senandung Timuran.* Second class sleepers, second and third class seats. Air-conditioned. No first class sleepers.

Trains 28 and 29: *Ekspress Senandung Wau.* Daily. First and second class sleepers, second and third class seats. Air-conditioned.

Trains 81–93: Third class slow train, much older train with basic seats, not air-conditioned. Please double-check the timetable for these trains locally, as it changes from time to time.

FARES

Malaysian rail fares are very cheap. Some key examples are shown in the table below.

One-way fare per person, in ringgits	3rd class seat	2nd class seat	1st class seat	2nd class sleeper	1st class sleeper	Deluxe sleeper, shower and WC
Singapore to Bangkok	The cost of a Singapore to Bangkok journey is the sum of the fares from Singapore to Kuala Lumpur, KL to Butterworth, Butterworth to Bangkok.					
Singapore to Kuala Lumpur*	–	RM34 (£7,$10)	RM68 (£14,$21)	RM43 (£9,$13)	RM86 (£18,$25)	RM131 (£27,$40) sharing, RM180 (£37,$55) sole occupancy
Singapore to Butterworth (Penang)*	–	RM60 (£12,$18)	RM127 (£26,$38)	–	–	–
Butterworth (Penang) to Bangkok	–	–	–	RM112 (£23,$34)	–	–
Butterworth (Penang) to Surat Thani	–	–	–	RM101 (£21,$30)	–	–
Kuala Lumpur to Butterworth (Penang)	RM17 (£4,$5)	RM34 (£7,$10)	RM67 (£14,$20)	RM43 (£9,$13)	RM85 (£18,$26)	–
Kuala Lumpur to Hat Yai	–	RM44 (£9,$13)	–	RM57 (£12,$17)	–	–
Kuala Lumpur to Tumpat / Wakaf Bharu	RM29 (£6,$9)	RM39 (£8,$12)	–	RM52 (£11,$16)	RM106 (£22,$32)	–
Singapore to Tumpat / Wakaf Bharu	RM30 (£6,$10)	RM41 (£9,$12)	–	RM54 (£11,$16)	–	–

* If your ticket starts in Singapore, or is bought or collected at the station in Singapore, it will cost twice the price shown, as explained below.

Children aged 0–3 travel free, children aged 4–11 travel at half fare, children aged 12 and over pay full fare.

There is a 50 per cent discount on Malaysian intercity train fares for anyone aged over 60, including foreigners.

Prices in this table are in US$, not S$.

You can check these and other fares on the KTM website, **www.ktmb.com.my**. Note that Kuala Lumpur is listed under 'S' as 'Sentral Kuala Lumpur'!

> When checking fares or booking online at **www.ktmb.com.my**, classes and class codes are as follows:
>
> AFC = air-conditioned first class seats (also known as Premier)
>
> ASC = air-conditioned second class seats (also known as Superior)
>
> AEC = air-conditioned economy (third class) seats
>
> ADNS = second class sleeper (also known as Superior Night)
>
> 2PLUS or ADNFB = first class 2-berth sleeper (also known as Premier Night Standard)
>
> ADNFD = deluxe 2-berth sleeper with private shower and toilet (also known as Premier Night Deluxe)

Tickets bought in Singapore are double the price

A strange (you might say unfair) quirk of the system is that for historical (and presumably now financial) reasons, tickets bought in Singapore must be paid for in Singapore dollars, but at the ringgit amount. In plain English, if the fare is 34 ringgits, you'll be charged 34 Singapore dollars if you buy it in Singapore, even though RM34 is £7 (US$10) whereas S$34 is £17 (US$24). Crazy, eh? This also applies to tickets for journeys starting in Singapore booked online using the e-ticketing facility on **www.ktmb.com.my** and to tickets booked through the Malaysian Railways call centre and collected in Singapore. In fact, if you book online it's even more confusing, as the online system converts the Singapore dollar amount back into ringgits again: it takes the RM34 fare, reads it as S$34, then converts the S$34 back into RM82 and (at current exchange rates) charges you RM82 for a RM34 fare. For most westerners this is not an insurmountable problem as the fares are so cheap anyway. Finding that £7 has become £17 won't have a huge impact on a £1,000 holiday. But here are some tips to avoid paying more than you have to.

- Tip number 1: If you want to make a return journey from Singapore to Kuala Lumpur, book this as two separate one-way trips so at least the return leg will be charged in ringgits at the ringgit amount. If you book it as a return, both legs of a return ticket starting in Singapore will be charged in Singapore dollars, but a one-way ticket starting in Malaysia is charged in ringgits.

- Tip number 2: If you are in Singapore and book all your trains for a multi-leg journey – say Singapore to Bangkok – by email or phone with Malaysian Railways, collect the Singapore–KL ticket in Singapore (biting the bullet and paying in Singapore dollars), but wait till you get to KL to collect your onward tickets (KL–Penang and Penang–Bangkok in this case) so you can pay for them in ringgits at the ringgit amount. If you collect all the tickets in Singapore, you'll have to pay for all of them in Singapore dollars.

- Tip number 3: For a one-way journey from Singapore to KL in (say) a deluxe sleeper, use the e-ticketing facility on **www.ktmb.com.my** to book a return journey consisting of a dummy outward trip from KL to Singapore in the cheapest second class seat (which you won't use), then a 'return' leg from Singapore to KL in the deluxe sleeper (which you will use). This way, it counts as a return journey starting in Malaysia, so you will be charged in ringgits, which in this case will save money compared with paying twice the price for a one-way deluxe sleeper starting in Singapore, even allowing for the cost of the unused seat ticket from KL to Singapore.

Some people go out of their way to avoid paying in Singapore dollars, taking local transport to Johor Bahru (the first station in Malaysia, just north of the causeway from Singapore Island) so they can take the train from there. But is the hassle really worth it? Even in Singapore dollars a train ticket to KL is a mere £17/US$24, so you're saving only £10/US$14 by doing this, and it's a shame to miss out on a classic departure from the historic art-deco 1932-built

Singapore station. This is an experience that won't last for ever, as the station is now due to close before July 2011. It remains to be seen whether KTM will still charge fares in Singapore dollars for trains leaving only a mile or two south of Johor Bahru.

Before you ask, the e-ticketing system unfortunately won't let you buy a Singapore to Johor Bahru ticket in Singapore dollars, then a Johor Bahru to KL ticket on the same train charged in ringgits – they've thought of that one!

HOW TO BUY TICKETS

Do I need a reservation?

Yes, you do. All long-distance trains in Malaysia are 'reservation compulsory', so you will need a seat or berth reservation for each train you take. Reservations open 56 days before departure. The Singapore to Bangkok journey is ticketed as two or three separate journeys, Singapore to Kuala Lumpur, Kuala Lumpur to Butterworth, and Butterworth to Bangkok, or possibly Singapore to Butterworth, Butterworth to Bangkok, depending on how you want to do it. Each ticket will have the travel date, train number and your seat or berth number printed on it.

Can I stop off along the way?

Yes, of course! But you cannot buy an open ticket and randomly hop on and off trains without a reservation. You must buy a separate ticket (which will include a seat or berth reservation on a specific date on a specific train) for each individual train journey. So if you want to stop off, simply book each leg of the journey for whatever dates you want. You can arrange all your tickets in advance or buy them as you go to keep your options open – it's entirely up to you. Kuala Lumpur and Penang are both well worth a stopover, and you could stop off in southern Thailand too, enjoying the beaches or maybe taking the ferry to Koh Samui.

What's the best way to buy tickets?

It's easy to buy train tickets for travel within Singapore and Malaysia either at the station, online at **www.ktmb.com.my**, or by phone or email to the KTM call centre. Take your pick! Advice on each method is given below.

If you are wanting to buy tickets for international travel (i.e. from Singapore or Malaysia into Thailand), bear in mind that the Butterworth to Bangkok International Express cannot be booked online, only by phone or email or at the station, so to prearrange a complete northbound Singapore–Bangkok journey either book your Singapore–Kuala Lumpur and Kuala Lumpur–Butterworth trains online at **www.ktmb.com.my**, then book the Butterworth–Bangkok train by email to the KTM call centre, or book all three trains by email to the KTM reservations centre. Incidentally, if your journey involves the Kuala Lumpur to Hat Yai train rather than the Butterworth–Bangkok train, this *can* be booked online on the KTM website all the way to Hat Yai, but tickets for Thai domestic trains northwards from Hat Yai cannot be booked by the Malaysians; you'll have to buy onward tickets when you get to Hat Yai.

If you are returning south from Bangkok to Singapore, remember that trains within or starting in Thailand cannot be booked through Malaysian stations or call centres, as the reservations are held on the Thai reservation computer, not accessible by Malaysian Railways. So book the Bangkok to Butterworth International Express either at the station when you get to Bangkok, or by email with the State Railways of Thailand, or through an agency such as **www.thailandtrainticket.com** (see the Thailand chapter, page 407). Then book the Butterworth–KL and KL–Singapore trains either at the station when you get to Butterworth or online in advance using **www.ktmb.com.my**.

Buying tickets at the station

You can buy tickets at Singapore station or any railway station in Malaysia up to 56 days in advance. KTM has a computerised reservation system, so the ticket offices at Singapore, Kuala Lumpur, Butterworth or any other Malaysian station (including the KTM ticket office at the Georgetown ferry terminal on

Penang Island) can sell tickets and make reservations for any train journey within Malaysia, or starting in Malaysia heading into Thailand, including Butterworth to Bangkok.

Singapore ticket office accepts American Express and Diners Club credit cards, but not Visa or MasterCard. There's no ATM at Singapore station – the nearest one is a 15-minute walk away, so get cash out beforehand if you need it. The ticket offices at Kuala Lumpur and Butterworth do accept MasterCard and Visa.

Stations in Malaysia and Singapore cannot book seats or berths on trains running wholly within Thailand, nor can they book return journeys from Thailand back to Malaysia, because they cannot access the Thai Railways reservation system.

You can buy all the tickets you need for a Singapore to Bangkok journey at Singapore station. However, tickets bought in Singapore will cost more than twice as much as tickets picked up and paid for in Malaysia (see page 357), so it is better to buy just your Singapore–Kuala Lumpur ticket at Singapore station, then pay for the Kuala Lumpur–Butterworth and Butterworth–Bangkok tickets when you get to Kuala Lumpur. You can still book the KL to Butterworth and Butterworth to Bangkok trains in advance, using internet or email as shown in the section below.

Buying tickets online at www.ktmb.com.my

You can book Malaysian train tickets online. Just go to the Malaysian railways (KTM) website **www.ktmb.com.my**. Use the journey planner on their home page to find a train, and on the results page click 'Proceed Purchase Ticket' (the direct link to their sales system is **https://intranet.ktmb.com.my/ e-ticket/Login.asp**). Book your train(s), pay by credit card and print the ticket on your own PC printer, or you can collect the tickets from any KTM railway station, including Singapore. The www.ktmb.com.my e-ticketing system will book any express train wholly within Singapore and Malaysia, and it can also book the KTM-run international train from Kuala Lumpur to Hat Yai in Thailand. However, it cannot book the Thai-run International Express from

Butterworth to Bangkok, which you should book either by email (see the next section) or in person at any KTM station.

Tips for using the **www.ktmb.com.my** *e-ticketing system*

- Bookings open 56 days in advance.

- Can't find Kuala Lumpur in the list of destinations? It's shown under 'S' as 'Sentral Kuala Lumpur'.

- The confusingly named 'Label/slot' field on the booking form allows you to pick your coach (for example, coach 'J1'), then when you click 'view' it will show you the available seats or berths in that coach, allowing you to pick one (for example, 5A, 5B, etc.).

- When booking second class sleepers, pick berths in the centre of the car, away from the end doors, as these will be quieter, away from the wheels, with no draughts from the door.

- When booking second class sleepers, remember lower berths are wider than upper ones, which is why they're a fraction more expensive.

- Classes are shown as follows:

    AFC = air-conditioned first class seats (Premier)

    ASC = air-conditioned second class seats (Superior)

    AEC = air-conditioned economy class (third class) seats (Economy)

    ADNS = second class sleeper (also known as Superior Night)

- 2PLUS or ADNFB = first class 2-berth sleeper (also known as Premier Night Standard)

- ADNFD = deluxe 2-berth sleeper with private shower and toilet (also known as Premier Night Deluxe)

- If you are booking tickets for a journey starting in Singapore, read the section on page 357, which explains why the KTM online system will charge you RM82 for what is shown as a RM34 fare, and gives some tips on how to minimise the extra cost.

- If you have any problems with the online system, you can call KTM reservations on +60 3 2267 1200.

Buying tickets by phone or by email

If you want to book a journey within Malaysia, a sleeper on the International Express from Butterworth to Bangkok, or a complete train journey from Singapore to Bangkok, simply email your booking request to the Malaysian Railways reservation office at callcenter@ktmb.com.my, or call the KTM call centre on +60 3 2267 1200 (calling from outside Malaysia) or 03 2267 1200 (calling from within Malaysia). You can book all your trains this way: Singapore–KL, KL–Butterworth and Butterworth–Bangkok – but please remember that you're not asking for 'a Singapore to Bangkok ticket', you're asking for three separate tickets on three specific trains, each reserved for whatever date you want. If you email the request, make sure your email includes all the details for each of the three trains you need to book for the whole journey from Singapore to Bangkok, including dates and class of travel. Malaysian Railways will reply with a reference number which you can quote when you pick up and pay for your tickets in Malaysia or Singapore. Remember that tickets picked up and paid for in Singapore will cost twice as much as those picked up in Malaysia, so it is best to pick up only your Singapore–Kuala Lumpur ticket at Singapore station, then wait until you get to Kuala Lumpur to pick up the remaining tickets so you can pay in ringgits.

Malaysian Railways can only book the northbound International Express from Butterworth to Bangkok. A southbound journey from Bangkok to Malaysia must either be booked at Bangkok station when you get there, or booked by email with the State Railways of Thailand or one of several recommended Thai travel agencies such as Traveller2000, as shown in the Thailand chapter, pages 406–7.

BUS AND FERRY CONNECTIONS WITHIN MALAYSIA

The Butterworth–Penang ferry

Penang is an island, and the main town on Penang Island is called Georgetown, once capital of British Malaya. The railway station for Penang is Butterworth, which is on the mainland directly opposite Georgetown. When you arrive by train at Butterworth station, you go up a short walkway from the platforms to the ferry terminal, and ferries from Butterworth to Penang (Georgetown) operate around the clock at frequent intervals, taking just 15 minutes. Georgetown has some excellent British colonial buildings, interesting museums and temples, and a large Chinatown. Well worth a visit! The most famous and historic place to stay in Penang is of course the historic Eastern and Oriental Hotel, around £110 for a double room.

Kuala Lumpur to Malacca (Melaka)

Malacca is well worth a day's visit, as it has some of the oldest colonial buildings in Southeast Asia. It is not on the rail network, but modern buses run from the main bus station in Kuala Lumpur every hour, taking about 3 hours and costing about RM8 (£2) one-way. Alternatively, take a train from Kuala Lumpur to Tampin station (see the train timetable page 354), then take a bus or taxi from there (38 km). A taxi from Tampin to Malacca costs between RM40 and RM60 (£8– £13 or US$11–US$19).

Singapore to Malacca (Melaka)

There are regular buses from Singapore to Malacca taking about 5½ hours. Alternatively, take a train from Singapore to Tampin station (see the train timetable page 354), then take a bus or taxi from there (38 km). A taxi from Tampin to Malacca costs between RM40 and RM60 (£8–£13 or US$11–US$19).

Alor Setar or Arau to Langkawi island

Ferries run from both Alor Setar and Arau to Langkawi Island: there is little to choose between the two. From Alor Setar it's a short bus ride or RM15 (£3) taxi ride to the ferry terminal at Kuala Kedah. A ferry sails from Kuala Kedah to Langkawi every 30 minutes between 07:00 and 19:00, no advance reservation necessary, see **www.langkawi-ferry.com**. Sailing time is 1 hour 30 minutes; the fare is RM23 (£5) each way.

If you decide to go via Arau, it's a short taxi ride to the ferry terminal at Kuala Perlis, which is slightly closer to Langkawi than Kuala Kedah. The ferry sails from Kuala Perlis to Langkawi about every 30 minutes between 07:00 and 19:00, see **www.langkawi-ferry.com**, sailing time 1 hour 15 mins, fare RM18 (£4) each way, no advance reservation necessary.

Alor Setar and Arau are both on the mainline railway between Butterworth and Padang Besar. From Kuala Lumpur you should take the overnight *Ekspress Senandung Langkawi* sleeper train; see the train timetable, page 350. If you are travelling from Singapore to Langkawi, take the morning train from Singapore to Kuala Lumpur, spend the afternoon in KL, then take the *Ekspress Senandung Langkawi* on to Alor Setar or Arau.

If you are travelling to Langkawi from Bangkok or southern Thailand, Arau is probably the better choice; to get there you can take the International Express direct from Bangkok.

Penang to Langkawi island

A daily fast ferry operates direct from Penang to Langkawi Island, leaving at 08:15 and taking 2 hours 45 minutes. The fare is about RM60 (£13 or US$17) one-way. For children aged 3–11 it is RM45 (£10); children under 3 travel free. The return departure from Langkawi to Penang is at 17:15. For times, fares and online booking, see **www.langkawi-ferry.com**. This ferry is the best option if you want to go to/from Penang itself.

Perhentian Islands

The Perhentian Islands are relatively undeveloped islands off Malaysia's northeastern coast, excellent for scuba diving. The ideal way to reach the Perhentians is by overnight sleeper train from Kuala Lumpur or Singapore, taxi transfer then ferry.

Take the overnight sleeper train from Kuala Lumpur or Singapore to either Tanah Merah or Wakaf Bharu stations; see the Jungle Line timetable on page 354 for train times. The train fare is about RM54 (£11 or US$16) including a second class sleeper. The overnight train from KL has both second class sleepers and first class 2-berth sleepers, while the overnight train from Singapore just has second class sleepers, but even second class sleepers are comfortable, air-conditioned and perfectly adequate. Taking the sleeper train saves a hotel bill, is an experience in itself, and can even save time compared with flying.

Take a taxi from Tanah Merah or Wakaf Bharu to the main ferry port at Kuala Besut. Local taxis will be waiting for the train at either station; the taxi fare is RM50 (£10 or US$15), the journey time about 50 minutes from Wakaf Bharu or 30 minutes from Tanah Merah.

Speedboats from Kuala Besut take about 30 minutes to reach the Perhentian Islands, and depart 4–5 times daily, 09:00–17:00, according to demand. The fare is about RM60 (£13 or US$20) return. There are also slow boats which leave Kuala Besut at 08:30 and 14:30, taking 1½ hours, fare about RM40 (£8) return. There's another (private) jetty at Tok Bali, but ferries from here are less frequent.

Cameron Highlands

There are no trains to the Cameron Highlands, only buses and taxis, but the nearest stations are either Tapah Road or Ipoh. Ipoh is the better railhead to use, as Tapah Road station is 9 km from Tapah town and the *Rakyat Ekspress* doesn't stop there, whereas all trains call at Ipoh.

Take an express train from Singapore, Kuala Lumpur or Penang (Butterworth) to Ipoh, then a bus from Ipoh to Tanah Rata in the Cameron Highlands. There are four buses daily, leaving Ipoh at 08:00, 11:00, 15:00 and 18:00, journey time 3½ hours, fare around RM11 (£2). The bus station is walking distance from the rail station, but as there are several bus stations in Ipoh, make sure you head for the right one. The road winds up into the hills, with great views over the fields.

As an alternative, you could take a private taxi from Ipoh to Tanah Rata; it should cost around RM80 (£17) per taxi.

MOVING ON FROM MALAYSIA

A ferry service operates from Penang to Medan on the island of Sumatra; see the Indonesia chapter, page 329.

Travelling north on the International Express into Thailand, you can connect with ferries to the Thai islands Koh Tao, Koh Samui and Koh Phangan at Surat Thani; see the Thailand chapter, pages 419–23.

To reach Bangkok, as well as the main route via Butterworth and Hat Yai already described, you have two possible options: taking the route via the Jungle Line, and travelling by luxury tour train.

Singapore or Kuala Lumpur to Bangkok, via the Jungle Line

Take the train from Singapore or Kuala Lumpur to Wakaf Bharu, as described on page 353.

Buses (RM2, 40p) and taxis (RM15, £3) are available from Wakaf Bharu to the Thai frontier; or, if you are making a stopover at Khota Bharu, bus 29 runs every half hour from Khota Bharu bus station near the central market to the Thai/Malay border point, fare RM5 (£1). You then walk across the border into Thailand and keep walking straight on for 800 metres to Sungai Kolok railway station for the Thai Railways trains to Hat Yai, Surat Thani and Bangkok (see the Thailand chapter, page 418, for times). Be aware of the security concerns on the Sungai Kolok line (see page 352).

The Eastern and Oriental Express

There's also a luxury train between Singapore, Kuala Lumpur, Penang and Bangkok. The ultra-luxurious *Eastern and Oriental Express* runs once, twice or sometimes three times each month between these cities, including a brief diversion via Kanchanaburi and the Bridge on the River Kwai. It's operated by the same company that runs the superb Venice Simplon Orient Express in Europe, and uses sleeping-cars originally built in Japan for the New Zealand Railways Wellington–Auckland *Silver Star* sleeper train, which ran from 1972 to 1979. A one-way ticket from Singapore to Bangkok costs at least £1,230, including meals, but excluding drinks, compared with around £40 for travel by regular daily trains (although admittedly meals on the regular trains are extra!). See **www.orient-expresstrains.com** or (in the UK) call 0845 077 2222 for times, dates, prices and online booking.

NEPAL

There are no trains in Nepal, other than the end of an obscure branch line from India which is of little interest to most travellers. However, it's possible to travel from India to Nepal by a combination of train and bus; or indeed to travel from Europe to Kathmandu mostly by train, via Istanbul, Tehran and Pakistan, in two to three weeks, although there are security concerns in southeast Iran and in Pakistan.

Train operator:	There are no trains in Nepal, other than an obscure branch line from India of limited interest to travellers.
Time:	GMT+5 hours 45 minutes
Currency:	£1 = approx. 114 Nepalese rupees, $1 = approx. 74 Nepalese rupees
Tourist information:	**www.welcomenepal.com**
Visas:	All except Indian citizens need a visa. Tourist visas can be bought at all official frontiers for around $30 (£20). The visa fee must be paid in US$ cash, and you'll need 2 passport photos. Alternatively, visas can be bought from Nepal embassies; the Nepalese London embassy website is **www.nepembassy.org.uk**.

INDIA TO NEPAL, overland

Delhi ➔ Kathmandu by train+bus

It's easy, cheap, and an adventure to do this journey overland.

Day 1: Take a train from **Delhi** to **Gorakhpur**. The *Vaishali Express* leaves Delhi at around 19:45 and arrives at Gorakhpur Junction at

09:10 next morning; or there's another train from New Delhi at 17:20, arriving at Gorakhpur at 06:35 next morning. The fare is around 2,440 Indian rupees (£35 or $53) in AC1 (air-conditioned first class sleeper), Rs1,240 (£18 or $27) in AC2 (air-conditioned 2-tier sleeper), Rs785 (£12 or $17) in AC3 (air-conditioned 3-tier sleeper) or Rs315 (£5 or $7) in non-air-conditioned sleeper class. Check current times and fares at **www.indianrail.gov.in** or **www.cleartrip.com** and see the India chapter, pages 317 and 320, for details of accommodation and how to book.

Day 2: Take a bus or jeep from **Gorakhpur** to the Nepalese frontier at (Indian side) **Sunauli/Bhairawa** (Nepalese side, but also often called Sunauli). Journey time is about 3 hours, fare around Rs55 (£1 or $2).

Walk across the frontier, and it's then a few minutes' walk to the Bhairawa bus station. Take a bus or jeep on from **Bhairawa** to **Kathmandu**. Buses take 9–12 hours, and cost about 120 Nepalese rupees or 230 Indian rupees (£1 or $2). There are many buses daily, either daytime buses leaving regularly until about 11:00 or overnight buses leaving regularly from about 16:00 until 19:00. Indian rupees may be accepted here in Bhairawa, but not further into Nepal.

It's also possible to travel via Varanasi. An overnight train links Delhi and Varanasi. Buses link Varanasi with the Nepalese border – see the next section.

Varanasi to Kathmandu by bus

Day 1: Direct buses run from **Varanasi** to the Nepalese border at **Sunauli** (Indian side)/**Bhairawa** (Nepalese side), running several times daily (exact times not known). They take 9 hours and cost about 100 Nepalese rupees (£1.50 or $2). Walk across the frontier, and spend the night in a hotel in Sunauli.

Day 2: The Sunauli bus station is a few minutes' walk from the frontier. Buses to **Kathmandu** take 9–12 hours, and cost about 120 Nepalese rupees (£1 or $2). There are many buses daily, either daytime buses leaving regularly until about 11:00 or overnight buses leaving regularly from about 16:00 until 19:00.

NEPAL TO TIBET (CHINA), overland

There is no regular bus service and certainly no train between Kathmandu and Lhasa (Tibet/China). The only way this journey can be done legally at present is to go on an organised overland tour run by a local travel agency, who will arrange all the necessary permits for you. The cheapest tours cost about £270/$400 (ask for a budget tour – there are more expensive options with better accommodation) and take eight days, seven nights for the 955-km journey. Try **www.heiantreks.com**, whose tours depart Kathmandu every Tuesday and Saturday, **www.trekkingtibet.com** (recommended by one seat61 corres-pondent), **www.richatours.com**, **www.visitnepal.com/getaway** (departing Kathmandu every Saturday, April–October, $450 + $100 Tibetan permit), or do a Google search for other agencies. Once in Lhasa, there are trains onwards to Xian, Beijing or Shanghai; see the China chapter, page 304.

NORTH KOREA

North Korea is the last remaining Stalinist dictatorship, and many people consider it the world's most isolated country, as the regime permits westerners to visit only as part of an organised tour. Nevertheless, you can travel there by train, and in fact there are direct trains to its capital Pyongyang from both Beijing and (via the Trans-Siberian railway) Moscow.

Train operator:	State Railways
Ferry operators to North Korea:	–
Time:	GMT+9 all year round
Currency:	£1 = approx. 206 North Korean won
Tourist information:	–
Visas:	A visa is required for a visit to North Korea.

VISITING NORTH KOREA

Visas are not normally granted to foreign independent travellers to North Korea, only to visitors on an organised tour with a guide. Several companies can arrange visits to North Korea. In the UK try Regent Holidays (**www.regent-holidays.co.uk**, telephone 0845 277 3317), who can arrange group or individual tours to North Korea, including booking the Beijing–Pyongyang and Moscow–Pyongyang trains. Also try Koryo Tours (Beijing-based) at **www.koryogroup.com**, VNC Travel at **www.vnc.nl** (in the Netherlands), or **www.northkorea1on1.com** (based in the USA). Each of these companies can book the Beijing–Pyongyang sleeper train and help with visas. Although there have been discussions, there are no trains (nor any access) across the border between North and South Korea.

MOSCOW TO PYONGYANG

There is a weekly service between Moscow and Pyongyang, capital of North Korea, which leaves Moscow Yaroslavski station at 23:55 on Friday, and arrives in Pyonyang at 19:30 the following Friday. This train consists of several through sleeping-cars from Moscow to Pyongyang, attached to the weekly Moscow–Beijing Trans-Manchurian train for most of the way. There are first class 2-berth and second class 4-berth compartments, and a restaurant car is available. You'll need Russian, Chinese and North Korean visas, as the train travels the Trans-Siberian Railway via Ekaterinburg, Irkutsk, Ulan Ude in Russia, then the Trans-Manchurian line via Harbin in China.

Westbound, the train departs Pyongyang at 10:10 on Saturday, arriving at Moscow Yaroslavski station at 18:13 the following Friday.

You can see a timetable of this train from Moscow as far as Harbin in the Trans-Siberian chapter, page 59. Russian/Chinese border points are Zabaikalsk and Manzhouli. The point of entry into North Korea is Sinuiji (on the same day you arrive/depart Pyongyang). For train travel between London and Moscow, see page 67.

Note that the above route is approved for foreigners. There's another through sleeping-car twice a month between Moscow and Pyongyang via Tumangan, attached to the Moscow–Vladivostok *Rossiya* for most of its journey. This crosses directly from Russia into North Korea, but this is not (normally) an approved route for foreigners. There's a blog by Helmut Uttenthaler, a westerner who did manage to travel this route, at vienna-pyongyang.blogspot.com.

BEIJING TO PYONGYANG

A sleeper train runs four days a week from Beijing to Pyongyang, departing Beijing at 17:30 on Monday, Wednesday, Thursday and Saturday, arriving at

Pyongyang at 19:30 next day. From Pyongyang it departs at 10:10 on Monday, Wednesday, Thursday and Saturday, arriving at Beijing at 08:29 next day.

The train has soft class 4-berth sleepers and restaurant car. A restaurant meal costs around €5 (£4). This train is approved for European and other non-US foreigners but it's reported as *not* permitted for US citizens – if you're American, please check. Taking this train gives an insight into the poor rural areas of North Korea not normally shown to tourists. You'll also pass the location of the Ryongchon train disaster, when a trainload of flammable cargo exploded in 2004, the effect still visible. For train travel between London, Moscow and Beijing, see the Trans-Siberian chapter, page 33.

PAKISTAN

Like its neighbour India, Pakistan inherited a British-built railway network from its colonial era. Every bit as evocative as their Indian counterparts, Pakistani trains link all the main cities, with a main line running from the capital Karachi through Lahore to Peshawar, near the fabled 'North West Frontier'. However, there are currently some security and visa issues associated with a visit to Pakistan, so check the latest situation at **www.fco.gov.uk** before you go.

Train operator:	Pakistan Railway Corporation, **www.pakrail.com**
Time:	GMT+5
Currency:	£1 = approx. 122 rupees, $1 = approx. 85 rupees
Tourist information:	**www.tourism.gov.pk**
Visas:	UK citizens and most other western nationalities need a visa for Pakistan, see the Pakistan High Commission website **www.phclondon.org**. Check travel advice at **www.fco.gov.uk** before visiting.

EUROPE TO PAKISTAN, overland

It's just about possible to travel overland from the UK to Pakistan, although there are some security concerns and visa issues along the way, making it more of an expedition than a straightforward way to travel. For details, see page 90.

TRAIN TRAVEL WITHIN PAKISTAN

Trains link most main towns and cities in Pakistan, and even run across the border to India. Westwards, they cross into Iran, and the track at least (if not the trains) now runs right through to Europe. This is the mainline across Pakistan, and route of Pakistan's most famous train, the *Khyber Mail*. There are lots of trains, but only the most important are shown here. All trains shown have a restaurant car.

Important: Check Foreign Office advice for travel to Pakistan at **www.fco.gov.uk**, as there are currently serious security concerns. At the time of writing it was also reported that Pakistan was not allowing westerners to use trains or other surface travel within Pakistan, to avoid the embarrassment of any westerner being involved in a terrorist incident. Visas have been refused for travellers proposing to enter Pakistan overland using surface transport. However, it was also reported that whilst the London and Birmingham consulates were applying this rule, the Bradford consulate was not. Please check before travelling.

What are Pakistani trains like?

Trains have several classes. In descending order of cost, these are:

Air-conditioned sleeper (recommended)

First class sleeper

Air-conditioned lower class (both seat and sleeper versions)

Parlour car (comfortable open-plan seating; recommended for daytime journeys)

Economy class seats

Second class (seat and sleeper versions)

Most important trains also have a restaurant car. You can check train times and availability at the Pakistan Railways site, **www.pakrail.com**.

KARACHI TO LAHORE AND PESHAWAR

Karachi → Lahore, Rawalpindi, Peshawar

Train number (see notes)		27	41	7	15	1	107	101	103
Classes		P,L,E	P,L,E	A,1,L,E	A,L,E	A,1,E	P,L,E	P,L,E	P,L,E
Karachi (Cantonment)	depart	07:00 day 1	16:00 day 1	17:00 day 1	18:00 day 1	22:00 day 1	–	–	–
Hyderabad	arr/dep	09:45 day 1	18:40 day 1	19:45 day 1	20:35 day 1	00:50 day 2	–	–	–
Rohri	arr/dep	14:50 day 1	23:20 day 1	00:40 day 2	01:05 day 2	05:40 day 2	–	–	–
Multan (Cantonment)	arr/dep	I	I	07:20 day 2	I	14:03 day 2	–	–	–
Lahore (Junction)	arr/dep	02:45 day 1	10:15 day 2	14:15 day 2	12:00 day 2	21:40 day 2	07:00	07:30	16:30
Rawalpindi	arr/dep	–	–	19:30 day 2	–	03:10 day 3	11:00	12:30	21:30
Attock	arr/dep	–	–	–	–	04:30 day 3	–	–	–
Peshawar (City)	arrive	–	–	–	–	06:20 day 3	–	–	–
Peshawar (Cantonment)	arrive	–	–	–	–	06:40 day 3	–	–	–

Peshawar, Rawalpindi, Lahore → Karachi

Train number (see notes)		28	2	8	42	16	104	102	108
Classes		P,L,E	A,1,E	A,1,L,E	P,L,E	A,L,E	P,L,E	P,L,E	P,L,E
Peshawar (Cantonment)	depart	–	22:30 day 1	–	–	–	–	–	–
Peshawar (City)	depart	–	22:42 day 1	–	–	–	–	–	–
Attock	arr/dep	–	00:12 day 2	–	–	–	–	–	–
Rawalpindi	arr/dep	–	02:40 day 2	08:15 day 1	–	–	07:30	16:30	18:00
Lahore (Junction)	arr/dep	07:00 day 1	08:30 day 2	13:50 day 1	16:00 day 1	18:00 day 1	12:30	21:30	21:30
Multan (Cantonment)	arr/dep	I	15:30 day 2	20:55 day 1	I	I	–	–	–
Rohri	arr/dep	19:20 day 1	23:50 day 2	04:00 day 2	03:20 day 2	05:25 day 2	–	–	–
Hyderabad	arr/dep	00:10 day 2	05:25 day 3	09:15 day 2	07:55 day 2	09:55 day 2	–	–	–
Karachi (Cantonment)	arrive	03:00 day 2	06:45 day 3	12:00 day 2	10:45 day 2	12:50 day 2	–	–	–

A = air-conditioned sleeper.

1 = first class sleeper.

L = air-conditioned lower class seats.

P = parlour car seats.

E = economy class seats.

Trains 1 and 2: *Khyber Mail*. Recommended for Karachi–Peshawar journeys.

Trains 7 and 8: *Tezgam*. Recommended for Karachi–Rawalpindi journeys.

Trains 15 and 16: *Karachi Express*. Recommended for Karachi–Lahore journeys.

Trains 27 and 28: *Shalimar Express*. Recommended for Karachi–Lahore journeys.

Trains 41 and 42: *Karakoram Express.* Modern spacious Chinese-built coaches, with AC lower class sleepers, no AC class sleepers.

Fares

Karachi to Rawalpindi in air-conditioned sleeper class costs about 2,600 Pakistani rupees (£21 or $30) per person one-way; in a seat in air-conditioned lower class it costs about Rs1,175 (£10 or $15); in an economy class seat it costs about Rs505 (£4 or $7).

The approximate fares for Karachi to Lahore, travelling on the *Karakoram Express*, are Rs1,945 (£16 or $23) one-way per person for a berth in an air-conditioned lower class sleeper; Rs1,315 (£11 or $17) for an air-conditioned lower class seat; Rs795 (£7 or $10) for a berth in an economy class sleeper; Rs715 (£6 or $8) for an economy class seat.

Children under 3 travel free; children aged 3 and up but under 12 travel for half fare.

KARACHI TO QUETTA

The *Bolan Mail* (trains 3 and 4) runs daily between Karachi and Quetta, departing Karachi (City) at 17:00 and Karachi (Cantonment) at 17:20, arriving at Quetta at 14:10 next day (train 3). From Quetta (train 4) it departs at 11:00, arriving at Karachi (Cantonment) at 08:00 next day and Karachi (City) at 08:25. The train has first class sleepers and economy class.

QUETTA TO PESHAWAR

Trains 23 and 24 link Quetta and Peshawar daily, with air-conditioned sleepers, first class sleepers and economy class. Train 23 departs Quetta at 10:00, arriving next day at Lahore at 10:00, Rawalpindi at 15:10, and Peshawar at 18:40. From Peshawar train 24 departs at 08:00, calling at Rawalpindi at 11:40, Lahore at 17:20, and arriving at Quetta at 17:00 next day.

KHYBER PASS

The line up the Khyber Pass from Peshawar to Landi Kotal, built by the British in 1920, is now officially closed to passenger trains, but special steam excursions operate from time to time.

MOVING ON FROM PAKISTAN

Lahore ➔ Amritsar (India) and Delhi, by train

A twice-weekly train leaves Lahore at 08:00 on Monday and Thursday (these are the confirmed days of running as at November 2008; previously it ran on Tuesday and Friday) for Wagah (the Pakistan side of the Pakistan/India frontier), arriving 09:15, departing again after customs checks at 11:30 (in practice usually after 12:00) for Atari on the Indian side of the frontier, arriving 20 minutes later. The train has second class non-air-conditioned seats only, and it's composed of Indian Railways carriages for half the year, Pakistani coaches for the other half (I suspect that the days of running may vary depending on which country is providing the coaches – it may run on Tuesday and Friday for part of the year when provided by Indian Railways; please double-check locally). There are connections from Atari for Amritsar, arriving around 15:00, and for Delhi (please double-check connecting times locally). The fare from Lahore to Wagah is 130 Pakistani rupees (£1). Tickets are not sold at Lahore's main station, but at Lahore Railway Headquarters, about 2 km from the station. You need your passport to buy a ticket. The fare from Wagah to Atari is 16 rupees.

For information on train travel within India, see the India chapter, page 308.

Lahore ➔ Amritsar (India) and Delhi, by bus or taxi

Lahore–Amritsar can also be done daily, and faster, by bus or taxi. Take a bus or taxi from Lahore to Wagah, walk through the frontier to Atari on the Indian side, then take a bus or taxi to Amritsar for daily trains to New Delhi. Going by bus or taxi also allows you to see the spectacular ceremony at sunset when the border closes. Indian and Pakistani guards try to outdo each other with their performances, watched by Indian and Pakistani crowds – as a tourist, you may get to sit in the VIP stand!

Karachi → Munabao (India) and Jodhpur

A new weekly international train called the *Thar Express* started on 17 February 2006, linking Karachi with Jodhpur.

Eastbound, the *Thar Express* leaves Karachi every Friday at 23:00, arriving at 'Zero Point' on the Pakistan/India frontier at around 08:00 next morning. After customs checks, the train goes forward to Munabao on the Indian side, arriving around 11:00. The Indian train departs Munabao at 19:00 after customs formalities, arriving at Jodhpur (Bhagat Ki Kothi station) at 23:50 on Saturday.

Westbound, the *Thar Express* leaves Jodhpur (Bhagat Ki Kothi station, about 4 km from the main station) every Friday night/Saturday morning at 01:00, arriving at Munabao at 07:00; then leaves Munabao at around 14:30 on Saturday, reaching Karachi at 02:15 on Sunday morning.

The sleeper fare from Jodhpur to Munabao/Zero Point is about Rs170, and from Munabao/Zero Point to Karachi is about Rs230. No more information is yet available, but feedback would be appreciated! The train has one sleeping-car and several economy cars.

Quetta → Zahedan (Iran)

Trains run from Quetta to Zahedan twice a month; see page 94.

SOUTH KOREA

South Korea has a good rail network linking all its main centres, including a new high-speed train service called 'KTX' between its capital, Seoul, and second city, Pusan, taking just 2 hours 50 minutes. You'll also find ferries linking Korea with both Japan and China, plus a new ferry to Vladivostok for the Trans-Siberian railway to Moscow.

Train operator:	Korean Railways, **www.korail.go.kr**
Ferry operators to Korea:	Japan–South Korea: **www.jrbeetle.co.jp** China–South Korea: **www.weidong.com** Russia–South Korea: **www.dbsferry.com/02_ticket/ticket03.asp**
Time:	GMT+9
Currency:	£1 = approx 1,805 won, $1 = approx. 1,250 won
Tourist information:	**http://english.tour2korea.com**
Visas:	UK, EU, US, NZ, Australian and some other nationalities do not need a visa to visit South Korea for up to 90 days, but an onward or return ticket must be held.

EUROPE TO SOUTH KOREA, without flying

It's possible to travel from the UK to South Korea overland using the Trans-Siberian Railway from Moscow either via Vladivostok and a ferry from Vladivostok to Donghae in Korea, or via Beijing, then a ferry from Tianjin in China to Incheon in Korea. The journey will take about 14 days. See the Trans-Siberian chapter, pages 66–70, for details of the London to Vladivostok and London to Beijing journeys, then see the Vladivostok–Korea or China–Korea sections below. You can also travel from Japan to Korea, using a ferry from Hakata to Pusan (see below).

VLADIVOSTOK TO KOREA, by ferry

A weekly ferry links Vladivostok in Russia with Donghae in South Korea. The ferry sails from Vladivostok on Wednesday at 15:00, arriving at Donghae at 10:00 on Thursday. Returning, it sails from Donghae at 15:00 on Monday, arriving at Vladivostok at 12:00 on Tuesday. Fares start at €150 (£126) one-way, rising to €310 (£260) for a deluxe cabin. The ferry is the 1993-built *Eastern Dream*, equipped to a good standard. The service is relatively new, having started in 2009. See the official site, **www.dbsferry.com/02_ticket/ticket03.asp**, for details and booking. Donghae has both rail and bus links with the rest of South Korea. Donghae to Seoul by train takes 5 hours 55 minutes with around six direct trains daily. For train times, see **www.korail.go.kr**; as these trains use Seoul Cheongnyangi station, not Seoul Main station, use 'Cheongnyangi' not 'Seoul' as your origin/destination.

CHINA TO KOREA, by ferry

There are several ferry services from China to South Korea, including one from Tianjin to Incheon twice a week, and one from Qingdao.

Beijing → Seoul via Tianjin

Air-conditioned trains link **Beijing** and **Tianjin** every hour or so. The journey time is 1 hour 15 minutes for the 137 km.

Ships sail from **Tianjin** to **Incheon** twice a week, taking 25 hours. For sailing dates and times, see **www.chinahotel.co.kr/ct/ferry3_english.html**.

Frequent trains link **Incheon** and **Seoul**, 39 km away, journey time 58 minutes.

Beijing ➜ *Seoul via Qingdao*

An overnight train (number T25) leaves **Beijing** Main station at 22:48 and arrives at **Qingdao** at 07:40. The train has soft and hard class sleepers. There is also now a range of fast daytime D-category trains from Beijing South station to Qingdao taking just 5½ hours.

The ship sails from **Qingdao** at 16:00 on Monday, Wednesday and Friday, arriving at **Incheon** at 10:00 next day. The one-way fare for the most basic berth is about 110,000 won (£61) or RMB750 (£75). The operator is Weidong Ferry – see **www.weidong.com** for sailing dates and fares.

Frequent trains link **Incheon** and **Seoul**, 39 km away, journey time 58 minutes.

Seoul ➜ *Beijing via Qingdao*

Frequent trains link **Seoul** and **Incheon**, 39 km away, journey time 58 minutes.

The ship sails from **Incheon** at 17:00 on Tuesday, Thursday and Saturday, arriving at **Qingdao** at 09:00 next day; see **www.weidong.com** for sailing dates and fares.

An overnight train (number T26) leaves **Qingdao** at 20:07, arriving at **Beijing** Main station at 05:38 next day. There are also now a range of fast daytime D-category trains to Beijing South station taking just 5½ hours.

JAPAN TO KOREA, by ferry

There are several ferry services between Japan and South Korea. The suggested options are:

> **Japan Kyushu Railway 'Beetle'** service from Fukuoka (Hakata) to Pusan. The 'Beetle' is a fast jetfoil, taking just 2 hours 55 minutes and running 4–5 times a day. It's also one of the few ferry companies with

a website in English, **www.jrbeetle.co.jp**. The fare is about ¥13,000 (£100) one-way, and from ¥24,000 (£184) return.

Kampu Ferry service from Shimonoseki (international port terminal) to Pusan. These are conventional ferries with cabins, sailing overnight. A ferry departs daily at 18:00, arriving at 08:30 next morning. Fares are around ¥9,000 (£69) second class (with tatami mat sleeping place), ¥12,000 (£92) first class (with bed in a western-style or Japanese-style cabin with shower and toilet), deluxe cabins and suites also available. It's 10 per cent cheaper to buy a return ticket, but it's reportedly cheaper still to buy another one-way ticket back when you get to Korea. The website, **www.kampuferry.co.jp**, is in Japanese but Google language tools (**www.google.co.uk/language_tools?hl=en**) can help you translate it.

Camellia Line service from Hakata to Pusan by conventional ferry, **www.koreaferry.co.kr** (only in Korean). Sailings are overnight (22:00–06:00) in one direction, by day (12:30–18:00) in the other. One-way fares start from 80,000 won (£44), or from 100,000 won (£55) with cabin berth.

Japan Railways offer inclusive train+ferry fares from Tokyo, Kyoto, Osaka, Hiroshima, Nagasaki and other stations in mainland Japan to Pusan, using either the Kampu Ferry from Shimonoseki or the fast Beetle jetfoil from Hakata (Hakata is at the end of the high-speed *shinkansen* line from Tokyo, Kyoto, Osaka and Hiroshima). For example, Tokyo to Pusan costs around ¥29,260 (£225). Tickets are sold from one month before departure up to two days (ferry) or seven days (jetfoil) before departure, so don't try to buy a ticket on the day of travel. See **www.hyperdia.com** (English button upper left) for train times and fares within Japan.

For the train service between Pusan and Seoul, see **www.korail.go.kr**.

TRAIN TRAVEL WITHIN SOUTH KOREA

All major towns and cities in South Korea are linked by an efficient railway. For train times and fares visit **www.korail.go.kr**.

In addition, Seoul and Pusan (also known as Busan) are linked by a new high-speed train service known as KTX. The KTX runs on a new high-speed line built using French TGV technology. Trains run frequently, taking just 2 hours 50 minutes. The fare is 45,000 won (£25) one-way second class, 63,000 won (£35) first class. For times, fares and online booking of KTX trains, see **www.korail.go.kr**.

SRI LANKA

Although a relatively small country, Sri Lanka has a good rail network. For visitors, trains are easily the best way to travel from the Sri Lankan capital Colombo up into the hills to Kandy and the hill station at Nuwara Eliya. Seen from a first class observation car – which is attached to the back of key trains – the scenery on this route is stunning.

Train operator:	Sri Lanka Government Railways, **www.railway.gov.lk** Also try **http://colombofort.com** or **www.reddottours.com**
Time:	GMT+5½
Currency:	£1 = approx. 163 Sri Lanka rupees, $1 = approx. 114 rupees
Tourist information:	**www.srilankatourism.org**, **www.srilankatourism.org.uk**
Visas:	UK, EU, US, NZ, Australian and some other nationalities do not need a visa to visit Sri Lanka for up to 30 days.

TRAVELLING TO SRI LANKA, without flying

There are no ships to Sri Lanka, and no ferries these days to or from India. Sadly, the only way to get to Sri Lanka, even from India, is to fly.

TRAIN TRAVEL WITHIN SRI LANKA

Once in Sri Lanka, trains are the cheap, safe and enjoyable way to get around. Trains link the major cities and have several classes:

> **First class sleepers:** A first class sleeping-car is available on several overnight trains. These have lockable 2-berth compartments with

separate toilet and washbasin. Bedding is provided.

First class observation car: Available on the best daytime trains on the amazingly scenic route from Colombo to Kandy and Badulla, and highly recommended. The observation car is normally at the rear of the train (occasionally behind the locomotive) and has comfortable, if slightly grubby, armchairs facing a large window looking back along the track. Seats must be reserved before departure; reservations open 10 days before travel. Book early, as the observation car is popular and often gets fully booked, especially during school holidays.

First class air-conditioned seats car: Only available on one or two InterCity Express trains from Colombo to Batticaloa and Vavunia.

Second class seats: Available on all trains. Second class seats come in several versions, depending on the train: (1) unreserved seats, where you buy a ticket, hop on and sit in any available seat, (2) reserved seats where you must make a reservation and you get an allocated seat, and (3) reserved 'sleeperette' reclining seats which are available on most overnight trains and which recline to about 45 degrees for sleeping. Second class seats are the recommended option on trains with no first class.

Third class seats: Available on most trains. These come in several versions, depending on the train: unreserved seats, reserved seats, and reserved 'sleeperette' reclining seats. Third class is very basic and gets very crowded, and it is not generally recommended for visitors.

Train times

Train times for some popular routes are shown below. You can check routes and timetables at the new Sri Lanka Railways website, **www.railway.gov.lk**, or in the Thomas Cook Overseas Timetable. There is also train information at **www.slrfc.org/sri-lanka-railways-time-table.html**, **http://colombofort.com** and **www.reddottours.com**.

How to buy tickets

It's easy to buy tickets when you get to Sri Lanka. There is a special ticket window for tourists at Colombo Fort station. Reservations for trains with reserved seating, such as InterCity Express trains, open 10–14 days in advance. Other trains (shown as having 'unreserved' seats) don't require a reservation; you just buy a ticket on and hop on. Seats in the first class observation car from Colombo to Kandy can get fully booked from time to time, so book a few days ahead if you can, but you may find seats available on the day of travel. If you want to pre-book a train before you get to Sri Lanka, and are prepared to pay a £10 booking fee, try **www.reddottours.com**.

COLOMBO TO KANDY AND BADULLA

This scenic train ride is *the* way to reach Kandy, 121 km by rail from Colombo. It's the best way too to get to Nuwara Eliya ('City of Lights'), a colonial hill station 2,000 metres above sea level, surrounded by tea plantations. The railway station you need is Nanu Oya, 6 km from central Nuwara Eliya, with plenty of taxis and auto-rickshaws available. It's also possible to walk. The journey onwards to Badulla, into the hill country, is also wonderful, and probably the best train ride in Sri Lanka. Travel in the first class observation car is recommended, and if possible on an InterCity Express train.

Colombo → Kandy, Nuwara Eliya, Badulla

Km	Classes (see notes)		3	0,2, 3,R*	ICE	0,2, 3,R**	2,3	2,3	ICE	2,3	2,3	Sleeper
0	Colombo (Fort)	depart	–	05:55	07:00	09:30	10:35	12:40	15:35	16:35	17:45	20:00
121	Kandy	arrive	–	|	09:34	|	13:52	15:58	18:08	19:42	20:58	|
121	Kandy	depart	03:30	|	–	|	–	–	–	–	–	|
207	Nanu Oya (for Nuwara Eliya)	arrive	09:33	12:27	–	15:25	–	–	–	–	–	03:21
246	Haputale	arrive	11:49	14:07	–	17:02	–	–	–	–	–	05:05
292	Badulla	arrive	14:10	15:55	–	18:55	–	–	–	–	–	07:10

Badulla, Nuwara Eliya, Kandy → Colombo

Classes (see notes)		2,3,R	ICE	2,3	2,3 3,R**	0,2,	ICE	2,3 3,R*	0,2,	3	Sleeper
Badulla	depart	–	–	–	–	05:45	–	–	08:50	12:00	18:20
Haputale	depart	–	–	–	–	07:48	–	–	10:51	14:38	20:33
Nanu Oya (for Nuwara Eliya)	depart	–	–	–	–	09:27	–	–	12:27	16:58	22:33
Kandy	arrive	–	–	–	–	I	–	–	I	21:38	I
Kandy	depart	05:00	06:10	06:30	10:40	I	15:00	15:30	I	–	I
Colombo (Fort)	arrive	08:16	08:47	09:45	14:00	15:40	17:38	18:55	19:28	–	05:35

All these trains run daily.

* This train is the *Podi Menike*.

** This train is the *Udarata Menike*.

ICE = InterCity Express. On this route, ICEs have a first class observation car with reserved seats, second and third class reserved seats.

Sleeper = *Night Mail*. First class sleepers (2-berth compartments), second and third class reserved sleeperettes (reclining seats), second and third class unreserved seats, buffet car.

0 = first class observation car with reserved seats.

2 = unreserved second class seats.

3 = unreserved third class seats.

R = buffet/restaurant car.

You can check train times using the official Sri Lanka Railways website, **www.railway.gov.lk**.

Fares

One-way adult fares	3rd class reserved seat	2nd class reserved seat	1st class observation car	1st class sleeper
Colombo to Kandy by InterCity Express	Rs150 (£1/$2)	Rs220 (£1.50/$2)	Rs360 (£2/$3)	Rs360 (£2/$3)
Colombo to Kandy by normal train	Rs105 (65p/$1)	Rs190 (£1/$2)	–	–
Colombo to Badulla	Rs270 (£2/$3)	Rs450 (£3/$5)	Rs750 (£5/$7)	Rs750 (£5/$7)

COLOMBO TO GALLE AND MATARA

A great way to reach the cities of Galle and Matara, by train along the coast. Second class is the recommended option, as third class gets too crowded.

Colombo → Galle, Matara

Km			2,3	2,3	2,3	2,3	2,3	2,3	3	3	3
0	Colombo (Maradana)	depart	06:30	–	–	13:40	15:40	16:40	17:10	17:50	18:45
2	Colombo (Fort)	depart	06:55	08:35	10:30	14:05	15:50	16:46	17:15	18:00	19:30
116	Galle	arrive	09:48	11:18	13:02	16:46	18:07	19:13	20:34	20:38	22:55
159	Matara	arrive	11:17	12:27	14:26	18:25	19:15	20:25	–	22:07	–

Matara, Galle → Colombo

		3	3	3	2,3	2,3	2,3	3	2,3	2,3	2,3	2,3
Matara	depart	–	–	–	04:20	05:20	05:50	–	09:30	–	13:10	14:05
Galle	depart	03:30	04:15	04:40	05:35	06:30	07:30	09:00	10:55	13:45	14:30	15:45
Colombo (Fort)	arrive	07:00	07:46	08:02	08:13	08:58	10:05	13:12	13:20	16:34	17:14	18:37
Colombo (Maradana)	arrive	07:07	07:50	08:10	08:20	09:05	10:12	13:35	–	16:40	–	18:45

Please double-check train times locally. There is no first class on this route.

2 = unreserved second class seats.

3 = unreserved second class seats.

You can check train times using the official Sri Lanka Railways website, **www.railway.gov.lk**.

Fares

The one-way fare for Colombo to Matara is Rs230 (£1.40 or $2) in a second class unreserved seat, Rs130 (80p or $1.20) in a third class unreserved seat. Colombo to Galle costs Rs180 (£1.10 or $1.65) in second class, Rs100 (60p or $0.90) in third.

COLOMBO TO POLONNARUWA AND TRINCOMALEE

Second class is recommended on this route, as third class is too crowded.

Colombo → *Trincomalee*

Km			2,3,R	2,3,R	ICE	Sleeper	Sleeper
0	Colombo (Fort)	depart	06:05	06:05	10:30	19:15	21:00
227	Galoya	arrive	12:00	12:00	15:16	00:20	02:54
260	Polonnaruwa	arrive	I	13:10	16:10	01:34	I
350	Batticaloa	arrive	I	15:00	18:25	04:00	I
296	Trincomalee	arrive	13:55	–	–	–	05:10

Trincomalee → *Colombo*

		ICE	2,3,R	Sleeper	Sleeper
Trincomalee	depart	–	10:00	19:30	–
Batticaloa	depart	07:45	I	I	20:15
Polonnaruwa	depart	09:58	I	I	22:25
Galoya	depart	10:55	12:40	21:55	23:20
Colombo (Fort)	arrive	15:40	19:00	04:05	04:52

All trains shown run daily.

Please double-check all train times locally.

ICE = InterCity Express. On this route, ICEs have second and third class reserved seats and a buffet car, plus a first class reserved observation car.

Sleeper = first class sleepers (2-berth compartments), second and third class reserved sleeperettes (reclining seats), second and third class unreserved seats, buffet car.

You can check train times using the official Sri Lanka Railways website, **www.railway.gov.lk**.

Fares

One-way adult fares	3rd class reserved seat	2nd class reserved seat	1st class sleeper berth
Colombo to Trincomalee	Rs205 (£1/$2)	Rs370 (£2/$3)	Rs750 (£5/$7)
Colombo to Batticaloa	Rs230 (£1.50/$2)	Rs420 (£3/$5)	Rs900 (£6/$9)
Colombo to Batticaloa by ICE	Rs320 (£2/$3)	Rs500 (£3/$5)	Rs900 (£6/$9)

COLOMBO TO ANURADHAPURA AND VAVUNIA

Trains link Colombo with Anuradhapura and Vavunia. However, since 1990 trains no longer operate as far as Jaffna or Talaimannar Pier (previously the ferry terminal for India) because of the security problems in that area.

Colombo → Vavunia

Km			ICE	2,3	2,3	ICE	Sleeper
0	Colombo (Fort)	depart	05:45	08:45	13:45	16:20	22:00
205	Anuradhapura	arr/dep	09:10	14:10	19:50	20:10	03:17
254	Vavunia	arrive	10:15	–	20:15	21:10	05:05

Vavunia → Colombo

		2,3	ICE	2,3	ICE	Sleeper
Vavunia	depart	03:20	05:45	07:45	15:30	22:00
Anuradhapura	arr/dep	05:00	06:40	09:30	16:55	23:40
Colombo (Fort)	arrive	09:55	10:25	15:25	20:30	04:35

ICE = InterCity Express. On this route, ICEs have second and third class reserved seats and a buffet car. The 16:20 from Colombo and the 05:45 from Vavunia also have an air-conditioned first class car.

Sleeper = *Night Mail*. First class sleepers (2-berth compartments), second and third class reserved sleeperettes (reclining seats), second and third class unreserved seats, buffet car.

2 = unreserved second class seats.

3 = unreserved third class seats.

R = buffet/restaurant car.

You can check train times using the official Sri Lanka Railways website, **www.railway.gov.lk**.

Fares

The one-way fare for Colombo to Vavunia travelling by InterCity Express is Rs650 (£4 or $6) in a first class reserved seat, Rs450 (£3 or $5) in a second class reserved seat, Rs270 (£2 or $3) in a third class reserved seat.

TAIWAN

Taiwan has a good and modern rail network linking all its major cities, and now boasts a new high-speed line between its capital Taipei and second city Kaohsiung. Intrepid overland travellers can even get there without flying, using one of the ferry services from mainland China.

Train operator:	Taiwan Railway Administration, **www.railway.gov.tw** (normal trains) Taiwan High Speed Rail Corporation, **www.thsrc.com.tw** (high-speed trains) Taipei metro: **http://english.trtc.com.tw/** Kaohsiung metro: **www.krtco.com.tw/en/e-index.aspx**
Time:	GMT+8
Currency:	£1 = approx. 47 new Taiwanese dollars, $1 = approx. NT$32
Tourist information:	**www.taiwan.net.tw**
Visas:	UK, EU, US, NZ, Australian and some other nationalities do not require visas for stays of up to 30 days. A return air or ferry ticket must be held.

EUROPE TO TAIWAN, without flying

There appear to be few or no passenger-carrying freighters from Europe to Taiwan, but it's possible to get there via the Trans-Siberian Railway to China, then a ferry to Taiwan.

London → Taipei, by train+ferry

Travel by train from **London** to **Moscow** as shown on page 67, journey time around 48 hours.

Take the Trans-Siberian Railway from **Moscow** to **Beijing**, as described in the Trans-Siberian chapter, page 68 (6 nights).

Travel by train from **Beijing** to **Fuzhou**: a modern 'Z' category sleeper train leaves Beijing West daily at 15:08, arriving in Fuzhou at 10:51 the next morning. In the other direction, the train leaves Fuzhou at 16:52, arriving at Beijing West at 12:38 next day. You can confirm train times at **www.chinatravelguide.com** or **www.chinahighlights.com**.

Take the ferry from **Fuzhou** to the Taiwanese **Matsu** island group, then the next day the ferry from **Matsu** to **Keelung** on mainland Taiwan; see below for details of these ferries. Travel by train from **Keelung** to **Taipei**; see below and **www.railway.gov.tw**. In all this journey will take around 14 days. You can also travel via the new weekly ferry from Xiamen on mainland China direct to the Taiwan mainland at Keelung, see below.

FERRIES TO TAIWAN

Japan to Taiwan by ferry

Sadly, the twice-weekly ferry run by Arimura Sangyo Lines between Japan and Taiwan was discontinued in 2008. For the record, the Arimura website is **www.arimuraline.co.jp** but it's in Japanese only; sailing times in English used to be posted on **www.tokai-kyowa.co.jp/english/i_ferry01.html**, which may have information on alternatives or any resumption in service, though this seems unlikely. It's reported that Star Cruises (**www.starcruises.com**) has occasional cruise sailings between Japan and Taiwan: you fill out a form and they contact you if they have anything suitable. But it's not cheap, and it's not clear whether they will allow one-way voyages.

China to Taiwan by ferry

You can travel between mainland China and mainland Taiwan in two stages, by first taking a short ferry ride from Fuzhou in China to the Matsu island group (part of Taiwan), then a ferry from Matsu to Keelung on mainland Taiwan. The ferry timetables and fares for these two services are given below. Alternatively, a new weekly ferry started in 2010 from Xiamen on mainland China direct to Keelung on mainland Taiwan; details are also shown below.

The Macau–Taiwan ferry has been permanently suspended; however, there are ferries operating from the Taiwanese outlying island of Kinmen to Xiamen in southern China (a 30-minute crossing, as the islands lie just off the Chinese coast), and also from the island of Matsu, although there are now no ferries between mainland Taiwan and Kinmen, over 200 kilometres away.

Fuzhou (China) to Matsu (Taiwan)

There are two sailings daily in either direction. From Fuzhou ferries depart Mawei ferry terminal at 09:15 and 14:40, arriving at Fu-ao in Matsu at 10:45 and 15:30 respectively. From Matsu ferries depart at 09:40 and 14:00, arriving at Mawei ferry terminal in Fuzhou at 11:10 and 15:30.

The fare is NT$1,300 (£28) one-way, NT$2,500 (£53) return.

Matsu to Keelung (mainland Taiwan)

The Taima-Iun Ferry service sails daily except Tuesday in either direction, leaving Matsu (Fu-ao) at 09:30, arriving at Keelung on mainland Taiwan at 18:30. Returning from Keelung it departs at 21:50 and arrives at Matsu at 08:30 next morning.

The one-way fare, per person, for Keelung to Matsu is NT$1,890 (£40) in a first class 2-berth cabin, NT$1,575 (£34) in a business class 4-berth cabin, NT$1,050 (£22) in an economy dormitory, NT$630 (£13) in an economy seat.

New ferry from mainland China to mainland Taiwan

A new weekly ferry started in 2010 between mainland China at Xiamen and mainland Taiwan at Keelung. The ferry sails from Xiamen on Saturday at 18:00, arriving in Keelung at 10:00 the next day. It sails from Keelung on Sunday at 18:00, arriving in Xiamen at 10:00 next day. The website is **www.coscotw.com.tw/cht/asp/star-main.asp** but it's in Chinese only. The fare is around NT$3,500 (£75 or US$110) per person in a 6-berth 'luxury' cabin. For information and booking contact gracewang@mail.coscotw.com.tw or try the emails shown on their website's contact page.

TRAIN TRAVEL WITHIN TAIWAN

A modern rail system links most large towns and cities in Taiwan, and a new high-speed (300km/h) railway opened in January 2007 between the two biggest cities, Taipei and Kaohsiung. There's a map of the Taiwan rail network at **http://johomaps.com/as/taiwan/taiwanrail.html**.

Taipei to Kaohsiung by 300km/h high-speed train

A new high-speed (300km/h) train service using Japanese bullet-train technology started running in January 2007 between Taipei and Kaohsiung. It is run by the Taiwan High Speed Rail Corporation, **www.thsrc.com.tw** (English button top right).

These trains run at least every 15 minutes throughout the day, at times more frequently. Journey time is 1 hour 40 minutes on the limited-stop trains, 1 hour 55 minutes on other services. There are three classes: unreserved economy, reserved seat economy and business class.

Full-price fares are NT$1,490 (£32 or US$48) in reserved economy, or NT$1,950 (£41 or US$61) for business class (off-peak departures offer 15–35 per cent discounts). To check train times and fares, and for online booking, go to **www.thsrc.com.tw**.

The station in Kaohsiung is actually at Zuoying in the north of the city. You can take a frequent Taiwan Railway Administration local train from New Zuoying station (in the same building as the Zuoying high-speed station) to Kaohsiung main station in the city centre, journey time 10 minutes, or you can take the Kaohsiung Metro (red line), also taking 10 minutes, metro website **www.krtco.com.tw**. You can buy tickets for the local train from the ticket machines or staffed kiosks, and metro tickets from the machines near the metro platforms. Buses and taxis are also available to the city centre. An extension of the high-speed line to a station in Kaohsiung city centre is planned for the future.

In Taipei, the high-speed trains use the same station as the Taiwan Railway

Administration conventional trains. Taipei metro information can be found at **http://english.trtc.com.tw/**.

Keelung–Taipei–Kaohsiung by conventional trains, western line

The western main line links Keelung, Taiwan's capital Taipei, and its second city and major port, Kaohsiung. For a route map, see **http://service.tra.gov.tw/EN/index.aspx** or **http://johomaps.com/as/taiwan/taiwanrail.html**; for train times, fares and online booking see the official Taiwan Railway Administration website, **www.railway.gov.tw** (English version available; online booking only available 06:00–21:00 Taiwan time). The best trains are the Tze Chiang expresses which run at up to 130km/h, are fully air-conditioned and take as little as 4 hours. Only one very comfortable class of seating is provided on these trains, with an at-seat trolley refreshment service. The Tze Chiang train fare from Taipei to Kaohsiung is NT$845 (£18 or US$27) one-way.

The next best train type, with slightly less comfortable seating but also air-conditioned, is the Chu Kuang train service, Taipei–Kaohsiung fare NT$544 (£12 or US$17), journey time 6½ hours. The next train type down the range is the Fu Shin, which has less legroom.

Taipei to Hualien and Taitung (eastern main line)

Taiwan Railway Administration provides more or less hourly express trains on the scenic eastern line. From late 2007 new Taroko Express high-speed (130km/h) electric tilting trains were introduced, providing an hourly service between Taipei and Hualien, with several services continuing along the scenic valley to Taitung. All seats must be reserved. For times, fares and online booking, see **www.railway.gov.tw**.

Tourist trains around Taiwan island

From May 2008, two daily tourist trains started running right around the island in one day. One service goes clockwise, leaving Taipei on the eastern main line via Hualien and Taitung, rounding the south coast and returning to Taipei via the western main line (train number 2080); the other travels anti-clockwise, down the western main line, around the south coast and along the eastern main line back to Taipei (train number 2079). These trains offer a higher class of travel with large aircraft-style first class seats, lounge and buffet car. The cost for the whole trip around the island is approximately NT$2,200 (£47 or US$70). There are also tours available in various places on the way for those wanting to stop off. Seats on the tourist train must be reserved. The train is a joint venture between Taiwan Railway Administration and a private company called EZ Travel; for information see **www.eztravel.com.tw/package1**.

Other scenic routes

Three scenic railway branches are also worth a visit. The Neiwan line takes in a river, Hakka museums, temples, Hakka culture cafés and restaurants. The Pingsi line takes in waterfalls, a river, a tourist coal mine, cafés and restaurants and various culture festivities. The Jiji line passes mountains, historical villages and houses, cafés and restaurants, several through-services being available from Taichung TRA railway station and Taichung high-speed rail station. These three lines offer a special tourist ticket, allowing tourists to get off where they like and reboard any train throughout the day for NT$80 (£2 or $3). This special tourist ticket is available at all major railway stations across Taiwan. All branch-line trains are air-conditioned.

THAILAND

Thailand has one of the best metre-gauge rail systems in the world, and Thai trains are easily the best way to get around and see the country at ground level. Train travel in Thailand is comfortable, safe, cheap and environmentally friendly. And unlike flying, it's a genuine Thai experience that makes the journeys as much part of your trip as the destinations. Taking the train is the ideal way to travel between Bangkok and Chiang Mai, and a train+ferry combo is a great way to get from Bangkok to Koh Samui. Train+bus is a good option for Bangkok to Krabi or Phuket.

You can also travel from Bangkok to neighbouring countries by rail. Bangkok to Singapore is an epic 1,946-km (1,249-mile) journey that can cost as little as £40 ($60), including sleepers for each of the two nights; see the Malaysia and Singapore chapter. A new rail line now crosses the Mekong River into Laos, facilitating train travel between Bangkok and the Laotian capital Vientiane; see the Laos chapter. And a bus+train combo will get you from Bangkok to Siem Reap or Phnom Penh in neighbouring Cambodia; see the Cambodia chapter.

Train operator:	State Railways of Thailand (SRT), **www.railway.co.th** (for train times and fares; for online booking go to **www.thairailwayticket.com**)
Time:	GMT+7
Currency:	£1 = approx. 48 baht, $1 = approx. 32 baht
Tourist information:	**www.tourismthailand.org**
Visas:	UK, US, Canadian, Australian, NZ and most EU citizens can visit Thailand for up to 30 days without a visa, or 15 days if entering overland.

EUROPE TO THAILAND, without flying

If you have the time, it's possible to reach Bangkok overland from the UK, using a twice-weekly Trans-Siberian train from Moscow to Beijing in China, then the twice-weekly Beijing–Hanoi sleeper train, then daily trains onwards to Saigon. See the Trans-Siberian and Vietnam chapters for details. The whole journey will take about two weeks. From Saigon, take a bus to Phnom Penh and another bus and train onwards to Bangkok; see the Cambodia chapter.

TRAIN TRAVEL WITHIN THAILAND

A map of train routes in Thailand and Southeast Asia is on page 260.

You can check timetables and fares for all State Railways of Thailand trains at **www.railway.co.th**: always select 'timetables' from the menu, as fares are shown at the bottom of each timetable page, and these include the appropriate air-conditioning supplement, sleeper and special express supplements. If you select the 'fares' option, the fares shown *don't* include those supplements. Online booking is available at a different site: see the 'How to buy tickets' section, page 405.

Which station in Bangkok?

Most trains use Bangkok's main Hualamphong station, a major landmark right in the city centre, although trains to Kanchanaburi leave from Bangkok Thonburi station (also known as Bangkok Noi) across the river in the west of the city. However, to ease congestion, State Railways of Thailand ultimately intends to move long-distance services out to a new terminal at Bang Sue junction station, 7 km north of Hualamphong station, and at some point all long-distance trains will start from there instead of Hualamphong. Suburban and short-distance trains will continue to run from Hualamphong, linking it to Bang Sue. The new Bangkok metro also links Bang Sue to the rest of Bangkok. For a metro map, see **www.bangkokmetro.co.th**. At the time of writing, all long-distance trains still use Hualamphong, but please double-check when you get to Bangkok.

Bangkok Airport Rail Link

A new modern rail link opened in August 2010 between Suvarnabhumi airport and central Bangkok, see **www.bangkokairporttrain.com**. Trains run every 15 minutes, journey time 30 minutes, fare 150 baht (£3 or $5). The new service links the airport to Bangkok City Air Terminal at Makkasan, and interchange stations with the MRT (metro) at Phetchaburi station and with the Skytrain at Phaya Thai station. It does not directly serve Bangkok's main Hualamphong station. State Railways of Thailand trains between Bangkok and Ayutthaya, Chiang Mai and Nong Khai (for Vientiane in Laos) call at Don Muang station, right next to the *old* Bangkok Airport, about 50 minutes (22 km) from central Bangkok. However, most commercial flights were transferred from the original Dong Muang Bangkok Airport to the new Bangkok Suvarnabhumi Airport in September 2006.

WHAT ARE THAI TRAINS LIKE?

Thai trains have three classes: first, second and third. First class exists only as modern air-conditioned sleeping-cars on overnight trains. Second class comes in seat and sleeper versions, in air-conditioned and non-air-conditioned varieties, and is very comfortable, especially on sleeper trains and the air-conditioned express railcars. Even third class is surprisingly clean and acceptable by European standards, and is an enjoyable way to travel for many shorter trips.

First class sleepers

First class sleeping-cars are modern and air-conditioned, with lockable 2-berth compartments with washbasin. Clean bedding, soap and towels are provided. The toilet at the end of the car even has a shower (cold or lukewarm water, but very welcome). Passengers travelling alone share with another passenger of the same sex, or can pay a higher supplement to secure sole occupancy. The berths convert to a sofa for evening and morning use. A very good choice if you want space and privacy, although the cheaper second class sleepers are perfectly adequate for most people. On key routes such as Bangkok–Chiang Mai, a steward or stewardess from the restaurant car will come round and take your food or drink order, which will be delivered to your compartment. You'll be offered a set menu with a few choices, costing around 150 baht (£3) for dinner and 100 baht (£2 or $3) for breakfast. If there are three or four of you travelling together, you can book two adjacent 2-berth sleepers with an interconnecting door.

Second class sleepers

Most western visitors are quite happy using second class sleepers, which are comfortable, safe and great fun. Berths are not in compartments, but are arranged open plan along the coach wall either side of a central aisle. During the evening and morning part of the journey, pairs of seats face each other on each side of the aisle. At night, each pair of seats pulls together to form the bottom bunk, and an upper bunk folds out from the wall. The attendant will make up your bunk with a proper mattress and fresh clean bedding, and will hook up the curtains which are provided for each bunk to give you privacy. Second class sleepers come in both air-conditioned and non-air-conditioned varieties. The fare for an upper berth is a fraction cheaper, but the upper bunks tend to be narrower. There's plenty of luggage room; take a bike lock if you want to chain up your luggage for peace of mind. Security is not a problem. It's a great way to travel which saves time even compared with flying, and saves a hotel bill too.

Second class seats on air-conditioned express railcars

The express railcar is an excellent option for daytime travel on routes such as Bangkok to Chiang Mai and Bangkok to Hua Hin and Surat Thani. These modern air-conditioned railcars have comfortable second class reclining seats. There is a hostess service of light meals and refreshments included in the fare. Relax and enjoy the journey as the scenery rolls by.

Second class seats on ordinary trains

A pleasant and comfortable way to travel for long-distance daytime journeys, although slower than the express railcars. There are both air-conditioned and non-air-conditioned varieties. The advantage of the non-air-conditioned coaches is the open windows and unrestricted views, a breeze wafting in as the train clickety-clacks through the Thai countryside.

Third class seats on ordinary and local trains

In spite of its name, third class is a perfectly good option for short trips such as Bangkok to Kanchanaburi or Ayutthaya, as it's generally clean, not usually crowded outside the commuter peaks, unbelievably cheap, and sitting next to an open window as the train passes through the countryside is a very pleasant experience. However, second class would be better for long trips such as Bangkok to Nong Khai or Chiang Mai. Third class may have wooden or padded seats, and is normally non-air-conditioned, though air-conditioned third class exists on a few long-distance routes.

HOW TO BUY TICKETS

How quickly do trains get fully booked?

People often ask, 'Will I be OK booking my Bangkok–Chiang Mai ticket at the station on the day?' It's normally fairly easy to find seats or berths available even on the day of travel (or more certainly on the day before), if you aren't fussy about which train you take or in which class. But trains do get fully booked at peak Thai holiday periods. If you're flexible and aren't travelling in a peak holiday period, you'll be fine buying tickets when you get to Thailand. But if it's important to be on a specific train in a specific class on a specific date, then book in advance through an agency or online; it's worth the small extra fee to be sure of a place.

There are a few holiday periods when booking ahead is strongly recommended under all circumstances. The two biggest are New Year (30 December to 3 January) and Songkran (Thai New Year, usually 11–16 April). If you want to travel around these dates you should definitely pre-book, preferably on the very day booking opens, 60 days before departure.

Buying tickets at the station

It's normally very easy to buy tickets yourself at the station when you get to Thailand. All long-distance express trains require a reservation, which can be made on the day of travel or up to 60 days in advance. Reservations are computerised, and the booking office at any main station can reserve seats or berths for any journey in Thailand. Your ticket will have the train time and your seat or berth number printed on it. Third class local trains such as Bangkok–Ayutthaya or Bangkok–Kanchanaburi don't require a reservation – you just turn up, buy a ticket from the ticket office and hop on.

Bangkok's main Hualamphong station has a well-organised reservation office, open daily 08:00–16:00. From the main entrance, walk towards the platforms, and the reservation office is tucked away on the extreme right, more or less level with the entrance to the platforms. There's a queuing system: when you enter, take a numbered ticket from the machine and wait until your number appears on the display, directing you to a particular reservation counter. The staff are friendly and helpful, and there are ticket counters for English-speaking customers. Bangkok also has a normal ticket office, open at all other times.

Buying tickets online at www.thairailwayticket.com

In early 2009, Thai Railways finally launched online booking, at **www.thairailwayticket.com** in conjunction with their partners Prida Pramote. The system will currently book second class sleepers or seats (but not first class sleepers) on a few key routes and trains, including for example all the main trains between Bangkok and Chiang Mai (trains 1, 2, 9, 10, 11, 12, 13, 14), trains 69 and 70 between Bangkok and Nong Khai, and most key trains between Bangkok and Surat Thani or Hat Yai. Once it is running successfully, they plan to extend it to other classes, routes and trains. So give it a go! Bookings open 60 days before departure; you can use this system from 60 days down to a minimum of three days before departure (less than three days and you'll need to book at the station). You need to register. It won't accept UK postcodes, so use that old favourite '12345'. You pay securely by Visa or MasterCard and print out your own ticket, which is valid for travel. You can buy tickets for one to four people at a time, but not for more than four people unless you repeat the process. It doesn't offer a choice of upper or lower berth, but if you get an upper at the end of the booking (before payment), simply go back and reselect the train and it may well offer you a lower. The emails that I receive now usually report success with this new system.

Buying tickets by email

To book with the State Railways of Thailand, email them at least 15 days (but less than 60 days) before your date of travel on passenger-ser@railway.co.th, or send a fax to +66 2 225 6068. Your fax or email must include the journey, date, train number, departure time, class, seat or sleeper (upper or lower berth), number of passengers, your name and email address. You eventually will receive an email confirmation, and you then collect and pay for your tickets at Bangkok Hualamphong station booking office at least one hour before departure. Bookings open 60 days before departure, but email bookings are only accepted more than 15 days before departure to give them time to respond. Thai railways charge 200 baht (£4 or $6) per email booking. Booking this way normally works well, but recently several people have said they waited up to two weeks for a reply, and one correspondent says he waited a month, so you may just have to be patient. Some people have reported that they haven't had a reply. If you have any problems, or need to make a booking less than 15 days before departure, try using an agency such as Traveller2000 or Thaifocus as shown below.

Buying tickets from a Thai travel agency

You can book train tickets through several reputable Thai travel agencies such as **www.thailandtrainticket.com**, **www.thaifocus.com**, or **www.asia-discovery.com**. These agencies will book trains for you and have the tickets waiting at your hotel in Bangkok, or they can send them to you in the UK by courier. Naturally, they charge a small fee for this. Thailandtrainticket charges the normal Thai Railways fare plus a 300 baht (£6 or $9) booking fee, but they'll reduce this to 150 baht (£3 or $5) if you say you've been referred by seat61.com. You can pick up tickets at their office or have them delivered to your hotel. They charge 500 baht (£10 or $15) for airport delivery, and for delivery to your home address they charge the actual overseas courier cost. Five seat61 correspondents have highly recommended Thailandtrainticket, saying they give good and reliable service, and two have recommended Thaifocus (though two others have reported that Thaifocus charges higher fees and fares). Shop around to check what fees each agency charges before you make the booking. Reservations open 60 days before departure, so you can't book before then.

BANGKOK TO CHIANG MAI

It's easy to travel from Bangkok to Chiang Mai by train, whether you choose an overnight sleeper or a daytime journey through the countryside on the air-conditioned express railcar. Travelling from Bangkok to Chiang Mai by sleeper is effectively faster than flying, less hassle, far more environmentally friendly, more of a real Thai experience, and saves you a hotel bill, too. The daytime train allows you to enjoy the scenery, which on the last third of the trip, up into the mountains approaching Chiang Mai, is particularly good – even on the sleeper, watching the sunrise from the train in the morning is a great experience.

The recommended trains are the overnight sleeper trains 1 and 2, which have the most modern cars, and the daytime express trains 9 and 12.

Bangkok → Chiang Mai

Km	Train number		9	3	109	1	11	13	51
	Classes		DRC	DRC	s,2,3	1,S	DRC	1,S	s,2,3
0	Bangkok (Hualamphong)	depart	08:30	10:50	14:30	18:10	18:00	19:35	22:00
22	Don Muang	depart	09:14	11:40	15:19	18:56	18:46	20:23	22:49
71	Ayutthaya	depart	09:43	12:15	16:00	19:31	19:25	21:01	23:30
133	Lopburi	arr/dep	10:29	13:00	17:00	20:24	20:15	21:55	00:28
389	Phitsanulok	arr/dep	13:19	16:06	20:44	I	23:06	01:34	04:20
751	Chiang Mai	arrive	20:30	–	05:30	07:25	06:15	09:45	12:45

Chiang Mai → Bangkok

Train number		106	102	12	52	14	2	10
Classes		2,3	2,3	DRC	s,2,3	1,S	1,S	DRC
Chiang Mai	depart	–	06:45	08:45	14:50	16:30	17:50	21:00
Phitsanulok	arr/dep	08:59	14:15	15:08	22:40	00:05	I	03:51
Lopburi	arr/dep	12:27	17:47	18:05	02:50	03:32	04:04	06:30
Ayutthaya	arrive	13:28	19:14	18:53	03:49	04:40	05:13	07:21
Don Muang	arrive	14:13	20:09	19:27	04:39	05:36	06:04	08:04
Bangkok (Hualamphong)	arrive	15:05	21:10	20:25	05:30	06:40	07:00	09:10

All trains run daily.

1 = first class sleeper.

S = second class air-conditioned sleeper.

s = second class sleeper (non-air-conditioned).

2 = second class seats.

3 = third class seats.

DRC = Diesel Railcar express with second class air-conditioned seats, meals included.

Fares

Bangkok to Chiang Mai one-way costs 1,353 baht (£28 or $42) per person in air-conditioned first class sleeper, sharing a 2-berth compartment. Sole occupancy of a first class sleeper compartment costs an extra 500 baht (£10 or $16). For a lower bunk in a second class air-conditioned sleeper the one-way fare is 881 baht (£18 or $27); a narrower upper bunk is 50–100 baht (£1–£2) less; a berth in a non-air-conditioned second class sleeper (available on a few trains) costs around 160–200 baht (£3–£4) less than the air-conditioned variety.

If you travel by the daytime air-conditioned Diesel Railcar express, the fare for a second class seat is 611 baht (£13 or $19), which includes meals. On an ordinary daytime train a second class seat costs 431 baht (£9 or $13), a third class seat 271 baht (£6 or $8).

Children aged 0 to 3 and less than 100 cm in height travel free; children aged 4 to 11 and under 150 cm travel at half fare; children 12 years old and upwards (or over 150 cm tall) pay full fare.

You can check fares and train times at **www.railway.co.th** (but remember to do this by selecting 'timetables', in order to see the total fare payable for your chosen train with any air-conditioning supplement, sleeper or special express supplement included).

BANGKOK TO NONG KHAI

Here are trains between Bangkok and Nong Khai, near the border with Laos. If you're wanting to travel on into Laos, see the Laos chapter, page 341. Trains 69 and 70, with air-conditioned sleeping-cars, are the recommended option; the other services have no sleeping-car, only seats, which are not recommended for an overnight journey. From Nong Khai to Bangkok the air-conditioned express (train 76) runs as a daytime service, and would also be a good choice.

Bangkok → Nong Khai

Km	Train number		133	77	69
	Classes		2,3	DRC	1,S
0	Bangkok (Hualamphong)	depart	20:45	18:30	20:00
22	Don Muang	depart	21:31	19:13	20:50
71	Ayutthaya	depart	22:17	19:47	21:41
624	Nong Khai	arrive	09:45	05:05	08:25

Nong Khai → Bangkok

Train number		76*	70*	134
Classes		DRC	1,S,3	2,3
Nong Khai	depart	06:00	18:20	19:15
Ayutthaya	arrive	15:30	04:23	05:50
Don Muang	arrive	16:12	05:22	06:52
Bangkok (Hualamphong)	arrive	17:10	06:25	08:00

All trains run daily.

1 = first class sleeper.

S = second class air-conditioned sleeper.

2 = second class seats.

3 = third class seats.

DRC = Diesel Railcar express with second class air-conditioned seats, meals included.

Fares

Bangkok to Nong Khai one-way costs 1,217 baht (£25 or $38) per person in air-conditioned first class sleeper, sharing a 2-berth compartment. Sole occupancy costs an extra 500 baht (£10 or $16). For a lower bunk in a second class air-conditioned sleeper the one-way fare is 778 baht (£16 or $24); a narrower upper bunk is 50–100 baht (£1–£2/$3–$5) less.

If you travel by the air-conditioned Diesel Railcar express, the fare for a second class seat is 498 baht (£10 or $15), which includes meals. On an ordinary (non-air-conditioned) train a second class seat costs 388 baht (£8 or $12), a third class seat 258 baht (£5 or $8).

Children aged 0 to 3 and less than 100 cm in height travel free; children aged 4 to 11 and under 150 cm travel at half fare; children 12 years old and upwards (or over 150 cm tall) pay full fare.

You can check fares and train times at **www.railway.co.th** (but remember to do this by selecting 'timetables', in order to see the total fare payable for your chosen train with any air-conditioning supplement, sleeper or special express supplement included).

BANGKOK TO UBON RATCHATHANI

On this route the recommended trains are trains 21 and 22 (for daytime travel), and trains 67 and 68 if you prefer to do the journey overnight.

Bangkok → Ubon Ratchathani

Km	Train number		21	135	139	67	141	
	Classes			DRC	2,3	2,3	1,S,2,3	2,3
0	Bangkok (Hualamphong)	depart	05:45	06:40	18:55	20:30	22:25	
22	Don Muang	depart	06:29	07:39	19:42	21:09	23:16	
71	Ayutthaya	depart	06:58	08:25	20:25	21:50	23:50	
575	Ubon Ratchathani	arrive	14:00	18:20	06:15	07:25	10:20	

Ubon Ratchathani → Bangkok

Train number		136	146	22	142	68	140
Classes		2,3	2,3	DRC	2,3	1,S,2,3	2,3
Ubon Ratchathani	depart	07:00	08:45	14:50	16:50	18:30	19:30
Ayutthaya	arrive	16:37	19:05	21:46	02:37	03:55	05:25
Don Muang	arrive	17:38	19:55	22:27	03:27	04:49	06:25
Bangkok (Hualamphong)	arrive	18:40	21:00	23:15	04:25	05:50	07:30

All trains run daily.

1 = first class sleeper.

S = second class air-conditioned sleeper.

2 = second class seats.

3 = third class seats.

DRC = Diesel Railcar express with second class air-conditioned seats, meals included.

Fares

Bangkok to Ubon Ratchathani one-way costs 1,180 baht (£25 or $37) per person in air-conditioned first class sleeper, sharing a 2-berth compartment. Sole occupancy costs an extra 500 baht (£10 or $16). For a lower bunk in a second class air-conditioned sleeper the one-way fare is 761 baht (£16 or $24); a narrower upper bunk is 50–100 baht (£1–£2) less.

If you travel by the air-conditioned Diesel Railcar express, the fare for a second class seat is 551 baht (£11 or $16), which includes meals. On an ordinary (non-air-conditioned) train a second class seat costs 388 baht (£8 or $12), a third class seat 245 baht (£5 or $8).

Children aged 0 to 3 and less than 100 cm in height travel free; children aged 4 to 11 and under 150 cm travel at half fare; children 12 years old and upwards (or over 150 cm tall) pay full fare.

You can check fares and train times at **www.railway.co.th** (but remember to do this by selecting 'timetables', in order to see the total fare payable for your chosen train with any air-conditioning supplement, sleeper or special express supplement included).

BANGKOK TO ARANYAPRATHET

Aranyaprathet, 255 km from Bangkok, is just 15 km from the Cambodian border post at Poiphet from where buses run to Siem Reap and to Battambang (with connecting buses to Phnom Penh). See the Cambodia chapter, pages 282–5, for more information on these routes and the bus onwards from Phnom Penh to Saigon in Vietnam.

Two trains a day run between Bangkok and Aranyaprathet. Eastbound, they leave Bangkok Hualamphong station at 05:55 (train 275) and 13:05 (train 279), arriving at Aranyaprathet at 11:35 and 17:35 respectively. Westbound trains depart Aranyaprathet at 06:40 (train 280) and 13:55 (train 276), arriving at Bangkok (Hualamphong) at 12:05 and 19:55. These trains have third class seats only, but Thai third class is quite clean and comfortable, and a pleasant way to travel. The fare is just 58 baht (£1.20 or $1.80) one-way. The seats are unreserved: just turn up at the station, buy a ticket and hop on.

BANGKOK TO KANCHANABURI AND THE BRIDGE ON THE RIVER KWAI

The best way to reach Kanchanaburi is by train, using the infamous 'Death Railway' itself, for just 100 baht, about £2 or $3! A regular State Railways of Thailand passenger service still runs over the Death Railway from Bangkok via

Kanchanaburi as far as Nam Tok, crossing the famous 'Bridge on the River Kwai' a few kilometres beyond Kanchanaburi. There are two trains a day from Bangkok Thonburi station (also known as Bangkok Noi, on the west side of the river in Bangkok) to Kanchanaburi and Nam Tok, calling at River Kwae Bridge station on the Bangkok side of the bridge a few minutes after Kanchanaburi.

The trains are third class only, but don't let this put you off – they are clean and comfortable, and sitting next to an open window whilst you travel through the Thai countryside is easily the most pleasant way to reach Kanchanaburi. The seats are all unreserved; you just buy a ticket at the station and hop on the train.

If you're coming from Singapore, Malaysia or southern Thailand, you can travel direct to Kanchanaburi and the River Kwai Bridge without going into Bangkok – just change trains at Nakhon Pathom (64 km west of Bangkok), where the branch line to Kanchanaburi leaves the main line.

There is also a special railcar (second class air-conditioned) for tourists at weekends, leaving Hualamphong station at 06:30 for Kanchanaburi at 09:30, Nam Tok 11:30, returning from Nam Tok at 14:25 and Kanchanaburi at 16:53, arriving at Bangkok at 19:30. Special fares apply, and reservation is required.

Bangkok → *Kanchanaburi, River Kwai, Nam Tok*

Train number		485	257	259
Classes		3	3	3
Bangkok (Thonburi/Noi station)	depart	–	07:45	13:35
Nakhon Pathom (connections from south)	depart	–	09:03	14:55
Kanchanaburi	depart	05:57	10:50	16:19
River Kwae Bridge	depart	06:13	10:55	16:26
Nam Tok	arrive	08:20	12:35	18:30

Nam Tok, River Kwai, Kanchanaburi → Bangkok

Train number		260	258	486
Classes		3	3	3
Nam Tok	depart	05:20	12:55	15:15
River Kwae Bridge	depart	07:12	14:36	17:35
Kanchanaburi	depart	07:19	14:44	17:41
Nakhon Pathom (for trains to the south)	arrive	08:50	16:23	–
Bangkok (Thonburi/Noi station)	arrive	10:10	17:35	–

The Bridge on the River Kwai

There is a small technical problem with the Bridge over the River Kwai: it crosses a river all right, but not the River Kwai! Pierre Boulle, who wrote the original book, had never been there. He knew that the Death Railway ran parallel to the River Kwae for many miles, and assumed that it was the Kwae which it crossed just north of Kanchanaburi. He was wrong – it actually crosses the Mae Khlung. When David Lean's blockbuster came out, the Thais faced something of a problem. Thousands of tourists flocked to see the bridge over the River Kwae, and they hadn't got one – all they had was a bridge over the Mae Khlung. So, with admirable lateral thinking, they renamed the river. The Mae Khlung is now the Kwae Yai ('Big Kwae') for several miles north of the confluence with the Kwae Noi ('Little Kwae'), including the bit under the bridge.

The bridge is about 5 km from the centre of Kanchanaburi. By all means wait for one of the three daily passenger trains, all of which call at the River Kwae Bridge station, but it's best to take a cycle rickshaw. The bridge is now surrounded on the Kanchanaburi side by a museum, cafés, shops and a couple of steam locomotives on static display. You're free to walk across the bridge on the wooden planks – though remember to stand aside for the passenger trains when one comes along. If this sounds foolhardy, remember that there is a 10km/h speed restriction for trains across the bridge, and they all hoot like mad!

There were actually two bridges here, both built by prisoners of war. The first (wooden) bridge was completed in February 1943, superseded a few months later by the steel bridge which you see today. The curved steel bridge spans are original, and were brought from Java by the Japanese. However, the two straight-sided spans come from Japan, and were installed after the war to replace spans destroyed by Allied bombing in 1945.

Hellfire Pass and Wampo Viaduct

Make sure you ride the train between Kanchanaburi (or River Kwae Bridge station) and the current terminus at Nam Tok: as well as crossing the famous bridge, the train runs along the beautifully scenic River Kwae, passing over the equally impressive Wampo Viaduct, also built by prisoners of war. Another must-see is Hellfire Pass, about 80 km north of Kanchanaburi, on the disused section beyond Nam Tok. Here, the Australian government has cleared about 7 km of the old track-bed as a memorial to the 13,000 Allied prisoners and 80,000 Asian labourers who died building the railway. The site includes the Hellfire Pass itself (Konyu Cutting, dubbed 'Hellfire Pass' by the PoWs for the way the worksite looked at night by torchlight). A taxi and driver for half a day from Kanchanaburi will cost about £35, and you can ask the driver to drop you at Nam Tok on the way back, to return to Kanchanaburi or Bangkok by the 12:50 or 15:15 train. There are one-day organised tours from Kanchanaburi, but these typically get only 30 minutes at Hellfire Pass, only enough to see the pass itself. If you go independently, you can walk all the way past the locations of 'Three Tier Bridge' and the 'Pack of Cards' bridge to Compressor Cutting, 7 km northwest of the visitor centre. The peaceful walk through the warm shady jungle along the disused track-bed, past small cuttings and dips where the wooden viaducts used to be, is a very moving experience.

BANGKOK TO AYUTTHAYA

Ayutthaya is the ancient capital of Thailand, with many impressive ruins to visit – a great day trip from Bangkok. It's easy to get there by train. There is a train from Bangkok (Hualamphong station) to Ayutthaya every hour or so with basic but clean third class seats. No reservation is necessary – just turn up, buy a ticket and hop on. Third class is not crowded outside peak times, and it's a very pleasant way to get there, sitting next to an open window with a cool breeze blowing in, as the train clickety-clacks along. See **www.railway.co.th** for exact train times if you really feel you need them. The fare for the 71-km journey is 15 baht (30p or 45¢).

You could also stop off at Ayutthaya on the way to or from Chiang Mai or Nong Khai. If so, it's easier to use third class local trains for the Bangkok–Ayutthaya section of your journey rather than an express (which you'd have to book), as the local trains are cheaper, more frequent and no reservation is necessary. Consult the Bangkok–Chiang Mai or Bangkok–Nong Khai timetable, pages 408 and 410, for express train times for the Ayutthaya–Chiang Mai or Ayutthaya–Nong Khai part of your journey.

BANGKOK TO SOUTHERN THAILAND

There are plenty of good trains from Bangkok to southern Thailand, with connections by bus or ferry to Thailand's beaches and islands. For trains between Bangkok, Penang, Kuala Lumpur and Singapore, see the Malaysia chapter, pages 348–52. The Bangkok–Singapore main line crosses into Malaysia at Padang Besar at the western end of the frontier. Sungai Kolok is at the eastern end of the border with Malaysia, and although trains don't cross into Malaysia here, you can walk across the border and get a bus to Kota Bharu just a few kilometres away. The railway station for Kota Bharu is Wakaf Bharu (5 km or so from Kota Bharu itself), from where there are daily trains to Singapore and Kuala Lumpur via the scenic 'Jungle Line'; see the Malaysia chapter, page 353. This jungle route makes an interesting alternative to the more usual mainline route from Bangkok to Kuala Lumpur and Singapore via Padang Besar.

Bangkok → Hua Hin, Surat Thani, Hat Yai, Sungai Kolok

Km	Train number		43*	261	171	35*	37*	169	83*	173	167	85*	41
	Classes		DRC	3	s,2,3	1,S,2	1,S,2,3	s,2,3	1,S,2,3	s,2,3	s,2,3	1,S,2,3	DRC
0	Bangkok (Hualamphong)	depart	08:05	09:20	13:00	14:45	15:10	15:35	17:05	17:35	18:20	19:30	22:50
64	Nakhon Pathom	depart	09:17	10:48	14:43	16:09	16:39	17:19	18:31	19:11	19:53	20:54	00:04
229	Hua Hin	arr/dep	11:11	13:35	17:13	18:24	19:08	20:15	20:46	21:40	22:05	23:19	02:11
485	Chumphon (for ferry to Koh Tao)	arrive	14:19	–	21:11	22:00	23:22	00:45	01:32	02:39	03:15	03:47	05:57
651	Surat Thani (for Koh Samui and Krabi)	arrive	16:30	–	00:10	00:50	01:53	03:21	04:05	05:29	05:58	06:27	08:11
845	Trang	arrive	–	–	l	l	l	l	07:55	–	10:25	–	l
945	Hat Yai	arrive	–	–	05:36	06:57	07:31	09:26	–	–	–	–	12:27
1159	Sungai Kolok	arrive	–	–	10:45	–	11:25	–	–	–	–	–	–

Sungai Kolok, Hat Yai, Surat Thani, Hua Hin → Bangkok

Train number		40*	174	86*	42	168	170	84*	172	38*	36*	262
Classes		DRC	s,2,3	1,S,2,3	DRC	s,2,3	s,2,3	1,S,2,3	s,2,3	1,S,2	1,S,2	3
Sungai Kolok	depart	–	–	–	–	–	–	–	11:30	14:20	–	–
Hat Yai	depart	–	–	–	16:20	–	14:35	–	15:26	18:05	18:20	–
Trang	depart	–	–	–	l	13:25	l	17:20	l	l	l	–
Surat Thani	depart	10:40	16:46	18:22	20:25	17:42	20:02	20:47	21:07	23:25	23:17	–
Chumphon	depart	12:46	19:24	20:44	22:31	20:32	23:31	23:24	00:01	02:32	01:57	–
Hua Hin	arr/dep	16:01	00:13	01:19	01:45	01:04	04:11	03:38	04:30	06:23	05:47	14:10
Nakhon Pathom	arrive	18:15	03:04	04:09	03:56	03:30	07:02	06:34	07:19	08:54	08:20	16:59
Bangkok (Hualamphong)	arrive	19:45	04:45	06:05	05:40	05:20	09:00	08:25	09:25	10:30	09:55	18:45

All trains run daily.

1 = first class sleeper.

S = second class air-conditioned sleeper.

s = second class sleeper (non-air-conditioned).

2 = second class seats.

3 = third class seats.

DRC = Diesel Railcar express with second class air-conditioned seats, meals included.

* Recommended trains – express railcar by day, the best air-conditioned sleepers overnight.

Fares

One-way fares in baht from Bangkok to	1st class sleeper a/c express train	2nd class sleeper a/c express train	2nd class seat a/c fast railcar	2nd class seat ordinary train	3rd class seat ordinary train
Hua Hin	–	–	382 (£8, $12)	292 (£6, $8)	234 (£5, $7)
Chumphon	1,134 (£24, $35)	770 (£16, $23)	480 (£10, $15)	380 (£8, $12)	272 (£5, $7)
Surat Thani	1,279 (£27, $40)	848 (£18, $27)	578 (£12, $18)	438 (£9, $13)	297 (£6, $9)
Hat Yai	1,494 (£31, $47)	945 (£20, $30)	675 (£14, $21)	535 (£11, $17)	339 (£7, $11)

Children aged 0–3 and less than 100 cm in height travel free; children aged 4–11 and under 150 cm travel at half fare; children 12 years old and upwards (or over 150 cm tall) pay full fare.

The first class fares are for sharing a 2-berth sleeper. Sole occupancy is available for an extra 500 baht (£10 or $16).

The second class sleeper fares shown here are for a lower bunk; a narrower upper bunk is 50–100 baht (£1–£2) less. Non-air-conditioned sleepers (available on trains 167–174 on this route) cost 160–200 baht (£3–£4) less than the air-con variety.

You can check fares at **www.railway.co.th** (but remember to do this by selecting 'timetables', in order to see the total fare payable for your chosen train with any air-conditioning supplement, sleeper or special express supplement included).

KOH TAO

You can take any train from Bangkok to Chumphon shown in the timetable above (Bangkok to southern Thailand), then hop on a ferry to Koh Tao. You can buy combined train+ferry tickets from State Railways of Thailand ticket offices.

Alternatively, there are ferries to Koh Tao from Surat Thani, the next stop south on the railway. This route is useful if you are travelling from further south – from Phuket, say, or from Malaysia or Singapore.

You can check ferry times at **www.kohtaoonline.com/timetable.htm**. There are also ferries from Koh Tao to Koh Samui, see **www.seatranferry.com** and look for 'Seatran Express'.

Chumphon ➜ *Koh Tao, by ferry*

Ferry operator		LC	KTC	SEB	LC	KJCF	NB
Chumphon	depart	07:00	07:00	07:00	13:00	23:00	24:00
Koh Tao	arrive	08:30	09:30	10:00	14:30	05:00	06:00

Koh Tao ➜ *Chumphon, by ferry*

Ferry operator		LC	KTC	LC	SEB	NB	KJCF
Koh Tao	depart	10:00	10:30	14:30	14:30	22:00	23:00
Chumphon	arrive	11:45	13:00	16:10	17:30	03:00	05:00

Ferry operators:

LC = Lomprayah Catamaran (**www.lomprayah.com**).

KTC = Koh Tao Cruiser.

SEB = Songserm Express Boat (**www.songserm-expressboat.com**).

KJCF = Ko Jaroen Car Ferry.

NB = Night Boat.

The Lomprayah Catamaran fare is 600 baht (£12 or $18) one-way.

Surat Thani to Koh Tao, by ferry

The Night Boat ferry departs Surat Thani Bandon Road pier at 23:00, arriving at Koh Tao at 08:30 next morning; it leaves Koh Tao at 20:30, arriving at Surat Thani at 05:30 next morning.

KOH SAMUI AND KOH PHANGAN ISLANDS

Ferries to Koh Samui and Koh Phangan leave the mainland from Surat Thani, which is on the Bangkok–Hat Yai–Singapore mainline railway, so it's easy to travel to either island by train+ferry. It's also safe, cheap, comfortable and the environmentally friendly way to get there, far better than cramped buses or short-haul flights. If you use an overnight sleeper it takes no more time out of your holiday than flying and is a lot more fun, and far more of an experience. See the Malaysia and Singapore chapter, page 350, for trains from Malaysia, and the Bangkok to southern Thailand timetable, page 418 for the full train service on the Thai portion of the line. The recommended combinations of train+ferry for Bangkok to Koh Samui are shown below.

For direct ferries between Surat Thani and Koh Phangan, and ferries from Koh Samui to Koh Phangan, see **www.kohphangan.com/travel/gethere.html**.

For ferries from Koh Samui to Koh Tao, see **www.seatranferry.com**.

Surat Thani to Koh Samui, by ferry

Several ferry companies operate from Surat Thani to Koh Samui, including the Seatran ferry (hourly sailings, 1½ hour crossing), the Songserm express catamaran (2 daily sailings, 1 hour crossing), and the Songserm overnight boat.

The Seatran ferry uses Don Sak pier in Surat Thani. Ferries depart on the hour every hour, from 06:00 to 19:00 Surat Thani–Koh Samui, and from 05:00 to 18:00 Koh Samui–Surat Thani, taking 1 hour 30 minutes for the journey. The fare is 110 baht (£2 or $3) one-way, or you can get a combined bus+ferry ticket from Surat Thani railway station to Koh Samui costing about 250 baht (£5 or $8). Surat Thani railway station is located at Phun Phin, 14 km from Surat Thani town centre, and shuttle buses run between the station and Don Sak ferry terminal (which is 60 km east of the town). You can check ferry times and fares at **www.seatranferry.com**.

The Songserm overnight boat can be useful if you arrive in Surat Thani after the last Seatran ferry. It sails from the Ban Don ferry pier close to central Surat Thani at 23:00, and arrives at Koh Samui at 05:00 next morning. Upper deck tickets give you a mattress and pillow, the lower deck just has straw mats.

Bangkok to Koh Samui by train+ferry

Option 1, overnight: Take train 85 from **Bangkok** (Hualamphong) to **Surat Thani**, departing Bangkok at 19:30 and arriving at Surat Thani at 06:27 next morning. This train has first and second class air-conditioned sleepers (recommended), and second and third class seats.

On arrival at Surat Thani railway station (located at Phun Phin, 14 km from Surat Thani town centre), shuttle buses meet the train and take you to the Don Sak ferry terminal 60 km east of Surat Thani.

The Seatran ferry departs at 08:00, arriving at **Koh Samui** at 09:30.

Option 2, daytime: Take the Diesel Railcar express train 43, departing **Bangkok** (Hualamphong) at 08:05 and arriving at **Surat Thani** at 16:30. This train has air-conditioned second class seats, and meals are included in the fare.

Travel by shuttle bus from Surat Thani railway station to Don Sak ferry terminal.

Take the 18:00 Seatran ferry, arriving at **Koh Samui** at 19:30.

Koh Samui to Bangkok by train+ferry

Option 1, overnight: Take the 17:00 Seatran ferry from **Koh Samui** to Don Sak ferry terminal, arriving at 18:30.

Transfer by shuttle bus to Surat Thani railway station (Phun Phin).

Take the overnight sleeper train 84 departing **Surat Thani** 20:47, arriving at Bangkok (Hualamphong) at 08:25 next morning.

Option 2, daytime: Take the 07:00 Seatran ferry from **Koh Samui** to Don Sak ferry terminal, arriving at 08:30.

Transfer by shuttle bus to Surat Thani railway station (Phun Phin).

Take the Diesel Railcar express train 40 departing **Surat Thani** 10:40, arriving at Bangkok (Hualamphong) at 19:45.

Fares

A combined train+bus+ferry ticket is available, which covers your whole journey Bangkok–Koh Samui. This combined fare is 1,379 baht (£29) per person one-way in a first class air-conditioned sleeper, 948 baht (£20) in a second class air-conditioned sleeper, 678 baht (£14) in an air-conditioned second class seat on a Diesel Railcar express; on an ordinary (non-air-conditioned) train the one-way fare is 568 baht (£12) in second class, 427 baht (£9) in third class.

You can buy the combined train+ferry tickets at Bangkok Hualamphong station reservations office, or online for a small handling fee from **www.traveller2000.com**.

PHUKET

Buses run to Phuket from Surat Thani and from Hat Yai, making a combination of train+bus the most comfortable and environmentally friendly way to travel there, whether you are coming from Bangkok or from Malaysia.

Bangkok to Phuket by train+bus, via Surat Thani

Take the overnight sleeper train from Bangkok to Surat Thani; see the timetable on page 418. Train 85 leaving central Bangkok at 19:30 is a good choice. Next morning, take a bus from Surat Thani to Phuket, journey time around 6 hours. There are about 14 buses a day between 05:00 and 15:30. The bus fare is unlikely to be more than about 280 baht (£6 or $9). Buses are run by the Thailand Transportation Co.

Returning, buses leave Phuket for Surat Thani at 04:45, 05:30, 07:00, 07:30, 08:00, 08:20, 09:00, 09:40, 10:00, 11:00, 12:00, 12:20, 13:50, 15:30. (Information on departure times from Surat Thani is not available, but times are likely to be similar.)

Hat Yai to Phuket by bus

The bus journey from Hat Yai to Phuket also takes about 6 hours. Buses leave Hat Yai at 05:45, 07:45, 08:45, 09:30, 10:05. Buses are run by Phuket Tour and Trang Tour, and the fare is in the region of 160 baht (£3 or $5).

Returning, there are buses from Phuket to Hat Yai at 06:20, 07:40, 08:00, 09:00, 09:30, 10:20, 11:20.

For information on trains between Hat Yai and Malaysia, see the Malaysia and Singapore chapter, page 351.

KOH PHI PHI

A ferry links Phuket and Koh Phi Phi. The ferry sails from Phuket at 08:30 and 13:30, and from Koh Phi Phi at 09:00 and 14:00. Crossing time is 90 minutes.

KRABI

Krabi hasn't got a railway station, but it's easy to get there using a train to Surat Thani or Hat Yai, and then travelling onward by bus. Detailed information on buses from Hat Yai to Krabi is not available; see the Malaysia and Singapore chapter, page 351, for information on trains between Hat Yai and Malaysia.

Bangkok to Krabi by train+bus, via Surat Thani

Using the comfortable overnight sleeper from Bangkok, the train+bus journey to Krabi takes no more time out of your holiday than flying, but is a lot more interesting, cheaper, and far more environmentally friendly. Take a comfortable train from Bangkok to Surat Thani – see the timetable on page 418. Train 85 leaving central Bangkok at 19:30 is a good choice. Then take a bus from Surat Thani station to Krabi. You're likely to find a number of buses to Krabi waiting at Surat Thani station after the arrival of your train. The bus fare is about 150 baht (£3 or $5); the journey time from Surat Thani to Krabi is about 2 hours.

State Railways of Thailand offers combined train+bus tickets from Bangkok to Krabi, which you can buy at Bangkok Hualamphong station reservations office, or online for a small handling fee from **www.traveller2000.com**. This combined fare is 1,379 baht (£29) per person one-way in an air-conditioned first class sleeper, or 850 baht (£18) in an air-conditioned second class sleeper.

MOVING ON FROM THAILAND

Train and bus travel between Bangkok and Phnom Penh in Cambodia or Saigon in Vietnam is described in the Cambodia chapter, pages 283–5. For travel between Bangkok and Vientiane in Laos, see the Laos chapter, page 339. Train travel between Bangkok and Malaysia or Singapore is shown in the Singapore and Malaysia chapter, page 348. The 1,946-km (1,249-mile) train ride from Bangkok to Singapore takes just 48 hours with changes of train at Butterworth (Penang) and Kuala Lumpur. It costs only around £40 or $60, including a sleeper berth with clean bedding for each of the two nights. By all means stop off in southern Thailand, Penang or Kuala Lumpur if you like – the cost is the same. If money is no object, there's also a regular luxury train between Bangkok and Singapore, the *Eastern and Oriental Express*. It's run by the same company as Europe's Venice Simplon Orient Express (page 367), see **www.orient-expresstrains.com** or call +44 (0) 207 921 4010.

VIETNAM

Vietnam's air-conditioned trains are safe, comfortable and inexpensive, the ideal way for independent travellers to get around and see Vietnam at ground level. The train journeys are an experience in themselves and you might get to meet some Vietnamese! Vietnam's rail network has improved dramatically over the last few decades, and several daily trains with air-conditioned sleeping-cars now link Saigon with the beaches at Nha Trang, Danang for the nearby town of Hoi An, the ruined palaces at Hué, and northern capital Hanoi. The scenery between Hué and Danang is stunning, as the train skirts the coast then climbs up into the hills and over the Hai Van pass. Trains also link Hanoi and Lao Cai for the hill station at Sapa, and there are even international trains from Hanoi to Nanning and Beijing in China.

Train operator:	Duong Sat Viet Nam (DSVN: Vietnam Railways), **www.vr.com.vn**
Time:	GMT+7
Currency:	£1 = approx. 27,500 dong, $1 = approx. 18,900 dong
Tourist information:	**www.vietnamtourism.com**
Visas:	Required by UK citizens and most other western nationalities. Vietnamese embassy visa section: 12–14 Victoria Road, London W8 5RD, telephone 020 7937 3222, fax 020 7937 6108, **www.vietnamembassy.org.uk**.

EUROPE TO VIETNAM, overland

If you have the time, it's perfectly possible to reach Vietnam overland from the UK, using the twice-weekly Trans-Siberian train from Moscow to Beijing, then the twice-weekly soft sleeper train from Beijing to Hanoi. See the Trans-

Siberian chapter, pages 66–9, for details of the London–Moscow–Beijing journey, then page 438 below for details of the Beijing–Hanoi train. The whole journey will take about two weeks.

TRAIN TRAVEL WITHIN VIETNAM

Inexperienced travellers often mistakenly think they'll save time by using internal flights – in fact, not only is an overnight train ride from Hanoi to Hué or Danang far more of an experience (and cheaper) than a flight, the train saves time compared with flying, because it leaves Hanoi city centre in the evening and arrives in Hué city centre next morning. Flying takes four or five hours out of your sightseeing day in getting to a remote airport, checking in, taking the flight itself, collecting your bags and getting back into the city centre. And the sleeper train saves a hotel bill, too. And what's the rush anyway?

Air-conditioned trains with sleepers and on-board catering link Hanoi, Hué, Danang, Nha Trang and Saigon (Ho Chi Minh City). You'll see some amazing scenery from the train between Hanoi and Saigon. Easily the best section is between Hué and Danang over the Hai Van Pass, where the train runs along the coast past bays and islands and through the hills. The train travels at low speed up the fierce gradients, with an assisting locomotive at the rear and people sitting on the roof! There's a map of train routes in Vietnam and Southeast Asia on page 260.

Hoi An has no station, but it's just 30 km by bus or taxi from Danang. There are also trains from Hanoi to Halong and Haiphong (for Halong Bay) and Hanoi to Lao Cai (for Sapa).

Is it Saigon or Ho Chi Minh?

Ho Chi Minh City (HCMC) is the official name for the whole conurbation. However, the city centre is still officially called 'Saigon', which is of course its time-honoured and traditional name. It is shown in all Vietnamese railway timetables and in big letters on Saigon station building itself as 'Sai Gon', and *not* Ho Chi Minh. So do what the locals do: call it Saigon!

The Reunification Express?

Trains between Hanoi and Saigon are sometimes referred to as the

'Reunification Express' by guide books or tourist agencies. However, there are now many trains on this route and no single train officially carries this name.

THE NORTH–SOUTH 'REUNIFICATION' LINE: HANOI, HUÉ, DANANG, SAIGON

Over the last decade the Hanoi–Saigon train service has been steadily improving and a whole range of daily air-conditioned trains now link Hanoi, Hué, Danang, Nha Trang and Saigon (HCMC). The timetable below shows the principal trains, all running daily. Look for the 'SE' numbered trains, as these are the best. The 'TN' trains are slower and older. There are additional trains at peak times, such as the Tet holiday period. You can check train times at the Vietnamese Railways website, **www.vr.com.vn**, although the English-language version doesn't always work well so you may need to try the Vietnamese version with a little help from Google Translate.

Hanoi → Hué, Danang, Saigon (Ho Chi Minh City)

Km	Train number		SE1*	SE3*	SE5*	SE7	TN1
0	Hanoi	depart	19:00 day 1	23:00 day 1	15:45 day 1	06:15 day 1	10:05 day 1
116	Ninh Binh				18:03 day 1	08:30 day 1	12:34 day 1
175	Thanh Hoa		22:15 day 1		19:19 day 1	09:40 day 1	14:09 day 1
319	Vinh		00:44 day 2	04:07 day 2	22:10 day 1	11:56 day 1	16:42 day 1
522	Dong Hoi		04:31 day 2	07:49 day 2	02:34 day 1	15:43 day 1	21:36 day 1
688	Hué		07:57 day 2	10:45 day 2	06:07 day 2	19:07 day 1	01:13 day 2
791	Da Nang (for Hoi An)		10:31 day 2	13:12 day 2	08:56 day 2	21:41 day 1	04:38 day 2
928	Quang Ngai		13:28 day 2		11:57 day 2	00:35 day 2	08:09 day 2
1,095	Dieu Tri (for Qui Nhon)		16:16 day 2	18:20 day 2	14:57 day 2	03:23 day 2	12:11 day 2
1,315	Nha Trang		20:28 day 2	22:03 day 2	19:40 day 2	07:37 day 2	16:46 day 2
1,551	Muong Man (for Phan Thiet)					11:41 day 2	21:57 day 3
1,726	Saigon	arrive	04:10 day 3	05:00 day 3	04:40 day 2	15:05 day 2	03:03 day 3

Saigon (Ho Chi Minh City) → *Danang, Hué, Hanoi*

Train number		SE2*	SE4*	SE6*	SE8	TN2
Saigon	depart	19:00 day 1	23:00 day 1	15:45 day 1	06:30 day 1	10:05 day 1
Muong Man (for Phan Thiet)		I	I	19:04 day 1	09:42 day 1	14:14 day 1
Nha Trang		02:31 day 2	05:33 day 2	23:49 day 1	13:23 day 1	18:24 day 1
Dieu Tri (for Qui Nhon)		06:17 day 2	09:14 day 2	04:08 day 2	17:13 day 1	23:32 day 2
Quang Ngai		09:13 day 2	I	07:19 day 2	20:31 day 1	03:21 day 2
Da Nang (for Hoi An)		11:51 day 2	14:30 day 2	10:18 day 2	23:12 day 1	06:38 day 2
Hué		14:43 day 2	17:06 day 2	13:21 day 2	02:07 day 2	10:38 day 2
Dong Hoi		17:44 day 2	19:56 day 2	17:02 day 2	05:21 day 2	14:06 day 2
Vinh		21:37 day 2	23:41 day 2	22:08 day 2	09:26 day 2	19:12 day 2
Thanh Hoa		00:16 day 3	I	00:58 day 3	11:56 day 2	22:49 day 2
Ninh Binh		I	I	02:25 day 3	13:07 day 2	00:11 day 3
Hanoi	arrive	04:02 day 3	05:00 day 3	04:45 day 3	15:28 day 2	03:05 day 3

* = recommended trains. All these trains run daily.

Trains SE1–SE6 have air-conditioned soft sleepers (4-berth), air-conditioned hard sleepers (6-berth), air-conditioned soft seats and air-conditioned restaurant car. Trains SE1 and SE2 now have a new luxury tourist sleeping-car attached between Hanoi, Hué and Danang run by private company Livitrans; see page 000.

Trains SE7–SE8 have air-conditioned hard sleepers (6-berth), air-conditioned soft seats and air-conditioned restaurant car. No soft sleepers.

Trains TN1 and TN2 have air-conditioned and non-air-conditioned hard sleepers (6-berth) and hard seats only.

Hoi An

Hoi An is about 30 km south of Danang, and it features on many visitors' itineraries. There is no railway station at Hoi An, but there are regular buses, minibuses and taxis from Danang to Hoi An, taking between 45 minutes and an hour. The bus fare is about £2 ($3); a taxi will cost in the region of £7–£10 ($10–$15), depending on your negotiation skills.

What are trains SE1–SE8 like?

The best trains are the ones with 'SE' train numbers, equipped with modern air-conditioned coaches and restaurant or buffet car. They have three classes of accommodation (plus a deluxe option on trains SE1 and SE2):

> Soft class air-conditioned sleepers (4 berths per compartment). In soft sleeper, simple tray meals are served in your compartment along with mineral water, included in the fare. Soft sleepers aren't available on train SE7/8.

> Hard class air-conditioned sleepers (6 berths per compartment).

> Air-conditioned soft class reclining seats.

> Trains SE1 and SE2 now have a new tourist sleeping-car attached between Hanoi, Hué and Danang, run by a private company called Livitrans. This has 4-berth sleeper compartments of a much higher standard than the regular Vietnamese Railways ones. Hanoi to Hué with Livitrans costs £33 ($49), Hanoi to Danang £39 ($59). See **www.livitrans.com** for fares and online booking.

The coaches on these SE trains have large picture windows, unobstructed by the wire mesh that protects other trains' windows from stones. Choose these trains if you can.

What are trains TN1 and TN2 like?

These are the slower, older trains. At peak periods, you may see a TN3, 4, 5 or 6 running, too. Trains TN1 and TN2 have three classes of accommodation:

> Air-conditioned hard class sleepers (6 berths per compartment).

> Hard class sleepers (6 berths per compartment, non-air-conditioned).

> Hard class seats (non-air-conditioned).

One advantage of these TN trains is that their non-air-conditioned cars have windows that open, better for photographing the scenery. However, bear in mind that they are much more basic than the SE trains.

Which class should you choose?

Air-conditioned soft sleeper is the recommended choice for most western travellers for any journey involving overnight travel. Air-conditioned soft sleeper cars have western-style toilets at the end of the corridor. However, air-conditioned hard sleeper is perfectly acceptable if you're on a budget or if all the soft sleepers are sold out, so don't rule it out. Some hard sleepers have squat-type toilets only, if that's an issue for you. Air-conditioned soft seat is a good choice for daytime journeys, but not for overnight trips as you can't sleep properly in a seat.

Fares

Train travel in Vietnam is cheap, and sleeper trains save on hotel bills, too. The old system of charging foreigners higher fares than Vietnamese citizens was abolished in 2002, and everyone now pays the cheaper Vietnamese fare. The table overleaf shows fares in 1000s of Vietnamese dong.

One way per person (000 dong)	Train type	Soft sleeper	Hard sleeper		Soft seat	Hard seat
		AC	AC	Non-AC	AC	Non-AC
Saigon–Hanoi (1,726 km)	SE	1,250 (£45, $67)	1,174 (£43, $63)	–	836 (£30, $45)	–
	TN	–	802 (£29, $43)	653 (£24, $35)	–	440 (£16, $24)
Saigon–Danang (935 km)	SE	774 (£28, $42)	727 (£26, $39)	–	503 (£18, $27)	–
	TN	–	497 (£18, $27)	393 (£14, $21)	–	265 (£10, $14)
Saigon–Hué (1,027 km)	SE	837 (£30, $45)	786 (£28, $42)	–	533 (£19, $29)	–
	TN	–	537 (£20, $29)	417 (£15, $22)	–	280 (£10, $15)
Saigon–Nha Trang (411 km)	SE	367 (£13, $20)	345 (£12, $19)	–	220 (£8, $12)	–
	TN	–	212 (£8, $11)	173 (£6, $9)	–	117 (£4, $6)
Hanoi–Hué (688 km)	SE	603 (£22, $33)	567 (£21, $31)	–	370 (£13, $20)	–
	TN	–	387 (£14, $21)	290 (£10, $16)	–	195 (£7, $11)
Hanoi–Danang (791 km)	SE	668 (£24, $36)	627 (£23, $34)	–	425 (£15, $23)	–
	TN	–	428 (£16, $23)	333 (£12, $18)	–	225 (£8, $12)
Hué–Danang (103 km)	SE	83 (£3, $5)	78 (£3, $4)	–	56 (£2, $3)	–
	TN	–	54 (£2, $3)	44 (£2, $2)	–	30 (£1, $2)
Danang–Nha Trang (524 km)	SE	420 (£15, $23)	396 (£14, $21)	–	282 (£10, $15)	–
	TN	–	270 (£10, $15)	220 (£8, $12)	–	150 (£5, $8)

Children aged 0–4 travel free; children aged 5–9 travel at half fare; children of 10 and over pay full fare.

The hard sleeper fares shown are for the middle bunk. Top bunks are roughly 15 per cent cheaper, bottom bunks roughly 5 per cent more expensive.

The soft sleeper fares shown are for lower berths. Upper berths are roughly 2 per cent cheaper.

Do I need a reservation? Can I stop off along the way? Can I hop on and off?

Yes, yes, and no. All trains require a reservation, so you need a specific ticket/reservation for each individual train journey you make. If you want to travel from Saigon to Hanoi (or vice versa) stopping off on the way, this is not a problem, but you will need to book it as a series of separate journeys, with a separate ticket for each leg either bought in advance or bought as you go along. You cannot buy an open ticket and hop on and off trains without a reservation.

How to buy tickets at the station

It's easy to buy train tickets at the station when you get to Vietnam. Apart from peak holiday periods such as Tet (the Vietnamese New Year, a major holiday period lasting several days around late January or early February), it's not difficult to book a soft sleeper a few days in advance, but be prepared to be flexible over your exact choice of class, train number or departure date. If you are booking for the same day or the following day, you might find the best-quality trains full, but other trains will probably have berths available. Reservations were computerised in 2002, and you can buy tickets for most train journeys within Vietnam at Saigon and Hanoi station booking offices. So, for example, you can buy both a Saigon–Hué ticket and a Hué–Hanoi ticket at Saigon station ticket office. However, at other stations such as Hué, Danang or Nha Trang, you can only book journeys starting at the station you're at. At ticket offices, you pay in Vietnamese dong; US dollars are not generally accepted. If you're sure of your itinerary and it's important to be on a specific train on a specific date in a specific class, then you can pre-book by email with a local Vietnamese travel agency – see below.

How to buy tickets by email through a travel agency

If you want to get some or all of your train reservations booked in advance before you get to Vietnam, there are several reputable travel agencies who will book trains for you for a small fee. Tickets can be waiting for you at your hotel when you get to Vietnam, or couriered overseas, with payment by Visa, MasterCard or other major credit card. Reliable Vietnamese travel agencies who will book train tickets by email include:

> Vietnamstay, **www.vietnamstay.com/service/sapatrain.htm**: This agency gets very good reports from travellers, although they can only book trains departing from Hanoi or Saigon, not journeys starting at intermediate stations. Their website now only seems to mention Hanoi–Sapa trains, but ask them for a quote for other routes.

> VietnamImpressive, **www.vietnamimpressive.com**: A new arrival, but has already had three very good reports from seat61 correspondents. Their prices look good: Hanoi to Danang in soft sleeper on SE1 costs £39 ($58), Danang to Saigon in soft sleeper on SE3 costs £35 ($52). If you pay by Onepay there's a 3 per cent credit card charge. They will deliver to any hotel in Vietnam or can courier your tickets to the UK by DHL for £43 ($65).

> Saigon Hotel, **www.saigonhotel.com** (formerly Viet-nam.net) has not had such good reports, but offers a comprehensive service, charging around £91 ($137) for Hanoi to Saigon or £45 ($73) Hanoi to Hué in soft sleeper.

Can I buy all 4 berths in a compartment to have a room to ourselves?

Privacy-loving westerners often ask this. The answer is that, in theory, yes, you can, but it can't be guaranteed that the train staff won't allocate additional passengers to the berths they know to be empty. My advice is don't bother – just book two beds in a 4-berth soft class sleeper. The Vietnamese may view it as selfish to take up four beds when you only need two, given that places on their national transport system can be in short supply at times. You'll be safe and comfortable sharing a 4-berth soft sleeper, and might actually meet some real Vietnamese people this way!

THE SLOW TRAIN TO SAPA: HANOI TO LAO CAI

If you want to head for the hills at Sapa, take the train from Hanoi to Lao Cai. Sapa has no railway station, but it's about 40 km from Lao Cai railway station and easily reached from there by tourist bus (£1, $2), jeep (£3, $4–5 per person) or hired motorbike. There are both daytime and overnight sleeper trains between Hanoi and Lao Cai, and some trains have higher-quality privately run sleeping-cars in addition to the regular DSVN (Vietnamese Railways) sleepers.

Trains to Lao Cai depart from a separate section of Hanoi's main railway station, sometimes called the 'B' station, usually platforms 10 or 11. Road access is on Tran Quay Cap street, on the opposite side of the tracks from the main 'A' station at 120 Le Duan street, so make sure you make this clear to your taxi driver. Or you can enter the main 'A' station and walk across the tracks on a walkway, but allow time to do this as it's a bit of a trek.

Hanoi → Lao Cai (for Sapa)

Train number		LC3	SP7	SP1	SP3	LC1
Hanoi	depart	06:10	20:35	21:10	21:50	22:05
Lao Cai	arrive	16:35	05:00	05:25	06:15	07:20

Lao Cai → Hanoi

Train number		LC4	LC2	SP8	SP2	SP4
Lao Cai	depart	09:15	18:45	19:30	20:15	21:00
Hanoi	arrive	20:15	04:00	04:30	04:35	05:10

Trains LC3, LC4: Daily. Soft seats and hard seats, not air-conditioned.

Trains LC1, LC2: Daily. Air-conditioned soft sleepers, air-conditioned hard sleepers, hard sleepers (non-air-conditioned), soft seats, hard seats.

Trains SP1, SP2, SP3, SP4: Daily. Air-conditioned soft sleepers, air-conditioned hard sleepers, hard sleepers (non-air-conditioned), air-conditioned soft seats, soft seats (non-air-conditioned), hard seats. These trains also have several privately run deluxe sleepers attached, see below.

Trains SP7, SP8: Privately run 'Livitrans' sleeping-cars, see below.

Hanoi–Lao Cai is 294 km (183 miles).

Fares and how to buy tickets

The fare for Hanoi to Lao Cai one-way on an 'SP' train is 300,000 dong (£11 or $17) in air-conditioned soft sleeper, 234,000 dong (£9, $14) in air-conditioned hard sleeper, 175,000 dong (£6 or $9) in non-air-conditioned hard sleeper, 168,000 dong (£6 or $9) in air-conditioned soft seat, 113,000 dong (£4 or $6) in non-air-conditioned soft seat, or 98,000 dong (£4 or $6) in hard seat (not air-conditioned). For the deluxe tourist coach fares, see below.

Tickets can be bought at the station or by email from a travel agency: see pages 433–4 for advice.

Hanoi to Sapa by luxury tourist train

The overnight trains between Hanoi and Lao Cai have several privately run deluxe sleeping-cars attached for tourists, as well as the normal sleepers and seats. If you want extra comfort and cleanliness and don't mind paying a bit more, go for one of these.

> **Livitrans:** This company operates private sleepers on trains SP7 and SP8. The fare is £22 ($33) in 'tourist' 4-berth sleeper, or £48 ($72) in 'VIP' 2-berth sleeper. See **www.livitrans.com**.

> **Tulico, Ratraco, TSC, Friendly, Royal, King**: These deluxe tourist cars run attached to trains SP3 and SP4. They're all significantly better than the regular Vietnamese Railways sleepers, and reportedly there's not a lot to choose between the different private operators. For example, the Tulico cars offer VIP 2-berth, first class 4-berth or second class 4-berth, aimed at mid-market tourists. The cost is around £40/$60 each way in 2-berth, £20/$30 each way in first class 4-berth

or £17/$25 in second class 4-berth. For more information on the various tourist sleepers, email booking and prices, see **www.vietnamstay.com/service/sapatrain.htm**. Once in Vietnam, you can book these tourist sleepers via local travel agencies, but not at the station, although there's an office selling tickets for the Ratraco sleepers to Lao Cai just inside the main station entrance.

Victoria train: This is a cut above the other tourist trains; in fact, it's the most luxurious way to reach Sapa, with wood-panelled 'Orient Express'-style carriages. However, you can only use it if you're staying at the deluxe Victoria Hotel in Sapa. It runs daily except Saturday, consisting of two deluxe sleeping-cars and a restaurant car attached to trains SP3 and SP4. Prices are around £93/$140 a round trip per person (£107/$160 including meals in the restaurant car) in 4-berth, or £147/$220 per person (£167/$250 with meals) in 2-berth. One-way fares are only about 25 per cent less than returns, so buy a return ticket if you're coming back to Hanoi. See **www.victoriahotels-asia.com/eng/hotels-in-vietnam/sapa-resort-spa/victoria-express-train** or **www.vietnamstay.com/service/sapatrain.htm** for details. The hotel can arrange a shuttle bus or private car transfer from the station.

HANOI TO HAIPHONG (FOR FERRY TO CAT BA ISLAND)

Hanoi → Haiphong

Hanoi	depart	06:00	–	15:25*	–
Hanoi Long Bien	depart	I	09:30	15:35	18:10
Haiphong	arrive	08:15	12:10	18:00	20:35

Hanoi → Haiphong

Haiphong	depart	06:10	08:55	15:10	18:40
Hanoi Long Bien	arrive	08:40	11:18	17:40	I
Hanoi	arrive	–	11:25	–	21:05

* Starts from Hanoi main station at weekends only, runs daily from Long Bien.

Hanoi–Haiphong trains have soft and hard class seats.

Hanoi Long Bien is 3 km from Hanoi main station. Hanoi to Haiphong is 102 km (63 miles).

Ferries to Cat Ba Island

Hydrofoils leave Haiphong ferry terminal at 08:50 and 09:00, journey time 45 minutes. Returning, hydrofoils leave Cat Ba ferry terminal at 06:45 and 15:00. Alternatively, there are ships taking 2 hours, with departures from Haiphong ferry terminal at 06:30 and 12:30. Returning, the ships leave Cat Ba Island at 05:45 and 12:30. Cat Ba town is a half-hour bus ride from where the ships arrive, but the hydrofoils arrive at a pier near Cat Ba town.

How to buy tickets

Buy tickets for the train locally, at the station. No advance reservation is necessary.

Buy your ferry ticket at the ticket offices at the port; the fare is around 100,000 dong (£4 or $6).

HANOI TO BEIJING, by train

There is a safe, comfortable and affordable twice-weekly train service between Beijing and Hanoi, taking two nights. A Chinese express train with modern air-conditioned 4-berth soft class sleepers and restaurant car runs from Beijing to Dong Dang on the Vietnamese frontier. At Dong Dang you pass through customs and passport control and board a connecting Vietnamese metre-gauge train for the final run to Hanoi. Note that at Nanning you may be asked to get off and wait on the platform for an hour or two while the train is shunted.

From Hanoi the train runs every Tuesday and Friday, departing at 18:30 and arriving at Dong Dang at 22:40. The Chinese train departs Dong Dang at 01:20 (day 2), arriving at Nanning at 07:00, then calling at Guilin at 13:28, Zhengzhou at 05:23 (day 3), arriving at Beijing (West) at 12:09.

From Beijing the train runs on Sunday and Thursday, departing at 16:08, calling at Zhengzhou 22:56, Guilin 14:58 (day 2), Nanning 21:15, arriving at Dong Dang at 00:11 (day 3). The Vietnamese train departs Dong Dang at 03:50, arriving at Hanoi at 08:10.

At Hanoi the train to Beijing departs from a separate section of the main railway station, sometimes called the 'B' station. Road access is on Tran Quay Cap street, on the opposite side of the tracks from the main 'A' station at 120 Le Duan street, so make sure you make this clear to your taxi driver. Or you can enter the main 'A' station and walk across the tracks on a walkway, but allow time to do this as it's a bit of a trek.

If you can't get tickets for this twice-weekly Hanoi–Beijing through train, or if you need to travel on one of the other days of the week, simply use the daily train between Hanoi and Nanning (see page 440), then one of the regular daily sleeper trains between Nanning and Beijing. For example, a train leaves Nanning at 10:50 and arrives at Beijing at 14:35 the following day. Southbound, a train leaves Beijing at 16:08 arriving at Nanning at 20:10 (you'll need to spend a night and day in Nanning).

Getting a Chinese visa in Hanoi

You'll need a visa to enter China, and indeed you will need to show your Chinese visa at Hanoi station when buying your train ticket to Beijing. It's reported that the Chinese embassy in Hanoi will *not* now issue visas for anyone who is not a Vietnamese citizen or resident (this may well be a new policy for 2010). So either get your visa in your home country before you leave, or arrange your Chinese visa in Hanoi through a suitable travel agency such as **www.hanoibackpackershostel.com**.

Fares and how to buy tickets

From Hanoi to Beijing one-way costs around 4,400,000 Vietnamese dong (about £160 or $240) per person in soft class 4-berth sleeper if you buy your ticket at Hanoi ticket office, window 10 (for foreigners and international trains). You will need to show your passport and a valid visa for China. You can pay in US dollars or dong; credit cards are reportedly not accepted, although there's a MasterCard sign. This train cannot be booked online, although you could try emailing local travel agencies in Vietnam.

The one-way fare from Beijing to Hanoi in soft class 4-berth sleeper is around RMB2,156 (£218 or $327) if bought from the ticket office or local agency in Beijing. (The price increased significantly in February 2009 for journeys in both directions.)

Alternatively, you can arrange a ticket from outside China via **www.chinatripadvisor.com**, who charge $389 (£259), or **www.chinatrain ticket.net**, who charge $406 (£270). Reliable Russian/British agency **www.realrussia.co.uk** can also book this train along with your Trans-Siberian tickets, but are more expensive, charging around £356 one-way.

HANOI TO NANNING, by train

Since January 2009, a daily overnight train has linked Hanoi and Nanning. This is a standard-gauge Chinese sleeper train, with soft and hard air-conditioned sleepers, that runs all the way from Nanning to Hanoi, train MR1/T872 Hanoi–Nanning, train T871/MR2 Nanning–Hanoi.

From Hanoi it departs Gia Lam station (6 km from Hanoi Main station, across the river) at 21:40 (day 1), arriving at Dang Dong, the border point, at 02:00 (day 2). It leaves Dong Dang at 03:00; arrives at the Chinese border point, Pinxiang, at 04:41; departs Pinxiang at 06:41, and arrives at Nanning at 10:12 (day 2).

From Nanning the train departs at 17:15, arriving at Pinxiang at 20:41. It then leaves Pinxiang at 22:41, arrives at Dong Dang at 23:22, leaves Dong Dang at 01:25 (day 2), and arrives at Hanoi Gia Lam station at 05:30.

You should always double-check these train times locally, as they are subject to change. The distance is 396 km.

The fare in soft sleeper, per person one-way, is 568,000 dong (£21 or $31) Hanoi to Nanning, and RMB229 (£23 or $34) Nanning to Hanoi. A metered taxi from Hanoi old quarter to the Gia Lam station is likely to cost around 100,000 dong (£3.70 or $5.50).

Tickets are sold in Nanning at the station reservations office counter 16 and at Hanoi Main Station ticket window 10. Tickets are also sold in Hanoi by Vietnam Hanoi Railways Tourist Company (Travel Agency – 152 Le Duan street, Hanoi, email haratour@fpt.vn, telephone (84 4) 3518 6782). In Hanoi, you'll need to show your passport and Chinese visa when buying tickets. See page 439 for advice on obtaining the visa.

Nanning to Hanoi by daytime bus

If the train is full or you prefer daytime travel, there are several daily buses between Nanning and Hanoi, using modern coaches. Buses reportedly leave Nanning bus station at 08:30, 09:00 and 09:30, journey time 7–8 hours, fare around RMB150 (£15 or $23). The scenery is reported as well worth the trip!

HANOI TO HONG KONG

There is no direct train service between Hanoi and Hong Kong, but you can travel overland fairly easily and cheaply with a change of train in Nanning and Guangzhou. You cannot buy a through-ticket; you generally need to buy tickets for each train as you go along, but it will cost around £70 or $105 one-way in total, and it's an experience in itself. Remember that you'll need a visa for China, and you'll need to satisfy any return/onward ticket requirements, which is usually more of a logistical headache than the actual travelling.

Travelling in the other direction it's a good idea to book the Hong Kong–Guangzhou and Guangzhou–Nanning trains in advance by email through an agency such as **www.chinatripadvisor.com**, **www.chinatraintickets.net** or **www.china-train-ticket.com**, or perhaps in person through a travel agency in Hong Kong. The other buses and trains can be paid for as you go along.

Hanoi → Hong Kong

Day 1, evening: Take the daily overnight train from **Hanoi** to **Nanning**: see the section above. It leaves Hanoi Gia Lam station at 21:40 and arrives at Nanning at 10:12 next morning. The soft sleeper fare is 568,000 dong (£21 or $31). Spend the day in Nanning. Alternatively, there are several modern buses from Hanoi to Nanning every morning.

Day 2, evening: Travel by overnight train from **Nanning** to **Guangzhou**. There are several possible trains: train 2572 leaving Nanning at 19:13 and arriving Guangzhou (main station) at 06:52 next morning; train 1234 leaving Nanning at 18:13 and arriving Guangzhou (East station) at 09:10; and train K366 (a higher-quality K-category train) leaving Nanning at 00:31 and arriving at Guangzhou (main station) at 11:50 on day 3. All three trains have soft and hard class sleepers. The fare is about RMB286 (£29 or $43) in a soft sleeper, or RMB184 (£19 or $29) in a hard sleeper. In an ideal world, you'd pre-book this train, and I suppose you could always try contacting a Chinese travel agency in Nanning, assuming they could somehow arrange for you to collect tickets. Otherwise, as there's no easy way to pre-book from Vietnam, just turn up and see what ticket you can get to Guangzhou.

Day 3: travel from **Guangzhou** (East/Dong station) to **Hong Kong** (Kowloon station) by train. (If you have arrived from Nanning at Guangzhou main station, a taxi to Guangzhou East station will cost about RMB30 (£3/$5).) There is a range of departures daily, including one at 14:00, arriving at 15:48. The fare is about HK$190 (£17 or $25).

Hong Kong ➜ *Hanoi*

Day 1, morning: Take a train from **Hong Kong** (Kowloon station) to **Guangzhou** (East station). There is a range of departures daily, including one leaving Kowloon at 11:17 and arriving at Guangzhou (East/Dong) at 12:58.

Day 1, evening: Take an overnight sleeper train from **Guangzhou** (main station) to **Nanning**: train number 2571 departing Guangzhou at 16:52 and arriving at Nanning the next morning (day 2) at 06:23. Soft and hard class sleepers are available. Spend the day in Nanning.

> **Day 2, evening:** Take the daily overnight train from **Nanning** to
> **Hanoi** (see the section above). It leaves Nanning at 17:15 and arrives
> Hanoi at 05:30 next morning. Soft and hard sleepers are available.
> Alternatively, there are several modern buses from Nanning to Hanoi
> every morning.

HANOI TO KUNMING

Some years ago, there was a direct metre-gauge sleeper train from Hanoi to
Kunming in China twice a week. Unfortunately, floods and landslides damaged
the Chinese part of the line in May 2002 and this train is currently suspended
– likely to remain so for many years. Because of a shortage of funds for repair,
it is not clear exactly when (or if) it will start running again, although there are
reports that work on a new fast standard-gauge line will start at some point. In
the meantime, use a train from Hanoi to the frontier then a sleeper bus as
shown below.

Hanoi → Kunming by sleeper train+sleeper bus

While the train remains suspended, take an overnight train from Hanoi to Lao
Cai: see the train times and fares on pages 435–7. Lao Cai is just 3 km from the
Chinese border. Use a local taxi to reach the border post and cross over to
Hekou on the Chinese side. Passing through both sets of customs takes about
an hour. Then travel overnight from Hekou to Kunming on one of several
sleeper buses (buses with sleeping-berths). One bus leaves Hekou bus station
(just a few blocks from the border post) at 19:00 and arrives in Kunming around
07:00, but there are earlier and maybe later departures. The bus fare is about
RMB87 (£9). You may want to stop off at Lao Cai to visit Sapa, 40 km away,
before going on into China.

Kunming → Hanoi by sleeper bus+sleeper train

Southbound, take an overnight sleeper bus from Kunming to Hekou on the
Vietnamese frontier. A bus leaves Kunming's East bus station around 19:30

each evening, arriving at Hekou early next morning. There may in fact be several other evening departures too. At Hekou, the border is a few blocks from the bus station. Cross over the border to the Vietnamese side and use a taxi to get to Lao Cai, 3 km from the border post. Then take an overnight train from Lao Cai to Hanoi: see pages 435–7 for train times and fares.

SAIGON TO PHNOM PENH (CAMBODIA) AND BANGKOK (THAILAND)

There is no railway (as yet) between Saigon and Phnom Penh, a distance of some 250 km. However, there is a daily bus service; and a number of local tour operators run a river boat+bus service from Saigon to Phnom Penh – a very enjoyable way to travel between the two cities. For details of the buses and onward travel to Bangkok by a combination of bus and Thai train, see the Cambodia chapter, page 285.

PART

6

THE AMERICAS

North America

CANADA

————— VIA Rail – *Canadian*

------ VIA Rail – other trains

—·—·— Rocky Mountaineer

xxxxx Ontario Northland

USA

— — Long-distance train with double-deck Superliner cars. 1 train daily

▪▪▪▪▪▪ Long-distance train with Viewliner, Amfleet or Horizon cars. 1 or 2 trains daily

·········· Inter-city-style service, with a range of trains daily

PACIFIC

OCEAN

U S A

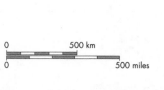

0   500 km

0   500 miles

N

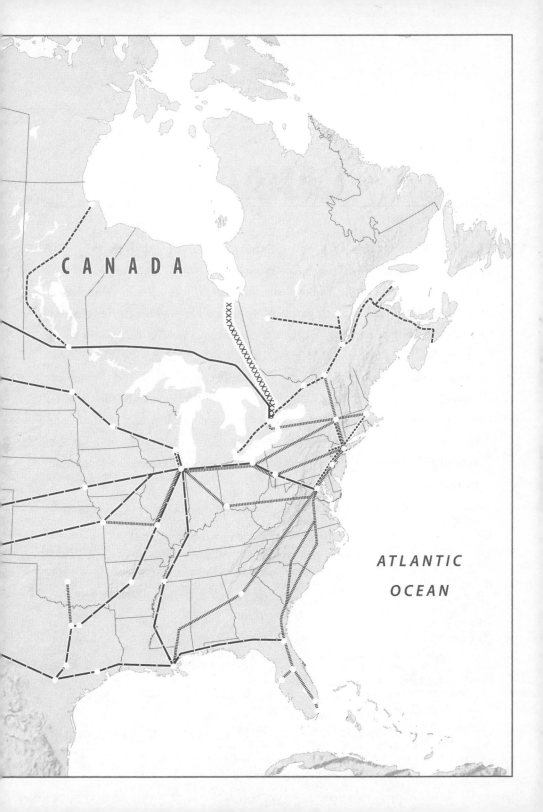

CANADA

Canada is home to some of the world's most epic and scenic train rides. VIA Rail's trans-continental train the *Canadian* links Toronto and Vancouver three times a week all year round through superb scenery in the Rocky Mountains – indeed, the train itself is an attraction, as it uses stainless-steel cars built in 1955 and inherited from Canadian Pacific's original *Canadian*. Further south on the Calgary–Banff–Vancouver route you'll find the superb Rocky Mountaineer running a rail cruise service twice a week between April and September, following the original 1885 Canadian Pacific route through the Rockies, through breathtaking mountain scenery that's the equal of any in the world. And even if all you want is A to B transportation between Toronto, Ottawa, Montreal and Québec, VIA Rail's intercity trains make an inexpensive, ground-level alternative to stressful flights.

Train operator:	VIA Rail, **www.viarail.ca** Other train operators: Ontario Northland, **www.ontc.on.ca** Rocky Mountaineer, **www.rockymountaineer.com** Algoma Central, **www.algomacentralrailway.com**
Time:	Halifax: GMT–4; Montreal/Toronto: GMT–5; Vancouver: GMT–8. Clocks go forward 1 hour from second Sunday in March to first Sunday in November.
Currency:	£1 = approx. 1.56 Canadian dollars. At the time of writing, US$ and Canadian dollars are roughly equivalent in value.
Tourist information:	**www.canadatourism.com** Montreal: **www.tourism-montreal.org**; Toronto: **www.city.toronto.on.ca**; Vancouver: **www.tourismvancouver.com**; Québec: **www.bonjourquebec.com**; Nova Scotia: **http://explore.gov.ns.ca**
Visas:	UK, EU, US, NZ and Australian citizens and many other nationalities don't require a visa to visit Canada.

EUROPE TO CANADA, without flying

There are two ways to cross the Atlantic without flying. You can cruise across on Cunard's *Queen Mary 2*, which runs a regular trans-Atlantic passenger service from Southampton to New York at least once a month between April and October, see **www.cunard.com** or call 0845 678 0013 (in the US or Canada; call 1-800-7-CUNARD). The crossing normally takes seven nights (slower than the five nights it typically took in the 1950s!), and you can expect to pay around £1,100 each way per person for the cheapest cabins, although this includes all meals and entertainment as well as accommodation. You can then take daily trains from New York to either Montreal or Toronto; see the section below. Or you can cross the Atlantic aboard a passenger-carrying freighter, which may take a bit longer, and probably won't be any cheaper, but there may be a wider choice of departures. For information about travel by freighter, try Strand Travel (**www.strandtravelltd.co.uk**, telephone +44 (0)20 7921 4340).

TRAINS BETWEEN THE USA AND CANADA

New York to Montreal and Toronto

Two daily trains link New York with Canada, run by Amtrak, jointly with VIA Rail in the case of the New York–Toronto train.

The New York–Toronto train – the *Maple Leaf*, with coach class and business class – departs New York at 07:15, calling at Niagara Falls (USA) at 16:33 and arriving at Toronto at 19:37. From Toronto it departs at 08:30, calling at Niagara Falls (USA) at 12:30 and arriving at New York at 22:05

The New York–Montreal train – the *Adirondack*, with coach class only – departs New York at 08:15, arriving at Montreal at 19:10; and southbound departs Montreal at 09:30, arriving at New York at 20:35

Both trains have comfortable air-conditioned reclining seats and a café car, and are a day well spent – highly recommended. Both trains travel right along the scenic Hudson River valley all the way from New York to Albany, with superb views of the river, including West Point Military Academy, Bannerman's Island and Storm King Mountain. Try to sit on the left-hand side of the train leaving New York. The *Adirondack* passes through more great scenery in the Adirondack mountains. A wonderful ride!

New York–Montreal costs US$62 (£41). New York to Toronto costs US$105 (£70). You can check times and fares and book online at **www.amtrak.com** (or you can call 1-800-USA-RAIL in the US or Canada).

Seattle to Vancouver

On the other side of the continent, two daily articulated Spanish-designed Talgo trains link Seattle with Vancouver, one in the morning, one in the evening. For details, see **www.amtrakcascades.com** or **www.amtrak.com**. You can also travel between Vancouver and Seattle via Victoria, the British Columbia provincial capital, on Vancouver Island: there is a daily catamaran service between Seattle and Victoria (see **www.victoriaclipper.com** for times and fares), and regular buses link Victoria with Vancouver (see **www.pacificcoach.com** for times and fares).

CANADIAN INTERCITY TRAINS

Montreal–Ottawa–Toronto

VIA Rail's fast modern intercity trains link Toronto, Ottawa and Montreal. Montreal to Toronto takes about 4 hours 40 minutes city centre to city centre, and the fare starts at around Can$78 (£50) if you book in advance, or Can$152 (£97) regular fare. Toronto to Ottawa takes about 4 hours 20 minutes and also costs from Can$78 (£50) booked in advance, regular fare Can$140 (£90). Montreal to Ottawa takes 1 hour 50 minutes, with advance fares from Can$35 (£22), regular fare Can$61 (£39). You can check times, fares and book online at **www.viarail.ca**.

Montreal to Québec

From Montreal to Québec, air-conditioned trains run several times daily, taking less than 3 hours. The fare is around Can$47 (£30) if you book in advance. You can check times, fares and book online at **www.viarail.ca**.

CANADA'S TRANS-CONTINENTAL *CANADIAN*

The greatest train in Canada, making one of the world's greatest train journeys, VIA Rail's *Canadian* runs three times a week all year round, linking Toronto, Winnipeg, Edmonton, Jasper and Vancouver. The journey takes four nights, and the train consists of the original 1955-built stainless-steel coaches from the Canadian Pacific Railway's *Canadian*. You can travel very affordably in economy class in a reclining seat, or in sleeper touring class (formerly 'Silver and Blue' class) with a private sleeping-car room and restaurant-car meals included. You can check times and fares for a specific date at **www.viarail.ca**. Remember that this route crosses four time zones; all train times shown in this chapter are local time.

Toronto → Winnipeg → Vancouver

Km	*Canadian*			
0	Toronto	depart	22:00 (day 1)	Tue, Thur, Sat
1,943	Winnipeg	arrive	08:01 (day 3)	Thur, Sat, Mon
		depart	12:00 (day 3)	Thur, Sat, Mon
2,702	Saskatoon	arr/dep	23:47 (day 3)	Thur, Sat, Mon
3,221	Edmonton	arrive	06:37 (day 4)	Fri, Sun, Tue
		depart	07:37 (day 4)	Fri, Sun, Tue
3,600	Jasper	arrive	13:00 (day 4)	Fri, Sun, Tue
		depart	14:30 (day 4)	Fri, Sun, Tue
4,052	Kamloops North	arr/dep	23:09 (day 4)	Fri, Sun, Tue
4,466	Vancouver	arrive	09:42 (day 5)	Sat, Mon, Wed

Vancouver → *Winnipeg* → *Toronto*

Canadian			
Vancouver	depart	20:30 (day 1)	Tue, Fri, Sun
Kamloops North	arr/dep	06:35 (day 2)	Wed, Sat, Mon
Jasper	arrive	16:00 (day 2)	Wed, Sat, Mon
	depart	17:30 (day 2)	Wed, Sat, Mon
Edmonton	arrive	23:00 (day 2)	Wed, Sat, Mon
	depart	23:45 (day 2)	Wed, Sat, Mon
Saskatoon	arr/dep	09:10 (day 3)	Thu, Sun, Tue
Winnipeg	arrive	20:30 (day 3)	Thu, Sun, Tue
	depart	23:30 (day 3)	Thu, Sun, Tue
Toronto	arrive	09:30 (day 5)	Sat, Tue, Thur

Fares

The fares vary by time of year, higher in July and August, at Easter and other peak periods, lower at other times. Toronto to Vancouver one-way costs Can$507–Can$596 (£325–£382) per person in an economy class reclining seat, Can$970–Can$1,541 (£622–£988) in a sleeper touring class 'section' sleeper, or Can$1,464–Can$2,324 (£938–£1,490) in a sleeper touring class 'roomette' or bedroom. (See the next section for a description of the various classes.) You can check the fares for your date of travel at **www.viarail.ca**.

Which class should I choose?

Economy class (reclining seats) (formerly known as comfort class): Travelling in this class you have a comfortable reclining seat and access to the economy class 'Skyline' car with coffee shop, lounge and 'vista dome'. Sleeping in a seat may not be as comfortable as having a proper sleeper, but the seats recline to about 40 degrees, have loads of legroom and leg-rests. An economy class seat costs a fraction of the price of a sleeper touring class berth, and with a coffee shop, lounge area and observation dome, the facilities in economy class are still excellent. It's an experience streets ahead of a mere flight, and infinitely more comfortable than bus travel.

Sleeper touring class (formerly known as Silver and Blue class): This is the luxury option. Sleeper touring class gives you the choice of having your own private 2-berth bedroom, a single-berth roomette, or a 'section' berth, all with comfortable beds and with hot showers at the end of the corridor. The fare includes all meals in the elegant sleeper touring class restaurant car, and you can use the famous 'Park' observation-lounge car at the rear of the train. The 'Park' car, 18 of which were built and all named after Canadian parks, features a classic north American 'vista dome' upstairs, the bullet lounge at the rear (complimentary tea and coffee always available) and the mural lounge downstairs underneath the dome.

Sections are the cheapest type of sleeper, also known simply as 'upper or lower berths'. Sections consist of open-plan seats arranged in pairs facing each other – a useful bit of information is that the person with the slightly more expensive lower berth gets the seat facing forward during the day. At night, the seats pull together to form a lower berth, and an upper berth folds out from the wall. Curtains are fitted to each bunk for privacy. If you've seen Marilyn Monroe in *Some Like it Hot*, then you'll have seen sections – the girl band travels from Chicago to Florida in a sleeping-car with sections. Bring your own Marilyn . . .

The next step up from a section is a *roomette* or a *bedroom*. If you are travelling alone, you'll be allocated a roomette. This is a very compact single room, just big enough for a large seat with plenty of legroom, and a leg-rest with a toilet bowl hidden underneath. There is a washbasin in the corner. At night, a bed folds down from behind the seat, taking up almost all of the roomette. If there are two of you, you'll get a bedroom. These are larger rooms for two people, with separate en suite washroom and toilet. An upper and lower berth convert to seats for daytime use. Bedrooms are the same price per person as a roomette.

How to buy tickets

The best and cheapest way to buy tickets is direct from VIA Rail, online at **www.viarail.ca**. You collect the tickets at the station before departure. Alternatively, you can make VIA Rail bookings in the UK by telephone through First Rail Ltd, 0845 644 3553.

Can you stop off on the way?

Yes, of course you can; just remember that every leg of your journey requires a seat or berth reservation for a specific train and date. You cannot buy an open ticket and hop on and off trains spontaneously. But it's easy to pre-book stopovers, as **www.viarail.ca** has a 'multi-city' option which allows you to specify a Toronto–Vancouver journey with one or more stopovers at places along the way, such as Winnipeg or Jasper (for Jasper National Park). Booking your trip using this 'multi-city' feature is cheaper than buying a separate ticket for each leg.

Canada's trans-continental trains: a brief history

There were (and are) two competing trans-continental rail routes across Canada. The Canadian Pacific Railway opened the first trans-continental line across Canada in 1885, running from Montreal/Toronto to Vancouver via Winnipeg, Calgary and Banff. Instead of taking the easiest route through the Rockies via the Yellowhead Pass, political tension with the United States led them to take a more difficult (and scenic) southerly route through the Kicking Horse Pass. The second and later line, built around 1917 by the Canadian Northern Railway (nationalised in 1921 as Canadian National Railways or CN, as in the CN Tower), runs from Montreal/Toronto to Vancouver to the north of the CPR route, via Winnipeg, Edmonton, Jasper and the easier Yellowhead pass.

VIA Rail was formed in 1978 as a government corporation to take over the passenger trains from these two private companies, which now only run freight trains. Initially, VIA Rail continued to run both the Canadian Pacific's *Canadian* and the Canadian National's *Super-Continental* daily on each of these two trans-continental routes, with the rolling stock getting progressively older and less reliable. However, in 1990, this was reduced to one train, the present-day *Canadian*, running from Toronto to Vancouver three times a week via the Canadian National route through Winnipeg, Edmonton and Jasper. VIA Rail lacked the funds to buy new cars, so they completely rebuilt and upgraded the original stainless-steel 'streamliner' coaches built in 1955 for the Canadian Pacific's *Canadian*, making this train a real classic in its own right as well as transportation from A to B. There are now no regular passenger services on the original 1885 Canadian Pacific route through Calgary or Banff, apart from the excellent Rocky Mountaineer train (see page 456) which runs between Calgary, Banff and Vancouver three times a week April–October.

VANCOUVER TO VICTORIA

If you're going to Vancouver, don't miss a trip to the British Columbia provincial capital, Victoria, on Vancouver Island. Regular buses link Vancouver with Victoria in about 3½ hours, going on board a ferry to reach the island. See **www.pacificcoach.com** for times and fares. To travel onwards to the States, you can use a daily fast catamaran service between Victoria and Seattle – see **www.victoriaclipper.com**. (For direct trains Vancouver–Seattle, see **www.amtrakcascades.com** or **www.amtrak.com**.)

MONTREAL TO HALIFAX BY THE *OCÉAN*

The overnight train *Océan* links Montreal and Halifax (a journey of 1,352 km) daily except Tuesday. Eastbound it departs Montreal at 18:30, arriving at Halifax at 16:35 next day. Westbound it departs Halifax at 12:30, arriving at Montreal at 08:29 next day. (Halifax is an hour ahead of Montreal.) Exact departure times may vary slightly in winter, November to April; check at **www.viarail.ca**.

The *Océan* has economy class reclining seats, sleeper class sleeping-cars, with restaurant car, coffee shop and lounge. As its name suggests, sleeper class gets you a comfortable private sleeper, but without including meals or other extras. However, in the summer tourist season from June to October the *Océan* also has sleeper touring class sleeping-cars and a 1955-vintage stainless-steel observation dome/lounge car at the back, like the one attached to the rear of the *Canadian*. This observation/lounge car is reserved exclusively for sleeper touring class passengers, and meals in the restaurant car are included in the sleeper touring class fare (meals extra for other passengers). In summer, all departures of the *Océan* use modern air-conditioned sleeping-cars (some with private toilet and shower) and reclining seat cars originally built in the UK for the abortive Channel Tunnel night trains, and now marketed by VIA Rail as 'Renaissance' cars. In winter (November–April), four departures per week use Renaissance cars; the remaining two departures per week use 1955-built stainless-steel cars (seats and sleepers), similar to those used on the Toronto–Vancouver *Canadian*.

Three times a week some coaches running direct between Montreal and Gaspé (1950s stainless-steel cars, forming the *Chaleur*) are attached to this train. See **www.viarail.ca** for more information, including fares and online booking.

Fares and how to buy tickets

You can check fares for the *Océan* at **www.viarail.ca**. To give you a rough idea, Montreal–Halifax costs about Can$148 (£95) in economy class, or Can$322 (£206) in sleeper class. You can book online at **www.viarail.ca**, picking up the tickets at the station before departure. Alternatively, you can make VIA Rail bookings by telephone in the UK through First Rail Ltd, 0845 644 3553.

THE ROCKY MOUNTAINEER

A private company called Rocky Mountaineer runs regular scenic trains on three different routes through the Canadian Rockies, with spectacular scenery and great on-board service. Although more of a 'tourist experience' than 'scheduled mode of transport', with prices to match, the trains offer regular scheduled departures from late April to early October and if you're travelling independently you can buy one-way tickets. Each trip takes two days, with an overnight hotel stop so that you travel the whole route in daylight. The Rocky Mountaineer is now the only passenger train using the famous Canadian Pacific main line between Calgary, Banff and Vancouver.

Which route to choose?

The Rocky Mountaineer runs on three different routes. Independent travellers can buy one-way or return tickets in either direction between Vancouver and Banff, Calgary or Jasper.

'First Passage to the West', Vancouver to Banff and Calgary: Previously and more accurately called the Kicking Horse route after the pass it uses to cross the Rocky Mountains, this is perhaps the most scenic and certainly the most historically significant route to choose, as it travels over the famous Canadian Pacific Railway, Canada's first trans-continental line, opened in 1885. It's the original Rocky Mountaineer route on which the company first started in 1990, when the last regular passenger trains on the line were discontinued. You'll pass Castle Mountain, the pretty station at Lake Louise, the Continental Divide, the much-photographed Stoney Creek bridge, the site of the 1885 'Last Spike' and the wonderfully scenic Thompson and Fraser River canyons. You're likely to see bald eagles, ospreys and maybe even bears. There are two departures a week from late April to early October, and the journey takes two full days with one overnight hotel stop included in the fare.

'Journey through the Clouds', Vancouver to Jasper: Previously (and again more accurately) called the Yellowhead route, this route takes you over the second and later of the two Canadian trans-continental railways, the Canadian Northern line, opened in 1917, nationalised as Canadian National in 1921. It's the same route as that taken by VIA

Rail's Toronto–Jasper–Vancouver *Canadian*. Between Vancouver and Kamloops, the Rocky Mountaineer Yellowhead and Kicking Horse routes are the same – in fact, the two trains usually run coupled together. Also note that this route and the Fraser Discovery route share the section of line past Mount Robson and through the Yellowhead Pass. So if you want to make a circular tour, the best combination is probably the Kicking Horse route Vancouver–Banff, then by bus between Jasper and Banff via the Columbia Icefields, then the Fraser Discovery route from Jasper back to Vancouver. The Rocky Mountaineer Yellowhead train also runs twice a week from late April to early October; the journey takes two full days with one overnight hotel stop included in the fare.

'Rainforest to Goldrush', Whistler to Jasper via Quesnel: Previously known as the Fraser Discovery route, this route is all about getting off the beaten track into gold-rush and timber country, rather than taking a famous trans-continental rail line. It takes you along the mighty Fraser River over the Pacific Great Eastern Railway (PGE), started in 1885 and only fully completed in 1952 – no wonder it was nicknamed the Prince George Eventually! The scenery is wonderful, especially the Fraser River canyon, and you may see bald eagles, ospreys and possibly bears. It runs once a week from late May to late September, and the journey takes two full days with one overnight hotel stop included in the fare. Most passengers travel from Vancouver to Whistler a day or two beforehand on the 'Whistler Sea to Sky' service run by the same company (see page 473).

On board the Rocky Mountaineer

The Rocky Mountaineer offers two classes of service: 'Red Leaf' and 'Gold Leaf'. This section explains the features of each class, and will help you choose.

Red Leaf service: On any other train worldwide, Red Leaf service would probably qualify as first class in its own right. There's certainly no need to pay extra for Gold Leaf service if you really can't afford it, and you're more likely to find other independent travellers and younger travellers in Red Leaf than Gold Leaf. Red Leaf consists of spacious reclining seats in classic 1950s ex-Canadian National coaches, refurbished to modern standards with plush carpet and air-conditioning. All seats face forward, although pairs of seats can be turned round to form a bay of four for families. There's loads of legroom, and seat backs have drop-down tables.

Each car has an attendant who provides a live commentary and keeps the complimentary tea, coffee and soft drinks coming. Alcoholic drinks cost extra, about Can\$7 (£4.50) per glass of wine or miniature of spirits. The fare includes a light breakfast and packed lunch each day, served at your seat.

All passengers get a copy of the *Rocky Mountaineer* newspaper, which features a route guide listing points of interest along the way (referenced by milepost), a map, and information about the train, the history of the route, and the wildlife you can see.

There's no observation car as such, just large picture windows, but in each coach vestibule the top half of the coach access doors swings inwards and locks into place, forming a semi-official sightseeing platform for reflection-free photography or just getting some fresh air.

The fare includes a hotel room for the overnight stop, and transfers by motor coach to and from the hotel.

On the 'Rainforest to Goldrush' route, there's usually a separate Red Leaf lounge car attached to the train, with armchairs and tables.

Travel tips

● On the 'Rainforest to Goldrush route', request a seat on the left-hand side of the train eastbound, right-hand side westbound, as that's where the best scenery will be.

- If you are going to travel in Gold Leaf and are booking by phone, request a seat towards the front of the leading Gold Leaf car, as the upper deck front windows in this car give great views forward over the roof of the rest of the train.

Gold Leaf service: This is the premium option. It's not cheap, and the scenery is the same as you'll see in Red Leaf, but the onboard experience is excellent and more than meets expectations. Is it worth the extra over Red Leaf? If you can afford it, yes, because of the food, wine, service, and not least those glass domes that give the best all-round view of the Canadian Rockies you can get.

Gold Leaf passengers travel in modern purpose-built double-decker dome cars. Upstairs under the glass roof there are 72 reclining seats with loads of legroom and drop-down tables. Downstairs, reached by spiral staircase or wheelchair lift, there are toilets, kitchens, a 36-seat restaurant for breakfast and lunch, and a small open-air viewing platform for fresh air and reflection-free photography.

A pair of attendants in each coach provide live commentary and keep the snacks and complimentary alcoholic and non-alcoholic drinks flowing. Rocky Mountaineer's excellent own-label Sumoc Ridge Merlot is very easy to drink – too easy, probably!

Breakfast and lunch are served downstairs in the restaurant in two sittings, included in the fare. There's a choice of excellent main courses freshly prepared in the kitchen and served on real china. Lunch comes complete with Rocky Mountaineer's own-label British Columbian red or white wine.

All passengers get a copy of the *Rocky Mountaineer* newspaper, which features a route guide listing points of interest along the way (referenced by milepost), a map, and information about the train, the history of the route, and the wildlife you might see.

The fare includes a hotel room for the overnight stop, and transfers by motor coach to and from the hotel.

What's the journey like?

This section gives you a flavour of what there is to see on each route. The route guide in your *Rocky Mountaineer* newspaper on board the train lists these and other highlights, quoting the nearest milepost – the mileposts are black numbers on small white signs placed next to the track every mile. The miles reset to zero at every railway divisional point. Approximate times are used here to give you a better idea of the journey.

'First Passage to the West' (Kicking Horse) route: *Calgary, Banff → Vancouver*

This is the most historic and arguably most scenic route operated by the Rocky Mountaineer: the original Canadian Pacific Railway through the Rockies, opened in 1885. You can make the journey in either direction, between Vancouver and either Banff (a resort town in the Rockies) or Calgary (a major city just east of the Rockies). This account assumes you travel westbound. You can, of course, travel each of these routes in the opposite direction to that described.

Day 1

06:10 Calgary: The train leaves Calgary around 6.30am and heads across the plain and up into the Rockies to Banff, 82 miles (131 km) away, where the majority of passengers join the train.

08:20 Banff: Originally known simply as 'siding 29' on the Canadian Pacific Railway; Lord Strathcona named it 'Banff' after his home town in Scotland in 1880. Banff station is just a few minutes' walk from the town centre and 30 minutes' walk from the famous (and highly recommended) Banff Springs Hotel. The station building dates from 1910, a replacement for the original 1886 log cabin. If you're joining the train here, you check in at the Rocky Mountaineer desk placed just outside the station waiting room; you're given your seat allocation and your luggage is taken from you. Tea and coffee are available inside the waiting room until the train arrives from Calgary, which is around 08:40, with departure around 09:00. The luggage travels by road and arrives at your overnight hotel before you do.

09:10 Castle Mountain: On leaving Banff, the train winds through the pine trees along the Bow River, with snow-capped mountains on either side of the broad valley. Look out for the impressive and imposing Castle Mountain to your right, around milepost 99. It's an appropriate name!

09:50 Morant's Curve: At milepost 113, 3 miles (5 km) east of Lake Louise, the train snakes through what has become known as 'Morant's Curve', although strangely it isn't mentioned anywhere in the Rocky Mountaineer route guide or on any map. Nicholas Morant was a photographer with the publicity department of the Canadian Pacific Railway, and this was one of his favourite spots for taking PR shots of CPR trains. If you've ever had a 'railway encyclopaedia' or 'boy's book of trains', the chances are that it has an illustration of a Canadian passenger or freight train on 'Morant's Curve', and even today, many of Rocky Mountaineer's brochure photos are taken here. The other classic location for PR shots of Canadian trains in the Rockies is the Stoney Creek Bridge, which we'll come to later.

09:55 Lake Louise: The Rocky Mountaineer passes the beautiful 'log cabin' style station at Lake Louise, on the left on a track slightly lower than the one that westbound trains now use. Lake Louise station was used for the station scenes in the film *Dr Zhivago*. The lake itself is up in the mountains, out of sight. The train now crosses and briefly runs alongside Highway 1, the Trans-Canada Highway.

10:05 Continental Divide: A small monument and wooden sign on the left mark the Continental Divide, and the boundary between Alberta and British Columbia. Rainwater falling east of the divide flows to the Atlantic, rainwater falling to the west makes its way to the Pacific. It's the highest point on the trip, 5,332 feet (1,625 metres) above sea level. Travelling west, you now put your watch back an hour, as BC is an hour behind Alberta.

09:20 (BC time) Spiral Tunnels: The train passes Wapta Lake and enters the first of the two famous 'Spiral Tunnels'. Inside the Upper Spiral Tunnel, the train describes a complete spiral and emerges further down the mountainside, facing the opposite way. The train then crosses the deep wooded valley and plunges into the Lower Spiral Tunnel to descend even further. Long freight trains can even cross over themselves here! There's a cut-away diagram of the spiral tunnels in your route guide, and the commentary from your carriage attendant will explain it, but it's still disorientating. The Spiral Tunnels were built in 1907, replacing a dangerously steep section of line known as the 'Big Hill', where many CPR trains and staff came to grief.

09:55 Kicking Horse canyon: The train calls at Field, an important operating centre for the Canadian Pacific Railway, then heads through the Kicking Horse canyon, crossing and re-crossing the Kicking Horse River several times. The river is narrow, fast-running, and blue with meltwater sediment. The train follows it for 30 scenic miles (48 km), with many bridges and tunnels.

11:20 Rocky Mountain Trench: The train now runs through a wide flat valley full of pines – the Rocky Mountain Trench. The Columbia River is on the left.

12:40 Stoney Creek Bridge: This is the other classic location for illustrations of trains crossing Canada. It's a beautiful arched steel girder bridge at milepost 76.2, 484 feet (148 metres) long and 325 feet (100 metres) above the creek bed below, built in 1929. It's the latest of three bridges built on this spot. The approach to the bridge is dead straight, so there's little opportunity to see or photograph the bridge, and although the line curves sharply to the left immediately afterwards, there are so many trees in the way that it's still difficult to get a clear view of it. A new tunnel (the 9-mile (14-km) long MacDonald Tunnel) was built in 1988 to increase capacity by bypassing both the Stoney Creek Bridge and the shorter 1916-built Connaught Tunnel, but the Rocky Mountaineer deliberately takes the original route.

15:35 The Last Spike: The train passes Craigellachie, where on 7 November 1885 the last ceremonial rail spike was driven in, completing the Canadian Pacific Railway and linking Montreal to Vancouver by rail. Here there's a monument and small museum by the tracks, on the right-hand side.

16:00 Lake Shuswap and Osprey Alley: The train passes
Sicamous, 'The houseboat capital of the world', and for some miles
runs along the shore of the huge and beautiful Lake Shuswap. It
passes 'Osprey Alley', a long line of osprey nests in the tops of
telegraph poles and trees by the lake. Watch out for bald eagles, too.
After Lake Shuswap comes Lake Mara.

18:30: The mountains give way to gentle hills along the South
Thompson River. The hills are volcanic, but at their feet lie sandstone
mounds or 'hoodoos', which are the moraines left by ancient glaciers.
The country is more arid here, rocky and sandy with fewer trees, very
different from the morning's scenery.

19:20 Kamloops: The train pulls into Kamloops for its overnight stop.
Motor coaches meet the train and transfer passengers to their hotels.
There is a choice of two evening entertainment shows (with food)
whilst in Kamloops, both bookable through Rocky Mountaineer, but
don't overestimate how sprightly you'll feel on arrival at your hotel at
8pm after a day travelling with so much to take in. Banff to Kamloops
is 309 miles (494 km).

Day 2

07:00 Kamloops: Motor coaches collect passengers from their hotels
and take them to the station.

07:30: The Rocky Mountaineer leaves Kamloops, now combined with
the Jasper–Vancouver train. It veers right and crosses the Thompson
River on to Indian ('first nation') territory, passing a small wooden
church on the left that was allegedly used in the film *Unforgiven* with
Clint Eastwood.

Between Kamloops and Vancouver, the 1885 Canadian Pacific (CP)
and the later 1917 Canadian National (CN) trans-continental railways
run parallel, usually on opposite sides of the river. For the first 58 miles
(93 km) west of Kamloops, the Rocky Mountaineer uses CN tracks in
both directions, but between Basque and Vancouver there is
'directional running' where CN and CP co-operate, sending all
westbound trains, including the westbound Rocky Mountaineer, down

CN tracks on one side of the river, and all eastbound trains, including the eastbound Rocky Mountaineer, down the CP tracks on the other side. You see the same scenery, of course, from a slightly different angle, but if you really want to travel on the original 1885 CP tracks (almost) all the way between Vancouver and Banff, you'll need to take an eastbound Rocky Mountaineer.

08:40 Kamloops Lake: The train runs along the shore of Kamloops Lake – watch out for more bald eagles, and for the coloured rocks at Painted Bluff on the right.

09:25: The train reaches the end of the lake and runs alongside the Thompson River. The countryside here is even more arid than before – indeed, the train passes Ashcroft, the driest town in Canada.

10:35 Black Canyon: The train passes Black Canyon, a section of black lava cliff on the right, with the Thompson River on the left. After Black Canyon Tunnel, the Rocky Mountaineer crosses the Thompson on a steel girder bridge.

11:30: The scenery now changes again, from dry and sandy back to rocky with pine trees. The train enters the Thompson River canyon, with CP tracks one side of the river, CN tracks on the other side.

11:55 Avalanche Alley: The Rocky Mountaineer travels at the very edge of the river under a sheer cliff wall with avalanche protection sheds in several places. One section of the rock wall is attractively coloured, known as Rainbow Canyon.

12:05 Confluence of Thompson and Fraser rivers: Just after Lytton the train curves to the left over a bridge across the Fraser River. The confluence of Thompson and Fraser rivers is now on the right.

12:15 Cisco crossing: At Cisco, CP and CN tracks swap sides of the river. The CN line crosses first on a distinctive arched orange-painted girder bridge, the CP tracks then crossing in the opposite direction on a squared-off black steel bridge lower down on the right. Being the first, the CP engineers built their line down whichever was the easier side of the canyon; the later CN engineers had to make do with the opposite, trickier side.

13:35 Hell's Gate: This is the narrowest and fastest-flowing point of the Fraser River. On the right on the far bank is the Hell's Gate café, with a suspension footbridge across the river below the train and a cable car over the river and up the mountain.

15:15: We're no longer right next to the Fraser River, which has become very broad. The train is in a wide flat valley, with farms and greenhouses starting to appear. The historic site of Fort Langley is just visible through the trees on the left.

16:50 Approaching Vancouver: The train slows through the freight cars in Thornton Yard, finally curving right over a very long, low steel bridge across the Fraser River with a much higher arched road bridge on the left, which also carries the Vancouver 'Skytrain' metro. Once across the river, the Rocky Mountaineer curves sharply right again, weaving its way through the Vancouver suburbs.

17:35 Vancouver: The Rocky Mountaineer slowly passes, then reverses into, the Rocky Mountaineer terminal, a block away from the Pacific Central station where VIA's *Canadian* arrives. Their impressive and spacious terminal building was once a diesel locomotive maintenance shed.

You've now travelled a total of 594 miles (950 km) from Banff or 676 miles (1,082 km) from Calgary.

'Journey through the Clouds' (Yellowhead) route:
Jasper ➔ Vancouver, via Kamloops

This train travels over the second trans-continental line built across Canada, the Canadian National route between Jasper (in Jasper National Park) and Vancouver, opened in 1917.

● The Rocky Mountaineer leaves Jasper station around 08:00 and heads up through the Yellowhead Pass. This is the easiest pass through the Rockies (in other words the lowest, at 3,718 feet (1,133 metres) above sea level). The Canadian Pacific chose a more difficult route through the Kicking Horse Pass to the south because of political tensions between Canada and the USA at the time, and a desire to safeguard Canadian territory.

- Look out for the highlight of the trip: views of snow-capped Mount Robson to the right of the train. At 12,972 feet (3,954 metres) it's the highest mountain in the Rockies.

- After running alongside Moose Lake, the train crosses the Fraser River.

- For almost 20 miles (32 km), the train passes some of Canada's most magnificent mountains in the Premier range, named after early Canadian prime ministers.

- The train passes the site, marked by a small cairn, where twelve members of the Royal Canadian Horse Artillery were killed when two CN trains collided.

- The train passes Pyramid Falls, where water cascades 300 feet (90 metres) beside the tracks.

- The train stops overnight at Kamloops.

- Day 2 is identical to the Kicking Horse route above – the two trains run coupled together between Kamloops and Vancouver.

'Rainforest to Goldrush' (Fraser Discovery) route: Whistler → Jasper, via Quesnel

This is a less well-known but truly remarkable route, through the goldrush and timber country of the Cariboo.

Vancouver–Whistler: You can travel from Vancouver to Whistler the previous day (or any day you like) using the daily 'Whistler Sea to Sky' (formerly Whistler Mountaineer): see page 473. Whistler is one of Canada's biggest ski resorts, a sort of North American Zermatt. Cable cars run up the mountains, seaplanes run scenic flights, and there are many outdoor activities in both summer and winter. The centre of

Whistler village is pedestrianised, with many bars and restaurants. Stay in Whistler overnight.

Day 1

07:30 Whistler: The Rocky Mountaineer Rainforest to Goldrush train leaves Whistler at 07:30 on day 1. Whistler station is in the Creekside area of Whistler between Alta and Nita lakes, a few minutes' taxi or motor coach transfer from Whistler village itself. Check-in opens at 06:30; you hand over your luggage (which travels by road) and you are given a boarding card with seat allocation.

08:10 Green River, Birkenhead River: Breakfast is served as you pass through snow-capped mountains and run alongside the Green River. The scenery is beautiful, although there are still houses and occasional timber yards here, not to mention a few power pylons! The Green River soon gives way to the Birkenhead River, also on the right, but flowing in the opposite direction.

08:35 Nairn Falls: The train crosses a low bridge just above the top of a waterfall in the pine trees, Nairn Falls.

10:00 Anderson Lake: The train skirts the blue waters of Anderson Lake right by the water along the cliffs. The tracks follow the shore for 15 miles (24 km), with many photo opportunities.

10:30 Lake Seton: The train passes the end of Anderson Lake and crosses the spit of land known as Seton Portage separating it from another lake, Lake Seton. Originally one big lake, lakes Anderson and Seton were separated by a landslide over 1,000 years ago. Lake Seton is a luminous turquoise colour, an effect caused by the sediment washed down by meltwater from the mountains. The train passes the BC Hydro Bridge River hydroelectric plant and a timber yard.

11:20 Lillooet: Lillooet is a major railway town, and there's a 10-minute locomotive crew rest stop here in the freight yards.

11:35 Fraser River canyon: After leaving Lillooet, the train crosses the wide and brown Fraser River on a massive and dramatic girder bridge, 800 feet (244 metres) long and 190 feet (58 metres) above the river. Immediately after the bridge, the train snakes left on to the Fraser's left bank and starts climbing a steep 2.2 per cent gradient for the next 30 miles (48 km). It's one of the longest sustained 2.2 per cent rail gradients in America. This 30-mile stretch is the highlight of the trip: the train follows the Fraser River canyon, high up on the mountainside with the river far below. The sheer scale of the canyon is spectacular. There are few trees; the landscape is arid and sandy here.

13:00 Cariboo Plateau: The train finally leaves the Fraser River canyon. It's now on the Cariboo plateau, and pine trees make a welcome reappearance. These are the gentle rolling hills of cattle country.

16:00–17:00: Still on the Cariboo plateau, this is also timber country. You can smell the sawdust from the many lumber yards. You pass Lac La Hache and Williams Lake.

18:00 Deep Creek Bridge: 1,194 feet (364 metres) long, 312 feet (95 metres) high, one of the highest rail bridges in North America (in fact, only the Stoney Creek Bridge on the Kicking Horse route is higher). You pass many cattle ranches, and can spot many deer in the wooded areas.

19:30 Quesnel: The train passes lumber yards and the occasional osprey nesting in a telegraph pole or tall tree, and arrives at Quesnel (pronounced 'kwanell') for the overnight hotel stop. Quesnel is the local centre for the Cariboo, and if you've never seen small-town Canada it's well worth an evening wander. This is easier to do if you're at a town centre hotel (Red Leaf passengers currently use the centrally located Best Western), less easy if you're in a hotel a few miles out (Gold Leaf passengers are currently bussed a few miles out to the Sandman's hotel in an industrial/retail area). Personally, I'd suggest you request the town-centre Best Western even if you're in Gold Leaf. In Quesnel you'll find the longest wooden truss footbridge in the world, across the wide and fast-flowing Fraser River – check out the steak house and pub on the hill the other side! There's also a Greek restaurant, a casino built to look like an old paddle steamer, and a gift shop by the river that's often open in the evenings when the train arrives. There's a town museum (complete with allegedly haunted doll 'Mandy') which you may or may not find open when the train comes in.

Day 2

07:10 Quesnel: Motor coaches transfer you from the hotel around 06:45, and the Rocky Mountaineer leaves Quesnel around 07:40 when everyone is on board.

08:00: The train crosses the dramatic Cottonwood Bridge, 1,023 feet (312 metres) long and 236 feet (72 metres) high, over a valley full of pine trees with a river racing beneath. The bridge was only completed in 1952, the last major link in the railway line from Vancouver to Prince George and Prince Rupert on which work had begun in 1912. The 'last spike' was driven in 8 miles (13 km) further on, at the slightly smaller Abhau Creek bridge, on 31 October 1952.

09:10: The Fraser River is sighted again, on the left. Endless pines and birch trees, and the odd sawmill, including a fully automated one at Dunkly.

10:20 Prince George (almost!): The Rocky Mountaineer makes slow progress through the yards approaching Prince George. The train heads for a long, low steel bridge across the Fraser into Prince George, which is the route passenger trains (when there were any) would normally take. But immediately before the bridge the train turns right at a triangular junction on to the line leading out of Prince George towards Jasper. The train is no longer on the Pacific Great Eastern but on the Grand Trunk Pacific. The GTP is Canada's third trans-continental line, built from Jasper through Prince George to the Pacific Ocean at the port of Prince Rupert. Although it is not in the same league as Vancouver, much freight is still shipped overseas via Prince Rupert. The GTP was nationalised after its bankruptcy in 1921 and is now part of Canadian National Railways.

12:30: Lunch is served as the train enters the Rocky Mountain Trench – a wide valley between the mountains. The train follows the meandering brown river through the pines and birches.

16:00: The train passes McBride, with agriculture now in evidence across the valley.

17:50 Mount Robson: Another highlight of the trip – the train passes Mount Robson, the highest mountain in the Rockies at 12,972 feet (3,954 metres).

18:10: The Fraser River is now narrower, cleaner and greener. The valley narrows, with snow-capped mountains on each side.

18:50: The train joins the Jasper–Kamloops–Vancouver main line, and passes through the Yellowhead Pass. This is the easiest and lowest pass through the Rockies at 3,718 feet (1,133 metres) above sea level. The train crosses from British Columbia into Alberta, and the clocks go forward an hour.

20:30 (Alberta time): The train arrives at Jasper, at the heart of Jasper National Park. The station is right at the front of this small town, which grew up around the railway.

Departure dates, times and fares

Here's a summary of Rocky Mountaineer departure dates, schedules and fares. The prices reflect a 'unique travel experience' rather than regular A to B transportation, but it's worth it for the scenery, the truly excellent on-board service and (especially in the case of the 'First Passage to the West' route via Kicking Horse Pass) the historical significance of the railway itself. You can check these times and fares at **www.rockymountaineer.com** – and should always double-check the departures for your dates of travel, as days sometimes vary.

First Passage to the West eastbound departs Vancouver on Monday and Friday from late April to early October, boarding time at the Rocky Mountaineer terminal 07:30. Arrival at Kamloops for the overnight hotel stop is 17:35, and the train departs next morning at 06:15, arriving at Banff at 19:20 and Calgary at 21:40. Westbound it runs from Calgary on Wednesday and Sunday from late April to early October, boarding time at Calgary 06:10, and at Banff 08:20. The train arrives at Kamloops at 19:20 for the overnight hotel stop, and departs next morning at 07:30, arriving at Vancouver at 17:35.

Journey through the Clouds eastbound departs Vancouver on Tuesday and Friday, from late April to early October, boarding time at the Rocky Mountaineer terminal 07:30. Arrival at Kamloops for the overnight hotel stop is 17:35, and the train departs next morning at 08:10, arriving at Jasper at 18:10. Westbound it runs from Jasper on Thursday and Sunday from late April to early October, boarding time 07:45. The train arrives at Kamloops at 16:10 for the overnight hotel stop, and departs next morning at 07:30, arriving at Vancouver at 17:35.

Rainforest to Goldrush eastbound departs Whistler most Mondays from May to mid-October, boarding time 07:10. The train arrives at Quesnel at 19:30 for the overnight hotel stop, and departs next morning at 07:10, arriving at Jasper at 20:30. Westbound it departs Jasper most Wednesdays from May to mid-October, boarding time 07:10. Arrival at Quesnel for the overnight hotel stop is at 18:30, and the train departs next morning at 07:10, arriving at Whistler at 19:30.

The fares for all three routes are the same. In Red Leaf, the one-way fare is Can$659–Can$909 (£411–£568) per person for two people travelling together, or Can$789–Can$979 (£493–£612) for a solo traveller. In Gold Leaf, the one-way fare is Can$1,159–Can$1,649 (£743–£1,030) per person for two people travelling together, or Can$1,239–Can$1,729 (£724–£1,080) for a solo traveller. All fares include train travel, meals, one night in a hotel and motor coach transfers.

How to buy tickets

If you're an independent traveller, the best way to buy tickets is direct from Rocky Mountaineer. You can book simple one-way train journeys between Vancouver and Whistler, Calgary, Banff or Jasper online at **www.rockymountaineer.com**.

If you prefer, you can book all Rocky Mountaineer's train journeys and tours by telephone: lines are open 04:00–22:00 Pacific Standard Time, seven days a week, and calls from the UK, Canada, USA, Australia and New Zealand are free. Telephone numbers are:

United Kingdom (freephone): 00 800 0606 7372

USA and Canada (toll free): 1-877-460-3200

Australia (toll free): 00-11-800-0606-7372

New Zealand (toll free): 00-800-0606-7372

Other countries (calls charged): 1 604 606 7245

VANCOUVER TO WHISTLER ON THE 'WHISTLER SEA TO SKY'

This service (previously called the Whistler Mountaineer) is a little scenic gem, the most comfortable way to travel the 74 miles (118 km) between Vancouver and Whistler. In both Whistler Classic and Whistler Dome class, coach attendants maintain a live commentary and serve drinks and snacks included in the fare. It's run by the same company that operates the Rocky Mountaineer. There are departures in both directions every day except Tuesday and Wednesday from late May to late September: northbound departing Vancouver at 08:30, arriving at Whistler at 12:00; southbound departing Whistler 15:00 and arriving at Vancouver at 18:30. In Vancouver the train uses the North Vancouver Whistler Mountaineer station. Motor coach transfers to and from hotels in central Vancouver and Whistler village are included in the fare.

Vancouver ➜ Whistler

07:15–07:45: Passengers are collected by motor coach from central Vancouver hotels, and driven through Stanley Park and across the Lion's Gate Bridge to the North Vancouver Whistler Mountaineer station, a simple siding a block or two away from the original BC Rail passenger station. BC Rail stopped normal passenger service on this route in 1999.

08:30: After leaving Vancouver, the train passes right under the Lion's Gate Bridge and over a girder bridge across the Capilano River

(Vancouver's famous Capilano footbridge, see **www.capbridge.com**, is out of sight further up the valley). In Whistler Dome class, sit back and enjoy some complimentary Bucks Fizz, then a welcome cooked breakfast. A packed light breakfast is served in Whistler Classic class, with complimentary tea or coffee.

The train runs alongside the sea (on the left-hand side) until it heads off into the mountains. It passes through the mile-long Horseshoe Bay Tunnel, built to eliminate a difficult section of line around the headland, emerging on to the banks of Howe Sound. For some miles the train runs along the banks of this beautiful sound (also on the left-hand side) past the BC Ferries terminal serving the islands. The train passes waterfalls and an old copper mine, once the largest copper mine in the British Empire and now a museum.

10:40: The train starts to climb, away from Howe Sound up into the hills. This is the most scenic part of the journey, as the train passes over several high trestle bridges along the Cheakamus Canyon with the narrow, fast-flowing river way down below.

The train passes over the top of Brandywine Falls, 195 feet (60 metres) high.

12:00: A few minutes later it arrives at Whistler station. This is in the Creekside area of Whistler, near Nita Lake. A fleet of buses meets the train and transfers passengers to their hotels in Whistler village a mile or two away.

A top tip on this route would be to request a seat on the left-hand side of the train northbound, right-hand side southbound, as both Howe Sound and the Cheakamus Canyon are on this side.

Fares and how to buy tickets

Vancouver to Whistler in Whistler Classic class costs Can$135 (£85) one-way or Can$235 (£147) return, or for a child aged 2–11 Can$70 (£45) one-way, Can$119 (£74) return; in Whistler Dome class the adult fare is Can$235 (£147) one-way or Can$335 (£209) return and the child fare Can$135 (£85) one-way,

Can\$219 (£137) return. These fares include breakfast or afternoon tea and motor coach transfers as well as train travel.

You can check times and fares, and buy tickets online, at **www.whistlermountaineer.com**. See page 473 for details of how to book by telephone.

OTHER TRAINS IN CANADA

Jasper–Prince George–Prince Rupert

The *Skeena* runs three times a week on this route, departing Wednesday, Friday and Sunday from both Jasper and Prince Rupert. It's an amazingly scenic two-day journey, the train stopping overnight at Prince George so you see it all in daylight (you will need to book a hotel separately; it's not included in the fare). Comfort class seating is available all year round, Totem class seating in panorama sightseeing cars is available mid-May to late September. There's a 'Park' lounge/observation-dome car attached at the rear, for all passengers off-season, only for Totem class passengers in peak season (May–September). For times, fares and online booking, see **www.viarail.ca**.

Winnipeg to Churchill

The *Hudson Bay* runs on this route three times a week, to the land where the polar bears live. See **www.viarail.ca**.

Montreal to Gaspé

The *Chaleur* runs three times a week, attached to the *Océan* for part of its journey (see pages 455–6). See **www.viarail.ca** for full information.

Vancouver Island: Victoria–Nanaimo–Courtenay

This is a local railcar service, the *Malahat*. It runs daily over its 140-mile (225-km) route, leaving Victoria at 08:00 Monday–Saturday, 10:00 on Sunday, returning in the afternoon. Journey time is 4 hours 45 minutes. See **www.viarail.ca**.

Toronto to North Bay and Cochrane, and Cochrane to Moosonee

There are a few long-distance train services due north out of Toronto, run by Ontario Northland, see **www.ontc.on.ca** for details.

Hearst–Oba–Saulte Sainte Marie

Algoma Central runs a three-times-a-week year-round scheduled train service on this route, plus snow train and canyon tour trains, see **www.algomacentralrailway.com**. Oba is served by VIA Rail's Toronto–Vancouver *Canadian*; see **www.viarail.ca** for connecting train times between Toronto or Vancouver and Oba.

RAILPASSES FOR CANADA

Good-value railpasses are available for Canada, worth checking out if you are planning a tour. The CanRail pass gives unlimited travel in a seat on all VIA Rail trains, including comfort class reclining seats on the *Canadian* and *Océan*. If you want a sleeper touring class or easterly class sleeper you must pay the difference between the seat price and the sleeper price. Note that even in seats on the *Canadian* and *Océan*, a seat reservation will need to be made either in advance or when you get to Canada, as you cannot hop on and travel on these trains without a reservation. Also be aware that the *Canadian* in particular can get fully booked at peak times. The passes do not cover non-VIA trains such as the Rocky Mountaineer.

CUBA

Cuba is a fantastic country to visit. You'll find Cubans very hospitable people, and Havana has to be one of the most vibrant cities in the world. It's a safe place to visit, too, unless of course you fall down one of the many potholes in the street. Cuba's rail network runs the length of the island, linking the main cities and towns – an interesting way to get around, especially if you want to travel with Cubans the way Cubans do, and not in a tourist bus. Don't expect western standards on the trains: take your own toilet paper, and allow for the odd breakdown – think of it as all part of the Cuba experience! In particular, the *Tren Francés* from Havana to Santiago is a safe, comfortable and (contrary to popular opinion) reasonably reliable way to make the trip from one end of Cuba to the other – much better than a cramped long-distance Viazul bus or a flight.

Train operator:	Ferrocarriles de Cuba. No official website, but see **www.fahrplancenter.com/ AlFFLAKubaNacionales04.html** or **www.cuba-individual.com/s_horario.htm**
Time:	GMT–5 hours (GMT–4 hours from first Sunday in April to last Sunday in October)
Currency:	Foreigners generally used to pay in US dollars, but in 2004 the Cuban government announced that US dollars would no longer be accepted. Instead, dollars, pounds or euros can be converted into 'convertible pesos' where 1 convertible peso = US$1. A 10 per cent tax applies to conversion of US dollars into convertible pesos, but not to conversion of euros or pounds sterling into pesos. Cuban citizens use 'ordinary' pesos.
Tourist information:	**www.travel2cuba.co.uk**
Visas:	UK citizens and most other western nationalities need a 'tourist card' to visit Cuba. You can get a tourist card direct from tour agencies and airlines serving Cuba, or you can buy one at Havana's José Martí airport.

GETTING TO CUBA, without flying

There are no passenger ships to Cuba, and no easy options for getting there without flying, unless you can find a suitable cruise or freighter.

TRAIN TRAVEL WITHIN CUBA

What are Cuban trains like?

Fast trains 3 and 4 between Havana and Santiago de Cuba (renumbered from trains 1 and 2 in 2007, for reasons known only to the Cubans) now use comfortable stainless-steel air-conditioned coaches bought second-hand from French Railways, and are now known accordingly as the *Tren Francés*. These coaches were originally used on the premier Trans-Europe Express (TEE) service between Paris, Brussels and Amsterdam before being replaced with high-speed Thalys trains. They were shipped to Cuba in 2001.

There are no sleeping-cars or couchettes, just seats in two classes – *primera* ('first' class) and *primera especial* ('special first' class). *Primera* is the old European second class, with vinyl padded seats two abreast on each side of the aisle. *Primera especial* is the old European first class, with much more space and fabric-covered seats arranged two abreast on one side of the aisle, one on the other side.

The train is getting a little worn and grubby, but the seats are comfortable, there is powerful air-conditioning, a café, and even piped music. A hostess looks after each coach. Bring your own toilet paper! This train is normally fairly reliable, with up to three locomotives hauling it – in fact, if the *Tren Francés* runs more than an hour late, Ferrocarriles de Cuba will refund your fare.

To quote one recent traveller, 'The journey from Havana to Santa Clara was very comfortable and there were only seven foreigners on a train full of friendly Cubans – a marked contrast to the rather grumpy "tourist only" bus network.'

Some services, such as trains 29 and 30 between Havana and Moron, are provided by railcars, either ex-Spanish Railways or stainless-steel Budd railcars bought second-hand from VIA Rail Canada. The latter are comfortable, carpeted, air-conditioned single-coach railcars with reclining seats, hostess service and refreshments.

Other trains, such as trains 7 and 8 between Havana and Santiago, consist of older cars, in many cases bought second-hand from Germany, Mexico or Japan. Although Ferrocarriles de Cuba operate overnight services, there are no sleeping-cars or sleeping accommodation of any kind – the trains just have reclining leatherette seats. These trains are an experience – don't expect them to be the cleanest or best maintained trains you will ever see!

HAVANA TO SANTIAGO DE CUBA

The timetable below shows services on the main line that runs from Havana east to Santa Clara, Camagüey and Santiago de Cuba, plus its branch lines to Sancti Spiritus, Cienfuegos, Moron, Bayamo and Guantanamo. Information on Cuban train services is difficult to confirm, so treat this as a guide and check exact times locally. The shortage of fuel in Cuba can sometimes affect buses and local trains, but these mainline trains have priority.

Havana → Santa Clara → Camagüey → Santiago de Cuba

Train number	1*	3	5	7	9	11	29
Notes	A	B	C	C	D	E	F
Havana (Estación Central)	18:20	16:30	20:30	18:45	21:40	–	17:40
Matanzas			19:00	23:01	21:24	00:24	–	19:47
Santa Clara	00:26	22:48	03:30	02:22	05:40	07:50	21:08
Cienfuegos**	|	|	|	|	|	|	|
Sancti Spiritus	|	|	|	|	08:50	|	|
Ciego de Avila	|	01:19	06:59	05:47	–	11:32	00:12
Moron	|	|	|	|	–	|	01:55
Camagüey	04:42	03:54	09:41	08:35	–	14:27	–
Bayamo	|	|	|	13:40	–	|	–
Cacocúm	|	07:19	13:59	–	–	19:17	–
Guantanamo	|	11:30	|	–	–	|	–
Santiago de Cuba	09:50	–	17:15	–	–	22:35	–

Santiago de Cuba → Camagüey → Santa Clara → Havana

Train number	2*	4	6	8	10	12	30
Notes	A	C	B	C	D	E	R
Santiago de Cuba	21.00	–	08:50	–	–	06:00	–
Guantanamo	I	11:40	I	–	–	I	–
Cacocúm	I	16:14	12:04	–	–	09:32	–
Bayamo	I	I	I	23:15	–	I	–
Camagüey	02:25	20:00	16:34	04:25	–	14:35	–
Moron	I	I	I	I	–	I	23:50
Ciego de Avila	I	21:54	19:01	06:56	–	17:19	??:??
Sancti Spiritus	I	I	I	I	16:40	I	I
Cienfuegos**	I	I	I	I	I	I	I
Santa Clara	06:38	00:35	22:37	10:38	20:17?	20:55	??:??
Matanzas	I	04:09	02:48	14:46	01:27	–	I
Havana (Estación Central)	12:15	06:30	05:15	17:20	04:05	–	08:00?

* = recommended train, see note A below.

** = it has been reported in October 2010 that there are currently no trains running to Cienfuegos.

? = estimated calling time, please check locally.

xx:xx = calling time unknown.

c = the train to/from Cienfuegos uses Havana La Coubre station, a short walk from Havana Central.

All trains, even overnight ones, only have seats. There are no couchettes or sleeping-cars in Cuba.

Note A: *Tren Francés* (the French Train). Since 2009 it's been running every third day, but you'll have to check locally which days it runs by asking at the information office or looking for posters. This is the recommended train to take, fast and reasonably reliable, using comfortable air-conditioned stainless-steel coaches with reclining seats bought second-hand from France. It offers two classes of seating, basic leatherette *primera* and quite luxurious (albeit grubby) *primera especial*.

Note B: Runs every third day, on days when the *Tren Francés* isn't running, so together trains 1/2 and 5/6 provide a Havana–Santiago service on two out of three days. However, trains 5 and 6 have much more basic passenger cars than the *Tren Francés*.

Note C: Runs every third day. *Primera* class seats only. Ask at the station to find which day it runs.

Note D: Runs every second day. *Primera* class seats only. Ask at the station to find which day it runs.

Note E: It's not clear when this runs, probably every two to three days. *Primera* class seats only.

Note R: Daily. Fast air-conditioned railcar, either Canadian or Spanish.

HAVANA TO PINAR DEL RIO

A train links Havana Central with Pinar del Rio every second day. Train 225 leaves Havana around 22:35, arriving Pinar del Rio at 04:20. Train 224 leaves Pinar del Rio at 08:45, arriving at Havana at 14:30.

FARES AND HOW TO BUY TICKETS

Foreigners pay higher fares than Cubans. Foreigners used to have to pay in US dollars, but since November 2004 US dollars are no longer accepted in Cuba and foreigners pay train fares in 'convertible pesos'. (Convertible pesos can be bought with pounds sterling or euros at the equivalent rate of 1 convertible peso = US$1, so 1 convertible peso = approx. £0.67. If you use US dollars to buy the convertible pesos a 10 per cent tax is levied on the transaction, making the de facto rate 1 convertible peso = US$1.10.)

One-way fares for foreigners, in convertible pesos		
Havana to Santiago de Cuba on train 3 or 4 (*Tren Francés*)	in *primera especial*	62 (£42 or $69)
	in *primera*	50 (£34 or $56)
Havana to Santiago de Cuba on train 7 or 8	in *primera*	30 (£20 or $33)
Havana to Sancti Spiritus	in *primera*	14 (£9 or $16)
Havana to Moron	in *primera*	24 (£16 or $27)
Havana to Pinar del Rio	in *primera*	7 (£5 or $8)
Havana to Bayamo/Manzanillo	in *primera*	26 (£17 or $29)
Havana to Guantanamo	in *primera*	32 (£21 or $36)

Children aged 0–4 travel free, children aged 5–11 travel at half fare, children aged 12 and over pay full fare.

Foreign visitors can buy train tickets at the special LADIS booking office on the side of Havana Estación Central. At other stations, you can book at the normal ticket office. It's best to book a day or two in advance if you can.

HAVANA TO HERSHEY AND MATANZAS, by the Hershey Railway

An electric railcar runs on a railway originally built by the Hershey Corporation (the chocolate company) from Havana (Casablanca station, across the harbour from Havana itself) to Hershey and Matanzas. To reach Havana Casablanca station, take the ferry across the harbour from the foot of Santa Clara Street in Havana old town. Once on the other side, Casablanca station is immediately west of the ferry dock, looking more like a tram stop than a conventional station, so just follow the overhead electric wires along the street. In Matanzas, the Hershey railway station is about 2 km from Matanzas mainline station. Foreigners pay their fares in convertible pesos; Havana to Hershey is about 1.50 pesos (£1 or $1.70), Havana to Matanzas about 2.8 pesos (£1.90 or $3.10). Tickets go on sale one hour before departure. The timetable changes every so often, so always double-check train times locally.

Havana → Hershey → Matanzas

Havana (Casablanca)	06:11	12:27	17:51
Hershey	07:46	14:00	19:18
Matanzas	10:10	16:24	21:52

Matanzas → Hershey → Havana

Matanzas	05:16	11:30	16:54
Hershey	07:46	14:00	19:28
Havana (Casablanca)	09:17	15:27	20:55

PERU

Peru's great tourist attraction is the ruined Inca city at Machu Picchu, and naturally you'll find a train to take you there. In fact, you'll find several different trains heading from Cusco to Machu Picchu in the morning and back in the late afternoon, all run by PeruRail and aimed at different budgets, from the Backpacker service to the deluxe *Hiram Bingham*. If you want to explore Peru further by train, PeruRail also run a service from Cusco to Lake Titicaca, and there is also the *Tren de Sierra* in the north, between Lima and Huancayo, run by the Ferrocarril Central.

Train operators:	PeruRail, **www.perurail.com** (trains to Machu Picchu and Lake Titicaca) Ferrocarril Central, **www.ferrocarrilcentral.com.pe** (Lima–Huancayo)
Time:	GMT–5
Currency:	£1 = approx. 4.35 nuevos soles, $1 = approx. 2.84 nuevos soles
Tourist information:	**www.peru.info**
Visas:	UK, US, Canadian, Australian, NZ and most EU citizens do not need a visa to visit Peru for up to 90 days.

EUROPE TO PERU, without flying

There are no passenger ships between Europe and South America, so there are no easy options for getting to Peru without flying, unless you can find a suitable cruise ship or freighter. For cruise and freighter travel, try Strand Travel (**www.strandtravelltd.co.uk**, telephone +44 (0)20 7921 4340).

TRAIN TRAVEL WITHIN PERU

Once you are in Peru, there are several train services of interest to visitors, including the famous train to Machu Picchu. There are two separate networks:

- The southern network, including Cusco to Machu Picchu and Cusco to Puno (Lake Titicaca), is run by a western company called PeruRail (**www.perurail.com**), part of the Venice Simplon Orient Express group.

- The northern network links Lima with Huancayo.

TRAINS TO MACHU PICCHU

There are four different trains from the northern city of Cusco to the Inca citadel at Machu Picchu every day, all run by PeruRail, **www.perurail.com**, part of the Venice Simplon Orient Express group which took over operation of this network from the Peruvian railway company ENAFER in 1999. Three of the four trains are aimed at tourists, each serving a different market:

The *Hiram Bingham*: This is the luxury option, from around £222 or $334 each way per person, including gourmet meals, cocktails, entertainment, bus connections and entrance to the Machu Picchu citadel plus guided tour. It departs daily at 09:10, arriving at Machu Picchu at 13:09; on the return journey it departs Machu Picchu at 18:07, arriving back at Poroy (the station for Cusco – see below) at 21:59.

The **Vistadome:** The mid-range option, costing around £47 or $71 each way per person, including complimentary snacks and non-alcoholic drinks served at your seat. It's a series of diesel railcars with panoramic windows, as its name suggests. It departs daily at 06:53, arriving at Machu Picchu at 10:38; it then leaves Machu Picchu at 16:00, and arrives back at Poroy at 19:42.

The **Expedition** (formerly known as the Backpacker): The budget option, from around £32 or $48 each way per person. It has basic but reasonably comfortable seating and a buffet car where you can buy non-alcoholic drinks and snacks. It departs daily at 07:42, arriving at Machu Picchu at 10:51; from Machu Picchu it departs at 17:03, arriving back at Poroy at 21:01.

The Local: A subsidised train service for the local Peruvian communities and (at certain times of year) Peruvian citizens only, leaving Cusco for Machu Picchu at 07:15.

In addition, there are extra shuttle trains between Sacred Valley (Ollantaytambo) and Machu Picchu at intervals through the day – see **www.perurail.com**.

The Vistadome and Backpacker trains used to leave from Cusco's main San Pedro station on the Avenida Sol and spent half an hour in a scenic but slow zigzag climb up the mountainside. However, as of 2009 all tourist trains leave from Poroy station, a local halt situated 13 kilometres (8 miles) west of Cusco, so miss this interesting section. To get to Poroy from Cusco takes about 20 minutes by taxi; a 3-seat taxi from Cusco to Poroy costs around 20–30 soles (£5–£7 or $7–$11) per taxi. There's also a bus, fare 6 soles (£1.50 or $2) per person.

After Poroy the train descends into the Sacred Valley and the Andean foothills, along the Urubamba River. You'll pass colourful villages and herds of llamas.

The station at Machu Picchu is in fact called Aguas Calientes, and is 8 km (5 miles) from the ruined Inca city itself. A bus link runs every 30 minutes from the station to the ruins, costing $10 (£7) return; the fare can be paid in US dollars or the local currency.

Useful links for the Inca site at Machu Picchu are **www.peru-machu-picchu.com**, **www.machupicchu.org**.

You can book the three tourist-orientated trains online at **www.perurail.com**.

CUSCO TO PUNO (LAKE TITICACA)

PeruRail also run the *Andean Explorer* three times each week from Cusco to Puno on Lake Titicaca, 385 kilometres in a 10-hour scenic daytime journey, fares from £95 or $143 per person. The train departs Cusco at 08:00 on Monday, Wednesday and Saturday. In the other direction it departs Puno at 08:00 on Monday, Wednesday and Saturday. See **www.perurail.com** for times, fares and online booking.

LIMA TO HUANCAYO

The air-conditioned *Tren de Sierra* links Lima and Huancayo once or twice a month, with *touristico* (first) class and *clásico* (second) class and bar car. *Touristico* fares (around 160–200 soles or £37–£46) include breakfast and complimentary tea, coffee, water and soft drinks. *Clásico* fares start at 100 soles (£23). You can check departure dates and book tickets online at **www.ferrocarrilcentral.com.pe**. In Lima, the train departs from either Desamparados or Monserrate station. Twice-daily trains link Huancayo with Huancavelica.

UNITED STATES

There are planes, of course, but you'll see nothing of America at 35,000 feet. And there are long-distance buses, but do you want to spend whole days on a bus? In fact, the USA has an excellent rail network, and although it's a skeleton network by European standards, it'll take you to most of the towns and cities a traveller is likely to visit. It'll even take you from coast to coast in comfort, by any one of half a dozen different routes, at remarkably affordable prices, through world-class scenery. And from the 'All aboard!' of the conductor to the plaintive wooooo, wooooo of the diesel locomotive as your train speeds across the prairie or winds its way along a Colorado canyon, the trains reflect America's great railroading tradition.

Train operator:	Amtrak, **www.amtrak.com**
Trans-Atlantic sea travel:	Cunard, **www.cunard.com**, telephone 0845 678 0013 Strand Travel, **www.strandtravelltd.co.uk**, telephone +44 (0)20 7921 4340
Time:	New York: GMT–5, Chicago: GMT–6, Los Angeles: GMT–8. Clocks go forward 1 hour from second Sunday in March to first Sunday in November.
Currency:	£1 = approx. 1.50 US dollars
Tourist information:	Each state has its own tourist agency, see **www.towd.com**
Visas:	UK and EU citizens must go to the US State Department ESTA website at **https://esta.cbp.dhs.gov** to obtain 'pre-approval' to visit the USA under the visa waiver system. Originally free of charge, a small $14 (£9) charge will be made as from late 2010.

EUROPE TO THE UNITED STATES, without flying

Southampton to New York, by scheduled trans-Atlantic liner service

Even in this day and age, Cunard maintains a scheduled trans-Atlantic passenger ship service linking the United States with Europe, with sailings from Southampton to New York at least once a month between April or May and November. It needn't cost much more than a business class airfare, and this includes seven nights' accommodation and all meals. You'll travel aboard the greatest liner of them all, Cunard's *Queen Mary 2*, and it really is the only way to arrive in New York.

Fares for two people sharing the cheapest Britannia class stateroom start at around £1,145 per person one-way, £2,290 per person round trip, with children going for around £470 each way. However, prices vary enormously according to sailing date and cabin grade. You can sometimes find special offers from as little as £769 one-way. Naturally, for the millionaires amongst us there are more luxurious suites, costing tens of thousands.

The *QM2* sails from one of four possible cruise terminals in Southampton docks (but no longer from the historic Ocean Terminal where the original *Queen Mary* and the *Titanic* would have sailed) at 17:00. Check-in is from 13:00 to around 15:45. The crossing lasts seven nights (a handful of crossings take only six nights), arriving in New York's Brooklyn cruise terminal bright and early at 07:00. You'll need to be on deck from about 04:30 to enjoy the complete approach to New York. And yes, it's a 'crossing' not a 'cruise', and feels like a real journey, with many passengers using it as a genuine form of transport.

Sailings from Southampton are scheduled in 2011 for 10 May, 3 June, 24 June, 20 July, 15 August, 29 August, 20 September, 16 October, 10 November, 12 December.

Sailings from New York are scheduled in 2011 for 26 April, 17 May, 10 June, 6 July, 27 July, 22 August, 5 September, 7 October, 23 October, 17 November. The ship normally sails from New York at 17:00 and arrives in Southampton at 06:30 seven nights later, although the odd sailing takes only six nights.

The last complete trans-Atlantic season for the 1967-built *Queen Elizabeth 2* was 2003. The brand-new *Queen Mary 2* took over the trans-Atlantic sailings from 2004.

You can check sailing dates, times and fares and book online at **www.cunard.com**. To check prices and book tickets in the UK, call Cunard on 0845 678 0013. In the USA or Canada, call 1-800-7-CUNARD. You can often find slightly cheaper fares from a cruise retailer. Try Iglu Cruise, **www.iglucruise.com**, 020 8544 7182; **www.cruise.co.uk** on 0800 408 6200; **www.cruisedirect.co.uk** on 0800 093 0622; or Strand Travel, **www.strandtravelltd.co.uk**, on 020 7921 4340. For the train service to and from Southampton, see **www.nationalrail.co.uk**.

Europe to the USA, by passenger-carrying freighter

In addition to Cunard's *QM2*, some regular freight ships carry a limited number of passengers, and there are occasional crossings by other cruise lines. UK agencies listing both freighter and cruise line voyages are Strand Travel (**www.strandtravelltd.co.uk**, telephone +44 (0)20 7921 4340) and **www.cruisepeople.co.uk**. A US agency booking passenger travel by freighter is **www.freightercruises.com**. Also try **www.freightertrips.com**.

TRAIN TRAVEL WITHIN THE UNITED STATES

Long-distance and intercity trains in the USA are operated by the National Railroad Passenger Corporation, more commonly known as Amtrak, and it's easy to check Amtrak schedules online at **www.amtrak.com**. It's impossible to list all trains here, but you can usually assume there is one train per day on each of the long trans-continental routes within the US shown on the map on page 446. Two notable exceptions are the New Orleans to Los Angeles *Sunset Limited*, which runs only three times a week, and the New York to Florida service, which has two or three trains per day. A more frequent intercity style service connects Boston, New York and Washington (and the cities in between), see page 492; and similar services run between the cities of California (see page 499), between Chicago and Milwaukee, and between Seattle and Portland.

WHAT ARE AMTRAK TRAINS LIKE?

Short-distance trains come in various types, all with comfortable air-conditioned seating and often with a café car. On the Boston–New York–Washington DC route there is now the premium-fare, 150mph Acela Express high-speed train, based on French TGV technology, but running on conventional tracks.

Long-distance trains east of Chicago, such as the New York–Chicago *Lake Shore Limited*, the New York to Florida *Silver Star* and *Silver Meteor* or the New York to New Orleans *Crescent* (but not the Washington to Chicago *Capitol Limited*), have Viewliner sleeping-cars (see the sleeper section below), Amfleet or Horizon reclining seat cars, an Amfleet lounge car serving snacks and drinks, and a 'heritage' restaurant car serving full meals at reasonable prices. If you have paid for a sleeper, all meals are included in the fare.

Long-distance trains west and south of Chicago (plus the Washington DC–Chicago *Capitol Limited*) use double-deck Superliner cars. Superliner trains have reclining seats, sleeping-cars, a dining car and an observation-lounge car. Reclining seats are spacious with lots of legroom, comparable to business class on an airliner. They recline to about 40 degrees, and are quite easy to sleep in. Pillows are provided at night, and you can either bring a blanket or buy an Amtrak blanket from the lounge car. Sleeping-cars are described below. The Superliner observation lounge is the social centre of the train, with a café downstairs and a large lounge with huge side and roof windows giving an unparalleled view of the scenery. Seats in the observation lounge are open to both reclining seat and sleeping-car passengers on a first come, first served basis. The dining car serves full meals at affordable prices – if you have paid for a sleeper, meals are included in the fare. A route guide is available free on these trains, telling you what to look out for along the way.

Travelling by sleeping-car

Travelling by Amtrak sleeper is a real treat. All sleeper passengers get complimentary meals in the dining car, morning tea or coffee and fruit juice when you wake up, shoeshine service, and complimentary newspapers. You return from dinner in the diner to find your bed made up for the night by the sleeper attendant. Hot showers are available, either at the end of the corridor if you're travelling in a roomette, or en suite if you are travelling in a bedroom. However, sleeper travel isn't cheap. In Europe you can pay a small supplement for a berth in a shared couchette or sleeper compartment. In the US, you have to pay for the whole room whether there are two of you or just one. To give you a rough idea, some sample sleeper supplements are shown in the fares section on page 500.

Viewliner sleeping-cars

Viewliner sleeping-cars operate on long-distance trains in the east. The distinctive double row of windows on these cars makes them light and airy during the day, and gives both upper and lower berths a window for star-gazing at night. Viewliners have three types of accommodation:

> **Roomettes** (formerly known as standard bedrooms): Very compact sleeper compartments just big enough for two seats facing each other which convert at night to an upper and lower berth – the beds take up most of the room. Rooms have a washbasin, toilet (your companion will have to leave the room while you use it), fold-out table and LCD video screen. There is a shower for roomette passengers at the end of the corridor.

> **Bedrooms** (formerly known as deluxe bedrooms): Much larger than roomettes, with an en suite shower and toilet. Bedrooms have freestanding chair and sofa in daytime mode, and upper and lower berths at night. The lower berth is extra wide, almost a double bed by UK standards!

> **Special bedrooms:** Similar to a bedroom, with private shower and toilet, but fully wheelchair-accessible.

Superliner sleeping-cars

Superliner sleeping-cars operate on Amtrak's long-distance trains west and south of Chicago, also on the Washington DC–Chicago *Capitol Limited*. These massive double-deck cars have bedrooms on both upper and lower levels. They offer four types of accommodation:

Roomettes (formerly known as standard bedrooms): Compartments just big enough for two seats facing each other across a small table by day, and two berths at night. Toilets are available along the corridor and there's a shower cubicle on the lower deck. There are ten roomettes on the upper level and four downstairs.

Bedrooms (formerly known as deluxe bedrooms): Much larger than roomettes, with an en suite shower and toilet. All five bedrooms in each car are on the upper level. Bedrooms have freestanding chair and sofa in daytime mode, and upper and lower berths at night. As in the Viewliner bedrooms, the lower berth is extra wide.

Family bedroom: Located at one end of the lower level, taking up the full width of the car, the family bedroom has two adult beds and two child beds. There is no shower or toilet in a family bedroom, but these are nearby outside the room.

Special bedroom: Located at the other end of the lower level, also taking up the full width of the car, the special bedroom is wheelchair-accessible, with two berths. There is no shower in a Superliner special bedroom.

BOSTON–NEW YORK–WASHINGTON

A fast and frequent intercity service links Boston, New York, Newark, Philadelphia, Baltimore and Washington DC. New York to Washington takes as little as 2 hours 48 minutes, New York to Boston just 3 hours 30 minutes. There are two types of train: premium-fare Acela Express 150mph high-speed trains with first class and business class, and regular North East

Regional trains with coach class and (in most cases) business class.

There are also connecting train services from Boston to Portland (Maine) and from Philadelphia to Harrisburg. See **www.amtrak.com** for times, fares and online booking.

CROSSING THE USA, by train, coast to coast

The 3,000-mile (4,800-km) journey across the United States by train is one of the world's great travel experiences. It is easy, comfortable, safe, and an affordable alternative to flying. In fact, the fare from New York to Los Angeles or San Francisco starts at an amazing $193 (£129) in a reclining seat if you book online at **www.amtrak.com**. There is a choice of half a dozen different coast-to-coast routes. Free route guides are available on board each train, telling you what to look out for along the way, and the scenery on many routes is absolutely world class.

If you make the whole journey in one go it will take three nights: one night from New York, Boston or Washington to Chicago, where you must change trains, then two nights from Chicago to Los Angeles, San Francisco or Seattle. You can also travel coast to coast via New Orleans, although this takes an extra night as you need to stay overnight in New Orleans. Below is a summary of coast-to-coast train times and a brief description of each train. Bear in mind that these trains run for over 2,000 miles and can arrive several hours late, so don't book any tight connections at the other end. You can see how your chosen trains have performed for punctuality over the last three weeks using **www.amtrakdelays.com**. This will give you a good idea of what to expect!

Which coast-to-coast route to choose?

All the trans-continental routes are scenic, and all have their own character. But if you have a choice, one particular route stands out as the most spectacular for both scenery and US historical significance. This is the *California Zephyr* from Chicago to San Francisco, in connection with either the *Lake Shore Limited* from New York or Boston to Chicago or the *Capitol Limited* from Washington DC to Chicago. The *California Zephyr's* route is one of the world's greatest train journeys, and in around 48 hours you will cross the farmlands of Nebraska, scale the Rockies beyond Denver while you eat ham and eggs for breakfast in the diner, snake through rocky river valleys in Colorado and pass through the Sierra Nevada mountains to reach Reno, Sacramento and the San Francisco Bay area. The route covers much of the very first historic trans-continental railroad route, and there's a commentary for the most significant section.

However, the other routes have great scenery too. The *Southwest Chief*, for example, will take you from Chicago to Los Angeles over the famous Santa Fe railroad, alongside the equally famous Route 66, through Navajo Indian country – another amazing trip.

Coast to coast by train via Chicago, westbound

All trains run daily			*Lake Shore Limited*	*Lake Shore Limited*	*Capitol Limited*	
New York (Penn Station)	depart	day 1	15:45	–	–	–
Boston	depart	day 1	I	11:55	–	–
Washington DC	depart	day 1	I	I	16:05	–
Chicago (Union Station)	arrive	day 2	09:45	09:45	08:45	–
Change trains in Chicago and take whichever onward train you want . . .						

All trains run daily			*Empire Builder*	*California Zephyr*	*Southwest Chief*	*Texas Eagle*
Chicago (Union Station)	depart	day 2	14:15	14:00	15:15	13:45
Portland	arrive	day 4	10:10	I	I	I
Seattle	arrive	day 4	10:25	I	I	I
Dallas	arrive	day 3	–	I	I	11:30
Denver	arrive	day 3	–	07:15	I	I
Salt Lake City	arrive	day 3	–	23:05	I	I
San Francisco (Emeryville*)	arrive	day 4	–	16:10	I	I
Flagstaff (for Grand Canyon)	arrive	day 3	–	–	20:57	I
Los Angeles	arrive	day 4	–	–	08:15	08:30**

sleeping-cars, reclining seats, observation lounge, café and dining-car

Coast to coast by train via Chicago, eastbound

All trains run daily			Empire Builder	California Zephyr	Southwest Chief	Texas Eagle
Los Angeles	depart	day 1	–	–	18:55	14:40**
Flagstaff (for Grand Canyon)	depart	day 2	–	–	05:21	│
San Francisco (Emeryville)	depart	day 1	–	09:50	│	│
Salt Lake City	depart	day 2	–	04:10	│	│
Denver	depart	day 2	–	19:50	│	│
Dallas	depart	day 2	–	│	│	15:40
Seattle	depart	day 1	16:40	│	│	│
Portland	depart	day 1	16:45	│	│	│
Chicago (Union Station)	arrive	day 3	15:55	15:30	15:10	13:52

Change trains in Chicago and take whichever onward train you want . . .

All trains run daily			Capitol Limited	Lake Shore Limited	Lake Shore Limited	–
Chicago (Union Station)	depart	day 3	18:40	21:30	21:30	–
Washington DC	arrive	day 4	13:10	│	│	–
Boston	arrive	day 4	–	21:10	│	–
New York (Penn Station)	arrive	day 4	–	–	18:25	–

* The *California Zephyr* westbound calls at Oakland, then terminates in Emeryville. An 'Amtrak Thruway' bus transfers passengers across the Bay Bridge between Emeryville and San Francisco proper.

** The *Texas Eagle* is extended to run to and from Los Angeles only, on three days a week (Tue, Thur and Sun from Chicago, Wed, Fri and Sun from Los Angeles). It takes a day longer than the more direct *Southwest Chief*, so in the westbound direction, arrival in Los Angeles is on day 5 from New York, not day 4. Departure in the eastbound direction also needs to be a day earlier if you take this train, on day '0' rather than day 1.

Treat these times as just a guide – always check times and fares at **www.amtrak.com** as they change from time to time.

The trains:

Capitol Limited: Washington DC–Chicago daily (764 miles/1,222 km, one night). Superliner train with sleeping-cars, reclining seats, observation lounge, café and dining-car.

California Zephyr: Chicago–San Francisco daily (2,438 miles/3,901 km, two nights). Superliner train with sleeping-cars, reclining seats, observation lounge, café and dining-car. This is one of the great train rides of the world, and if you are planning a coast-to-coast trip, this is the best route to take. The train actually starts/finishes in Emeryville, Oakland, just across the Bay Bridge from San Francisco proper. There is an Amtrak bus transfer between central San Francisco and Emeryville.

Empire Builder: Chicago–Seattle/Portland (2,206 miles/3,530 km Chicago–Seattle, two nights). Superliner train with sleeping-cars, reclining seats, observation lounge, café and dining-car. This train winds its way past Glacier National Park and through the mountains of Washington state.

Lake Shore Limited: New York–Chicago daily (959 miles/1,534 km, one night), with through cars Boston–Chicago daily. Amfleet coaches, Viewliner sleeping-cars, Amfleet lounge-café, heritage dining-car. This train takes the scenic route up the Hudson River out of New York, with the train tracks running right alongside the river, past Storm King Mountain and West Point Military Academy. Try to get a seat on the left-hand side of the train out of New York, right-hand side heading to New York.

Southwest Chief: Chicago–Los Angeles (2,256 miles/3,610 km, two nights). Superliner train with sleeping-cars, reclining seats, observation lounge, café and dining-car. This train mostly travels via the Santa Fe railroad, once used by the famous Chicago–Los Angeles *Super Chief*, the film stars' favourite. It will take you through Apache Canyon and right through Navajo Indian country, with a live commentary from an Indian guide over the train's public address system for the relevant section of line. The train serves Flagstaff, which is one hour by connecting bus from the Grand Canyon, with day tours available.

Texas Eagle: Runs daily Chicago–Dallas–San Antonio, but only three times a week between Chicago and Los Angeles (westbound from Chicago on Tuesday, Thursday and Sunday, eastbound from LA on Wednesday, Friday and Sunday). Superliner train with sleeping-cars, reclining seats, observation lounge, café and dining-car. (2,728 miles/4,365 km Chicago–LA, 3 nights.)

Coast to coast by train via New Orleans, westbound

Runs daily			Crescent
New York (Penn Station)	depart	day 1	14:15
Washington DC	depart	day 1	18:30
Atlanta	arrive	day 2	08:13
New Orleans	arrive	day 2	19:38
Change trains and overnight stop . . .			

Runs on Mon, Wed, Fri only			*Sunset Limited*
New Orleans	depart	day 3	11:55
Houston	arrive	day 3	21:50
San Antonio	arrive	day 4	03:00
El Paso	arrive	day 4	16:15
Los Angeles	arrive	day 5	08:30

Coast to coast by train via New Orleans, eastbound

Runs on Wed, Fri, Sun only			*Sunset Limited*
Los Angeles	depart	day 1	14:40
El Paso	depart	day 2	08:15
San Antonio	depart	day 2	23:55
Houston	depart	day 3	06:15
New Orleans	arrive	day 3	14:55
Change trains and overnight stop . . .			

Runs daily			*Crescent*
New Orleans	depart	day 4	07:05
Atlanta	depart	day 4	20:21
Washington DC	arrive	day 5	10:10
New York (Penn Station)	arrive	day 5	14:02

The trains:

Crescent: New York–New Orleans daily (1,377 miles/2,203 km, one night). Amfleet reclining seats, Viewliner sleeping-cars, Amfleet lounge-café, heritage dining-car.

Sunset Limited: Three times weekly New Orleans–Los Angeles (1,995 miles/3,192 km, two nights). Superliner train with sleeping-cars, reclining seats, observation lounge, café and dining-car.

NEW YORK TO NIAGARA FALLS

Three daily trains link New York via Albany with Niagara Falls. Journey time is a leisurely 8 hours 30 minutes, a relaxing journey along the Hudson River Valley out of New York, past Storm King Mountain and West Point Military Academy – a very scenic route, highly recommended. See **www.amtrak.com** for times, fares and online booking.

NEW YORK TO TORONTO AND MONTREAL (CANADA)

A daily train (the *Maple Leaf*) links New York with Toronto via Niagara Falls, and another daily train (the *Adirondack*) links New York with Montreal via the scenic Adirondack mountains. Both trains travel along the Hudson River Valley out of New York, past Storm King Mountain and West Point Military Academy – a very scenic route, highly recommended. See the Canada chapter, page 449, for train times.

NEW YORK AND WASHINGTON TO FLORIDA

New York → Miami

Both trains run daily			Silver Star	Silver Meteor
New York	depart	day 1	10:52	15:15
Washington DC	depart	day 1	15:00	19:30
Jacksonville	arrive	day 2	06:55	09:23
Orlando	arrive	day 2	10:31	13:10
Tampa	arrive	day 2	12:45	I
Ft Lauderdale	arrive	day 2	17:12	18:02
Miami	arrive	day 2	18:05	18:55

Miami → New York

Both trains run daily			*Silver Meteor*	*Silver Star*
Miami	depart	day 1	08:40	11:50
Ft Lauderdale	depart	day 1	09:20	12:30
Tampa	depart	day 1	I	17:17
Orlando	depart	day 1	13:57	19:24
Jacksonville	depart	day 1	17:33	22:57
Washington DC	arrive	day 2	07:46	15:14
New York	arrive	day 2	11:36	19:16

Silver Meteor: Daily. Amfleet reclining seats, Viewliner sleeping-car, dining-car.

Silver Star: Daily. Amfleet reclining seats, Viewliner sleeping-car, dining-car.

INTERCITY TRAINS IN CALIFORNIA

Regular trains link Los Angeles, Anaheim (for Disneyland) and San Diego. Regular trains link San Francisco (Oakland) with Sacramento, Bakersfield and San Jose. A daily train, the *Coast Starlight*, links Los Angeles with San Francisco (or rather, with Oakland across the bay) and Seattle. See **www.amtrak.com** for times, fares and online booking.

AMTRAK FARES

It's easy to check fares at **www.amtrak.com**: just click 'Reservations'. The table overleaf shows some sample fares to give you an idea of cost. (3,000 miles coast-to-coast overland for as little as £131/$197 has to be one of the world's greatest travel bargains!)

Normal one-way fares	Basic fare for a reclining seat (per person)	Supplement for a 'roomette' (per 2-bed room)	Supplement for a 'bedroom' (per 2-bed room)
New York to Los Angeles or San Francisco	$197 (£132)	$490–$880 (£328–£590)	$800–$1400 (£536–£938)
New York to Chicago	$86 (£58)	$188–$450 (126–£301)	$550–$700 (£368–£469)
New York to Washington DC (normal train)	$49 (£33)	–	–
New York to Washington DC (150mph Acela Express)	$135 (£90)	–	–
New York to Boston	$49 (£33)	–	–
New York to Miami	$122 (£82)	$202–$350 (£135–£234)	$498–$750 (£334–£500)
New York to New Orleans	$128 (£86)	$182–$360 (£122–£240)	$335–$700 (£224–£469)
New York to Montreal	$62 (£42)	–	–
New York to Toronto	$105 (£70)	–	–
Chicago to Los Angeles or San Francisco	$146 (£98)	$301–$600 (£200–£400)	$617–$900 (£411–£600)

Children 2–15 (inclusive) travel at reduced fare; children under 2 travel free (limit one child under 2 per adult).

Return fares are twice the one-way fare.

For sleeper travel, you add the basic seat fare for each passenger to one sleeper supplement for the whole room. Sleeper supplements are per room per journey, not per person, so you pay one supplement for the room whether two of you occupy it or just one, in addition to a basic coach fare (or railpass) for each passenger. Sleeper supplements vary enormously by season and in accordance with demand, which is why a range is shown. The sleeper supplements include all meals in the dining car, morning tea or coffee and fruit juice and various other first class privileges. Roomettes are very small 1- or 2-berth rooms; bedrooms are larger 2-berth rooms with en suite shower and toilet.

HOW TO BUY TICKETS

If you live outside the United States, you can buy tickets online at **www.amtrak.com**, or by telephone to Amtrak's 24-hour number (001) 215 856 7953. You pick up the tickets at the station before departure, either from the staffed ticket office or from the self-service ticket machines. You simply pass the barcode on your booking printout under the machine's scanner, confirm the journey details and it will print out your tickets.

When you're in the United States, you can book online at **www.amtrak.com**, or you can call Amtrak 24 hours a day on 1-800-USA RAIL, picking up your tickets at the station on departure.

RAILPASSES

One of the best ways to see America is with an Amtrak USA railpass, as long as you are aware of its limitations.

- A 15-day (maximum 8-segment) railpass costs $389 (£259).

- A 30-day (maximum 12-segment) railpass costs $579 (£386).

- A 45-day (maximum 18-segment) railpass costs $749 (£600).

- Children aged 2–15 get passes for half price; children under 2 travel free.

- Unfortunately, the USA railpass no longer gives unlimited travel. 'Maximum 8-segment' (or 12- or 18-segment) refers to the maximum number of individual train rides you can take during your 15-, 30- or 45-day pass duration. A 2-day 1,500-mile train trip counts as one segment; so does a 30-minute 30-mile one. A journey involving a change of train counts as 2 segments.

- Railpasses are valid for any Amtrak train in the USA except Acela Express high-speed services and the Auto-Train car-carrying service.

- If you want to travel in a sleeping-car room, you need to pay the relevant room charge in addition to your railpass. For an idea of sleeper room charges, see the fares table on page 500.

- Reservations are required: the railpass is not a ticket; you must make a (free) reservation before boarding any train. You can make reservations as you travel around the States at stations or by calling Amtrak's 24-hour freephone number, 1-800-USA RAIL. Alternatively, you can make some or all of your reservations in advance from outside the States by calling Amtrak on (001) 215 856 7953.

- Although in theory you can make a reservation even on the day of travel, trans-continental trains get busy in summer and at Thanksgiving, for example, and pass holder places are limited by quota. The quota for railpass holders is reportedly set to zero when a train becomes 75 per cent full, so you might find trains 'full' for railpass holders, when seats remain available for customers paying cash. You will have a better chance of securing reservations if you book several days in advance. Bear this in mind if you have a specific itinerary.

OTHER COUNTRIES IN CENTRAL AND SOUTH AMERICA

TRAVELLING TO CENTRAL OR SOUTH AMERICA, without flying

There are no regular passenger ships between Europe and South America, though it's possible to get there by passenger-carrying freighter or the occasional cruise. Try Strand Travel, **www.strandtravelltd.co.uk**, +44 (0)20 7921 4340.

TRAIN TRAVEL AROUND CENTRAL AND SOUTH AMERICA

Unlike Europe or even parts of Asia and Africa, Central and South America do not have a developed international rail network. International train services are almost non-existent, and most journeys must be made by long-distance bus or plane. However, there are various domestic train routes within some South American countries that are of interest to travellers. Here's a summary by country.

TRAIN TRAVEL WITHIN ARGENTINA

There are intercity services on quite a number of routes, run by various different operators. Trains in Argentina are experiencing something of a revival, since the government intends to re-establish long-distance passenger trains between all major cities. For information, see **www.sateliteferroviario.com.ar/horarios/** (in Spanish only), which has information on all Argentinian train services.

One of the largest operators is Ferrobaires, **www.ferrobaires.gba.gov.ar**, which runs the trains south from Buenos Aires to cities such as Mar del Plata and Bahia Blanca. Their site is in Spanish only, but click 'Horarios y Tarifas' for fares and timetables, 'Destinos' for a route map, and get help from Google translate, **www.google.co.uk/language_tools?hl=en**.

The *Train to the Clouds* (*El Tren a las Nubes*) is a tourist service from Salta in northern Argentina, see **www.trenalasnubes.com.ar**.

TRAIN TRAVEL WITHIN BOLIVIA

There are a few train services in Bolivia, operated by two train companies, eastern (**www.ferroviariaoriental.com**) and western (**www.fca.com.bo**). The western network is more tourist-orientated, with trains from Oruro to Tupiza. There are two types of train, the *expresso* and WaraWara (the slower train makes more stops). There are three or four classes, *ejecutivo* being the best. It can get very cold in the train, with trips in both directions mainly made at night.

There is also a working branch line to Calama in Chile, but this runs only rarely – perhaps once a week. The main line from Oruro to Tupiza runs almost daily.

In the east of Bolivia, the rail hub is Santa Cruz, and trains go east to the Brazilian border and south to the Argentine border. There is a train every day from Santa Cruz east to Puerto Suarez. However, it is a mix of services. There is a normal train that locals use, which takes the longest. There is an express train. And there is an expensive and fast *ferrobus*, which is a modern railcar, fare about 150 bolivianos (£14 or $21) per person. Different services go on different days but every day there is some service eastbound. Tickets can only be bought on the day of departure at the train ticket counter (train and bus stations are together); this opens at 08:00 but the queue starts to form earlier. The service south to Villamontes has similar service and a complicated schedule and goes almost every day. The train is comfortable and for the eastbound journey pretty much the only way to go overland. There is no website or any other way of getting information in advance: you just find things out when you arrive in Santa Cruz.

TRAIN TRAVEL WITHIN BRAZIL

Vitoria to Belo Horizonte

Intercity train services operate on one route, from Vitoria to Belo Horizonte. This train is cheaper and more comfortable than a bus. It leaves daily at 07:00 from Vitoria and at 07:30 from Belo Horizonte, arriving at its destination around 19:30–20:00. The train has two classes: *executivo* is the better, with air-conditioning and aircraft-style seating with a decent amount of legroom; fare 70 reals (£25); the more basic is *econômica*, which costs 46 reals (£16). There's a restaurant car, although the food does not get good reports. Operated by the most prosperous freight railway in Brazil, the route is very scenic and it's a pleasant way to spend a day. The train information part of their website is **www.vale.com/vale_us/cgi/cgilua.exe/sys/start.htm?infoid=152&sid=66** (the English version appears to omit the train information, so stick with Portuguese and remember that *preços* is 'prices' and *horarios* means 'timetables').

The other operating train is a tourist-orientated steam train, but it offers transport between two important Brazilian tourist towns, São João del Rei and Tiradentes. The steam train makes a nice alternative to the bus. The trip takes an hour and is about 20 km. The train runs daily, leaving São João del Rei at 10:00 and returning in the afternoon. The train ticket gives free entry to the train museum at the station in São João del Rei. Information can be found at **www.antt.gov.br/destaques/anexos/TremDelreiTiradentes.htm**.

There is now no train service at all between Rio de Janeiro and São Paulo. There's a list of all Brazilian train services (regular and tourist-orientated) at **www.antt.gov.br/destaques/TrensDePassageiros.asp**.

TRAIN TRAVEL WITHIN CHILE

The Chilean state railways official website (in Spanish only) is **www.efe.cl**. Seven 'Terrasur' trains per day on weekdays, four at weekends, link Santiago (Alamada station) with Curicó, Talca, Linares and Chillán on the electrified main line. The trains are air-conditioned, one class only, and have a refreshment car. Three of these trains have a bus connection from Chillán to Concepción. Sadly, the rest of Chile's main line south from Chillán towards Temuco and Puerto Montt is currently not working, though there are plans afoot to restore service in the future. There are odd trains on a few other routes, such as Valparaiso to Limache (which crazily no longer goes on to Santiago).

TRAIN TRAVEL WITHIN ECUADOR

The famous 445-km Quito to Guayaquil railway no longer runs from end to end, but parts of this route are open with occasional train services. A tourist train called the *Chiva Express* runs four times a week from Quito to El Boliche (45 km); there's also a mixed freight/passenger train three times a week. Another tourist train runs three times a week from Riobamba to Alausí, and yet another from Huigra to Bucay with bus connection to Guayaquil. See **www.efe.gov.ec**.

TRAIN TRAVEL WITHIN MEXICO

Mexico used to have a good train service linking all major cities, using restaurant cars, sleeping-cars and observation cars, many bought second-hand from the USA. Sadly, the Mexican government pulled the plug on almost all long-distance passenger train services some years ago, and buses and planes are now the only way to get around Mexico. A couple of minor services exist in certain areas, including the famous scenic 'Copper Canyon' service. For a summary of remaining Mexican train services, see **www.mexlist.com/pass.htm**.

Copper Canyon train from Chihuahua to Los Mochis

The famous Copper Canyon train from Chihuahua to Los Mochis deserves a special mention. In fact, there are two trains, the daily first class train with reclining seats, bar and restaurant car leaving both Los Mochis and Chihuahua at 06:00 and arriving around 20:45 that night, and the three-times-a-week economy train leaving Chihuahua at 07:00 on Monday, Thursday and Saturday, arriving at Los Mochis at 21:58, and leaving Los Mochis at 07:00 on Tuesday, Friday and Sunday, arriving at Chihuahua at 22:42. The fare is 991 pesos

(£53/$77) on the economy class train, 1,981 pesos (£107/$140) on the first class train. The distance is 653 km (408 miles). For information on the Copper Canyon train service see **www.chepe.com.mx/ing_html/index.html**. There's no online booking, but their website gives phone numbers and email addresses.

TRAIN TRAVEL WITHIN PANAMA

The Panama Canal Railway provides one daily train between Ciudad de Panama and Colón on Monday to Friday. It leaves Ciudad de Panama at 07:15 Monday to Friday only, arriving at Colón at 08:15. It leaves Colón Monday to Friday only at 17:15, arriving back in Panama City at 18:15. It has air-conditioned executive class coaches with refreshments available. The new station for Panama City is in the northern suburb of Allbrook, not far from the domestic airport – the old station in Panama City is now a McDonald's! The distance is 77 km (48 miles). See **www.panarail.com** for more information.

TRAIN TRAVEL WITHIN PARAGUAY

There are no passenger trains in Paraguay, other than a tourist steam train on Sundays from Asunción botanical gardens station.

TRAIN TRAVEL WITHIN URUGUAY

There are few operational trains in Uruguay, although a suburban service has restarted in Montevideo.

PART
7

AUSTRALASIA

AUSTRALIA

Australia is a huge country. And the best way to appreciate its vastness is to cross it at ground level in the civilised comfort of a train. The famous *Indian Pacific* links Sydney, Adelaide and Perth in three days, crossing the great Nullarbor Plain in the process. Don't miss out on a visit to the 'red centre' of Australia around Alice Springs, and there's no better way to reach Alice Springs or Darwin than by the equally famous *Ghan* from Adelaide. In the east, comfortable XPT trains link Sydney with Melbourne and Brisbane. Queensland Railways trains link Brisbane with Townsville and Cairns.

Train operators:	www.railaustralia.com.au for times and fares for all Australian trains Sydney to Melbourne, Brisbane, Canberra: www.countrylink.info Sydney/Melbourne–Adelaide–Perth, Alice Springs, Darwin: www.gsr.com.au Brisbane–Townsville–Cairns: www.traveltrain.com.au V-Line (Victoria regional trains): www.vline.com.au Kalgoorlie–Perth: www.transwa.wa.gov.au Ferry service Melbourne–Tasmania: www.spiritoftasmania.com.au
Time:	Sydney, Melbourne: GMT+10 (+11 Oct–March), Cairns: GMT+10 all year, Adelaide: GMT+9½ (+10½ Oct–March), Alice Springs: GMT+9½ all year, Perth: GMT+8 (+9 Oct–March)
Currency:	£1 = approx. 1.66 Australian dollars, $1 = approx. 1.10 Australian dollars
Tourist information:	www.australia.com
Visas:	UK, EU, US and Canadian citizens need a visa to visit Australia. This can be issued in 'electronic' form, arranged online at www.eta.immi.gov.au or by flight booking agencies such as Trailfinders and Travelbag.

EUROPE TO AUSTRALIA, without flying

It's a long way to Oz, but if you really want to get there without flying, there are two approaches.

Option 1 is to travel there all the way by sea. Air travel has devastated long-distance passenger ships, but you can still use the occasional cruise or a few freighter lines whose ships take a handful of passengers. Expect the voyages to take 32–40 days and cost at least £3,500 one-way, including cabin and meals. To find a cruise or freighter, try Strand Travel (**www.strandtravelltd.co.uk**, +44 (0)20 7921 4340), a UK agency which handles both cruises and freighters, including several UK–Australia passenger-carrying freighter lines. You'll find an online guide to travel by freighter at **www.seaplus.com**.

Option 2 is to travel from Europe to the Far East using the Trans-Siberian Railway, then take a freighter to Australia. You can travel by train from London to Moscow (two nights), take one of the twice-weekly Trans-Siberian Railway trains to Beijing in China (six or seven nights) and the twice-weekly onward train to Hanoi in Vietnam (two nights). Then take a daily train to Saigon (two nights) and a succession of buses and a train onwards via Cambodia to Bangkok. From Bangkok to Singapore a train runs daily and takes two nights. Several freighter companies run freighters once or twice a month out of Singapore for Australia, taking around 7–10 nights. This is a real adventure, with lots to see on the way. See the Trans-Siberian, Vietnam, Cambodia and Thailand chapters of this book, and for the final leg by freighter try Strand Travel (**www.strandtravelltd.co.uk**, +44 (0)20 7921 4340) or freighter companies **www.globoship.ch** and **www.hanjin.com**.

SYDNEY–ADELAIDE–PERTH ON THE *INDIAN PACIFIC*

This is a fabulous journey, giving you a real sense of the vastness of Australia which a flight simply doesn't deliver. With a cosy bed at night, a restaurant for your meals and a lounge in which to relax during the day, it's a rolling hotel. Now run by a private company called Great Southern Rail (**www.gsr.com.au**), the *Indian Pacific* now links Sydney, Adelaide and Perth once a week all year round, twice a week in peak periods. The *Indian Pacific* has only existed since

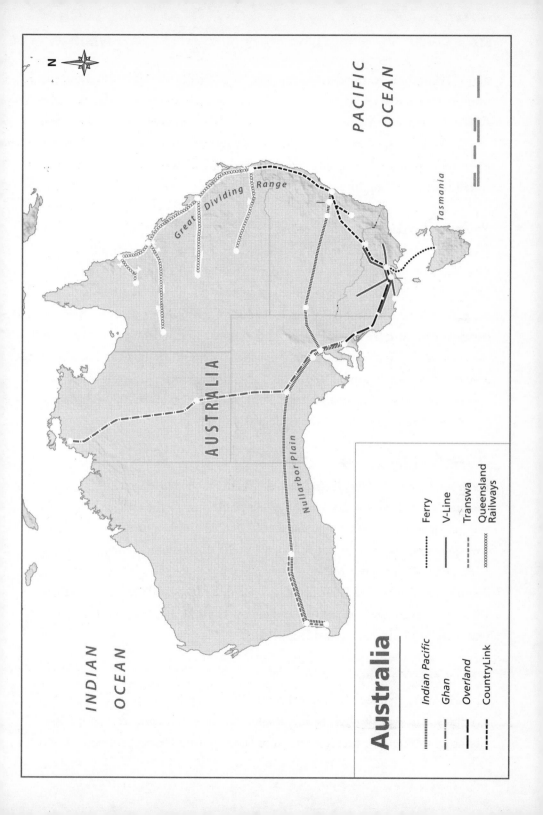

the 1970s, when a standard-gauge line was finally completed across the continent from Sydney to Perth, some 4,343 km or 2,698 miles. Today, both the *Indian Pacific* and its sister train the *Ghan* use the original stainless-steel coaches built by the American Budd company for the first *Indian Pacific* trains when they started running in 1973. Suitably modernised, of course! This train is well worth building into your Australian tour.

Sydney → Adelaide → Perth

Westbound, the *Indian Pacific* departs Sydney Central station at 14:55 every Saturday year-round, and on Wednesday from the end of August to the end of November and January to March (though with the economic recession some departures have been cancelled in 2010/2011 – check your dates of travel at **www.gsr.com.au**). It calls at Broken Hill at 06:40 next morning, and arrives at Adelaide at 15:05. Departure from Adelaide is at 18:40 (Sunday or Thursday), and the following evening the train calls at Kalgoorlie (arriving at 19:10, departing at 22:40), finally arriving at Perth East station at 08:10 next morning (Tuesday or Saturday, day 4 from Sydney).

Perth → Adelaide → Sydney

Eastbound, the *Indian Pacific* leaves Perth East station at 11:55 every Wednesday, and on Sunday from the end of August to the end of November and January to March (though you should double-check your dates of travel at **www.gsr.com.au**). It arrives at Kalgoorlie at 22:15 the same evening, departing again at 01:40. Just over 24 hours later it reaches Adelaide at 07:20 (Friday or Tuesday, day 3 from Perth). It departs Adelaide at 10:00, calls at Broken Hill at 18:30 that evening, and arrives at Sydney Central at 10:15 next morning (Saturday or Wednesday, day 4 from Perth).

About the journey

The 'IP' leaves Sydney Central station in downtown Sydney in mid afternoon and threads its way through Sydney's suburban commuterland. As night falls it climbs up through the scenic Blue Mountains, passing through Katoomba, and next morning you'll wake up in arid outback country around Broken Hill. Look out for kangaroo and emu over breakfast! The train arrives in Adelaide in the afternoon, with time for a city tour even if you're not stopping off, and leaves again for Perth in the early evening. The day after leaving Adelaide the *Indian Pacific* crosses the hot, dusty emptiness of the famous Nullarbor Plain on the longest stretch of straight railway line in the world. It stops long enough for you to visit the tiny community of Cook. If you've ever wondered what the Middle of Nowhere looks like, this is it! Once off the Nullarbor you can play 'spot the koala' over dinner as the beautiful evening sun plays over the leafy eucalyptus trees. After dinner that evening the train stops at the gold-rush town of Kalgoorlie for 3½ hours, long enough for a walkabout. Next morning after breakfast the train rolls into the pleasant and modern city of Perth, capital of Western Australia. You've crossed a continent!

What's it like on board the Indian Pacific?

The *Indian Pacific* has three classes of accommodation: Gold Service sleeper (formerly called 'first class'), Red Service sleeper (which used to be 'holiday class') and Red Service reclining seat (which used to be 'economy class'). Which should you choose? If you want the 'experience of a lifetime' and can afford it, go Gold Service sleeper for all the comforts, complete with restaurant car meals included. At the other extreme, if you're on a very tight budget, Red Service seats allow you to experience one of the world's great train journeys for not much more than you'd pay for a flight plus a hotel room or two – but see if you can afford a Red Service sleeper, as travelling such a long distance in a seat isn't as comfortable as having a private room and a bed for the night.

Gold Service sleeper passengers travel in private sleepers, either single-berth 'roomettes' for passengers travelling alone or 2-berth 'twinettes' for passengers travelling in twos. Both roomettes and twinettes come with comfortable freshly made-up beds, towels, and a complimentary toiletries pack with soap, shampoo, razor, toothbrush, toothpaste, etc. The fare includes excellent meals served in the exclusive Gold Service restaurant car. There's a Gold Service lounge car (sometimes two of them) with bar and armchairs, with complimentary tea and coffee always available. The lounge car's bar serves cocktails, beer and wine, although drinks are extra. Twinette sleeping-cars have a fairly conventional layout with side corridor. Each twinette 2-berth sleeper has an upper and lower bed which fold away to reveal a sofa for daytime use. Twinettes have a tiny private bathroom with hot shower, toilet and washbasin. Roomette sleeping-cars have a rather strange 'wavy' corridor snaking along the middle of the car with doors to the roomettes opening off both sides of it (the S-curves in the corridor maximise the space in each roomette). Each roomette is about 7 feet long by 4 feet wide (about 2.15 metres by 1.2 metres), just big enough for a comfy armchair, a table, and a sink unit in one corner with a drop-down sink and (yes, really) a drop-down flush toilet underneath it. At night, the bed folds down from behind the seat and takes up most of the room. There's an excellent hot shower at the end of the corridor.

Red Service sleeper passengers travel in economy 2-berth sleepers. As in Europe, passengers travelling alone in Red Service sleepers will share with another passenger of the same sex. The sleeping-car layout is identical to the Gold Service roomette cars, with a corridor snaking along the centre of the car in a series of shallow S-bends, with doors to the various sleeper compartments opening off both sides of it. Each room is the same size as a Gold Service single-berth roomette (about 7 feet by 4 feet/2.15 metres by 1.2 metres), but this time there are two armchairs facing each other, plus the washstand in the corner. At night, a lower bed folds down from behind one seat, taking up most of the room, and an upper berth folds out from the wall with just enough space still free beside it to climb in. Red Service passengers can use the Red Service self-service restaurant car, where they can buy snacks, soft and alcoholic drinks and complete meals, and rent personal DVD players and feature films. Meals and drinks are extra. If you find the Gold Service prices too expensive, this is a much more economical way to see Australia by train with the comfort of a proper bed in a private room at night, and you still get a convivial lounge and restaurant car during the day.

Red Service reclining seat passengers travel in comfortable reclining 'dayniter' seats with plenty of legroom and adjustable leg-rests. Bring your own rug and pillow if required. There's a hot shower at the end of the coach, with soap and towels provided for each passenger. Seats passengers can use the Red Service self-service restaurant car, where they can buy snacks, soft and alcoholic drinks and complete meals, and rent personal DVD players and feature films. Naturally, sleeping in a seat is a bit 'rough' compared with the comforts of a proper bed in a cosy sleeper, especially if you are doing the whole three-night journey in one go and not stopping off (which would be my first suggestion, to break the journey up). However, you're not stuck in a seat as you would be on a bus, as during the day you've got the same restaurant car as Red Service sleeper passengers, and of course the scenery is just as good! Travelling in Red Service seats makes this journey an affordable option for budget travellers if you compare it with the cost of flying plus a hotel room for three nights. And even in a seat, the experience of a train journey across Australia has to be worth more than the mundane non-experience of a flight. In other words, you might find a journey on the *Indian Pacific* in a seat enjoyable or you might find it a bit uncomfortable, but either way you'll have loads to write home about, whereas if you fly you won't.

Fares and how to buy tickets

One-way fares, per person		Gold Service sleeper	Red Service sleeper	Red Service reclining seat
Sydney to Perth	Adult	Aus$2,008 (£1,210)	Aus$1,362 (£820)	Aus$716 (£431)
	Child (under 16)	Aus$1,399 (£843)	Aus$887 (£534)	Aus$286 (£172)
Sydney to Adelaide	Adult	Aus$694 (£418)	Aus$501 (£302)	Aus$308 (£186)
	Child (under 16)	Aus$527 (£317)	Aus$365 (£220)	Aus$130 (£78)
Adelaide to Perth	Adult	Aus$1,514 (£912)	Aus$1,036 (£624)	Aus$458 (£276)
	Child (under 16)	Aus$1,022 (£616)	Aus$628 (£378)	Aus$211 (£127)

Children under 4 go free.

Note that the Pensioner fares shown on the GSR website are for Australian senior citizens only.

You can check fares and book online at **www.gsr.com.au**. Alternatively, call GSR's UK agent, International Rail (**www.internationalrail.com**) on 0871 231 0791. Return fares are twice the one-way fare, but check railpass prices as these can be cheaper. Gold Service fares include all meals. A small fuel surcharge is now being added (around Aus$10–30/£6–£18).

VISITING ADELAIDE

Named after the wife of King William IV, Adelaide is a much smaller city than Sydney or Melbourne and much more relaxed. Admirably well laid out by its founder, Colonel William Light, the city centre is surrounded by parkland. On Montefiore Hill to the north of the centre, you can see 'Light's vision', where Colonel Light stood to map out his plan for the city. For city-visit information see **www.cityofadelaide.com.au**. It's worth hiring a car for a few days to visit some of the wine regions nearby, including the famous Barossa Valley, see **www.barossa.com** or **www.barossa-valley-australia.com.au**.

VISITING PERTH AND FREMANTLE

Perth is the capital of Western Australia, a clean, modern city. For visitor information, see **www.cityofperth.wa.gov.au**. Frequent electric trains link Perth with Fremantle, see **www.transperth.wa.gov.au** for times and fares. Don't miss the excellent maritime museum in Fremantle, see **www.museum.wa.gov.au**.

ADELAIDE TO ALICE SPRINGS AND DARWIN ON THE *GHAN*

This is the best way to reach Australia's fabulous 'red centre'. Australia's second most famous train, the legendary *Ghan*, links Adelaide, Alice Springs and (since 2004) Darwin, once a week all year round, twice a week from April to October. By using the train you get a real feel for the scale of the Australian outback, which you simply don't on a plane. Like the *Indian Pacific*, the *Ghan* is now run by Great Southern Rail, and has the same classes of accommodation and facilities: Gold Service sleepers, lounge and restaurant, Red Service sleepers, reclining 'dayniter' seats, lounge and self-service restaurant (see pages 515–7).

Most departures of the *Ghan* now have an additional class of accommodation, the new super-deluxe Platinum service, complete with double (or twin lower) beds.

The *Ghan* gets its name from the (supposedly) Afghan camels and camel drivers who used to carry supplies up to Alice Springs before the railway came. The first railway was narrow-gauge, and the speed of the old *Ghan* was notoriously slow, taking 48 hours from Adelaide to Alice. Only in the early 1980s was the new standard-gauge line opened via a more direct route. The journey time has been cut to an afternoon and a night, and the service doubled to twice weekly from April to October. Connections are available to/from Sydney using the *Indian Pacific* and to/from Melbourne using the *Overland* (see pages 514 and 521). The railway onwards to Darwin was completed in January 2004, and in February 2004 the *Ghan's* service was extended to/from Darwin once a week, doubled to twice-weekly from April to October in 2006. Book early, as there has been massive interest in the service to Darwin and bookings have exceeded even Great Southern Rail's expectations.

Adelaide → Alice Springs → Darwin

Northbound, the *Ghan* departs Adelaide at 12:20 on Sunday year-round, and on Wednesday April–October, and arrives at Alice Springs at 13:45 next day. After a 4-hour stop, it departs Alice Springs at 18:00 and arrives at Darwin at 18:30 next day (Tuesday or Friday).

Darwin → Alice Springs → Adelaide

Southbound, the *Ghan* departs Darwin at 10:00 every Wednesday, and arrives at Alice Springs at 09:10 next day. It then departs Alice Springs at 12:45 and arrives at Adelaide at 13:10 next day (Friday).

April to October there is also a departure on Saturday at 09:00, which arrives at Alice Springs at 11:15 on Sunday, leaves Alice Springs at 15:15, and arrives at Adelaide at 13:10 on Monday.

Fares and how to buy tickets

One-way fares, per person		Platinum sleeper	Gold Service sleeper	Red Service sleeper	Red Service reclining seat
Adelaide to Alice Springs	Adult	Aus$2,365 (£1,425)	Aus$1,019 (£614)	Aus$656 (£395)	Aus$358 (£216)
	Child (under 16)	n/a	Aus$701 (£422)	Aus$400 (£241)	Aus$166 (£100)
Adelaide to Darwin	Adult	Aus$2,987 (£1,787)	Aus$1,973 (£1,189)	Aus$1,312 (£790)	Aus$716 (£431)
	Child (under 16)	n/a	Aus$1,357 (£817)	Aus$800 (£482)	Aus$331 (£200)

Children under 4 go free.

Note that the Pensioner fares shown on the GSR website are for Australian senior citizens only.

The Platinum fare is for two people sharing, per person. Solo passengers in Platinum class must pay for two tickets as there are no single-berth sleepers.

You can check fares and book online at **www.gsr.com.au**. Alternatively, call GSR's UK agent, International Rail (**www.internationalrail.com**) on 0871 231 0791. Return fares are twice the one-way fare, but check railpass prices as these can be cheaper. Gold Service fares include all meals. A small fuel surcharge is now being added (around Aus$10–30/£6–£18).

VISITING ALICE SPRINGS

Alice, as it's usually known, still has a frontier feel to it. Originally called Stuart and only officially renamed Alice Springs in 1933, it grew up around a telegraph station on the overland telegraph linking southern Australia with London. The site for the telegraph station was chosen because there was water, a spring which was named after the wife of Charles Todd, superintendent of telegraphs in Adelaide. You can still see the telegraph station, now a museum, at the north end of the town. Next to it is the very birthplace of the town – the original, now dried-up 'Alice spring'.

Ayer's Rock (Uluru)

You'll want to explore the outback while in Alice Springs, including Uluru, the world's largest sandstone monolith. It's some 440 km (275 miles) southwest of Alice – the outback is a big place! It's a fabulous area with lots to see besides Uluru, including the Olgas (Kata Tjuta, a group of 36 large domed rock formations) and King's Canyon. You can see Uluru and Kata Tjuta as a 17-hour day trip from Alice (which includes a 5-hour drive each way), but it's far better to book a 2-, 3- or 4-day 4-wheel-drive camping safari to see more in less of a hurry. For Uluru and outback tours from Alice, try **www.wayoutback.com.au**. You're still allowed to climb Uluru, a steep scramble along the tourist track up the least perpendicular part of its sandstone sides – however, aboriginal people request that you don't. The website for Uluru-Kata Tjuta National Park is **www.environment.gov.au/parks/uluru**.

MELBOURNE TO ADELAIDE ON THE *OVERLAND*

The third of the three trains run by Great Southern Rail, the *Overland* links Melbourne and Adelaide three times a week, all year round. Forget domestic flights: the *Overland* is easily the most civilised way to travel between these cities.

Westbound, it departs Melbourne Southern Cross station (the new name for the refurbished Spencer Street station) at 08:05 on Tuesday and Thursday, and at 08:40 on Saturday, and arrives at Adelaide (Keswick) at 17:45.

Eastbound, it departs Adelaide (Keswick) at 07:40 on Monday, Wednesday and Friday, and arrives at Melbourne (Southern Cross) at 18:40.

The *Overland* doesn't run from Adelaide on 25 December or from Melbourne on 26 December.

The one-way adult fare is Aus$134 (£81) in a Red Premium (first class) seat or Aus$90 (£54) in a Red (standard class) seat; the child fare (under 16) is Aus$95 (£57) in Red Premium or Aus$45 (£27) in Red.

To check times and fares, visit **www.gsr.com.au**. To buy tickets for the *Overland* in the UK, you can contact the UK sales agent International Rail (**www.internationalrail.com**) on 0871 231 0791 or book online at **www.gsr.com.au**.

VISITING MELBOURNE

In Melbourne, don't forget to visit the museum in the old gaol, **www.oldmelbournegaol.com.au**. Ned Kelly, Australia's most infamous outlaw, was imprisoned and hanged in Melbourne gaol, and his unique armour is still displayed there. Take a ride on Melbourne's trams (there's even a restaurant in a tram – eat your dinner travelling round the Melbourne streets; see **www.tramrestaurant.com.au**). For general tourist information, see **www.visitmelbourne.com**. For a day or two out of town, drive the famous Great Ocean Road. You can do this as a day tour by bus from Melbourne, or you can hire a car for a day or two. See **www.greatoceanrd.org.au**.

SYDNEY TO MELBOURNE, CANBERRA AND BRISBANE

Trains in New South Wales, including the interstate trains from Sydney to Melbourne and Brisbane, are run by CountryLink, formerly the State Rail Authority of New South Wales, a division of RailCorp. CountryLink run two comfortable XPT trains every day from Sydney to Melbourne, one by day and the other overnight. A similar service runs from Sydney to Brisbane, although as trains alternate between Brisbane and Casino, a bus connection is needed to Brisbane on one of the two. Equally comfortable Xplorer trains link Sydney with Canberra.

XPT trains might look familiar to us Brits. That's because they're based on the UK's InterCity 125, but re-geared to 100mph and with (you'll be pleased to learn) beefed-up air-conditioning. XPTs have first and economy class reclining seats. First and economy class seating is identical (even the legroom), so there is no advantage whatsoever in paying for first class unless economy is full. XPTs have a buffet car selling food and drink, including wine. Xplorers have similar seating to XPTs and a buffet-bar.

The overnight Sydney–Melbourne and Sydney–Brisbane XPT trains have one sleeping-car with 2-berth rooms. A sofa converts to an upper and lower berth, and there's a hot shower and toilet shared between each pair of adjacent compartments. Book early, as there's only one sleeping-car per train and it gets booked up fast.

Sydney to Melbourne

Southbound, the daytime train departs Sydney Central station daily at 07:42, arriving at Melbourne Southern Cross station (formerly Spencer Street) at 18:53. The overnight train departs Sydney Central daily at 20:40 and arrives at Melbourne at 07:35 next morning.

Northbound, the daytime train departs Melbourne Southern Cross station daily at 08:30, arriving at Sydney Central station at 19:54. The overnight train departs Melbourne daily at 19:55 and arrives at Sydney at 06:55 next morning.

All trains are XPTs run by CountryLink, with first and economy class seating and buffet-bar; the overnight trains also have one sleeping-car with 2-berth rooms. You should check times before travel at **www.countrylink.info**, as they may vary.

Sydney to Brisbane (or Casino)

Northbound, the daytime train departs Sydney Central station daily at 07:15, arriving at Casino at 18:44 (17:44 during daylight saving time); a bus connection will get you to Brisbane (Roma Street) at 22:31 (21:31 during daylight saving time). The overnight train departs Sydney daily at 16:12, arriving at Brisbane Roma Street station at 06:30 next morning (05:30 during daylight saving time).

Southbound, the daytime train departs Brisbane Roma Street station daily at 07:30 (06:30 during daylight saving time), and arrives at Sydney Central station at 21:06. The overnight train starts from Casino: a connecting bus leaves Brisbane Roma Street at 15:20 (14:20 during daylight saving time). The train departs Casino daily at 19:25 (18:25 during daylight saving time) and arrives at Sydney at 06:52 next morning.

All trains are XPTs run by CountryLink, with first and economy class seating and buffet-bar; the overnight trains also have one sleeping-car with 2-berth rooms. You should check times before travel at **www.countrylink.info**, as they may vary.

Sydney → Canberra

		Daily	Daily	Note A
Sydney Central	depart	06:58	12:05	18:11
Canberra	arrive	11:23	16:32	22:29

Canberra → Sydney

		Daily	Mon–Fri	Sat, Sun	Note B
Canberra	depart	06:43	11:56	11:55	17:03
Sydney Central	arrive	11:02	16:21	16:25	21:23

CountryLink Xplorer trains, with first and economy class with buffet-bar.

Note A: Runs Monday, Wednesday, Friday, Sunday.

Note B: Runs Tuesday, Thursday, Saturday, Sunday.

Please double-check times at **www.countrylink.info**, as times can vary.

Fares and how to buy tickets

One-way fares, per person		Economy seat	1st class seat	1st class sleeper
Sydney to Melbourne	Low season fare	Aus$91 (£55)	Aus$128 (£77)	Aus$216 (£130)
	High season fare	Aus$130 (£78)	Aus$183 (£110)	Aus$271 (£163)
Sydney to Brisbane	Low season fare	Aus$91 (£55)	Aus$128 (£77)	Aus$216 (£130)
	High season fare	Aus$130 (£78)	Aus$183 (£110)	Aus$271 (£163)
Sydney to Canberra	Low season fare	Aus$39 (£23)	Aus$56 (£34)	–
	High season fare	Aus$57 (£34)	Aus$80 (£48)	–

To check fares and train times and buy tickets online, see **www.countrylink.info**. Tickets bought online are sent by email. Note that sleepers can't be booked online. Alternatively, to book by telephone in the UK, contact the UK sales agent, **www.internationalrail.com** on 0871 231 0790.

VISITING SYDNEY

Sydney is a fantastic city. Take a tour of the opera house (**www.sydneyoperahouse.com**). Wander through the botanic gardens. Visit the observation deck of the Centrepoint Tower (**www.sydneytower.com.au**). Take a ferry from Circular Quay to Watson's Bay for fish and chips at Doyle's famous refreshment rooms (**www.doyles.com.au** – look for 'Doyles on the beach'; for Sydney ferry information see **www.sydneyferries.info**). For general city tourist information, see **www.sydney.com.au**.

Why not do the incredible Sydney Harbour Bridge climb? From Aus$179 (£107), you are briefed and equipped for a walk up the girders of Sydney Harbour Bridge for some fantastic views across the city, from the Pacific Ocean in the east to the Blue Mountains in the west. The bridge climb tour has been operating since October 1998. To book a climb, see **www.bridgeclimb.com**.

The Blue Mountains

If you'd like a scenic day out from Sydney, hop on a double-deck suburban train from Sydney to Katoomba in the Blue Mountains, 110km (69 miles) away – trains run about every hour, journey time 2 hours, fare around Aus$7.80 (£4.70) each way, or Aus$10.80 (£6.50) for an off-peak day return valid any time after 09:00 Monday–Friday or any time at weekends. Children under 16 go at half fare, children under 4 free. A short walk from the station brings you to the Three Sisters rock formation, overlooking the breathtaking Jamieson Valley, with lots of great scenic walks. For information and a guide to walks, see **www.bluemts.com.au** or **www.infobluemountains.net.au**. For Sydney suburban train times and fares, see **www.cityrail.info** (select 'Blue Mountains Line' in the journey planner, and remember that Sydney Central is shown as just 'Central'.

BRISBANE TO TOWNSVILLE AND CAIRNS

Queensland Railways (**www.traveltrain.com.au**) operates two trains between Brisbane and Cairns: the *Sunlander* sleeper train (three times a week), and a 100mph tilt train (twice a week) with business class seats only. Between

Brisbane and Rockhampton there are other trains besides the trains shown below, including a 100mph tilting daytime train; see **www.traveltrain.com.au**.

Brisbane → Townsville, Cairns

		Sunlander	*Sunlander*	100mph tilt train
Brisbane (Roma St)	depart	08:55 (Tue, Sun)	13:25 (Thur)	18:25 (Mon, Fri)
Rockhampton	depart	20:30 (Tue, Sun)	23:55 (Thur)	02:15 (Tue, Sat)
Townsville	arrive	08:35 (Wed, Mon)	11:50 (Fri)	11:55 (Tue, Sat)
	depart	09:00 (Wed, Mon)	12:15 (Fri)	12:05 (Tue, Sat)
Cairns	arrive	16:15 (Wed, Mon)	19:15 (Fri)	18:20 (Tue, Sat)

Cairns, Townsville → Brisbane

		Sunlander	100mph tilt train
Cairns	depart	09:15 (Tue, Thur, Sat)	09:15 (Wed, Sun)
Townsville	arrive	16:10 (Tue, Thur, Sat)	15:15 (Wed, Sun)
	depart	16:35 (Tue, Thur, Sat)	15:30 (Wed, Sun)
Rockhampton	arrive	04:50 (Wed, Fri, Sun)	01:10 (Thur, Mon)
Brisbane (Roma St)	arrive	15:55 (Wed, Fri, Sun)	09:10 (Thur, Mon)

Sunlander: First class sleepers (private 1- and 2-berth sleepers), economy berths (shared 3-berth sleepers) and economy reclining seats, lounge and restaurant. On Thursday and Sunday from Brisbane, Tuesday and Saturday from Cairns and Townsville, this train also has deluxe Queensland class sleepers, restaurant and lounge.

Tilt train: Introduced in 2003, this is an all-new 100mph tilting diesel train. It has business class reclining seats with video entertainment and a buffet-bar. Unfortunately, there are no sleepers, just seats.

Fares and how to buy tickets

One-way adult fare, per person	*Sunlander.* Queenslander class sleeper	*Sunlander.* First class sleeper	*Sunlander.* Economy berth	*Sunlander.* Economy seat	Tilt train: Business class seat
Brisbane to Townsville	Aus$714 (£430)	Aus$385 (£232)	Aus$249 (£150)	Aus$189 (£114)	Aus$283 (£170)
Brisbane to Cairns	Aus$784 (£472)	Aus$429 (£258)	Aus$279 (£168)	Aus$219 (£132)	Aus$328 (£198)

Children 3 years and under go free, children 15 years and under pay half the adult fare.

To check train times and fares and book online, see **www.traveltrain.com.au**. To book Queensland Railways trains from the UK, visit **www.internationalrail.com** or call 0871 231 0790.

Brisbane to Longreach

A Queensland Railways train called the *Spirit of the Outback* runs twice a week Brisbane–Rockhampton–Longreach, with first class and economy sleepers, economy seats, and restaurant car. See **www.traveltrain.com.au** for details.

Cairns to Forsayth

A little 1963-vintage stainless-steel railcar works the Savannahlander train from Cairns to Forsayth, which departs at 06:30 every Wednesday with an overnight hotel stop in Almaden, arriving in Forsayth on Thursday evening. It returns from Forsayth at 08:30 on Friday, also with an overnight hotel stop in Almaden, arriving at Cairns at 18:40 on Saturday. A 4-day outback rail experience! It runs from March to December, no service in late December, January or February or the first few days of March. See **www.savannahlander.com.au** for timetable, fares and booking.

KALGOORLIE TO PERTH ON THE *PROSPECTOR*

Transwa (formerly known as Westrail) introduced brand-new express diesel trains on the Perth–Kalgoorlie *Prospector* services in September 2003, running at up to 100mph. Within a few years, track will be upgraded to 125mph (200km/h), making these trains the fastest in Australia.

Perth → Kalgoorlie

Prospector		Mon–Sat	Sun	Mon, Fri
Perth (East)	depart	07:05	14:05	15:00
Kalgoorlie	arrive	13:45	20:40	21:45

Kalgoorlie → Perth

Prospector		Mon–Sat	Sun	Mon	Fri
Kalgoorlie	depart	07:15	14:15	15:15	15:25
Perth (East)	arrive	14:00	21:00	22:00	22:05

This route is also served by the *Indian Pacific*, see page 512. Transwa also runs trains between Perth and Bunbury, see **www.transwa.wa.gov.au**.

Perth to Kalgoorlie costs Aus$81.55 (£49) each way. Children under 5 travel free, children 5 to 15 (inclusive) at half fare. You can book online at **www.transwa.wa.gov.au**.

RAILPASSES FOR AUSTRALIA

There are two pass ranges: the Great Southern Railpass for travel only on GSR's three trains (the *Indian Pacific*, *Ghan* and *Overland*), and the Australia Flexi Pass, which includes nationwide travel on all three GSR trains plus CountryLink trains and most Queensland Railways trains. Just remember that you still need a reservation to travel on most long-distance trains with a pass. To travel in a sleeper with a railpass, you pay the difference between seat and sleeper prices. To check prices and buy a pass, contact **www.internationalrail.com** or call 0871 231 0790.

Rail Explorer Pass: gives unlimited Red Service reclining seat travel on the *Indian Pacific*, *Ghan* and *Overland* for six months for £422 or US$523 (adult rate), £260 or US$447 (student/backpacker/child rate).

Austrail Pass: gives unlimited nationwide Australian train travel on the *Indian Pacific*, the *Ghan*, the *Overland*, CountryLink trains between Sydney, Melbourne, Brisbane and Canberra, and most Queensland Railways trains, for six months.

NEW ZEALAND

Whether you're an overseas visitor or a born-and-bred New Zealander, trains are easily the best way to travel between New Zealand's three main cities, Auckland, Wellington and (with a little help from the Interislander ferry) Christchurch. Trains are also the best way to reach the North Island's Tongariro National Park, the South Island's west coast at Greymouth, the whale-watching and dolphin-swimming centre at Kaikoura or the Marlborough vineyards at Blenheim. Unlike domestic flights, the trains take you at ground level past superb scenery that can't be seen by road, in civilised comfort that cramped and uncivilised long-distance buses can't match. New Zealand's long-distance trains are operated by Tranz Scenic, once privatised but back in public ownership as part of KiwiRail as from 2008.

Train operator:	Long-distance trains: Tranz Scenic, **www.tranzscenic.co.nz**
	Interislander ferry Wellington–Picton: **www.interislandline.co.nz**
	Auckland suburban trains: **www.maxx.co.nz**
	Wellington suburban trains: **www.tranzmetro.co.nz**
	Taieri Gorge Railway: **www.taieri.co.nz**
Time:	GMT+12 (GMT+13 from last Sunday in September to first Sunday in April)
Currency:	£1 = approx. 2.13 NZ dollars, US$1 = approx. 1.46 NZ dollars
Tourist information:	**www.tourisminfo.govt.nz**
Visas:	UK, EU, US, Canadian and Australian citizens do not need a visa to visit New Zealand.

EUROPE TO NEW ZEALAND, without flying

To look into travel by passenger-carrying freighter or the occasional cruise, try calling Strand Travel (**www.strandtravelltd.co.uk**, telephone +44 (0)20 7921 4340), a UK agency which handles both cruises and freighters.

AUCKLAND TO WELLINGTON ON THE *OVERLANDER*

The famous *Overlander* train is easily the best way to get from downtown Auckland to city centre Wellington, stress-free and in comfort at ground level, stopping off if you like at the Tongariro National Park. The *Overlander* is an epic 681-km (423-mile) journey across the whole interior of the North Island, taking you in a single day past every kind of scenery there is, from coastline to volcanoes to mountains, from lush green farmland to thick New Zealand bush. It will take you the length of the historic North Island Main Trunk Railway, started in 1885 and completed in 1908, over such feats of engineering as the Raurimu Spiral, Turangarere Horseshoe and Makatote Viaduct. It's one of the world's great railway journeys, and one of my favourite train journeys anywhere, so ditch that domestic flight to Wellington and take the train!

Timetable, fares and how to buy tickets

The *Overlander* runs daily in the summer season from late September to early May, but runs only on Friday, Saturday and Sunday in winter.

From Auckland it departs at 07:25, calls at Hamilton at 09:50, arrives at National Park at 12:50, where it makes a half-hour stop, departing at 13:20, calls at Palmerston North at 17:00, and arrives at Wellington at 19:25.

From Wellington it departs at 07:25, calls at Palmerston North at 09:45, arrives at National Park at 13:40, departing at 13:45, calls at Hamilton at 17:00, and arrives at Auckland at 19:20.

A second train service, the *Capital Connection*, runs Monday to Friday between Palmerston North and Wellington, departing Palmerston North at 06:20, arriving at Wellington at 08:21, and on the return journey departing Wellington at 17:17, arriving at Palmerston North at 19:27.

The one-way fare for Auckland to Wellington on the *Overlander* is NZ$129

(£60 or US$88). Children aged 2–14 travel at reduced fare, infants under 2 travel free. For an unbeatable day's travel experience, this is a bargain.

It's easy to buy tickets for the *Overlander* online at **www.tranzscenic.co.nz** whether you live in NZ or overseas. You pay by credit card and print out your own ticket. Or when you're in New Zealand you can call 0800 TRAINS (0800 872 467); calls are free. From outside New Zealand call 00 64 4 495 0775. This is the cheapest way to buy tickets for the *Overlander*, direct from the train's operator and not through an intermediate agency. There are no discounts for seniors or students on the *Overlander*, although there are discounts on the other Tranz Scenic trains.

What's it like on board the Overlander?

The *Overlander* has reclining seats, all facing direction of travel, all lining up with huge panoramic windows, with loads of legroom even if you're over six feet tall. Seats recline to about 40 degrees. Seats are not allocated at booking, but by the train manager before departure. However, if you book by phone (or book online and then call Tranz Scenic's freephone number when you get to NZ and quote your booking reference) you can make a seating request. For example, four friends or family travelling together could request one of the very few bays of four seats facing each other around a table; keen photographers could request a seat at the front of the train close to the viewing platform; or you might prefer a seat in the rear coach near the observation lounge. Requests can't be guaranteed, of course, but it doesn't hurt to ask! All your heavy baggage is checked in to the baggage van; only hand luggage may be taken into the seating coaches.

At the back of the train is a small lounge with glass observation window so you can look back along the track. Great for socialising! Seats in the lounge are not allocated but are free for all passengers to use. You are asked not to hog the lounge seats for the whole trip.

At the front of the train at the rear of the baggage car is a small open-air viewing platform, ideal for seeing and photographing the scenery, with no glass in between you and it. Children must be accompanied.

In the centre of the train is a café counter selling tea, coffee, wine, beer, spirits, snacks and light microwaveable meals at reasonable prices. I can recommend the Devonshire cream tea in the afternoon, and a glass of Montana Sauvignon Blanc! You take your food and drink back to your seat.

The *Overlander's* coaches have been rebuilt from traditional New Zealand Railways coaches, to a design which first appeared in 1938. That's why they may appear strangely antiquated from the outside (apart from their new panoramic windows), but inside the coaches have been refurbished to a very high standard.

What is the journey like?

The crew of the *Overlander* provide a commentary over the train's public address system, pointing out things of interest, but here's a summary of what to look out for on the journey from Auckland to Wellington.

In **Auckland** the *Overlander* leaves from the shiny new Britomart Transportation Centre. Unlike the airport 23 km away, the station couldn't be more convenient. It's right at the top of Queen Street (Auckland's main street), just across the road from the Devonport and Islands ferry terminal, and a few minutes' walk from all the city centre hotels and the Sky Tower. You should check in at least 20 minutes before departure at platform 3. The train manager sets up a podium on the platform, allocates seats to passengers with reservations and sells tickets to any last-minute passengers. His assistant will take your heavy bags and check them in to the baggage car.

The Britomart Transportation Centre was opened in 2003, and the building that forms its main hall was originally Auckland's General Post Office, built in 1912 and used as a post office until the 1990s. Auckland's suburban trains and the *Overlander* now use five underground railway platforms, reached by two short escalators at the back of the main hall. Funnily enough, this was the site of Auckland's original railway station (albeit on the surface), right behind the post office, opened in 1885 on land reclaimed from the sea. This was closed in 1930 when an imposing new railway terminal was opened on Beach Road, an inconvenient 15 minutes' walk from the town centre. Only in 2003 was this 1930 station closed and the trains once more diverted into the city centre to the new Britomart station. The impressive 1930 station still stands – now a university accommodation centre. It's virtually a clone of the railway station at Wellington, which you'll see later!

The *Overlander* departs at 07:25 and the diesel struggles up the steep incline out of the station before emerging into the daylight. You'll see Auckland harbour and container terminal to the left, and a glimpse of the derelict platforms of Auckland's 1930 station to the right. The train swings right on to a causeway across the Orakei Basin (the submerged crater of an extinct volcano), passing occasional local trains as it snakes its way through the Auckland suburbs.

From Auckland to the first major stop, the *Overlander* passes towns, villages, light industry and farmland. There are some very scenic sections, with extinct volcanoes dotted in places over the landscape. The train runs along the Waikato River and passes right by Mount Taupiri (287 metres), the sacred mountain of the Waikato people. Many ancestors and chiefs are buried on Taupiri, including all the Maori kings.

Hamilton is the *Overlander*'s first major stop, where there's time to get off and stretch your legs. Here, the diesel locomotive is usually changed for an electric. The central part of the Auckland–Wellington North Island Main Trunk Railway between Hamilton and Palmerston North was electrified in 1988, allowing heavier loads to be hauled over the difficult terrain. Several new bits of track ('deviations') were also constructed in the 1980s, easing the most severe curves and gradients.

Beyond Hamilton, the scenery starts to hot up. The flat farmland immediately south of Hamilton is among the richest in the world, grazed by sheep, cattle and red deer. You'll cross the boundary between Waikato and King Country, and see the volcano Mount Pirongia (959 metres high) in the distance. King Country is the area once ruled by the Maori kings. In the 1870s, the New Zealand government admitted that it had no real control over this area. However, after 1882 an agreement was reached with the kings which allowed a railway to be constructed. Surveying started in 1883 and construction in 1885, though it would be another 23 years before Auckland and Wellington were finally linked by rail.

The train calls at **Te Kuiti** (alight here for the Waitomo glow-worm caves) and on the left as it leaves the station you'll see a king-size statue of a man shearing a sheep. Te Kuiti bills itself as the sheep-shearing capital of the world! A few minutes later the *Overlander* crosses the Waititi viaduct, built in 1887 and the oldest viaduct on the North Island Main Trunk Railway.

For the next hour or two, you'll start to appreciate just how lush and green New Zealand is. The train winds its way through valleys, hills, rivers, and you can almost see those hobbit holes in the hillocks! Indeed, Peter Jackson (filmmaker and producer of the *Lord of the Rings* films) has said that it was on board an Auckland–Wellington train, aged eighteen and reading Tolkien for the first time, that he realised how like Tolkien's Middle Earth the New Zealand landscape is. The train follows the picturesque Ongarue River all the way to **Taumarunui**.

About 30 minutes after departing Taumarunui, the traincrew will make an announcement that the *Overlander* is about to enter the world-famous Raurimu Spiral. Actually a couple of major hairpin bends, then a couple of loops and two tunnels, all built through thick rainforest, the Raurimu Spiral is how the railway engineers building the North Island Main Trunk got the line to climb 221 metres (700 feet) in less than 6 km (3½ miles). The train twists, turns, and doubles back on itself as it climbs. As a result of the spiral, Raurimu to National Park is 11 km by rail, though only 5.6 km as the crow flies! Designed in 1898, the spiral was adopted rather than an earlier proposal for a longer way round that would have been 19 km long and involved several difficult viaducts.

Just after clearing the top of the Raurimu Spiral, the train arrives at **National Park** station, 7 km by road from Tongariro National Park

Village. Southbound, the train stops for 30 minutes and you can stretch your legs, take photographs, or use the station's excellent buffet (northbound, the stop here is only 5 minutes). Be warned: a huge queue will form at the buffet counter minutes after the train's arrival! On a clear day, you can see the huge volcanoes in the distance.

After the train leaves National Park, you pass over a succession of imposing viaducts, in thick bush over huge river gorges. The first is the famous Makatote Viaduct, 11 km south of National Park, the highest of the lot and a huge steel structure 262 metres (860 feet) long and 79 metres (258 feet) above the river.

A minute or two later, the *Overlander* passes the site at Manganuioteao where engineers building the North Island Main Trunk from Wellington northwards and from Auckland southwards finally met and New Zealand's Prime Minister Joseph Ward drove in the final spike in 1908. When completed, the new railway reduced the Auckland to Wellington journey from three days of train, stagecoach, river steamer and train, to just 14 hours by direct train. A small grey obelisk marks the spot on the right, though you may not notice it as the *Overlander* swishes by.

A few viaducts further on, the huge Hapuawhenua viaduct was replaced in 1985 and is now a concrete structure, taking a shorter route across the valley. You can see the original 1908 (now disused) steel viaduct curving round the valley on your left.

At **Ohakune** you'll see another New Zealand peculiarity – small wooden houses originally built by New Zealand Railways for employees. There are thousands of these houses, all built to the same handful of designs, all over New Zealand. In the northbound direction, there's a 35-minute stop here and you can stretch your legs.

Ten minutes after Ohakune the *Overlander* passes over the Tangiwai Bridge, across the Whangaehu River. After the huge viaducts in the Tongariro National Park, this seems a very small and unimpressive bridge, but it was the scene of New Zealand's worst ever rail disaster in 1953. A small memorial stands next to the track on the right. It was Christmas Eve 1953, and a lake had formed in the crater of Mount Ruapehu. The wall of this crater burst, sending a 'lahar' or 6-metre-high torrent of water, mud and volcanic rock down the mountainside and along the river. The lahar washed away a bridge pier, just before the 3pm Wellington to Auckland express reached the bridge at around 10:21pm, with 285 people on board. 151 people died as the locomotive and five second class coaches plunged into the river and were washed downstream. A sixth, first class car teetered on the brink, allowing time for all but one passenger to be rescued, then plunged into the river. Today, bridge piers have been strengthened and early warning devices have been placed upstream.

Ten minutes later, the train passes the army camp at Waiouru, running through barren country some 800 metres above sea level. There is little vegetation here except grass, because of the altitude. After another 15–20 minutes the train doubles back on itself around the Turangarere Horseshoe, a huge hairpin bend around a small green valley.

Soon, the train starts following the massive and dramatic Rangitikei River gorge, and passes over a series of huge viaducts and through the occasional tunnel. Once in **Mangaweka**, look out on the left for the café with a DC3 Dakota aircraft stuck on top of it, painted in 'Cookie Time' colours.

The *Overlander* descends off the volcanic plateau to **Marton**, named after the birthplace of Captain Cook near Middlesbrough. Marton is on the Wellington–New Plymouth railway, and it is the point where they started building the North Island Main Trunk into the interior.

The train descends further down the side of a hill, curves around a golf course and crosses the Rangitikei River. Shortly afterwards it stops at **Feilding**, which has won many 'best kept town' competitions and is proclaimed on the station signs as 'Friendly Feilding, New Zealand's most beautiful town'.

Twenty minutes after Feilding, the train arrives at **Palmerston North**'s

Franklin station. Until 1963, the railway ran right through the middle of Palmerston North's main square. This was not very convenient for either New Zealand Railways or the townspeople, so a new station on a deviation around the outskirts of the town was constructed. Here, the electric locomotive is usually exchanged for a diesel, and you have a few minutes to stretch your legs on the platform.

An hour or two of rich green farmland follows, before the train reaches the coast. The *Overlander* runs along a very scenic stretch of coastline for a fair way, with great views of the sand and the breaking waves. It may be dark by now, but on the northbound journey the coastal views in the early morning sun are wonderful.

The coastline gives way to the picturesque Porirua Harbour and a stop at **Porirua** station.

The *Overlander* heads on to finish its run at **Wellington**'s imposing railway station, opened in 1937 and a stone's throw from the New Zealand Parliament buildings and city centre. You've done it: you've travelled overland between New Zealand's two biggest cities, all 681 km (423 miles) of it. I hope you'll agree, it was an epic trip.

A bit of history . . .

Surveys for the route of the North Island Main Trunk Railway started in 1883, led by one John Rochfort. Building work started in 1885, and the line was finally completed in 1908.

From the 1920s to the 1950s, the most prestigious train on the route was the *Night Limited*, an overnight sleeping-car train that would have been used by businessmen, politicians, in fact anyone who was anyone travelling between Auckland and Wellington. With fewer stops and a lighter load, it could manage the journey in about 12 hours. There was usually also a slower overnight train with more stops, leaving Auckland and Wellington around 15:00 and getting in next day in the early morning. This had seats but no sleepers, and it was the train involved in the accident at Tangiwai. The third of the three main daily Auckland–Wellington trains was the *Daylight Limited*, also a fast limited-stop train, which, as its name suggests, ran during the day, from morning till night. When it switched from steam to diesel haulage in 1963, it was renamed the *Scenic Daylight*.

In 1968, the *Scenic Daylight* was replaced by fast railcars with refurbished interiors, built by Fiat. This was successful, and New Zealand Railways bought several brand-new stainless-steel railcars from Japan, which it named *Silver Fern*. With comfortable seats and hostess service, these fast railcars ran the daytime service between Auckland and Wellington from 1971 until 1991, when they were replaced by the *Overlander*. You can still see *Silver Fern* railcars around, as at least one has been preserved and runs occasional charter trains.

In 1971, the *Night Limited* was replaced by the *Silver Star*, a prestige sleeping-car train which used brand-new stainless-steel sleepers and dining-car also bought from Japan. Unfortunately, airline competition forced this service to close before the decade was out, and in 1979 it was replaced by the *Northerner*. You can still travel in the stainless-steel *Silver Star* coaches between Singapore and Bangkok, as they were bought and rebuilt for the luxurious Eastern and Oriental Express tourist train (see page 367).

The *Northerner* had both seats and sleepers until 1987, when the last sleeping-cars between Auckland and Wellington were withdrawn. The *Northerner* continued with seats only until it was withdrawn in 2004. There is now no convenient overnight train between Auckland and Wellington.

The *Overlander* was introduced in 1991, increasing capacity over the *Silver Fern* railcars it replaced. It was almost withdrawn itself in 2006, but was saved, albeit reduced to three times a week (as opposed to daily) in the off-peak season. It now remains as the only train between Auckland and Wellington.

WELLINGTON TO PICTON BY INTERISLANDER FERRY

It's one of the most scenic ferry crossings in the world, and *the* way to travel between New Zealand's North and South Islands. The 92-km (58-mile) voyage across the Cook Strait between Wellington and Picton takes three hours. There are Interislander sailings from Wellington daily at 01:55, 08:25, 14:15, 18:15, and from Picton at 05:45, 09:50, 13:15, 18:05, 22:05. Times may vary, so check ferry fares and timetables at **www.interislandline.co.nz**.

In Wellington, the Interislander terminal is a long walk north of the railway station, but a shuttle bus clearly marked 'Interislander' leaves from platform 9 at the railway station 50 minutes before each sailing. The journey time is 5 minutes, the fare is NZ$2 (£1) per person, children under 5 free. Foot passengers must check in at the terminal at least 30 minutes before sailing time. All heavy baggage is checked in, so only hand luggage is carried on board. Passengers connecting with the train to Christchurch can check in bags in Wellington all the way through to Christchurch.

In Picton, the Interislander terminal is 200 metres from the station. All heavy baggage is checked in, so only hand luggage needs to be carried on board.

The 08:25 sailing from Wellington and 13:15 sailing from Picton connect with the *TranzCoastal* train to and from Christchurch. You can book combined Wellington–Christchurch ferry and train tickets online at **www.tranzscenic.co.nz**. Both these sailings are normally operated by the *Kaitaki*, the largest ferry in New Zealand waters. The *Kaitaki* may look familiar to ferry travellers from Ireland or the UK – she started life in 1995 as the *Isle of Innisfree* on the Irish Ferries Holyhead–Dublin and Pembroke–Rosslare routes, and later became P&O's *Pride of Cherbourg* on the Portsmouth–Cherbourg route!

The Interislander ferry company itself started life as the Union Steamship Co., and was later part of New Zealand Railways before being privatised, hence its close connections with the train service to Christchurch. Another ferry company also operates several daily ferries between Wellington and Picton – **www.bluebridge.co.nz** – but these ferries don't connect with the train to Christchurch.

A voyage on the Interislander . . .

The ship sails out of the Interislander terminal at Wellington and describes a wide arc out of Wellington harbour, with views of Wellington's seafront. It passes the suburb of Seatoun on the right and exits the harbour into the Cook

Strait separating the North and South Islands. Also on the right are some wicked-looking rocks, including the Barrett Reef, where the Lyttleton–Wellington overnight ferry *Wahine* came to grief in a storm in 1968.

The crossing of the Cook Strait itself only lasts an hour, and at the other side the ferry passes between narrow headlands into the Tory Channel. Named after the *Tory*, a migrant ship which passed through the channel in 1840, the Tory Channel is one of the Marlborough Sounds, a narrow channel between Arapawa Island on the right and a strip of mainland on the left. The ship slowly follows this channel, through an S-bend, entering the larger Queen Charlotte Sound and finally arriving at Picton, a small town and the railhead for the South Island.

Travel tips for the ferry connection

- **Shuttle bus for ferry departures and arrivals at Wellington:** The Interislander terminal is a long walk north of Wellington city centre, but a shuttle bus (clearly marked 'Interislander') operates from platform 9 at the railway station 50 minutes before each ferry leaves. The journey time is 5 minutes, the fare is NZ$2 (£1) per person, children under 5 free. Tickets can be bought with cash or credit card from the ticketing station. Similarly, a shuttle bus meets each ferry arrival and will take you to the railway station as soon as everyone has reclaimed their baggage (although there's no shuttle bus for ferry arrivals after 21:00).

- The Interislander ferry and connecting *TranzCoastal* train are easily the most comfortable and scenic way to travel from Wellington to Christchurch. It's also very cheap, with inclusive train+ferry fares from just NZ$130 (£60). The ferry sailings that connect with the train are the 08:25 sailing from Wellington (arriving in Picton at 11:35), and the 13:15 sailing from Picton (arriving in Wellington at 16:25).

- **Check-in and baggage:** You must check in to the Wellington Interislander ferry terminal at least 30 minutes before departure. At the ferry terminal, all bags except hand baggage must be checked in. If you're connecting with the *TranzCoastal* train, you can check your bags all the way through to Christchurch. Similarly, when checking in at Christchurch, you can check your bags all the way through to Wellington Interislander ferry terminal. Your bags will automatically be transferred between ferry and train at Picton, and you reclaim them at your final destination, either Wellington or Christchurch.

PICTON TO CHRISTCHURCH ON THE *TRANZCOASTAL*

Whether you are travelling straight through from Wellington to Christchurch or touring the South Island, the *TranzCoastal* train – which links Picton on Queen Charlotte Sound, via the Marlborough wine country and the whale-watching and wildlife centre at Kaikoura, with South Island's principal city – is the most comfortable and scenic way to do it.

The *TranzCoastal* runs daily. Southbound, it departs Picton at 13:00, calling at Blenheim 13:33, Kaikoura 15:28, Waipara 17:30, and arriving at Christchurch at 18:21. Northbound, it departs Christchurch at 07:00, calling at Waipara 07:58, Kaikoura 09:54, Blenheim 11:46, and arriving at Picton at 12:13.

It has comfortable seats, arranged in bays of four around tables. All seats line up with wide panoramic windows. A café-bar serves snacks, drinks, tea, coffee, wine, beer, spirits and light microwaveable meals, at reasonable prices. I can recommend the breakfast roll in the morning (NZ$7.50/£3.50) and the Devonshire cream tea in the afternoon (NZ$6/£3). There is a full-length open-air viewing platform, ideal for photographers or just for watching the scenery.

Fares and how to buy tickets

The normal one-way fare for Picton to Christchurch is NZ$118 (£56 or US$84). A combined train+ferry fare is available, at NZ$130 (£61 or US$91) for Wellington to Christchurch, or NZ$95 (£45 or US$67) for Wellington to Kaikoura. Children aged 2–14 travel at reduced fare, infants under 2 travel free.

It's easy to buy tickets online at **www.tranzscenic.co.nz**, whether you live in NZ or overseas. You pay by credit card and simply print out your own ticket. Or when you're in New Zealand you can telephone 0800 TRAINS (0800 872 467); calls are free. From outside New Zealand you can call 00 64 4 495 0775. There are discounts for anyone over 60 and for students on the *TranzCoastal*, though to get these you need to book by phone.

Travel tips

- **Free shuttle bus for *TranzCoastal* departures from Christchurch:** At Christchurch, a free Tranz Scenic shuttle (shuttle = shared minibus taxi) operates to a set timetable from most hotels and guesthouses in central Christchurch out to the railway station to connect with the *TranzCoastal* departure for Picton and Wellington. There's no need to book; just ask your guesthouse (or freephone and ask Tranz Scenic) what time the shuttle leaves which hotel. It departs between 05:55 and 06:40: for example, it leaves the Croydon B&B on Armagh Road at 06:07. There is no free shuttle meeting train *arrivals* in Christchurch, but a fleet of normal shuttles to the city centre will be waiting for the train and cost about NZ$6 (£3) per person.

- **Make a seating request:** If you book by phone (or book online and then call Tranz Scenic's freephone number when you get to NZ at least the day before travel, quoting your booking reference) you can make a seating request. The obvious request to make is for seats on the left-hand side of the train going south from Picton, or the right-hand side coming north from Christchurch, as this puts you on the coastal side of the train where most of the scenery is. Keen photographers could also request seats at the front of the train close to the viewing platform. Requests can't be guaranteed, of course, but it doesn't hurt to ask!

What you see on the journey

When you arrive at Picton by Interislander ferry, the station is just a 200-metre walk straight ahead of you. Look out for the *Edwin Fox*, a preserved nineteenth-century sailing ship in a museum on the left. It's the ninth oldest wooden sailing ship in the world, and you can see it from the road even if you don't have time to go into the museum. The small wooden station building now houses a Subway fast food place, a travel agency, and a small check-in desk for the train. Seats on the train are allocated there.

The train leaves Picton station and curves around the valley out of the town. Within half an hour you're in the middle of vineyards in the Marlborough wine region. You'll pass one of the main Montana wineries, with its huge stainless-steel tanks. The train calls at Blenheim, the region's main town. Soon after Blenheim, the train climbs hard up a long, gentle pass through grassy hills.

Within an hour of leaving Picton, snow-capped mountains appear in the distance on your right, and you pass over the unusual double-decker combined road and rail bridge over the Awatere River, with the railway on top and roadway underneath. There used to be several such bridges on this line, until new road bridges were built. Indeed a replacement road bridge is now under construction next to this one.

Just over an hour from Picton you skirt Lake Grassmere. Salt is produced here, by letting sea water evaporate in large salt pans. You'll see piles of harvested salt on the right. Within the next half-hour the train reaches the sea. It now runs right along the coastline for about 98 km. You'll see beaches, cliffs, rocky headlands, in places draped with low-lying sea mist.

Although parts of the line are much older, the Picton–Christchurch railway was only completed in 1945; work on this coastal section started in the 1930s. Until then, overnight ferries had linked Lyttleton (the port of Christchurch) direct with Wellington.

The train stops at Kaikoura, the South Island's main whale-watching and dolphin-swimming centre. The whale-watching centre is now housed in the old station building. The train stops for several minutes here and you can get out and stretch your legs. The train then continues along the coast. Watch out for the seal colonies just feet from the train. The seals tend to be the same colour as the rocks, but with a bit of practice you can spot huge numbers of them!

Just over 3 hours from Picton, the train swings inland again, through green hills and pretty valleys. It passes through the Christchurch suburbs and arrives at Christchurch station. This is now a small modern single-platform rail terminal, opened in 1993. This new station is some 3 km from the city centre, but taxis and shuttles (shared minibus taxis) are available.

CHRISTCHURCH TO GREYMOUTH ON THE *TRANZALPINE*

This is perhaps the most scenic train trip in New Zealand, and one of the most scenic train rides anywhere in the world. The *TranzAlpine* runs once a day each way between Christchurch, Arthur's Pass and Greymouth on the South Island's west coast, through the amazing misty mountain scenery of the Southern Alps. The 240-km (140-mile) journey takes 4½ hours, and if you like you can go there and back in a day with an hour in Greymouth. Or take the *TranzAlpine* one-way, and connect with buses down the west coast to Franz-Josef Glacier. Although I rate the North Island's *Overlander* from Auckland to Wellington as a far more historic and epic route, and in many ways almost equally scenic, you certainly won't regret buying a ticket for the *TranzAlpine*!

The train departs Christchurch daily at 08:15, calling at Arthur's Pass at 10:42 and arriving at Greymouth at 12:45. It departs Greymouth for the return journey at 13:45, calling at Arthur's Pass at 15:57 and arriving at Christchurch at 18:05.

The *TranzAlpine* has comfortable seats, mostly arranged in bays of four around tables, but there's some unidirectional seating. All seats line up with wide panoramic windows. Seat numbers are not allocated at booking, but at check-in. A café-bar serves snacks, drinks, tea, coffee, wine, beer, spirits and light microwaveable meals, at reasonable prices. I can recommend the breakfast roll in the morning (NZ$7.50/£3.50) and the Devonshire cream tea in the afternoon (NZ$6/£3). There is a full-length open-air viewing platform in the centre of the train, ideal for taking photographs or just for watching the scenery, with nothing between you and the view.

The *TranzAlpine's* coaches have been rebuilt from traditional New Zealand Railways coaches, to a design which first appeared in 1938. That's why they may appear antiquated from the outside, apart from their new panoramic windows, but inside the coaches have been refurbished to a very high standard.

Fares and how to buy tickets

The normal one-way fare for Christchurch to Greymouth is NZ$161 (£76 or US$113). A same-day return ticket costs NZ$199 (£93 or US$140). Children aged 2–14 travel at reduced fare, infants under 2 travel free.

Usually, the cheapest way to buy tickets for the *TranzAlpine* is online direct from the operator, Tranz Scenic, at **www.tranzscenic.co.nz**. You pay by credit card and simply print out your own ticket, wherever you are in the world. Or when you're in New Zealand you can telephone 0800 TRAINS (0800 872 467); calls are free. From outside New Zealand you can call 00 64 4 495 0775. There are discounts for anyone over 60 and for students on the *TranzAlpine*, though to get these you need to book by phone.

Several reports suggest that you can get cheaper fares by phone than online. So if you don't see any cheap promotional deals available online, only the full fare, try calling Christchurch i-SITE Visitor Centre on +64 3 379 9629 or Christchurch railway station on +64 4 341 2588, as discounted tickets might still be available through them.

Travel tips

- **Free shuttle bus for *TranzAlpine* departures from Christchurch:** At Christchurch a free Tranz–Scenic shuttle (shuttle = shared minibus taxi) operates to a set timetable from most hotels and guesthouses in central Christchurch out to the railway station to connect with the *TranzAlpine* departure for Greymouth. There's no need to book; just ask your guesthouse (or freephone and ask Tranz Scenic) what time the shuttle leaves which hotel. It departs between 07:00 and 07:40: for example, it leaves the Croydon B&B on Armagh Road at 07:13. There is no free shuttle meeting train *arrivals* in Christchurch, but a fleet of normal shuttles to the city centre will be waiting for the train and cost about NZ$6 (£3) per person.

- **Make a seating request:** Seats are not allocated at booking, but on departure. If you book by phone (or book online and then call Tranz Scenic's freephone number when you get to NZ at least the day before travel, quoting your booking reference) you can make a seating request. Seats on the right-hand side of the train going to Greymouth probably get the best views, or the left-hand side returning to Christchurch. Keen photographers could also request seats close to the viewing platform. Families or small groups may prefer a bay of 4 seats around a table to unidirectional seats. Requests can't be guaranteed, of course, but it doesn't hurt to ask!

What is the journey like?

You should check in at least 20 minutes before departure at Christchurch's Tranz Scenic railway station. This small modern rail terminal opened in 1993 in the suburb of Addington, about 3 km (1.5 miles) southwest of Christchurch city centre. You check in at the desks in the main entrance hall, where you are allocated your seat numbers. Heavy baggage must be checked in to the baggage car. The station stands in the middle of an unremarkable industrial estate, but this whole area was once the massive Addington Railway Works where many of New Zealand Railways' locomotives and rolling stock were made. There's little left to show for it now! Christchurch's original railway station was located on Moorhouse Avenue, immediately to the south of the city centre. The old station building, completed in 1960 to a design first published in 1938, still stands and is now the 'Science Alive' entertainment centre. If you take the free shuttle taxi to the station, you may drive past it.

The *TranzAlpine* leaves Christchurch at 08:15, and within 10 minutes the Addington cement works and freight yards give way to small wooden suburban bungalows. Minutes later the train is crossing flat open farmland, doing 60mph across the Canterbury Plain, heading relentlessly towards the snow-capped Southern Alps on the horizon.

The train passes fields of sheep, cattle and red deer, passes the small commuter town of Darfield, and the first tentative foothills appear. At around 09:00 the train calls at Springfield, where fresh muffins are loaded aboard for the café-bar.

At around 09:20 the *TranzAlpine* starts its climb into the Southern Alps, with views of the stunning Waimakiriri River gorge to the right. As it climbs, the train crosses a series of steel-girder bridges over deep gorges and goes through a series of short tunnels. The highest viaduct is the famous 'Staircase', 73 metres (237 feet) above the river. The scenery here is spectacular.

By about 09.40, the train has reached a grassy plateau dotted with hills. Hills give way to more mountains, liberally hung with mist. At 10:15 the *TranzAlpine* stops at Arthur's Pass station, surrounded by yet more mist-laden mountains, and there's time to get out, stretch your legs and take photographs.

Almost immediately after leaving Arthur's Pass, the train enters the Otira Tunnel. At 8.6 kilometres (5.3 miles) long, it's one of the longest tunnels in New Zealand. It was only completed in 1923, allowing direct train travel from east to west across the South Island. This section of line was once electrified, but now a door closes behind each train, allowing the train to act as a huge piston, forcing the diesel fumes out. Just the other side of the tunnel is Otira itself, where the *TranzAlpine* makes a very brief call. Otira was a railway town, running the railway that kept the coal flowing from the west coast coalfields to Christchurch and the rest of New Zealand.

The train now follows a deep valley containing a broad, shallow river. It crosses that river on a low bridge several times. Ever more mist-laden mountains flank the valley – a wonderful part of the journey. Watch out for waterfalls.

At around 12:00 the *TranzAlpine* passes the site of the Old Brunner Mine, just across the valley on the other side of the Grey River. This was the site of New Zealand's worst mining disaster in 1896. An ancient suspension bridge links the railway side of the river with the mine. The train passes Dobson, an old coal-mining town, though all the mines are now closed.

At 12:45 the *TranzAlpine* reaches Greymouth, a small town even by New Zealand standards, but it's the west coast's main centre. Even if it was warm and sunny in Christchurch, don't be surprised if you need your umbrella in Greymouth! Greymouth's wooden station building now houses an extensive gift shop and travel centre. Buses leave from just outside the station for destinations down the west coast, including Franz Josef Glacier. If you're returning to Christchurch the same day, you have an hour to explore the town or find some food – try the Café 124, on the main road just along from the station. The town clock is on the river bank, originally housed in the tower of the impressive colonial post office. The post office and its tower were demolished as they were thought to be an earthquake risk, and the clock now stands in its own short wooden tower. Next to it on the river bank is a sign which warns against eating fish caught next to the nearby sewer outlet. Welcome to Greymouth!

CHRISTCHURCH TO DUNEDIN AND INVERCARGILL, by bus

Once important cities, Dunedin and Invercargill apparently no longer justify a proper train service to the rest of New Zealand. The last Christchurch–Dunedin–Invercargill train service, the daily *Southerner* over the South Island Main Trunk Line, was withdrawn in 2004. Nowadays, anyone wishing to reach these towns must endure a long bus journey from Christchurch. There are two main bus services (an additional bus may run on Friday and Sunday).

Christchurch → Dunedin, Invercargill

Bus service		Daily InterCity	Daily InterCity
Christchurch	depart	08:00	14:00
Timaru	arr/dep	10:30	17:00
Oumaru	arr/dep	12:05	18:15
Dunedin	arr/dep	13:45	19:50
Invercargill	arrive	17:40	–

Invercargill, Dunedin → Christchurch

Bus service		Daily InterCity	Daily InterCity
Invercargill	depart	–	08:45
Dunedin	arr/dep	07:45	12:50
Oumaru	arr/dep	09:30	15:00
Timaru	arr/dep	11:20	16:20
Christchurch	arrive	13:45	18:40

Fares and how to buy tickets

Christchurch to Dunedin costs NZ$33–NZ$46 (£15–£22). Christchurch to Invercargill costs NZ$35–NZ$67 (£16–£31). You can check bus times and fares and book tickets online at **www.intercitycoach.co.nz**.

CHRISTCHURCH TO QUEENSTOWN AND MILFORD SOUND, by bus

There were never any train services to Queenstown, although historically you might have taken a slow train from Invercargill to Kingston (the preserved *Kingston Flyer* train uses part of this route, or did until the preservation company went bankrupt), then a steamer across Lake Wakatipu to Queenstown, a route on which Queenstown's famous 100-year-old working steamship *Earnslaw* would have operated. Today, there are bus services run by several companies. You need to change buses and stay overnight in Queenstown if you are travelling to/from Milford Sound.

Christchurch → Queenstown, Milford Sound

Bus service		Daily InterCity	Daily Newmans	Daily Newmans	Daily Topline
Christchurch	depart	08:20	08:20	–	–
Mount Cook	arrive	I	14:00	–	–
	depart	I	14:40	–	–
Queenstown	arrive	16:20	18:20	–	–
	depart	–	–	07:15	14:00
Te Anau	arrive	–	–	09:25	16:15
	depart	–	–	10:05	–
Milford Sound	arrive	–	–	12:45	–

Milford Sound, Queenstown → Christchurch

Bus service		Daily Topline	Daily Newmans	Daily Newmans	Daily InterCity
Milford Sound	depart	–	15:15	–	–
Te Anau	arrive	–	17:10	–	–
	depart	10:00	17:25	–	–
Queenstown	arrive	12:20	19:30	–	–
	depart	–	–	07:30	09:30
Mount Cook	arrive	–	–	11:30	I
	depart	–	–	12:10	I
Christchurch	arrive	–	–	17:30	17:30

Fares and how to buy tickets

You can check times, fares and book bus tickets online at **www.intercitycoach. co.nz**, **www.newmanscoach.co.nz** and **www.toplinetours.co.nz**.

DUNEDIN TO QUEENSTOWN, by train and bus

The most rewarding way to travel between Dunedin and Queenstown is via the Taieri Gorge Railway's 'Track & Trail' train/bus link. The Taieri Gorge Railway (**www.taieri.co.nz**) is a preserved railway running daily year-round tourist trains through spectacular scenery over part of the old Dunedin–Cromwell branch railway. Leaving from the beautiful and much-photographed 1906 railway station in Dunedin's town centre, it travels a few kilometres south over the South Island Main Trunk Line (still well used for freight but sadly with no passenger service) before branching off inland through the scenic gorge that gives the line its name. The train terminates at Pukerangi (58 km from Dunedin) and a minibus connection takes pre-booked passengers onwards to Queenstown. Highly recommended!

Dunedin → Queenstown

Train+bus service		Daily May-Sept	Daily Oct-April
Dunedin, by train	depart	12:30	14:30
Pukerangi, by train	arrive	14:35	16:35
Pukerangi, by bus	depart	14:45	16:45
Queenstown, by bus	arrive	18:45	20:45

Queenstown → Dunedin

Train+bus service		Daily May-Sept	Daily Oct-April
Queenstown, by bus	depart	10:00	12:00
Pukerangi, by bus	arrive	14:30	16:30
Pukerangi, by train	depart	14:45	16:45
Dunedin, by train	arrive	16:30	18:30

Fares and how to buy tickets

The combined 'Track & Trail' fare for Dunedin to Queenstown is NZ$115 (£54) for an adult, NZ$58 (£27) for a child. To check fares and buy tickets, contact the Taieri Gorge Railway via **www.taieri.co.nz** or call (03) 477 4449.

RAILPASSES FOR NEW ZEALAND

There is an excellent Tranz Scenic Railpass giving unlimited travel on all Tranz Scenic trains, including the *TranzAlpine*, *Overlander* and *TranzCoastal* and (if you buy the ferry-inclusive version) the Interislander ferry too. If you're going to travel on all three trains from Auckland to Wellington, across on the ferry, down to Christchurch and on to Greymouth, the 7-day pass works out cheaper than buying normal tickets, although you still need (free) seat reservations on each train. To buy a pass online in the UK, see **www.internationalrail.com** or call 0871 231 0790. For more information, see **www.tranzscenic.co.nz**. Once you have a railpass, it's easy to make seat reservations simply by calling Tranz Scenic on 0800 TRAINS (0800 872 467) when you're in New Zealand or from outside New Zealand by calling 00 64 4 495 0775.

Russian (Cyrillic) alphabet

If you're travelling to Russia, Ukraine, Serbia or Bulgaria, knowing the Cyrillic alphabet can make things much easier, as you can read place names and decipher many familiar words.

А	а	a as in car
Б	б	b as in boat
В	в	v as in vine
Г	г	g as in get
Д	д	d as in do
Е	е	ye as in yet
Ё	ё	yo as in yolk
Ж	ж	s as in pleasure, or zh
З	з	z as in zoo
И	и	ee as in see
Й	й	y as in yes
К	к	k as in kitten
Л	л	l as in lamp
М	м	m as in my
Н	н	n as in November
О	о	o as in hot
П	п	p as in pot
Р	р	rolled r
С	с	s as in see
Т	т	t as in top
У	у	oo as in boot
Ф	ф	f as in ferry
Х	х	ch as in the Scottish loch
Ц	ц	ts as in hits
Ч	ч	ch as in chip
Ш	ш	sh as in ship
Щ	щ	sh as in sheer, sometimes followed by the ch in chip as in fresh cheese
Ъ	ъ	the 'hard sign', with no sound of its own
Ы	ы	i as in ill
Ь	ь	the 'soft sign', a symbol which softens the preceding consonant
Э	э	e as in met
Ю	ю	u as in use or duke
Я	я	ya as in yard

World rail operator websites (outside Europe)

You are recommended to consult the relevant country page of **www.seat61.com**, where you may find additional or updated information, as well as going to the rail operator's official site.

COUNTRY	WEBSITE	REMARKS
Argentina		Train services in Argentina are experiencing something of a revival. Try **www.sateliteferroviario.com.ar/horarios/** (in Spanish only) for information about all Argentinian train operators.
Australia	All Australian train operators jointly: **www.railaustralia.com.au**	Provided by all train operators jointly, **www.railaustralia.com.au** is a good place to start for routes, times and fares to get around Australia by train.
	Great Southern Railway (GSR), **www.gsr.com.au**	GSR operates the *Indian Pacific* (Sydney–Adelaide–Perth), the *Ghan* (Adelaide–Alice Springs–Darwin) and the *Overland* (Melbourne–Adelaide). UK agents for GSR: International Rail, **www.internationalrail.com**, 0871 231 0790.
	CountryLink, **www.countrylink.info**	CountryLink operates trains Sydney–Melbourne, Sydney–Brisbane, Sydney–Canberra. Online booking possible at **www.countrylink.info** (not sleepers). UK agents for CountryLink: International Rail, **www.internationalrail.com**, 0871 231 0790.
	Queensland Railways, **www.traveltrain.com.au**	Brisbane–Rockhampton–Townsville–Cairns and other routes in Queensland. UK agents for QR: International Rail, **www.internationalrail.com**, 0871 231 0790.
	V/Line, **www.vline.com.au**	Internal trains in Victoria.
	Transwa, **www.transwa.wa.gov.au**	Perth–Kalgoorlie and Bunbury. Formerly Westrail.
Bangladesh	Bangladesh Railways Corporation, **www.railway.gov.bd**	

COUNTRY	WEBSITE	REMARKS
Bolivia		Bolivian eastern line: **www.ferroviariaoriental.com** Bolivian western line: **www.fca.com.bo**
Botswana	Botswana Railway	No official website.
Burma (Myanmar)	Myanmar Railways Corporation	No official website, but see **www.burma-travels.com/ trains.htm**. To arrange tickets from outside Burma, contact **www.yangonow.com**.
Cambodia	Chemin de Fer du Cambodge	No official website, and currently no trains operating.
Canada	VIA Rail, **www.viarail.ca**	Canada's national rail network. Times, fares and online booking for VIA Rail Canada's trains. UK agents for VIA Rail: First Rail, call 0845 644 3553.
	BC Rail	No longer provides Vancouver–Prince George passenger trains. Rocky Mountaineer now operates over some of their route.
	Ontario Northland, **www.ontc.on.ca**	Trains between Toronto and northern Ontario.
	Rocky Mountaineer, **www. rockymountaineer.com**	Rocky Mountaineer tourist trains running Calgary–Banff–Vancouver, Jasper–Vancouver, Vancouver–Whistler.
Chile	Chilean State Railways (EFE), **www.efe.cl**	Chilean State Railways official website (Spanish only).
China	Chinese Railways, **www.china-mor.gov.cn**	Official website in Chinese only. For train times in English, see **www.chinatravelguide.com/ctgwiki/ Special:CNTrainSearch?method=1**. To book Chinese trains from outside China, see **www.chinatripadvisor.com**. You can check times, fares and buy tickets for Beijing–Hong Kong, Beijing–Shanghai and Shanghai–Hong Kong trains at **www.train-ticket.net**.
Cuba	Ferrocarriles de Cuba	No official website.
Egypt	Egyptian National Railways (ENR), **www.egyptrail.gov.eg**	Sleeping-car trains from Cairo–Luxor and Aswan are run by a private company, see **www.sleepingtrains.com** for times, fares and booking.

COUNTRY	WEBSITE	REMARKS
Ethiopia	Chemin de Fer Djibouti Ethiopien (CFDE)	No official website.
India	Indian Railways, **www.indianrail.gov.in**	The UK agent for Indian Railways, including Indian railpasses, is the excellent SD Enterprises in Wembley. Call 020 8903 3411 or visit **www.indiarail.co.uk**. Online Indian train booking: **www.cleartrip.com**.
Indonesia	Indonesian railways (Kereta Api Indonesia), **www.kereta-api.co.id**	Website currently only available in Indonesian.
Iran	Iranian Islamic Republic Railways, **www.raja.ir**	Official site of the 'Raja Trains' passenger department. Times and fares for Iran and for international trains Tehran–Damascus and Tehran–Istanbul. Click the 'house' logo then 'English' top right.
Iraq	Iraq Republic Railways, **www.iraqrailways.com**	Train service Baghdad–Mosul, Baghdad–Basra.
Israel	Israel Railways, **www.israrail.org.il**	Times and fares for train travel in Israel.
Japan	Japan Railways (JR)	For a rail timetable in English visit **www.hyperdia.com** (the English button is upper left). Also see **www.japanrail.com**.
Jordan	Hedjaz Jordan Railway, **www.jhr.gov.jo**	Only limited passenger service.
Kazakhstan	Kazakh Railways, **www.railways.kz**	Official interactive timetable, in Cyrillic script, for Kazakhstan Railways. Also try **www.poezda.net**.
Kenya	Kenya Railways	No official website, but **www.eastafricashuttles.com/train.htm** has information on train times and fares between Mombasa and Nairobi.
Korea (South)	Korean National Railroad, **www.korail.go.kr**	Times and fares for South Korea.
Madagascar	FCE, **www.fce-madagascar.com**	There is just one (tourist-orientated) rail route on Madagascar.

COUNTRY	WEBSITE	REMARKS
Malaysia and Singapore	Keretapi Tanah Melayu (KTM), **www.ktmb.com.my**	Train times, fares and online booking for mainline trains within Malaysia and Singapore.
Mali	Transrail	Canadian consortium that has taken over the Malian (and Senegalese) railways. Trains operating Bayes–Kamako.
Mexico		The Mexican government discontinued virtually all long-distance passenger trains some years ago. For a summary of what's left, see **www.mexlist.com/ pass.htm**. For the famous 'Copper Canyon' train see **www.chepe.com.mx**.
Morocco	Office Nationale des Chemins de Fer Maroccains (ONCFM), **www.oncf.ma**	Train times and fares for Morocco.
Mozambique	Caminhos de Ferro do Moçambique (CFM), **www.cfmnet.co.mz**	Train times and fares for Mozambique.
Namibia	Transnamib, **www.transnamib.com.na**	Select 'Products and services' then look for 'Passenger services'. Also see **www.desertexpress.com.na**, a deluxe tourist service run by Transnamib.
New Zealand	Tranz Scenic, **www.tranzscenic.co.nz**	Tranz Scenic operates long-distance passenger trains in New Zealand, with online booking. For the Interislander ferry see **www.interislandline.co.nz**.
Pakistan	Pakistan Railway Corporation, **www.pakrail.com**	Official site, with train times and availability check.
Panama	Panama Canal Railway, **www.panarail.com**	One train service, Ciudad de Panama–Colón.
Peru	PeruRail., **www.perurail.com**	Peruvian passenger trains, including trains to Machu Picchu.
	Ferrocarril Central, **www. ferrocarrilcentral.com.pe**	Train service Lima–Huancayo.
Philippines	Philippine National Railroad, **www.pnr.gov.ph**	Philippine passenger trains.

COUNTRY	WEBSITE	REMARKS
Saudi Arabia	Saudi Government Railways, **www.saudirailways.org**	Saudi train times and fares Dammam–Riyadh.
South Africa	Shosholoza Meyl, **www.shosholozameyl.co.za**	Train times for long-distance passenger trains in South Africa.
	Premier Classe, **www.premierclasse.co.za**	Affordable deluxe long-distance passenger trains in South Africa.
	The *Blue Train*, **www.bluetrain.co.za**	South Africa's famous *Blue Train*, Cape Town–Pretoria.
Sri Lanka	Sri Lanka Railways, **www.railway.gov.lk**	Also see **http://colombofort.com** or **www.reddottours.com**.
Sudan	Sudan Railways Corporation, **www.sudanrailways.gov.sd**	
Syria	CFS (Chemins de Fer Syriens), **www.cfssyria.sy**	
Taiwan	Taiwan Railway Administration, **www.railway.gov.tw**	Train times and fares for rail travel in Taiwan.
Tanzania	Tanzania Railway Corporation, **www.trctz.com**	Train services from Dar es Salaam–Kigoma/Mwanza.
	Tanzania and Zambia Railway Authority (TAZARA), **www.tazarasite.com**.	Train service between Zambia and Tanzania, Dar es Salaam–Mbeya–Kapiri Mposhi.
Thailand	State Railways of Thailand, **www.railway.co.th**	Train times and fares for Thailand.
Tunisia	Société Nationale des Chemins de Fer Tunisiens (SNCFT), **www.sncft.com.tn**	Tunisian Railways official site.
Turkey	TCDD (Türkiye Cumhuryeti Devlet Demiryollan), **www.tcdd.gov.tr**	For Turkish train times and fares.

COUNTRY	WEBSITE	REMARKS
USA	Amtrak, **www.amtrak.com**	Train times, fares and online booking for rail travel in the USA.
	Alaska Railroad, **www.akrr.com**	
Uzbekistan	Uzbekistan State Railways, **www.uzrailway.uz**	In Uzbek and Russian only. For train times, try **www.poezda.net**. For Moscow–Uzbekistan trains.
Vietnam	DSVN (Duong Sat Viet Nam), **www.vr.com.vn**	Official website with train times for the Hanoi–Saigon line.
Zambia	Tanzania and Zambia Railway Authority (TAZARA), **www.tazarasite.com.**	Train service between Zambia and Tanzania.
	Rail Systems of Zambia	Train service Livingstone–Lusaka–Kapiri–Mposhi. No official website.
Zimbabwe	National Railways of Zimbabwe, **www.planet.nu/ sunshinecity/nrz/ railinfo.html**	One page of information on train times for the National Railways of Zimbabwe (including Bulawayo–Harare, Bulawayo–Victoria Falls).

Index

Page numbers in *italics* refer to a timetable. Return journeys are incorporated within outgoing journey entry.